Film Censorship
in America

Film Censorship in America

A State-by-State History

JEREMY GELTZER

McFarland & Company, Inc., Publishers

Jefferson, North Carolina

ISBN (print) 978-1-4766-6952-6
ISBN (ebook) 978-1-4766-3012-0

LIBRARY OF CONGRESS CATALOGUING-IN-PUBLICATION DATA

BRITISH LIBRARY CATALOGUING DATA ARE AVAILABLE

Front cover: Poster art for the 1936 film *Marihuana*
(Roadshow Attractions)

Printed in the United States of America

McFarland & Company, Inc., Publishers
Box 611, Jefferson, North Carolina 28640
www.mcfarlandpub.com

Acknowledgments

To my wife Heather, who provides encouragement, support, optimism, and endless strength, beauty, and poise. And Jackson, my son and best friend, full of curiosity and eager to learn, your intense energy is an inspiration. I could never have written this book without you both.

From my earliest memory my family has always nurtured a deep love of movies, media, and debate. Ranging the spectrum from Bogie to Bunuel, conversations with Mom, Dad and Gabe always flow with insight—and provided the foundation for my scholarship.

This book demonstrates that across America everyone loves the movies. While films entertain us, regional censors have strived to silence unpopular, controversial, risqué, and challenging voices. Free speech is a powerful right but it is vulnerable and must be protected.

Table of Contents

We don't have to give our reasons.
—Memphis censor Lloyd T. Binford on banning
Charlie Chaplin's *Monsieur Verdoux*[1]

Introduction

Motion pictures flickered to life in 1891. Edison's first viewing device, the Kineto-scope, sold for $300—about $7,500 today.[1] As early spectators peered into the peephole projector they were drawn into a hypnotic world of images in action. Scenes of dancers twirl-ing, boxers sparring, and musclemen flexing shimmered by. These enticing images and visions of light announced the coming era of mass media and electronic entertainment.

An updated generation of picture devices—now projecting images on a screen—left Edison's laboratory in 1896.[2] As the rebranded Vitascope began generating revenue, an ecosystem emerged around the new medium and experimenting engineers gave way to a corporate structure of producers, distributors, exhibitors, and executives. By 1905 amusement parlors teemed with eager audiences. Young people and women found a safe space to gather in the picture arcade. Working-class folks appreciated the cheap nickel-and-dime entertainment. Immigrants saw silent photoplays as an informative illustrated primer on living in America. Motion pictures such as *President McKinley's Inauguration* (1901), *A Trip to the Moon* (1902), *The Great Train Robbery* (1903), and *Opening Ceremon-ies, St. Louis Exposition* (1904) thrilled and captivated, entertained and educated. The emerg-ing technology had a unique ability to touch people on a personal, even spiritual level.

But not everyone loved the movies. Civic authorities felt threatened by the emergence of a mass media that took power and influence out of their hands and beyond their con-trol. Women and children mingling with the working class and immigrants unsupervised in a darkened auditorium upset the social order. Some concerns bordered on the ridicu-lous. In 1910 John Holcend interrupted fellow audience members at a Brooklyn theater. Newspapers reported that "ushers started to take [Holcend] out when he fell on the floor laughing. He was taken home still laughing and died several hours later still laughing hysterically."[3] Other concerns were more reality-based than fears of death by laughter. Many of the pop-up film parlors were unlicensed, unregulated, and unsafe firetraps easily ignited by the highly flammable nitrate film stock. Perhaps the most troublesome issue was triggered by film content. Popular pictures often contained scenes considered inap-propriate to a society still bound by the vestiges of Victorian values, Edwardian etiquette, and proper public behavior. Hip-shaking dancers risked arousing male viewers, stripped-down prizefighters exposed women to muscular male anatomy, off-color comedies lam-pooned authority figures, and voyeurism once improper was now commonplace.

As the film industry grew so did the mechanisms of state censorship. By the early 1920s the major film studios, Universal, Paramount, Fox, MGM, and Warner Bros., were well established in California and New York. Tracking with this expansion, film censor boards were convened throughout America. These moral authorities had the sworn duty to shield their communities from the moral corruption potentially posed by Hollywood movies.

1

Their names are forgotten today, but in their time film censors held sway over pop culture. Maj. Metellus Lucullus Cicero Funkhouser in Chicago, the Rev. Festus Foster in Kansas, and Dr. Ellis Paxson Oberholtzer in Pennsylvania were among the earliest. Lloyd T. Binford in Memphis, Christine Smith Gilliam in Atlanta, and Mary Avara in Baltimore were among the most outspoken and opinionated. Some regulators were vastly unqualified for their positions. In 1922 Ohio appointed the Rev. Wallace W. Foust as a state censor despite his own admission that he hadn't seen a film in five and a half years—or perhaps ever.[4] These state censors were not advisory; rather, they held actual legal authority to cut, edit, abridge, and even ban motion pictures before they ever reached their audiences. A film that ran in Philadelphia would be different in Peoria and Pasadena, and secondary markets like Pascagoula received the remnants of multiple rounds of censor cuts.

The decision of what material to excise from films could be arbitrary, unpredictable, and often based on the personal predilections of political appointees. Over time guidelines arose. The most forbidden elements included scenes of sensual kissing over three seconds in duration, nudity, birth control, abortion, drunkenness, drug use, prostitution, profanity, criminal modus operandi, and gunplay.[5] Municipal regulators intimidated many filmmakers into reluctant acquiescence. One of the most influential voices crying out against censorship was director D.W. Griffith, who authored a pamphlet entitled "The Rise and Fall of Free Speech in America." In his films Griffith created suspense and dramatic tension with well-timed violence and last-minute rescues. In interviews he pooh-poohed the censors, stating that "crime cannot be eliminated from the movies without barring all the classics of civilization."[6]

Cinema has always been provocative. From the moment the first motion pictures unspooled there has coexisted both an enthusiastic adoration of screen icons as well as a near-puritanical drive to control content. Over the past century moviemakers pushed cultural boundaries, empowered women, spoke out against fascism, wrestled with issues of race, and gave voice to troubled teens. State censors pushed back, dedicating their efforts to upholding conservative values, accepted conventions, and prudish decorum—an old guard waging war against changing times.

Journeying from state to state and looking at the effects of local censors, a hidden history of regional cinemas comes to light. Forgotten film studios in Chicago, Fort Lee (NJ), Tallahassee, Providence, Austin, Chadron (NE), and Upper Priest Lake (ID) came to life. While anyone with a smartphone today has the ability to create content, the drive to tell personal stories has existed from the earliest days of filmmaking. Many of these filmmakers have become shrouded in mystery, obscured by time, and erased by the mainstream industry. Ironically, some of these lost films have been rediscovered in archives where they had been mothballed by censors of an earlier era. In seeking to eradicate content, the censors' cuts could have an unintended consequence: the edits meant to erase content ending up saving it, storing scenes, preserving clips, and even protecting entire movies.

The tension between producers and regulators remains alive. Censorship is not locked in the past. Content regulation thrives today within issues of copyright and Fair Use, Net neutrality, zoning, privacy rights, revenge porn, and "ag-gag" laws. Meanwhile, emerging channels of communication such as the Dark Web, over-the-top (OTT) networks, BitTorrent peer-to-peer file sharing, and app-based content distribution create new avenues around regulators. The battle between freedom and control continues. As media evolves so does our responsibility to fight against forces that seek to silence indecent, inappropriate, and uncomfortable content.

Alabama

Many of Hollywood's most memorable motion pictures take place in Alabama. *To Kill a Mockingbird* (1962) helped personalize the civil rights movement. The adaptation of Harper Lee's Pulitzer Prize–winning novel was set in fictional Maycomb, Alabama. Picking up a floating feather, a simpleminded man reminisces about his childhood in *Forrest Gump* (1994). Set in fictional Greenbow, the film went on to claim six Academy Awards, including Best Picture, Actor, Director, and Adapted Screenplay.

Bette Davis embodied the privileged life of a plantation owner's daughter in *The Little Foxes* (1941), while Dorothy Dandridge and Harry Belafonte brought the struggles of African American schoolteachers in rural Alabama to the screen in *Bright Road* (1953). When murder was involved, *The Phenix City Story* (1955) delivered moody film noir, and *My Cousin Vinny* (1992) brought sidesplitting humor to a surreal small-town trial. When the subject was history, the struggle of Alabama's strongest daughter, Helen Keller, was reenacted in *The Miracle Worker* (1962), and Martin Luther King, Jr.'s march was brought to life in *Selma* (2014). Alabama is a notable place in the history of film.

Motion pictures first arrived in the heart of Dixie before 1903. J.T. Amberson was one of Birmingham's earliest projectionists. He began hand cranking flickering images across makeshift screens in 1905, working at playhouses across the city. Thirty-five years later, this magnificent Amberson recalled his early days to the *Birmingham News*. Waxing nostalgic about the early filmmaking technology, Amberson described working six-hour shifts in a cramped, unventilated, fireproof booth that could heat up to 105 degrees.[1] On busy nights the theater manager would send word to "jazz it up"—meaning crank the film faster. Amberson could whirl through a seven-minute film in four minutes. "The audience going in met itself coming out," he chuckled. It was all part of the showmanship, the hucksterism of a new entertainment medium.

As a pioneering film exhibitor, Amberson witnessed the development of new experimental techniques. As early as 1907, sound pictures were introduced. It was a primitive system to be sure: needle drops on a phonograph. Still, the effect could give early audiences a thrill—when it worked. Decades later, Amberson laughed over memorable mistakes: "While the wild west hero's burning guns would be blasting a death volley ... the screen might be showing a tender love scene."[2] In the first decade of commercial film exhibition, sync sound was a future dream, but Alabama's motion picture theaters pushed the limits of the medium's potential.

Movies were a thrilling new attraction. By the 1910s, Birmingham teemed with screens. The Marvel Theater sat four hundred people. The Amuse-You, the Capitol, Theaterium, and the Vaudette entertained audiences. While everybody loved the movies, not everyone was treated alike; African American moviegoers climbed to the balcony or sat segregated to one side of the screen.

3

Despite the intrusion of certain realities of the outside world, movie theaters gave Alabamians a great escape. Movies were new, exciting, and vivid and could even be progressive. Moral authorities saw the screen images as a threat to the social order that had to be controlled.

Government censors quickly set their sights on monitoring the movies. Birmingham's city council declared motion pictures a nuisance in 1906.[3] Mobile banned boxing films in 1910, and Albany installed a film censor board in 1917.[4] By the 1920s, Birmingham formed a film commission and appointed the uncompromising Myrtelle Snell as "chief amusements inspector." Snell had previously chaired Birmingham's Better Films Committee, a grassroots organization that lobbied for morally uplifting motion pictures. As city inspector, she had formal authority to enforce her decrees.[5]

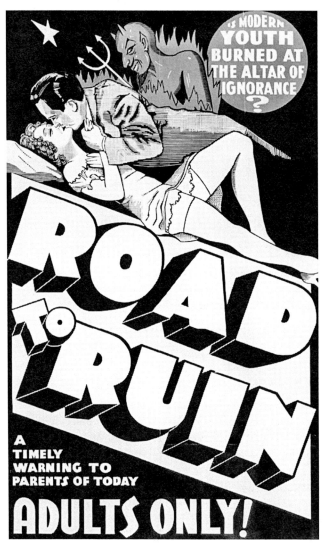

After the drug-related death of her husband, silent screen heartthrob Wallace Reid, Dorothy Davenport co-directed *The Road to Ruin* (1928).

When *The Road to Ruin* (1928) came to Birmingham, Snell shut it down. Directed by Dorothy Davenport, *Ruin* was a cautionary tale about the dangers of drug and alcohol abuse. Davenport was the widow of Wallace Reid, a major movie heartthrob in the early twenties. After he was injured during a stunt, Reid was prescribed morphine. As his pain increased, so did his addiction. Reid's movie career soon floundered, and he died in 1923.[6] On his deathbed the actor revealed his substance abuse.

Road to Ruin exposed—and glamorized—the dangers of fast living, sex, drugs, adventure, and alcohol. The low-budget film thrilled audiences with scenes of a booze-fueled co-ed kissing party, bare-legged dancing to jazzy jitterbug music, strip poker, and even a moonlight swim with girls stripped down to their bloomers. The city of Birmingham sued to stop the racy film. Snell cited the city code, which prohibited "the human female in a nude state or condition, or draped or clothed with transparent or partially transparent garments, draperies, or clothing which shows or represents any indecent, obscene, lewd, filthy, vulgar, lascivious, or suggestive act, [or] scene … [as well as] any moving picture show, theater, or other place of amusement [that shows] any scene depicting drunkenness of any female."[7]

When the film ban was challenged in court, Alabama stood by its censors. Judge Henry Clayton ruled that the city was merely exercising police power to protect the morals, health, and safety of its Dixie denizens.[8] Snell's censor board prevailed and *The Road to Ruin* bypassed Birmingham.

The Birmingham film committee continued to cut and ban racy films—until they went too far. Mae West, famous for her titillating sexual innuendos, pushed the lines of decency but delivered droves of audiences to the box office. In 1937 Snell's replacement, Harriet Adams, rejected the curvaceous actress's *Go West Young Man* (1936). This time Police Chief Luther Hollums, a fan of Mae, pushed back. Shutting the film commission down, Hollums commented, "Evil minded persons can always interpret things the wrong way."[9]

Hollums's police force took over as the city's movie censors, but Adams remained on call for her expertise in forbidden films. In her parting comments she cautioned theater managers to stay away from the evils of horror films, and with that the most active censor board in Alabama closed its doors.[10]

Even without a formal board in place, authorities could still crack down on bothersome movies. Mobile's mayor decided not to fund a formal censor board, relying instead on the outraged voices of various civic clubs. The Mobile Ministerial Association, the Knights of Columbus, the Mobile County League of Women Voters, and the Mobile District Council of the National Council of Catholic Women each had very clear ideas of which films should be tabooed. While the city did not enact a censorship law, these groups were influential enough to pressure local theater owners to avoid questionable pictures. As a result Otto Preminger's *Forever Amber* (1947), based on a seventeenth-century bodice ripper; Elia Kazan's *Baby Doll* (1956), a revenge-rape drama; and Arthur Penn's *The Graduate* (1967), with adulterous seduction, were each unwelcome in the Port City.[11]

A decade later Governor Albert Brewer took matters into his own hands by ordering raids on adult theaters throughout the state. Enforcement agents were set loose to confiscate various cinematic treasures. Among the films seized were *Inga* (1968), torn from a Montgomery grind house; *Thar She Blows* (1968), confiscated from a Jefferson County drive-in; *The Secret Sex Lives of Romeo and Juliet* (1969), taken from a Tuscaloosa theater; and *Starlet!* (1969), picked up from a Birmingham drive-in.[12]

But times had changed. This time the Alabama court looked at the governor's haul and declared the warrantless searches and seizures invalid and the censorship statute unconstitutional. Refusing to even see the films, a panel of three judges enjoined Alabama's authorities from interfering with the exhibitions.[13] *The Secret Sex Lives of Romeo and Juliet*, which claimed to have won Best Erotic Film at the Cannes Film Festival—an award that never existed—played on.

A new law was quickly drafted and ratified and morality police were back in business. The censors received another setback when they tried to deport *Last Tango in Paris* (1973). Directed by Bernardo Bertolucci and featuring Marlon Brando, *Tango*'s artistic erotica lit up censor boards across the country. Montgomery's chief of police, E.L. Wright Jr., challenged the picture. Once again Alabama's court declared the film censorship law invalid, unconstitutional, and void.[14]

State legislators enacted new laws and the cat-and-mouse game continued. In 2012,

ADULT
MOTION
PICTURES
HAVE COME
OF AGE...!

a story of
men and
women who
GO DOWN
to the sea
in ships...

THAR SHE BLOWS

FILMED IN COLOR ABOARD A 100 FOOT TWIN-SCREW CRUISER
PRODUCED BY DAVID F. FRIEDMAN and WILLIAM ALLEN CASTLEMAN ╱ DIRECTED BY RICHARD KANTER
SCREENPLAY BY RICHARD KANTER and DAVID F. FRIEDMAN ╱ AN ADO PRODUCTION ╱ RELEASED BY ENTERTAINMENT VENTURES, INC.
© MCMLXIX ENTERTAINMENT VENTURES, INC.

Thar She Blows (1968), a softcore sexploitation film, was too much for Alabama's authorities.

a Norwegian sex comedy entitled *Turn Me On, Dammit!* (2011) rankled several pastors in the state, and they organized protests.[15] *Turn Me On* was a coming-of-age tale about a teenage Scandinavian girl as she begins to explore her sexuality. No sleazy skin flick, *Dammit* was recognized with an award for its screenplay at the Tribeca Film Festival. Unlike in earlier eras, when inappropriate films were raided and run out of town, *Turn*

Censorship backfired when the banning of the Norwegian film *Turn Me On Dammit!* (2011) only attracted greater crowds.

Me On played to capacity crowds at a Tuscaloosa theater. The cries for censorship had backfired, becoming instead provocative promotion for the picture. The notion of "banned in Alabama" drew audiences curious to see forbidden fare.

The power to control film exhibition can shape public opinion and steer cultural direction. State censors like Myrtelle Snell truly believed in their mission to protect Alabama's values from on-screen dangers. But shutting down films based on personal bias only chills discussion and prevents social progress. In the end, Alabama's moral authorities drew greater attention to the screenings they wished to silence.

Alaska

Alaska was the final frontier for American filmmakers. Movies didn't reach the nation's northernmost territory until 1903. San Francisco–based producers the Miles brothers commissioned a crew to record several scenes there, including *Winter Sport on*

Snake River, Nome (1903) and *First Snow Storm of the Season, Valdez* (1903). The frozen north became more familiar to film audiences when the magic lantern operator turned cameraman Oscar B. Depue developed a travelogue on life in the wild country.

Depue began his career with Burton Holmes, one of the earliest travelogue presenters. In 1892 Holmes hired Depue as a freelance photographer. For the next ten years the two men traveled the world, returning periodically to the States to exhibit striking images in American theaters. As motion picture technology developed Depue added new equipment to his repertoire. He later recalled their expedition to the northern lands: "In 1903 we toured Alaska, taking the railroad over the White Horse Pass … and then a sternwheel steamer down the Yukon to Dawson. There we filmed the gold miners and their sluicing and hydraulic operations. During the remainder of our journey down the Yukon and on to Nome, we travelled and slept on a barge lashed to a river steamer."[1] Holmes and Depue's scenes included *Slavonian Miners Running to Dinner, Treadwell Mine, Alaska* (1905), *Camp Life of the Esquimaux at Cape Nome* (1905), *Dog Teams, Dawson City* (1905), and *Panoramic Approach to Taku Glacier* (1905).

By the end of the decade the Arctic region had become an attractive location for filmmakers intent on capturing diverse images. Pathé Frères sent a crew to record *The Polar Bear Hunt in the Arctic Seas* (1909) and *Chasing a Sea Lion in the Arctic* (1909). Raleigh et Robert, a Paris-based partnership of the Englishman Charles Raleigh and the German Robert Schwobthaler, commissioned *A Trip to the Arctic* (1909) and *Seal and Walrus Hunting* (1910).[2]

One of the most successful wildlife filmmakers of the era was Capt. Frank E. Kleinschmidt, a renowned big game hunter and naturalist. Commissioned by the Carnegie Museum, Kleinschmidt journeyed north and returned with stunning pictures of moose swimming across icy rivers and polar bears caring for their cubs in *Alaskan-Siberian Expedition* (1912). The intrepid traveler headed back into the area to film *Captain F.E. Kleinschmidt's Arctic Hunt* (1914), *Adventures in the Far North* (1923), and an ethnographic look at Inuit customs, *Primitive Love* (1927).[3] In *Primitive Love*, Kleinschmidt enlisted a fourteen-year-old Inuit boy named Mala as translator, production assistant, cameraman, and on-screen extra.[4] Mala would become the region's most important link to Hollywood.

Although Robert Flaherty of *Nanook of the North* (1922) fame has been given credit as the father of documentary film, a filmmaker named Edward S. Curtis was working on similar ethnographic projects. Curtis began photographing Native Americans in the late 1890s and developed a fascination with indigenous cultures. By 1912 he secured financing to shoot *In the Land of the Head Hunters* (1914) and set out to document "vision quest, love, witchcraft, war, ceremony, revenge, rescue, escape, and triumph" among the Kwakiutl peoples in Alaska and British Columbia.[5] The *New York Times* appreciated Curtis's images of "whaling, sealion [sic] hunting, dancing by Indians costumed as mythic animals and monsters … [and] sea fights between 80-man canoes."[6] Curtis followed *Head Hunters* with a short film entitled *The Alaskan Indians* (1916). For a brief period, film production in Alaska was vibrant. A regional production company called the Alaskan Film Corp. under the guidance of Leonard S. Sugden made several pictures, including *The Lure of Alaska* (1915) and *Way Up Yonder* (1920).

Following the scenic and ethnographic documentaries came a spate of now classic comedies that drew on the snowbound land for laughs. Charlie Chaplin went prospecting in *The Gold Rush* (1925). His hilarious misadventures saw the Little Tramp eating his shoe for sustenance and dancing the famous "Oceana roll," in which two dinner biscuits forked become little legs for a diminutive dance routine. Buster Keaton exited a subway at the last stop to find nothing but tundra in *The Frozen North* (1922). Mae West took suggestive comedy to the limit in several films, but *Klondike Annie* (1936) went over the edge—William Randolph Hearst banned advertisements for the film in his newspapers and Australia banned the film altogether.[7]

These Yukon-themed comedies were shot in the relative safety of studio soundstages, not under the harsh conditions of the northern territory. The Alaskan frontier was best suited for thrilling outdoor dramas produced by filmmakers prepared to brave the elements. Norman Dawn left his staff position at Universal Pictures to shoot *Lure of the Yukon* (1924), a drama set in the Alaskan goldfields.[8] He followed up with *Justice of the Far North* (1925), the story of an Inuit chief who falls into a crevice while hunting and is rescued by an Arctic explorer.[9] Earl Rossman directed and photographed *Kivalina of the Ice Lands* (1925) in color, capturing the prismatic aurora borealis on film. *Kivalina* was the tale of an Inuit hunter fighting the elements to obtain animal hides as a dowry for

ENSAMRÄTT: UNIVERSAL FILM A-B. STOCKHOLM

With an all–Inuit cast, *Igloo* (1932) documented the lives of indigenous Alaskans.

his betrothed.[10] Ewing Scott, who spent the bulk of his career as a second unit director at Fox, was able to move into the director's chair for *Igloo* (1932). *Igloo* was a docudrama that employed a native Inuit cast, including the now nineteen-year-old Mala, who had previously worked with Capt. Kleinschmidt on *Primitive Love*.

Scott's *Igloo* follows an Inuit tribe as springtime breaks the Arctic winter. Life returns to the region as temperatures warm and the hunting season resumes.[11] A year after *Igloo* was released, one of MGM's most reliable staff directors, W.S. Van Dyke, set out to film his own version of native life in Alaska. Once again Mala was the go-to Hollywood-Inuit fixer. Van Dyke's *Eskimo* (1933) took realism one step further, not only casting an indigenous actor but also recording large portions of the early talkie in Inupiat, the language of the indigenous peoples. Although it won an Academy Award for Editing, *Eskimo* is an overlooked accomplishment. Van Dyke, a director best remembered for classics of Golden Era Hollywood such as *Tarzan the Ape Man* (1932) and *The Thin Man* (1934), contributed a valuable record with *Eskimo*, capturing a vanishing way of life.[12]

Mala, star of *Igloo* and *Eskimo*, was a unique performer. Far from his upbringing in the Alaska Territory wilderness, he joined the Hollywood studio system. Mala worked on-screen for the Poverty Row powerhouse Republic Pictures, appearing in serial chapter plays such as *Robinson Crusoe of Clipper Island* (1936) and *Hawk of the Wilderness* (1938). He also continued to work behind the lens as an assistant cameraman on notable films, including Alfred Hitchcock's *Shadow of a Doubt* (1943).[13] In the early 1940s Mala and Ewing Scott discussed an on-film reunion. Together they planned a picture called *Son of Nanook* to be shot on location in Alaska with an indigenous cast, but the picture never came to pass.[14] Instead Scott continued his northern film odyssey with *Harpoon* (1948) and *Arctic Manhunt* (1949), mixing adventure plotlines with docudrama footage.

Similarly, Norman Dawn was no longer satisfied with the soundstages of Universal City. He was drawn back to Alaska, independently producing low-budget thrillers such as *Dangers of the Arctic* (1932), *Tundra: A Saga of the Alaskan Wilderness* (1936), *Taku* (1937), *Orphans of the North* (1940), and *Arctic Fury* (1949).

While the vistas of the northern frontier were wide open and free, territorial authorities imposed film regulation as early as 1913. That year the district passed a licensing provision that required film exhibitors to obtain permits. One exhibitor located in Seward protested the one-hundred-dollar fee, comparing it to a utility tax that levied half that amount. The court quickly dispensed with his claim: "A picture show might conduct a very large and profitable business, and a waterworks might conduct a very small and losing business. It seems that these picture shows should bear their reasonable share of taxation."[15] The authorities did not pass judgment on the content of films shown as long

Ray Mala (1906–1952) was a unique figure in Hollywood, both as an actor and a behind-the-scenes technician.

as exhibitors were current in their payment of assessed fees.

Filmmakers have been drawn to Alaska's wilderness for over one hundred years. Courageous cameramen have captured images of virgin forests, grazing caribou, calving glaciers, and smoking volcanoes.[16] The earliest cinematographers also celebrated industrial mining projects to showcase the power of modernity. In contemporary movies, the harsh terrain has exposed man's vulnerability against the merciless power of nature. An idealistic college grad was no match for the elements in the stunning *Into the Wild* (2007). Environmentalist Timothy Treadwell discovered too late that the bears he sought to protect bore allegiance to no one in Werner Herzog's *Grizzly Man* (2005). Alaska provides filmmakers with the hypnotic lure of danger and beauty. Although many early films have been lost, the scenes that survive open a window on an untouched world.

W.S. "Woody" Van Dyke ventured into the Arctic to direct *Eskimo* (1933).

Arizona

The idea started over lunch. The year was 1913 and a frustrated actor named Cecil B. DeMille sat down for a bite to eat with his friends, a San Francisco–born vaudeville producer named Jesse Lasky and his colleague, Samuel Goldfish. Their discussion turned to moviemaking.[1] By the end of the meal they had devised a plan. In December 1913 *Moving Picture World* announced the formation of the Jesse L. Lasky Feature Film Company, with Lasky as president, Goldfish as treasurer and business manager, and DeMille as general stage manager. Oscar Apfel, a director more familiar with the technical aspects of film-making, was poached from Edison Manufacturing Co. Lasky Film's first project would be an adaptation of a popular Western stage play called *The Squaw Man*.[2] The *World* noted that DeMille and Apfel left the East Coast with their actors to seek out authentic locations for the filming.

DeMille and his crew arrived in Arizona. By some accounts they set out to film in Flagstaff; by others it was Prescott. In one version of the behind-the-scenes story the mountains were too close—DeMille wanted them in the distance. In another, a blizzard delayed filming or it was too hot or the terrain was too bleak and desert like.[3] What was clear was that Arizona would not be DeMille's location. The crew loaded back onto the train and headed to Los Angeles, where *The Squaw Man* (1914) was produced in a developing neighborhood called Hollywood.[4]

The Lasky players were not the first film people to arrive in Arizona. The earliest picture show in Flagstaff dates to 1897, when the Bittner Theater Company toured the state with a Triograph.[5] By 1900 movie machines were common at carnivals, and traveling exhibitors such as the Beaty Bros. introduced robust programs with news, comedies, and headlining features. Among the Beatys' offerings were color films like *Jack and the Beanstalk* (1902), topical events such as *Assassination of President McKinley* (1901) and *Capture of the Biddle Brothers Outlaws* (1902), and slapstick laffers like *A Fat and Lean Man's Wrestling Match* (1901) and *Casey and the Steam Roller* (1902).[6]

Producers began arriving in the Grand Canyon State around 1910. Director Frank Beal, working for Flying "A," the American Film Manufacturing Co., an early studio that focused on Westerns, put local scenery to good use in *An Arizona Romance* (1911), *The Mission in the Desert* (1911), and *Bertie's Bandit* (1911). Rollin S. Sturgeon, a director for Vitagraph Studios, shot *The Better Man* (1912), *Omens of the Mesa* (1912), and *Angel of the Desert* (1913) on location. Edison Manufacturing Co. and Lubin Film commissioned scenic documentaries, such as *Hopi Indians Dance for Theodore Roosevelt at Walpi, Arizona* (1913) and *San Xavier Mission, Tucson* (1913), respectively. The most prolific Arizona filmmaker during this pre–Hollywood period was Webster Cullison, who churned out over thirty-five films in the Tucson area for Éclair American, including *The Cross in the Cacti* (1914), *The Caballero's Way* (1914), and the techno-thriller *Saved by Telephone* (1915).[7]

As movies became more popular, city administrators took notice. Phoenix mayor Lloyd B. Christie signed Ordinance No. 501 to regulate moving picture shows and create a board of censors on January 19, 1912. The film law required a licensing fee for the exhibitor and featured a permit process that banned nudity, indecent dress, and immoral language.[8] By 1918 Phoenix theater owners prepared to step into line as the city's cinema cop Avery Thompson took office. But Thompson's film enforcement remained lax. One of the few films banned in Phoenix was a crime underworld/prostitution thriller entitled *Who's Your Neighbor?* (1917), directed by S. Rankin Drew. Drew, a member of the Barrymore clan, died the following year, shot down in an aerial dogfight over World War I France.[9]

Arizona remained a film-friendly state. Moviemakers seeking authentic landscapes were frequent visitors. The most famous screen cowboys were seen against Arizona backdrops: William S. Hart in *The Silent Man* (1917), Douglas Fairbanks in *A Modern Musketeer* (1917), Tom Mix in *The Daredevil* (1920), stone-faced silent comedian Buster Keaton in *Go West* (1925), and steely Gary Cooper in *Arizona Bound* (1927). In the coming years B-movie cowpokes, such as Hoot Gibson in *Arizona Whirlwind* (1944), Lash LaRue in *Law of the Lash* (1947), and Whip Wilson in *Arizona Territory* (1950), were shot on location,

The anti-prostitution picture *Who's Your Neighbor?* (1917) was too hot for censors from Arizona to Washington State.

as well as singing cowboys Gene Autry in *The Man from Music Mountain* (1938), Tex Ritter in *Westbound State* (1939), and Roy Rogers in *Song of Arizona* (1946).

Director John Ford made a star out of the Monument Valley mesas on the Utah border in a series of John Wayne classics, including *Stagecoach* (1939), *Fort Apache* (1948), and *The Searchers* (1956). Ford focused on the lawless town of Tombstone in *My Darling Clementine* (1946) and on the vast desert in *3 Godfathers* (1948). By the 1950s, women were bringing a feminist edge to the traditionally male-dominated genre, with Joan Crawford starring in *Johnny Guitar* (1954) and Barbara Stanwyck appearing in *Forty Guns* (1957). None of these films ran into any trouble with the censors.

Then came *The Girls*. The Greek comedy *Lysistrata* was written by Aristophanes in the fifth century BC, but the theme is timelessly funny. The women of a town object to the warmongering of their husbands and boyfriends. In order to put a stop to the continuing battles, the ladies withhold all sexual favors until the men behave themselves. A motion picture adaptation entitled *The Girls* was released in 1968 as the Vietnam War raged on. Director Mai Zetterling produced a meta-film that focused on a theater group staging the play and wrestling with their homelife commitments and challenges. Having worked with the Swedish master filmmaker Ingmar Bergman on two pictures, Zetterling cast the frequent Bergman player Bibi Andersson. *The Girls* was not porn. It was an arthouse film that focused on feminist issues as interpreted by a woman director.

This pedigree did not sway Tucson's city attorney. After *The Girls* opened at Apache

Drive-In Theatre, the city became concerned the picture would distract drivers. Tucson cherry-picked the film's most salacious moments to show the judge and argued that *The Girls* contained scenes of nudity and hints of heterosexual intercourse.[10] The city attorney trotted out a child psychiatrist who testified that the material could be potentially harmful to minors as well as offensive to residents who could see the images from outside the theater.[11] The court agreed: the screening was a nuisance. *The Girls* was shut down. A 2,500-year-old comedy satirizing the stupidity of war was acceptable in ancient Athens but objectionable in Pima County.

A different result came out of a case involving the Northern Drive In. This Phoenix-area theater scheduled Peter Bogdanovich's *The Last Picture Show* (1971). Bogdanovich is a filmmaker steeped in motion picture history, having interviewed great directors such as John Ford and Howard Hawks and even entertaining Orson Welles as an extended houseguest. *Last Picture Show* followed a group of teenagers coming of age in a declining western town. Bogdanovich assembled an ensemble cast that included Jeff Bridges, Cybill Shepherd, Ellen Burstyn, Randy Quaid, Ben Johnson, and Cloris Leachman. The picture was nominated for eight Academy Awards, including Picture, Director, Adapted Screenplay, and Cinematography. *Last Picture Show* was an accomplished artistic achievement by any measure. There was one problem.

In one scene Cybill Shepherd attends a naked pool party. The attractive, innocent blonde girl is pressured to disrobe. She pulls off her dress to reveal underwear and a garter belt. Then she peels those garments off and steps up to the diving board, bare naked and self-consciously keeping her legs together. A moment later she's in the pool. This scene was racy, but brief nudity was not uncommon in coming-of-age films. The city of Phoenix saw things differently.

The city attorney, Joseph Purcell, brought charges. He claimed the four-second segment of frontal female nudity was a violation of Arizona's obscenity statute.[12] The three-judge panel took a measured look at the naked girl. They carefully considered Ms. Shepherd's pubic hair. Then they turned to the books and the legal definition of "genitalia." The word was clear to them when applied to male body parts, but the female anatomy was more of a mystery. They arrived at a delicate conclusion. A woman's pubic hair alone would not be considered "genitalia." Since Shepherd's slender legs remained together, *The Last Picture Show* did not technically violate the statute. The award-winning picture played on, entertaining Arizona audiences newly interested in lessons in female anatomy.

Arizona provided a picturesque landscape, attracting B-movie cowboys, sagebrush soap stars, and country-western crooners. Film censorship was considered in the early days but rarely invoked. When films became racier in the 1970s, censors became more active. It is ironic that a suggestive antiwar feminist art film would fall victim to the censor's ban as obscene, while the bottomless frolicking of *The Last Picture Show* could survive to skinny-dip another day on desert screens.

Arkansas

Film's first multihyphenate star hailed from Arkansas. Broncho Billy Anderson wrote, produced, directed, and starred in over four hundred motion pictures between 1907 and 1918.[1]

Born Gilbert Maxwell Aronson in 1880 in Little Rock, the aspiring actor moved to New York City around 1900. It was on a rooftop at 41 East Twenty-First Street in the open-air studio of Edison Manufacturing Co. that Aronson met Edwin S. Porter. Porter was on the rise as Edison's top film director. He was planning a Western and asked the Arkansas up-and-comer if he could ride a horse.[2] Aronson couldn't really, but it didn't stop him from signing on to appear in *The Great Train Robbery* (1903). The picture was a huge hit. The *New York Times* printed one of its earliest film reviews, reporting, "The series of moving pictures has proved a thriller in nearly all the cities of the United States." The *Times* made special note of "the lonely telegraph station in which the operator … is overcome with the butt of a pistol, bound hand and foot, gagged, and left unconscious on the floor by the desperadoes."[3] That pistol-whipped character was none other than Aronson, who also played a train passenger who is shot, as well as a lawman riding in pursuit of the railway robbers. With a literal bang Aronson made his entrance.

After appearing in *The Great Train Robbery* (1903), Broncho Billy Anderson (1880–1971) became a film executive, writing, directing, producing, and starring in many films.

The actor from Arkansas transformed to fill numerous roles, both in front of and behind the camera; as Broncho Billy Anderson, he was a creative force on-screen. Under Porter's direction, Broncho Billy appeared as a kissing masher in *What Happened in the Tunnel* (1903), a bumbling courier in *The Messenger Boy's Mistake* (1903), and the titular super sleuth in *Adventures of Sherlock Holmes* (1905). Broncho Billy was also a comedy innovator, credited with directing the first-known instance of the pie-in-the-face gag in *Mr. Flip* (1909).[4] Pushing west, Broncho Billy's film crew arrived in California in 1912—one of the first to open up a studio in the Golden State.

Broncho Billy wasn't Arkansas's only film innovator. Pine Bluff native Freeman Owens became interested in the movies around 1902 when he was twelve years old. The boy learned the business from the bottom up, hired by a theater manager to turn the crank for a one-armed projectionist.[5] In addition to being able-bodied, Owens was a curious tinkerer who built his own patented Camerascope as early as 1910.[6] His machine stood out from the other early film innovations because it could produce talking pictures—nearly two decades before *The Jazz Singer* took Hollywood by storm.[7] Owens advertised his freelance filmmaking services in the *Daily Arkansas Gazette*: "I am prepared to make motion pictures … of all kinds of industrial subjects, such as rice, cotton, etc.… All work guaranteed."[8]

While Freeman Owens was advertising his film skills, Arkansas authorities were beginning to crack down on problematic pictures. In 1910 heavyweight Jack Johnson became the first African American boxer champion after besting Jim Jeffries. Mayor W.R. Duley of Little Rock issued a proclamation against showing Jeffries-Johnson fight films, concerned the nickelodeon attraction could spark racial violence.[9] Within eight months Little Rock's city council took steps toward putting a censor board in place.[10]

More trouble was on the way to Arkansas theaters. Universal Pictures released *Traffic in Souls* (1913), a controversial drama that focused on inner city prostitution. A year before *The Birth of a Nation* (1915) swept across the United States, *Traffic in Souls* was a provocative sensation. Made for $5,700, the picture took in $475,000.[11] Such titillating fare did not sit well with Little Rock's authorities. When the picture arrived in town, Mayor Charles E. Taylor called for a special private screening with the chief of police Fred M. Cogswell, the city attorney Harry Hale, and a coterie of judges, ministers, and newspapermen in attendance. Once city officials were satisfied of the film's suitability for exhibition, the cinema Sanhedrin issued a permit for the film to play. The *Arkansas Daily Gazette* commented, "The only change suggested was in the name, *The Rescue* being suggested to replace *The Traffic in Souls*."[12]

Next, a film with a wholesome title left a disagreeable taste in the mouths of Little Rock's moral authorities. *Purity* (1916) featured supermodel Audrey Munson fully nude on screen in artistic posings. The plot was pure O. Henry: a girl poses for an artist. Her beau, a sensitive poet, becomes distraught at her shameless display but discovers that she only disrobed to earn money to publish his poetry. Once again Mayor Taylor called for a private screening.[13] Trimmed of several scenes, *Purity* was permitted to play at the Palace Theater, provided no children were admitted.[14]

Once Mayor Taylor left office in 1918, Frank B. Gregg stepped in as Little Rock's chief censor. A hardware shop owner before becoming the town's cinema cop, Gregg handled censorship with a pragmatic approach.[15] When exploitation filmmaker Ivan Abramson submitted *Enlighten Thy Daughter* (1917) for a permit, Gregg considered the picture. Abramson's film recounted the tale of a girl who lives fast, ends up pregnant, and dies after an abortion. There were educational possibilities with this content. Gregg demanded several cuts but allowed the film to play at the Palace Theater.[16]

Tensions ran hot the following week when *Cleopatra* (1917) came to town. The picture starred Theda Bara, a sex symbol like none other previously seen on-screen. Bara played a voracious man-eater in films such as *The Devil's Daughter* (1915), *The Galley Slave* (1915), and *The Vixen* (1916). Although there was no explicit nudity in *Cleopatra*, as there had been in *Purity*, or outright discussion of sex, as in *Enlighten Thy Daughter*, Bara's histrionic display of uninhibited lust drove the censor into a frenzy. Gregg banned the film and had the Palace Theater's manager, E.D. Brewer, arrested when he disobeyed the ruling. Brewer challenged the order and the case went before Judge John Martineau. Martineau surprisingly sided with the theater manager, refusing to grant an injunction against the film.[17] Popular with film buffs, Martineau would later be elected governor of Arkansas in 1927. Brewer, on the other hand, remained in hot water, charged the following year with assaulting a sixteen-year-old girl on a sofa at the Palace.

When *Cleopatra* passed, Gregg was broken. Powerless to do his job, he stepped down from the censor board. The *Daily Arkansas Gazette* reported, "The resignation was the result of the failure of the board to prohibit the exhibition of the *Cleopatra* film. Other members of the board … will resign unless the City Council gives the board authority to enforce its orders."[18] Within a month the mayor directed the city council to better define the duties of the censor board.[19] As the film industry gathered momentum, Little Rock prepared to keep its screens clean of racy, unauthorized motion pictures.

And the onslaught of inappropriate movies continued. *Ingagi* (1930) was a shockumentary that followed a British adventurer in Africa. The explorer treks deep into the jungle to investigate a tribal ritual in which women are given to gorillas as sex slaves. The film was scheduled at Little Rock's Arkansas Theater, but City Attorney Linwood L. Brickhouse stormed the box office to arrest the manager and confiscate the film and promotional posters as "lewd, lascivious, and indecent" materials.[20]

Arkansas's battle against smut was still raging three decades later when the Italian film *The Libertine* (1968) opened in Fort Smith. In the picture, a recently widowed woman discovers that her deceased husband kept a secret apartment for the fulfillment of kinky desires. She takes possession and uses the room for her own carnal discovery. In June 1970 a trio of ministers visited the Minitek Theater to view *The Libertine*. After the closing credits rolled, they headed straight for the sheriff to lodge their complaints. The film was seized, banned, and challenged, and censorship was upheld. There would be no *Libertine* in the Natural State.[21]

The following year the Joy Twin, an adult theater in North Little Rock, was raided. The owners were arrested for exhibiting indecent,

Theda Bara (1885–1955) brought a new type of woman to the screen in *Cleopatra* (1917), aggressively independent and sexually voracious.

immoral, and obscene pictures, and the grind house was shuttered.[22] But even with these two victories Arkansas censors recognized they were fighting a losing battle. Like Gregg decades earlier, the next generation of moralists realized that despite decisions in their favor, their time was limited. *Last Tango in Paris* (1972) and *Deep Throat* (1972) opened without incident, and Little Rock's chief censor, William M. Apple Jr., petitioned the mayor to deactivate the board. Apple opined sadly, "Pornography apparently doesn't have a high priority in the offices of city government."[23]

Rock City's fight against filth limped on until 1980. Owners of the Wild Cinemas of Little Rock challenged the state's obscenity act. The act banned nudity, including "the post-pubertal human female breast below a point immediately above the top of the areola," and limited depictions of sexual excitement.[24] Judge William Overton struck the law as unconstitutionally overbroad, and the smokers at Wild Cinema were permitted to play on.

While censors waged an ongoing battle against inappropriate pictures, filmmakers made Arkansas an important location. When the director King Vidor convinced MGM to produce the first talkie on location, he took his crews to eastern Arkansas to shoot *Hallelujah!* (1929). Elia Kazan's prophetic account of reality-TV stardom, *A Face in the Crowd* (1957), was set in the state and based on Budd Schulberg's short story "Your

Arkansas Traveler." B-movie maestro Roger Corman found Arkansas the perfect spot for low-budget movies. He sent a young Martin Scorsese to shoot *Boxcar Bertha* (1972), and Jonathan Demme to film *Crazy Mama* (1975) and *Fighting Mad* (1976). Malvern native Billy Bob Thornton brought his towering naïf Karl Childers to life in Arkansas for the writer-director's debut, *Sling Blade* (1996). Each of these pictures with Arkansas ambience has earned a rightful place in film history.

While Arkansas filmmakers from Broncho Billy to Billy Bob Thornton made their mark, state officials found they could not fight changing times. The censors' attempts to control increasingly defiant content were not compatible with free speech. Arkansas censors stepped aside, and the ribbon of movies continued to unspool.

California

Since the first films flickered to life, movies seem to have had a magnetic attraction to California. But Los Angeles was not the first film capital—San Francisco was.

In April 1894 the first Edison Kinetoscopes were installed in the Holland brothers' arcade in New York City.[1] Sixty days later the peep-show amusement arrived on the West Coast. The *San Francisco Chronicle* reported, "Only twenty-five of these machines [are] in existence, ten of which are in New York, ten in Chicago, and the remaining five right here in the city at 644 Market Street."[2] The program was limited, but still the *Chronicle* raved, "There are some fourteen different scenes, one more wonderful than the other."[3]

As wonderful as these moving pictures were, the City by the Bay had its skeptics. By October 1894 an ordinance was proposed to regulate and censor the new technology. The concern was over immoral and profane content, and San Fran's police commissioner took a proactive approach: "The kinetoscope had not as yet sinned, but why wait until it does?"[4] As movie parlors spread down the coast of California, so did the concern for improper content. Decades before it was a film town, Los Angeles enacted an anti–Kinetoscope ordinance in 1897 aimed at prohibiting prizefighting pictures.[5]

Despite the threat of municipal censorship, California was an attractive location. In 1897 Thomas Edison's director of film production, James H. White, set out on a world tour with a Kinetoscope crew in tow. They arrived in San Francisco that autumn to shoot local subjects, seen in shorts such as *Fisherman's Wharf* (1897) and *Arrest in Chinatown* (1897). Moving down the coast, California's first filmmakers rolled on the luxurious *Hotel Vendome, San Jose* (1897) and the impressive *Surf at Monterey* (1897). A twenty-five-second clip of an unpaved road teeming with horse-drawn carriages, trolleys, and bowler-hatted men captured the frontier ambience of *South Spring Street, Los Angeles* (1897). Continuing south, White's crew filmed *Street Scene, San Diego* (1898) before heading into Mexico.[6]

Four San Francisco siblings, Harry, Herbert, Joseph, and Earle Miles, took the West Coast film industry to a new level. The brothers started off as itinerant exhibitors and by 1902 moved into distribution, renting out titles to create a film exchange.[7] The following year they began producing their own pictures. The Miles Brothers Motion Picture Company built out a studio space at 1139 Market Street in 1906. One notable picture that sur-

The Miles brothers captured footage of San Francisco on the eve of destruction in *A Trip Down Market Street Before the Fire* (1906).

vives is *A Trip Down Market Street Before the Fire* (1906). Setting their camera on a trolley, the brothers captured a street scene of everyday life on the precipice of disaster. Just four days after filming a devastating earthquake and fire destroyed the city.[8] The catastrophe also ruined the Miles brothers' studio and their chance of making a greater impact on film history. The filmmaking center shifted to Los Angeles.

Francis Boggs, a theater man and native of Santa Rosa, was hired as a director at Chicago-based Selig Polyscope in 1907. Looking for authentic exterior locations, he took a crew to California. Since San Francisco was still rebuilding from the destruction two years earlier, Boggs set up shop in Los Angeles. By 1909 he established a film studio—Los Angeles's first—in a neighborhood called Edendale (now Los Feliz).[9]

Other filmmakers followed. The New York Motion Picture Co. dispatched their western division, Bison Films, to Edendale in 1909. Biograph approved D.W. Griffith's plan to shoot *In Old California* (1910) in a remote area called Hollywood. The orange groves of Hollywood became an attractive address when Nestor Motion Picture Co., under the management of Al Christie, established the first studio in the neighborhood in 1911. Nestor was located at the corner of Sunset and Gower. In 1912 the newly formed Universal Film Manufacturing Co. opened up across the street from Nestor but transitioned three years later to a large tract of land the company acquired over the Cahuenga Pass.[10] Inceville, Thomas Ince's expansive back lot, went up in 1911–1912 at Sunset Blvd.

and the Pacific Coast Highway. By the end of the decade Ince relocated to Culver City to build a studio complex that would become MGM in 1924, then Sony in 1981, and Amazon Studios in 2018. In Echo Park, at 1712 Glendale Blvd. Mack Sennett established his laugh factory in 1912 and began to churn out Keystone Comedies.[11]

The Jesse L. Lasky Feature Play Co. arrived in 1913, leasing a barn on Selma and Vine to produce *The Squaw Man* (1914) and laying the foundation for Paramount Pictures. The Fiction Film Co. took over the corner of Melrose and Bronson in 1916, a spot that would later transform into the Paramount lot. Fox Film acquired the Edendale Selig Polyscope studio and put cowboy star Tom Mix to work on oaters. Within five years, from 1909 to 1914, Los Angeles evolved from an obscure backwater to a movie mecca.

LA was a popular filmmaking destination, but it was not the only movie hub in California. The Chicago-based American Film Manufacturing Co. sent director Allan Dwan westward. Establishing the Flying "A" Studio in Santa Barbara, the production house began grinding out Westerns and in 1913 built a permanent facility at West Mission and State Street. Flying "A" was extremely productive, quickly becoming one of the largest studios in the United States—and establishing Santa Barbara as a rival for the title of film capital for nearly a decade, from 1912 to 1921. Sadly, most of the films produced during

Cecil B. DeMille (1881–1959) launched his film career—and Paramount Pictures—with *The Squaw Man* (1914).

Starring Beatriz Michelena, *Salomy Jane* (1914) was the big budget debut feature produced by the Marin County–based California Motion Picture Co.

that time have been lost.[12] After a century of neglect, the Santa Barbara studio was restored and partially preserved by a local architect as a living and working space.[13]

In 1912 the California Motion Picture Co. began modestly in the San Rafael area. George Middleton dabbled in promotional films for his auto dealership until convincing Herbert Payne, a wealthy San Francisco resident and scion of a mining family fortune, to provide seed money.[14] With funding secured, Middleton revised his production slate with greater aspirations. He trained his camera on the talents of his Latina wife, a former opera prima donna named Beatriz Michelena. The couple produced large-scale films such as *Salomy Jane* (1914), *Mrs. Wiggs of the Cabbage Patch* (1914), and *The Lily of Poverty Flat* (1915), which made Michelena into a star comparable to Florence Lawrence and Mary Pickford.[15] The couple's films were popular, but Middleton was too extravagant, building an entire mining town as the set for Michelena's on-screen adventures. The quality of Michelena's films was praised, but they failed to return on their investment. Production slowed in 1916 after nine films and ceased altogether by 1920. Michelena returned to the opera stage. While on tour in 1931 she received news that her film archive had spontaneously ignited, a victim of the highly flammable nitrate film stock. The remnants of Michelena's film career went up in flames. But that is not where her story ends. Sixty-five years later, in 1996, a surviving print of *Salomy Jane* was discovered in an

Australian archive. Returned to the Library of Congress, the film has been preserved and Michelena's work as a pioneering Latina film star and female producer restored to its rightful place in history. In 2002 President George W. Bush recognized Michelena's importance during National Hispanic Heritage Month.[16]

While Beatriz Michelena's California Motion Picture Co. turned out highbrow films with top-notch production values at a deficit, two other studios successfully turned out popular lowbrow Westerns and comedies: Essanay, in Niles, just south of San Francisco, and Balboa Studios, in Long Beach, just south of Los Angeles.

There is a lingering myth that filmmakers fled to California to escape Thomas Edison's aggressive patent litigation. There may be some truth to this theory, but Essanay was a charter member of Edison's Motion Picture Patent Co. Set up by Broncho Billy Anderson, an actor who parlayed a performance in *The Great Train Robbery* (1903) into stardom, Essanay was incorporated in Chicago in 1907. Seeking a longer outdoor shooting season, Broncho Billy moved operations west, arriving in Fremont in 1912 and erecting a studio in the township of Niles the following year.[17] From this facility Essanay churned out cheap but lucrative Westerns, such as *Broncho Billy's Last Hold-Up* (1912) and *Alkali Ike's Close Shave* (1912). By 1915 Essanay transferred its up-and-coming comedian on contract—Charlie Chaplin—to the Niles facility. In a single productive season Chaplin made *The Tramp* (1915), *The Champion* (1915), and *A Night Out* (1915), among other films. When his contract came up for renewal at the end of the year, the Little Tramp demanded an increase from $1,250 a week to $10,000 a week, plus a $150,000 signing bonus. Essanay thanked him for his work and showed him the door. It might not have been the best business decision. Two months later, on February 16, 1916, the Niles studio received a telegram from its corporate office in Chicago with orders to cease all production.[18]

A similar situation was playing out with Balboa Studios. The Horkheimer brothers—Elwood, "E.D.," and Herbert, "H.M."—set out from Wheeling, West Virginia, in 1912, flush with cash from an inheritance. More skilled salesmen than aspiring movie moguls, they arrived in Long Beach on the cusp of a movie boom.[19] Edison Manufacturing Co. had rented studio space to produce several films on location, including *Dances of the Ages* (1913) and *The Old Monk's Tale* (1913), but pulled out five months into their yearlong commitment. The Horkheimers assumed Edison's lease and Balboa Studios was born.[20] Between 1913 and 1918 Balboa was immensely prolific and competitive with the leading Hollywood studios. Active on the Balboa stages were Roscoe "Fatty" Arbuckle and Buster Keaton, who made *The Bell Boy* (1918) and *The Cook* (1918) on location.

For a brief two-year period, San Diego was also a contender in the film game. Lubin Film set up an outpost at Coronado in 1914. Once up and running, the plant was turning out almost ten films a month, many directed by the branch manager, Wilbert Melville, such as the crime drama *The Diamond Thieves* (1916) and the woman's hysteria/divorce picture *The Scarlet Chastity* (1916).[21] When Lubin, one of the industry's original pioneers, went out of business in 1916, so did the dreams of a San Diego studio.

By the end of the 1910s Los Angeles assumed a dominant position in the California film industry. As Hollywood thrived, establishing vertically integrated studios that controlled systems of production, distribution, and exhibition, the smaller facilities in San Francisco, Niles, Long Beach, and San Diego ceded control. By the time the 1920s dawned, Hollywood was the clear California capital.

Even as film studios in California were consolidating their power, the specter of state-authorized censorship threatened the emerging industry. In 1907 Long Beach passed an ordinance prohibiting motion pictures that depicted murder, suicide, burglary, drunkenness, wife beating, and nudity.[22] In 1909 San Francisco forbade pictures containing crime, violence, and "improper scenes."[23] The following year film laws were put in place in Los Angeles in January, in Pasadena in April, in Berkeley in June, and in Oakland in July.[24] On top of these municipal measures, the state senate passed a film censorship bill in 1913 over the resistance of motion picture industry lobbyists.[25]

Not only were film censorship laws passed, they were also enforced. A San Francisco theater owner screened a Vitagraph thriller entitled *A Dead Man's Honor* (1911) starring Maurice Costello and Mabel Normand. The picture depicted a holdup and a shooting murder. The theater owner was arrested, found guilty, and fined one hundred dollars or sentenced to fifty days in the county jail.[26] In Los Angeles, censors disapproved of Charlie Chaplin's cross-dressing comedy *A Woman* (1915) and ordered police to seize the film.[27] But as the movies became more lucrative, moviemakers became more powerful. In 1916 the Los Angeles city council voted to abolish film censorship. After the studios promised to bring productions to the Bay Area, San Francisco followed LA and repealed its own censorship ordinance.[28]

With state censorship in California under control, the studios cooperated on a system intended to keep regional censors across the country at bay. A production code was hammered out and enforced by Joseph Breen on all studio pictures. Breen's code limited the movies' subject matter and the maturity of the themes, squelching gangster dramas like *Scarface* (1932) and silencing cunning sexual innuendoes from the likes of Mae West. Hollywood filmmakers were forced to convey naughty moments with elliptical references: a tight embrace, a fade to black, a train going through a tunnel. On the other hand, the code attempted to preempt state censorship and avoid overlap between overseers of content. The studios sacrificed autonomy to avoid governmental regulators.

Still, there were films made outside the jurisdiction of the Production Code that called for censorship. One Czech film entitled *Ecstasy* (1933) featured a nubile fräulein skinny-dipping in a pond and streaking across fields of edelweiss. The picture was stopped at U.S. Customs and barred from entering the country.[29] Though the picture had been halted, its starlet was recruited by Louis B. Mayer and transformed into Hedy Lamarr, one of MGM's great glamour girls of the 1940s. Other pictures were not as fortunate. The Soviet propaganda film *Oblomok imperii* (*Fragment of an Empire*, 1929) was banned in Laguna Beach.[30] Upton Sinclair's screen adaptation of his novel *It Can't Happen Here* was killed in preproduction by Breen, censored on the basis that "it might offend Adolph Hitler or Benito Mussolini."[31]

By the 1960s film content had become more sexually explicit and outrageously extreme. Obscenity statutes could be used to rein in hard-core pornography, but certain films could present horrific debauchery without being technically or legally obscene. One of these was an exploitation film by grind house mavens Michael and Roberta Findlay. The Findlays pioneered innovative fetishistic cinema slaughter in low-budget slasher/horror flicks such as *Body of a Female* (1964), *Take Me Naked* (1966), and the pre–*Scream* trilogy of *The Touch of Her Flesh* (1967), *The Curse of Her Flesh* (1968), and *The Kiss of Her Flesh* (1968).

The Findlays' masterwork of marketing was *Snuff* (1976), a film that put fear in the hearts of many despite being seen by few. *Snuff* played off chilling rumors that real murders of young girls were being filmed for depraved entertainment. The movie caused alarm, motivating groups like Women Against Violence Against Women to take action.

The picture they said could *NEVER* be shown...

The Bloodiest thing that ever happened in front of a camera!!

SNUFF

The film that could only be made in South America... where Life is *CHEAP!*

Snuff (1975) was the brainchild of film provocateurs Michael and Roberta Findlay. It sent shockwaves through America with a slasher scenario that many thought was true.

In Orange County, Judge Paul Mast called the Findlays' film "grossly sickening" and issued an injunction banning it from exhibition.[32] The Findlays' film was merely fictional snuff, but even the description of such psycho-horror shocked audiences to their core. So dire was the crisis that the California state legislature was moved to pass an anti-snuff-film bill.[33]

From the earliest days California has been an incubator for filmmakers. Within months of the first motion picture exhibition, peephole Kinetoscopes attracted long lines of eager audiences in San Francisco. During the 1910s emerging studios dotted the West Coast, but a decade later these producers consolidated in and around Los Angeles. From that hub, Hollywood generated an industry—a dream factory—with attractive, persuasive, and hypnotic images that changed the world. While California encouraged the lucrative movie business, the flickering images presented a dilemma for morally minded authorities. This tension between creative freedom and administrative control shaped the media and the minds of generations of viewers. While the First Amendment and the power of a bountiful box office have encouraged free expression, that liberty remains fragile. It can be undone by the mania caused by a midnight movie.

Colorado

Rushing rivers, quiet valleys, and soaring mountains call out to photographers. Harry H. Buckwalter was one of the first to capture motion pictures of Colorado's rugged Rocky Mountain landscape.

Buckwalter began his career as a Denver-based newspaper and commercial photographer.[1] When motion picture equipment became available in the 1890s, Buckwalter leaped at the opportunity to experiment with the new medium. Meanwhile, a Chicago-based film mogul named Col. William Selig understood the cinematic potential of Colorado's natural beauty and signed on Buckwalter's services. Buckwalter's first films included panoramas, such as *Lava Slides in Red Rock Canyon* (1902); industrial scenes, such as *Where Golden Bars Are Cast* (1902), showing the Globeville smelter refining ore from slag to valuable bullion; and Western slices of life, such as *Runaway Stagecoach* (1902). With daredevil style he captured distinctive shots. One local newspaper reported, "H.H. Buckwalter, the moving picture man, is planning to take a balloon flight from the top of Pike's Peak, photographing the scenes as he floats down toward Manitou."[2]

After *The Great Train Robbery* (1903) captivated audiences, Buckwalter raised the level of excitement in his own films. *Tracked by Bloodhounds; or, A Lynching at Cripple Creek* (1904) depicted a woman killed and her husband's quest for vengeance. Buckwalter re-created a stage-

Tom Mix and his horse Tony starred in *The Great K&A Train Robbery* (1926), shot in Glenwood Springs, Colorado.

coach robbery for *The Hold Up of the Leadville Stage* (1904), a picture that was billed as "the most exciting film ever made in the mountains in Colorado."[3] Buckwalter next considered a film based on the labor strikes by the Western Federation of Miners. In June 1904 an explosion rocked the Independence, Colorado, train depot, killing thirteen nonunion men crossing the line. While a ripped-from-the-headlines story was exciting material, Buckwalter ultimately passed on the project. His first thought in making the film, he informed a reporter, had been "only the sensational feature. Such pictures are very popular in the [E]ast in all the summer resorts and theaters. But several very warm friends called my attention to the harm the picture would do Colorado and I at once agreed … to abandon it."[4] Buckwalter was nearing the end of his Colorado motion picture production days. He left the Rocky Mountains for Central America in 1912 when Selig commissioned a documentary on the Panama Canal, released as *Across the Isthmus of Panama* (1912).[5]

As Buckwalter was heading out, Colorado's censors were closing in. Denver's mayor,

James M. Perkins, stumped for film regulation: "I want to see excluded from all moving picture houses any films that are indecent; any that show wanton slaughter of animals or birds, [and] pictures that show … drunken men."[6] By 1916 women's clubs in Boulder, Greeley, and Fort Collins pressured their own mayors and city councils to enact film ordinances. These outspoken voices grew powerful. Like censors in many other states, Colorado's watchdogs shut down some films for moral issues, but Boulder's censors went further. *The Battle Cry of Peace* (1915) was a pacifistic response to the growing pressures of World War I. Boulder banned the peace-loving propaganda picture. But these activists were not solely concerned with antiwar films. Even Paramount's cartoon comedies found disfavor with Colorado's self-styled censors when the animated shorts were seen as advocating for the manufacture of armaments and against American Isolationism.[7] By 1919 a formal censorship law in Boulder outlawed scenes of safecracking, narcotics use, and counterfeiting. Women were permitted to smoke on-screen only in a "manner approved by the censor; kissing scenes may be cut by the censors or the length of the kiss shortened."[8]

Also in 1919, a bill was introduced to the Colorado legislature to control motion pictures on a statewide basis.[9] The controversial proposal had strong-minded advocates on both sides of the issue, but as it moved through the statehouse on its way to approval, disaster struck. The text of the Colorado censorship law was cribbed from a similar law in neighboring Omaha, Nebraska. The Colorado state stenographer charged with copying the legal text noticed a clerical error: the law as approved read, "Be It Enacted By the State Of Nebraska."[10] The typo proved fatal. The Colorado censorship statute was a dead letter.

Although a censorship law was out, innovative methods of controlling improper content were on the horizon. In 2000, a company called Clean Flicks of Colorado went into the business of creating altered versions of Hollywood films, editing out sex, nudity, profanity, and violence. Clean Flicks cropped offending footage or digitally inserted a black bar to obscure unsuitable images. It didn't take long for major motion picture studios and leading filmmakers to respond. Disney, DreamWorks, Fox, MGM, Paramount, Sony, and Warner Bros. brought suit, along with a who's who of A-list directors that included Steven Soderbergh, Robert Altman, Martin Scorsese, and Steven Spielberg.

Before the Colorado court Clean Flicks claimed they were creating derivative works that qualified as "Fair Use" because they transformed the original movie. Senior District Judge Richard Paul Matsch saw things differently: "The fair use defense is not applicable to this case … because the infringing copies of these movies are not used in a transformative manner."[11] Judge Matsch turned to the Supreme Court's definition of transformative and identified the requirement that "something new [must be added], with a further purpose or different character, altering the first with new expression, meaning or message."[12] Clean Flicks was not creating new movies, just neutering the naughty bits from selected titles. The family-friendly censoring service reworked their business model in 2007 but ultimately shut down entirely in 2013.[13]

In 2013 Colorado became the nexus of a series of lawsuits centered on a new method of distribution that disrupted the status quo: BitTorrent. BitTorrent is a peer-to-peer file-sharing system. A file transfer begins when one user accesses the Internet and makes a digital file freely available to the public from his or her computer. Because the torrent is a decentralized network where copyrighted works can be shared without authorization, it presents "a tough nut to crack for copyright holders."[14]

Torrent-sharing technology began around 2005, but litigation picked up as streaming technology improved. In 2011 producers of *The Hurt Locker* (2009) sued twenty-five thousand BitTorrent users but found their claims dismissed because of difficulties in tracking down defendants by their IP addresses.[15] Around the country BitTorrent lawsuits were filed, creating a dramatic increase in copyright litigation between 2010 and 2015. By going after multitudes of anonymous file-sharing defendants, copyright owners could economize on filing fees. But the courts became skeptical of such mass joinders, finding the technique ripe for copyright trolling and opportunistic litigation.[16]

Shortly after *Dallas Buyers Club* (2013) scored three Academy Awards—for stars Matthew McConaughey and Jared Leto and for the film's artistry of hair and makeup— the picture's producers began enforcing their rights. They filed over one hundred suits against alleged BitTorrent pirates, several of whom were based in Colorado. The complaint addressed the independent filmmakers' desire to recoup revenue from unauthorized downloaders.[17]

Twenty "John Doe" defendants were charged with copyright infringement, and by 2015 three Colorado residents were identified: Lisa Hudson of Thornton, Douglas Eldridge of Fountain, and Leonard Cordova of Colorado Springs.[18] Producers of *Dallas Buyers Club* claimed that the defendants had participated in a BitTorrent "swarm" with other peers, accessing, distributing, and exploiting the copyrighted film. While each of the defendants was found guilty of direct infringement and fined $2,250, the producers could not demonstrate that each of the defendants had accessed the film file on the same date. If they hadn't connected to the digital files simultaneously, they couldn't have been part of the same swarm. The significance of this decision was that the defendants could be held individually accountable, but grouping infringers together—to streamline and economize on litigation fees—would be far more difficult to prove. After the *Dallas Buyers Club* cases, courts around the country became less tolerant of actions targeting large numbers of anonymous file sharers.[19] The solution to the copyright challenges raised by file-sharing peer-to-peer technology would require innovative and strategic thinking as opposed to aggressive and impersonal litigation.

While Colorado audiences have enjoyed motion pictures since the early days of filmmaking, the state has spent decades attempting to control the medium. Clean Flicks tried to abridge Hollywood films and bring them to a potentially wider audience, but Colorado's courts found that the organization's methods violated copyright law. Producers of *Dallas Buyers Club* wanted that wider audience—they just wanted viewers to pay for their entertainment. Here Colorado's courts pushed back, requiring copyright holders to target specific infringers. The film history of the Mile High State demonstrates a precarious balance between free speech and censorship and the challenges of protecting copyrights against new and developing technologies.

Connecticut

The American film industry was born in New Jersey and grew up in New York. Less than fifty miles north, Connecticut brought a hint of New England to the tri-state area. Film depictions of Connecticut offered a cozy suburban lifestyle, but this oasis from the rat race could also hide a sinister reality.

When D.W. Griffith took his first directing assignment, the aspiring filmmaker headed for Norwalk to shoot *The Adventures of Dollie* (1908), a domestic thriller.[1] A family out on a stroll encounters two gypsies, who kidnap their child. The girl is placed in a barrel and sent down a river. Griffith's location at Sound Beach was a departure from studio-made pictures shot on rickety rooftop sets. The director returned to Connecticut, to Cos Cob outside Greenwich to shoot two more films: *Ingomar, the Barbarian* (1908), a drama set in ancient Gaul; and *The Ingrate* (1908), a story of fur trappers. Both featured Florence Lawrence, a starlet on her way to becoming recognizable as "the Biograph Girl."[2]

Within ten years of Griffith's films, the shadow of censorship emerged in Connecticut. At a time when New York, Pennsylvania, Ohio, and Maryland had passed or considered film regulations, the *Bridgeport Telegram* editorialized against the trend: "Censorship leads to woeful abuse of power. Sooner or later the job of censoring falls into the hands of some petty, narrow minded autocrat, who starts immediately to misuse his office, either to gratify his personal vanity, feed his spite, or line his pocketbook."[3]

Despite the *Telegram*'s warning, in 1925 a statewide film censorship bill was approved. The governor was granted the power to appoint a board charged with monitoring movies for content considered "obscene, indecent, immoral, inhuman, sacrilegious, or of such character as to tend to corrupt morals to incite crime."[4] Exhibitors would submit a film, pay a fee, and, if approved, be issued a permit. This much was similar with other state agencies, but the Connecticut censorship scheme had an additional element: a film tax. The regulation entitled "An act providing for the imposition of a tax on films from which motion pictures are to be exhibited within the state" levied a ten-percent duty on exhibition based on seating capacity. By the end of the year the state's 238 theaters contributed $192,000 to the state's coffers.[5]

Alarms sounded within the film community. Will Hays, newly hired to head the Motion Picture Producers and Distributors Association, was dispatched to Hartford. Hays threatened to close theaters throughout the state and cease distribution.[6] Fox Film went further. They sued to enjoin the tax.

Hays's appeal fell on deaf ears; similarly, Fox's action was fated for failure. The *Mutual* decision (see Ohio) handed down ten years earlier by the Supreme Court had ruled that motion pictures were "a business pure and simple" and subject to regulation under the police powers of a state.[7] Deferring to local administrators and Supreme Court precedent, the Connecticut court found that regulations on film would not infringe upon the First Amendment's protection of speech. Next the court looked at the tax. Here the issue of offending the Interstate Commerce Clause of the Constitution was raised. Once again the Connecticut court found that the tax did not discriminate, applying equally to films produced in state as well as those imported: "Whatever burden or restriction the law imposes is purely incidental insofar as interstate commerce is concerned."[8] Whether the Connecticut law was positioned as a revenue measure or a police regulation, it was a valid method of controlling the medium. The tax law was upheld and Fox's prayer for injunction denied.[9]

The Motion Picture Theatre Owners of Connecticut reluctantly contributed to a fund to cover the tax. Two years later a torrential downpour flooded the region, and the owners' association redirected its funding to the Red Cross for relief work.[10] This maneuver put the owners in a positive light. As the floodwaters abated, the film tax was repealed.

Unlike many states that were concerned with moral issues and representations of sex and crime in cinema, Connecticut eyed the movies as a source of income. Perhaps this use of state censorship—for greed—was even more insidious than the pretension of morality. The film law in Connecticut functioned less to protect audiences from inappropriate images and more as a method of fleecing filmmakers.

Connecticut took its place as the symbol of suburbia on screen. From Stamford to New Haven and Middletown to Manchester, the state seemed to be populated by eccentric aristocrats as well as average Joes making the bridge-and-tunnel commute to work in Manhattan.

In Howard Hawks's superb screwball comedy *Bringing Up Baby* (1938), Cary Grant played a buttoned-up paleontologist. Entering Katharine Hepburn's madcap orbit, he is taken on a roller-coaster ride of misadventure. Grant ends up in a rustic country house in Westport wearing a women's bathrobe and caring for a semi-domesticated leopard. Ten years later Cary returned to Connecticut for *Mr. Blandings Builds His Dream House* (1948), this time renovating an abode in fictional Lansdale County. Teaming with Myrna Loy, he experiences a far more relatable domestic horror story—the money pit of a house remodel.

How could it be that a Jewish man from the Russian empire could compose America's greatest Christmas song? Irving Berlin did just that for *Holiday Inn* (1942), the story of retired Broadway performers (Bing Crosby and Fred Astaire) who cool their heels in a Connecticut bed-and-breakfast. Berlin's high-concept scenario marked the B&B's seasonal festivities with musical numbers—and won the composer an Academy Award for "White

Christmas." Several songs, including "Happy Holidays" and "Easter Parade," were instant classics, while others, like the minstrel show performed in blackface for Lincoln's birthday, are best forgotten. In another film destined to become a Yule time chestnut, Barbara Stanwyck played a hard-boiled journalist forced to masquerade as Suzy Homemaker in *Christmas in Connecticut* (1945).

Despite Connecticut's quirky gentry, stressed-out working men, and idyllic wintertime locations, a darker current ran beneath the normality. In *The Stranger* (1946) Edward G. Robinson played a Nazi hunter. A trail leads to the quiet hamlet of Harper and an unrepentant war criminal. Directed by Orson Welles, who also played the villain, *The Stranger* revealed gothic horror in a quiet all-American town.

Director Elia Kazan made two Connecticut-set films that both dug beneath surface appearances to reveal criminal corruption and bigoted hatred. *Boomerang!* (1947) was based on true events. After a priest is murdered in Stamford, a frantic manhunt scapegoats a

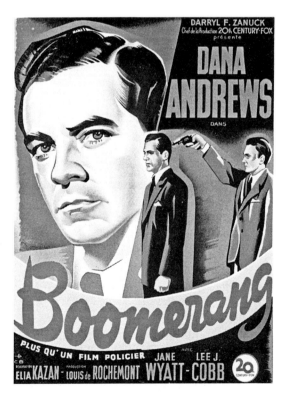

Based on a true story, Elia Kazan's *Boomerang!* (1947) was a socially conscious film that questioned the criminal justice system.

vagrant war veteran, condemning him on shreds of evidence. Dana Andrews played a district attorney whose challenge is to stand up for justice against an angry mob's need for revenge. Kazan's second film set in Connecticut was the Academy Award–winning *Gentleman's Agreement* (1947). Here a WASP-y journalist (Gregory Peck) goes undercover as a Jewish man in Darien. Posing as Phil Greenberg, he experiences the invisible anti–Semitism baked into American culture.

The quintessential horror story of surface appearances is *The Stepford Wives* (1975). In a pristine Connecticut neighborhood everything seems perfect. Leafy green streets are lined with comfortable houses tended by beautiful women. But when Joanna (Katharine Ross) relocates to Stepford with her family, she begins to suspect something is wrong. Glassy-eyed submissive trophy wives are revealed to be automatons. The film—a dated melodrama by itself—outgrew its B-movie credentials to become cultural shorthand for a certain type of woman.

While many states enacted film regulation bureaus to ward off the debauchery pictured in Hollywood movies, Connecticut's legislators saw inappropriate pictures as a good way to fill civic coffers. The film-luxury tax was withdrawn after exhibitors redirected their fund to philanthropy—and scored a valuable public relations coup. In the coming decades the state would take its place as a cinema suburb. The portrayal of Connecticut's shady lanes and upscale houses changed with the times, evolving from a fashionable address to a calm façade concealing deep-rooted secrets.

Delaware

Only one hundred miles from Edison's lab in Menlo Park, New Jersey, motion pictures arrived early in Delaware. The *Wilmington Evening Journal* raved about the new technology in 1894, describing how the Kinetoscope "is set a-going when a nickel is put into the slot." The reporter was dazzled as he peered through a peephole at *The Barbershop* (1894): "One of the lilliputian actors rises and walks across the picture to a chair, sits down and is tilted back … and then begins a 5 cent shave that resembles the swing of a scythe in the hands of a farmer."[1]

Soon a variety of devices, such as the "Great Projectoscope" and Lubin's "Cineograph," were spinning at parlors across the state.[2] Edison's production crews captured a slice of life in the First State in *Miniature Railway at Wilmington Springs* (1903), an interracial youth boxing bout in *A Scrap in Black and White* (1903), and a soapbox derby scene in *Tub Race* (1903). As local playhouses generated interest and income, municipal authorities began to enact regulations.

On June 9, 1909, a Wilmington exhibitor named John Wesley Morris opened the Hyrup Amusement Co. at 411 Market Street. City inspectors paid a visit to the playhouse and demanded a fee for operation. Morris studied the statute and refused. The law stated that a license was needed for operators of circuses and theatrical performances. The movie man reasoned that since there was no live entertainment in Hyrup's program of projected images, the law should not apply. Judge William Boyce of the Delaware Superior Court disagreed. He found that the medium of motion pictures, while not explicitly contemplated by the code, "did constitute the exhibiting of a circus within the meaning of said statute."[3] This was a significant decision. A year after Chicago had passed down the first case on film censorship (see Illinois), Delaware's court expanded the rule. Judge Boyce determined that statutes regulating public performances could be interpreted broadly to reach the new medium of motion pictures. This would set the stage for censorship battles in the next four decades.

Only two months after the Hyrup case, Wilmington considered banning the popular but racially charged Jeffries-Johnson boxing film. Before the city council could act, local exhibitors found that the film's rental costs for the "Fight of the Century" proved too prohibitive.[4] Market factors regulated motion picture exhibition, alleviating the need for state interference. Delaware boxing fans would have to travel to Philadelphia, Baltimore, or Washington, D.C., to see footage of the bout.

While access to a premium title like the Jeffries-Johnson film could be limited by market factors, Delaware wrestled with the issue of content regulation. The *Wilmington News* advocated pruning out certain subjects as early as 1911. Included on their taboo list were pictures that dealt with crime and infidelity or that made a joke of drunkenness or a farce of robbery. The paper editorialized, "It is certainly discouraging to see young girls, either not out of their teens or not out of school, laughing at and applauding dialogues and stage scenes that would naturally shock them in real life." The editors further added that "that sort of thing is demoralizing when served to those of immature minds."[5] By February 1915, State Senator Edward Gormley proposed a film ordinance: "An Act to Create a Board of Censors for Exhibitions of Moving Pictures."[6] As it headed for a vote, the bill was suddenly rescinded and replaced with a call for a prohibition on concealed weapons.[7] Film regulation was de-prioritized against gun control.

The issue of municipal censorship was under review in Wilmington city hall two months later. John O. Hopkins suggested an ordinance "to prohibit the exhibition of any moving picture likely to cause ill feeling between the white and black races."[8] Councilman Hopkins's proposal was likely aimed at the incendiary content of D.W. Griffith's *The Birth of a Nation* (1915), which was road-showing around the country, breaking box office records but also leaving a wake of racial disturbances. The Hopkins bill was passed and sent to Mayor Harrison W. Howell. Mayor Howell stamped a veto on the bill.[9]

Two years later the issue of censorship was live again, this time with an interesting wrinkle. State legislators conceded that Delaware was too small for its own dedicated censor board. As an alternative, one proposal required any film screening in the state to be approved by the censors of Pennsylvania or Maryland. The "Pennsylvania-Maryland-Censorship-for-Delaware" proposal was sent to committee, where it disappeared from discussion.[10] The proposal demonstrated creative thinking to be sure—allocating censorship to the political appointees of neighboring states as a cost-saving maneuver.

While Delaware's flirtation with censorship was brief, the state became a vital hub for the film industry's corporate activities. Delaware has long been attractive to businesses for several reasons, including limitations on liability and a Court of Chancery able to offer jurists with in-depth experience in matters of corporate law. Simultaneous with the film industry itself, Delaware emerged in the early 1900s as the preeminent venue for businesses to incorporate, based on the state's flexible corporate law and beneficial tax structure.[11]

When master exhibitor Marcus Loew acquired three studios and merged them into Metro-Goldwyn-Mayer, the consolidated entity was incorporated in Delaware on

October 18, 1919.[12] United Artists, brought together by Charlie Chaplin, Mary Pickford, Douglas Fairbanks, and D.W. Griffith, filed its certification for incorporation in Delaware on April 17, 1919.[13] Harry, Al, Sam, and Jack Warner had been in the movie business since 1903; when they created a corporate entity on April 4, 1923, Warner Bros. was incorporated in Delaware.[14] According to the companies' U.S. Securities and Exchange Commission filing papers, the Walt Disney Company; News Corp., the parent of Fox Films; Comcast, the parent of Universal Pictures; Viacom, the parent of Paramount; and Netflix were all incorporated in Delaware.

For over a century major motion picture studios logged their corporate records in Delaware, but one case rises above the others. This case pitted the Walt Disney Company against its onetime chief executive officer Michael Ovitz. After working his way through the corporate offices of Universal and Fox, Ovitz found his calling at the William Morris Agency. After six years as an agent Ovitz left in 1974 with four colleagues to form Creative Artists Agency. CAA quickly became an industry powerhouse, packaging stars, writers, and directors and selling projects, essentially replacing in-house studio development departments. Creative Artists reshaped the entertainment industry as studios were engulfed by diversified mega-corporations.[15]

In 1995 Disney's chief executive, Michael Eisner, began courting Ovitz for a position as studio head at the Mouse House. At first Ovitz was reluctant, unwilling to give up his $25 million salary as an agent without specific assurances, but several months of negotiations brought Ovitz and Disney closer to a deal. Ultimately the "Ovitz Employment Agreement" would specify a five-year term that guaranteed the super-agent $50 million unless he breached the agreement, in which case he would forfeit the remuneration. If Disney fired Ovitz for any reason other than gross negligence or malfeasance, Ovitz could claim his remaining salary plus an additional $7.5 million a year for bonuses and a $10 million severance payout.[16] The deal was sweet to say the least. The agreement was inked.

The Disney-Ovitz relationship began on a positive note in January 1995, but cracks in the façade quickly began to show. Ovitz turned out to be a poor fit with the company culture. He demanded preferential treatment, such as limousine transport at a corporate retreat while his colleagues loaded onto a bus, as well as questionable expense reimbursements. Under Ovitz's watch the studio produced Martin Scorsese's *Kundun* (1997). *Kundun* was a biopic that focused on the life of the Dalai Lama, a topic toxic for the Chinese government. The People's Republic of China reacted aggressively, calling a temporary halt on the development of Disney's lucrative theme parks on the mainland.[17]

Eisner sat on the pink slip for his studio boss for months. When the ax finally fell terminating Ovitz's regime at Disney, trouble was just beginning. Ovitz left with his treasure trove, and Disney shareholders filed an action in Delaware's Court of Chancery against both Ovitz and the company's board of directors. The shareholders claimed the $130 million severance payout was excessive—both a breach of fiduciary duty and a waste of corporate assets.[18]

Chancellor William B. Chandler III considered the tortuous tale of corporate indulgence and invoked the business judgment rule. This Delaware precedent was a policy of nonintervention, leaving a business's board to manage their own operations. The rule, wrote Chandler, was not actually "a substantive rule of law, but instead it is a presumption that in making a business decision the directors of a corporation acted on an informed basis … and in the honest belief that the action taken was in the best interests of the company [and its shareholders]."[19] In the course of business the court would step aside to give the C-suite broad latitude to exercise its judgment for better or worse.

The money was extravagant. The duty of care may have been played fast and loose. The duty of loyalty to the shareholders may not have been carefully considered. But ultimately Chandler ruled for the defendants, concluding that Disney's board of directors acted in a manner they believed was in the best interests of the corporation.[20] The chancellor's decision was appealed but found no quarter with the Supreme Court of Delaware. While everyone agreed the termination provision in Ovitz's employment agreement may have been prodigal, imprudent, and ill-informed, it was not a breach of fiduciary duty or business care, or a case of corporate corruption. The court's message was clear: the C-suite is allowed to make bad decisions.

In a world of increasing production costs, unpredictable box office income, erratic state censorship, and corporate mismanagement, Delaware was an oasis. Censors were sent packing and all but the most flagrant business bungling would be left alone. Delaware would step aside and allow the market to decide whether a studio would survive.

In the aftermath of the Ovitz fiasco, Bob Iger stepped into the studio's top slot. Iger's regime at Disney would be marked by remarkably sound corporate judgment. He acquired Pixar in 2006 for $7.4 billion, Marvel Entertainment in 2009 for $4 billion, and Lucasfilm in 2012 for $4.05 billion.[21] These purchases cemented Disney's position as an industry leader with blockbuster productions perfectly synced with the company's theme-park division.

Florida

Five years before the first scenes were cranked out of Hollywood's industrial film factories, Florida was the warm-weather movie location of choice. In 1916, while California was still a distant destination for many filmmakers, as many as thirty studios were operating in the Sunshine State. But as the twenties began to roar, Florida's stages quickly became a memory and California claimed the title of movie capital.

The story of filmmaking in Florida shows the rise and fall of a regional industry. From 1915 to 1919 Jacksonville was a media hub that buzzed with activity. But J-ville wasn't alone; movies also came out of Miami, Palm Beach, St. Augustine, and Tampa. For a brief period Florida attracted both major studios and aspiring independents that produced mainstream fare as well as niche content tailored to African American or Latino audiences. When political sympathies shifted, movie men found themselves unwanted in Jacksonville at a time when Hollywood was drawing in filmmakers. As quickly as its rise, so was the fall of the onetime self-proclaimed "World's Winter Film Capital."

Cameramen first arrived in Florida as part of the front line in the media war against Spain. Edison dispatched William "Daddy" Paley to cover Florida, America's staging point to invade Cuba. The cinematographer produced patriotic actualities on location, including *Burial of the "Maine" Victims* (1898), *9th U.S. Cavalry Watering Horses* (1898), and *Colored Troops Disembarking* (1898). Edison's main competitor, American Mutoscope and Biograph, followed with their own military pictures, including *With the Army at*

Tampa (1898), as well as domestic slice-of-life scenes, such as *Lawn Tennis in Florida* (1898), *Feeding the Ducks at Tampa Bay* (1898), and *Fighting Roosters in Florida* (1898).[1] One notable Biograph film takes on a sinister aspect to modern eyes: *An Execution by Hanging* (1898) appears to record the actual death of an African American man.[2] From everyday scenes to military preparedness to simmering racial tensions, early filmmakers were able to capture shadows of an era.

Each of these Edison and Biograph pictures were "actualities," or one-shot slice-of-life proto-documentaries. Narrative "story" filmmaking began when Col. William Selig sent a crew to shoot *A Trip to St. Augustine, Florida* (1906).[3] It was the Kalem Company that established deeper roots. Kalem built a studio in Jacksonville that operated from 1908 to 1917. As the Kalem crew prepared to embark on their southern expedition, the *Moving Picture World* announced, "Real Southern scenes taken among the palms and moss-covered pines will soon be shown all over the country."[4] Kalem's star-director Sidney Olcott captured local flavor in *The Ponce de Leon Fete* (1909), *The Seminole's Vengeance: or, The Slave Catchers of Florida* (1909), and *A Florida Feud: or, Love in the Everglades* (1909).

Other studios followed Kalem. Philadelphia-based Lubin Manufacturing Company sent a production team to Jacksonville in 1909 and opened a permanent facility by 1913, putting out such titles as *A Honeymoon Through Snow to Sunshine* (1910), *A Gay Time in Jacksonville Florida* (1912), and *A Florida Romance* (1913).[5] Thanhouser, a studio with its main offices in New Rochelle, New York, opened a winter plant in Jacksonville in 1912, releasing a series of costume dramas starring Florence La Badie: *The Arab's Bride* (1912), *A Love of Long Ago* (1912), and *The Ring of a Spanish Grandee* (1912).[6] Vitagraph set up in St. Augustine to shoot *A Florida Enchantment* (1914).

While Jacksonville was the state's filmmaking center, turnover there was high. When Lubin closed shop in 1915, Mark Dintenfass, one of Universal Pictures' early investors, purchased the lot for the Vim Comedy Company.[7] Louis Burstein's New York Motion Picture Company took over Lubin's contract star Billy Reeves, a popular Chaplin knockoff, to produce a slate of comedies under the King Bee Films banner.[8] Vim and King Bee were soon folded into Amber Star, the southern division of Rhode Island–based Eastern Film Company.[9] The film business in the Florida market was transient; to survive in front of the lens or behind the scenes, workers had to be flexible.

Oliver Hardy's pre–Laurel film career demonstrates the itinerant life of a film actor in Jacksonville. Hardy was born in Georgia and migrated south in 1914 when he was twenty-two years old.[10] As the Florida film scene was burgeoning, the young "Babe" Hardy signed with Lubin and began churning out nearly a film a week for two years from 1914 to 1915. The plus-size comedian appeared in Arbuckle-Keystone knockoff films, such as *The Honor of the Force* (1914) and *The Prize Baby* (1915). When Lubin Film folded, Hardy didn't skip a beat. His slapstick shorts were picked up by Vim, and the comedian continued to show up to work at the same studio; only the management had changed. At Vim, Hardy paired with a diminutive former trapeze artist named Billy Ruge for dozens of films in the "Plump and Runt" comedy series. When Vim rolled up the rug, King Bee took over and Hardy maintained his frantic output of funny films. The film industry moved around Babe Hardy as he continued his shtick. In 1918 King Bee transferred the corpulent comedian to Hollywood, where three years later he met Stan Laurel.

For Oliver Hardy, it was business as usual as the studio letterhead changed. The saga of the Eagle-Norman Studios shows a very different development. The Eagle Film

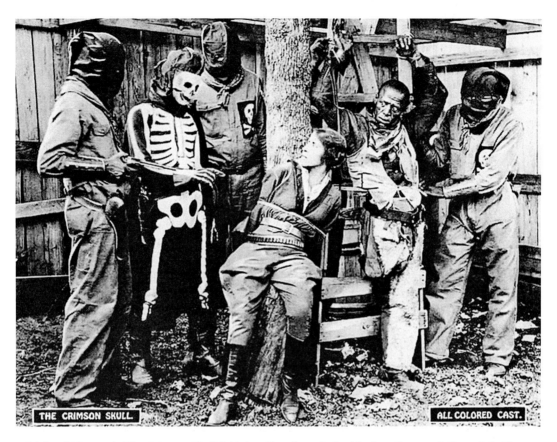

THE CRIMSON SKULL   ALL COLORED CAST.

Richard Norman's *The Crimson Skull* (1922), tailored-made for black audiences, delivered thrills and excitement on a modest budget.

Manufacturing and Production Company was a short-lived film factory that produced a dozen pictures. The majority of these titles featured a Spanish comedian named Marcel Fernández Peréz. Peréz was a popular draw in Europe but left the Continent as World War I heated up. Based in Jacksonville, he developed a Chaplin-esque character named "Tweedledum," who appeared in *Tweedledum Torpedoed by Cupid* (1916) and *A Lucky Tramp* (1916). But Perez's brand of stunt-based humor and trick camerawork was too costly for the small studio. Eagle failed and Richard E. Norman stepped in.

Norman was the owner of a film-processing laboratory. He entered the production end of the business with an action film called *The Green-Eyed Monster* a.k.a. *The Wrecker* a.k.a. *The Man at the Throttle* (1916). *Monster* centered on competition between two trainmen and their rivalry for the same woman. To increase nail-biting thrills, Norman cut into the film real-life footage of an actual train wreck. He road-showed the picture around the South, quickly earning back his investment. Recognizing an alternative film market that was not being adequately served, Norman acquired the Eagle facility and moved into the niche of "race" filmmaking.

Race films were movies that catered to African American audiences, with black actors and themes tailored to minority issues. While Oscar Micheaux (see South Dakota) was the poster child for this specialized industry, there were several white producers of race films, such as Reol Productions in Harlem, New York. Norman realigned his production slate to appeal to African American audiences. He remade *The Green-Eyed Monster* in 1919 as a race film—using the same train-wreck sequence. From its Jacksonville headquarters, Norman Films released *The Bull-Dogger* (1921), a black Western starring rodeo star Bill Pickett; and *The Flying Ace* (1926), a World War I aviation picture with stock footage of an aerial dogfight.[11] Norman Films was one of the longest-running race film shingles and one of the final studios remaining active in Florida, in production as late as 1928. The transition to talking pictures proved too costly and Norman folded. Unlike many regional studios that have all but disappeared, Norman's studio was rediscovered and restored. In 2002 the city of Jacksonville purchased the Eagle-Norman lot and dedicated a museum to recalling the city's golden era as a moviemaking capital.

While many of Florida's studios may have been fleeting operations, the state also provided locations for film houses destined to become Hollywood majors. Famous Players–Lasky, on the verge of restructuring itself to become Paramount Pictures, produced *My Lady Incog* (1916) in Palm Beach.[12] Fox Films sent their resident sex bomb Theda Bara to St. Augustine for *A Fool There Was* (1915) and to Miami for *A Woman There Was* (1919).[13] Back in Jacksonville, the Technicolor Film Corporation showcased its new system in *The Gulf Between* (1917), the first feature film shot in Technicolor.

Theda Bara burst on the screen as the first film "Vampire" in *A Fool There Was* (1915) shot in St. Augustine, Florida, and Fort Lee, New Jersey.

Florida was attractive to silent film producers for practical reasons: the Sunbelt allowed for year-round exteriors and ample light in an era before electric lighting was widespread. The diversity of landscape permitted producers to shoot seaside stories as well as exotic tales in the state's swampy interior. Jacksonville was a major hub on the vaudeville circuit, well serviced by train lines. Furthermore, the city actively courted business from film producers. In January 1916 Mayor J.E.T. Bowden extended an invitation to filmmakers to relocate to Jacksonville.[14] Bowden was an opportunistic city manager; in addition to the film business, he also supported Jacksonville's thriving bordello district.[15] The next mayoral election saw the political pendulum swing in a different direction. John W. Martin was elected mayor of Jacksonville in 1917 based on a more conservative platform. Both brothels and moviemakers were no longer welcome in Jax.[16]

The news got worse for filmmakers. In May 1921 Governor Cary Hardee ratified a film regulation code that covered the whole state.[17] When Hardee left office in 1925 he was succeeded by Martin. Martin had been no friend to the film industry when he served as mayor of Jacksonville, and his conservative policies didn't change when he relocated to the state capitol.

While Pennsylvania, Ohio, Kansas, Maryland, and New York had also enacted statewide censorship laws before 1921, Florida's code was different. Instead of creating a homegrown board of regulators, the Florida method looked to two out-of-state authorities for guidance. In order to legally play in Florida, a film had to have been passed by either the New York State Censor Board or the National Board of Review.[18] This was a cost-efficient way to regulate, but it surrendered Florida's moral authority to external organizations.

In practice Florida rarely moved to take action and censor a motion picture until obscenity became an issue in the 1960s. By the time George W. Bush commissioned the Obscenity Prosecution Task Force in 2005, Florida and the Eleventh Circuit emerged as one of the Department of Justice's favorite jurisdictions. Florida courts saw the successful prosecutions of Joe Francis, the producer of the *Girls Gone Wild* soft-core series; Danilo Simões Croce, an importer of fetish films, including the Internet sensation *2 Girls 1 Cup*; and Paul Little a.k.a. Max Hardcore, a pornographer specializing in demeaning and violent pornography.[19]

With the exception of extreme and outrageous fringe content, Florida's authorities maintained a hands-off approach to regulating motion pictures. Even after passing a censorship statute in 1921, the state left the business of barring films to other agencies. This policy of non-involvement saved money and resources. It was only when the federal government prioritized obscenity prosecutions that Florida became an important venue in the United States of censorship.

Florida has a vibrant film history. For a five-year period the state could claim to be one of America's most important production hubs. Sadly, many of the players in this regional industry have become obscure. The stages of Florida's once thriving film scene—such studios as Klever Pictures, Hialeah Studios–Miami, and Klutho Studios—have grown silent and forgotten, awaiting rediscovery.

Georgia

It was no ordinary day in Piedmont Park. At six thirty on the evening of September 18, 1895, President Grover Cleveland punched a golden button and the Cotton States and International Exposition in Atlanta came to life. "Cannon blazed and thundered, 60,000 people cheered," the *New York Times* reported, "[and] a thousand flags fluttered from the tops of the many buildings."[1]

But one booth was sadly overlooked. Two Washington, D.C.–based inventors,

Charles Francis Jenkins and Thomas Armat, had carted their Phantoscope—patent pending—to the expo hoping to make a grand introduction. Here an audience could have witnessed the first commercial motion picture exhibition in America. Except that no one showed up. The eager inventors "opened their doors to what they hoped would be an eager crowd. But there was no consuming desire on the part of the public to witness what was inside."[2]

In his autobiography Jenkins recalled that movies were "at the time understood or appreciated by but few, the few who casually visited the Phantoscope building."[3] He hired a carnival barker who sang and strummed a banjo, tempting crowds with the promise that for a modest sum they could witness an electrical miracle, since the terms for motion pictures, films, or photoplays had not yet been coined. The busker attracted a modest crowd, enough to keep the exhibit running. Six weeks later in early November a fire broke out and the Phantoscope was incinerated.[4] With their device lying charred in the embers, Jenkins and Armat deemed their experiment a failure.[5]

Motion pictures, of course, were not dead. Only two years later a series of wildly popular boxing films, such as *The Corbett-Fitzsimmons Fight* (1897), drew enthusiastic crowds to newly opened nickelodeon theaters. Georgia authorities were so threatened by the new medium of entertainment that by 1897 a bill was introduced to the state senate to prohibit Kinetoscopes of prizefighting pictures.[6] A decade later Atlanta mayor Lester Maddox declared his disapproval of boxing loops.[7] The battle over boxing films remained an issue in Atlanta. Reels of the Jack Dempsey–Gene Tunney match were seized from the Howard Theater (a few blocks from today's CNN Center) in 1927.[8] The exhibitor challenged the search warrant but to no avail. A prohibition on prizefighting films stayed on the books long after the genre faded in popularity.

Atlanta's authorities passed a flurry of laws to regulate local movie houses. Highly flammable film stock became a convenient excuse for stricter oversight. In 1911 Mayor Maddox pressured his fire chief to make careful inspections of theaters; Atlanta's police commissioner followed up with a series of raids.[9] Other actions aimed to harass theater goers. The city council considered a law requiring ladies to remove their hats at shows after 6:00 p.m. The "Hats Off" regulation stipulated that at daytime performances "they can wear any kind of hat they want to."[10] By the mid–1910s a chapter of the Better Films Bureau was founded by Mrs. Alonzo Richardson, and Atlanta organized a board of city censors led by J.W. Pattillo.[11] With the singular focus of monitoring obscene or inappropriate pictures, Atlanta's official film mavens were intermittently active between 1915 and 1944.[12]

Films that were scrutinized during this pre–World War II period ranged from the sexually titillating to the politically provocative. *Three Weeks* (1914), a suggestive picture that foreshadowed *9½ Weeks* (1986) by seven decades, was challenged by Atlanta's censors but ultimately passed.[13] An anti-birth-control film entitled *The Unborn* (1916) courted controversy, but the pro-life message found acceptance with Atlanta's movie-morality militia.[14] Race issues on film found less tolerance. Fox's *The New Governor* aka *The Nigger* (1915) was banned, with the *Atlanta Constitution* reporting that the picture "incurred resentment … because of alleged misrepresentation of the South."[15]

George K. Rolands and Samuel Q. Edelstein of the New York Photoplay Company announced a motion picture entitled *The History of the Leo Frank Case* (1915).[16] Their project was ripped from the headlines, based on an Atlanta murder case. The trial made national news when anti–Semitic sentiment was injected into the legal proceedings. The resulting mistrial further aggravated tensions. While the picture was still in production Atlanta's police department banned any film on the subject.[17] *The Leo Frank Case* played in nearby Charlotte but was never permitted to screen in the City Too Busy to Hate.

Similarly controversial, *Auction of Souls* a.k.a. *Ravished Armenia* (1919) focused on ethnic cleansing in Turkey. Written by and starring Aurora Mardiganian, a survivor of the Armenian genocide, *Auction* was produced while many of the horrific events depicted were still occurring overseas.[18] Notwithstanding its newsworthiness, Mardiganian's docudrama would not be permitted to educate Atlanta's audiences. Peachtree City censors barred *Auction* based on its shocking imagery.[19]

In December 1944 Atlanta's aldermen assembled a permanent review board. They appointed Christine Smith, a graduate of Emory University and a former director of the Atlanta League of Women Voters, to the position of chief censor.[20] Smith launched into her new post by barring Fritz Lang's unrelentingly bleak film noir *Scarlet Street* (1945). *Scarlet Street* starred Edward G. Robinson

Before the "It Girl," writer Elinor Glyn created a modern—liberated—woman in *Three Weeks* (1924).

as a henpecked store clerk. On his walk home one evening he rescues a beautiful femme fatale (Joan Bennett). Robinson's well-timed assistance leads him into a spiral of deceit and murder. Typical of Fritz Lang's fatalistic film visions, *Scarlet Street* is uncompromised by a Hollywood ending: each of its characters is punished for their amoral actions. Christine Smith was equally unbending. She banned the film, finding it indecent and improper: "The film deals with an immoral woman and illicit love, shows the enactment of a murder, and permits the man who commits the murder to go unpunished except by his own conscience."[21]

Walter Wanger produced *Scarlet Street*. His objection to the ban was personal; he was concerned not only for the box office but for the career of the film's female lead, Joan Bennett—his wife. "Atlanta is the only place in the country that has forbidden this picture," Wanger told the local Universal Pictures representative after arriving in the Southern city. "My interest in *Scarlet Street* is more than profession[al]. The picture stars the woman I love."[22] Wanger convinced the panel to review the picture a second time. The appeal

Aurora Mardiganian brought the Armenian genocide to the screen in her controversial *Auction of Souls* (1919).

locked in a tie vote and went to the city attorney. On February 15, 1946, the city attorney voted to uphold the censor's ban. *Scarlet Street* was frozen out of Hotlanta.[23]

Christine Smith put theater owners on the defensive. When the Paramount Theatre applied for a permit to revive *Imitation of Life* (1934), an Academy Award–winning melodrama starring Claudette Colbert, Louise Beavers, and Fredi Washington, Smith rejected the application. The picture centered on a light-skinned African American girl who conceals her heritage to pass as white. Twenty years after its original release the censor found the film still "cross[ed] the line."[24] *Swell Guy* (1946), written by Richard Brooks, focused on a two-faced scoundrel whose sunny disposition masks deceitful behavior. Smith objected to an illicit love affair in the film, and *Swell Guy* was banned.[25] Hitchcock's *Rope* (1948) was cut from schedules when Smith demanded deletion of the film's strangulation scene and the director refused.[26]

The following year, two films proved to be particularly controversial: *Lost Boundaries* and *Pinky*. Both confronted the issue of African American characters "passing" as white. In 1945, a decade after its original release, *Imitation of Life* had demonstrated Smith's sensitivity toward racial themes was still a raw nerve. By the end of the decade she was challenged to rethink her position. Smith stood firm on banning *Lost Boundaries* (1949), concerned it "would adversely affect the peace, morals, and the good order of the city."[27] *Pinky* (1949), on the other hand, served as an important antidote to outdated values. Smith passed *Pinky*, commenting, "I know this picture is going to be painful to a great many Southerners. It will make them squirm, but at the same time it will make them realize how unlovely their attitudes are."[28]

Pinky was directed by Elia Kazan, who had won a Best Director Academy Award the previous year for his exposé of anti–Semitic behavior in everyday life in *Gentleman's Agreement* (1948). Once again, with *Pinky*, Kazan produced a picture with undeniable artistic pedigree: Jeanne Crain was nominated for an Academy Award for leading actress, and Ethel Waters and Ethel Barrymore for their roles as supporting actresses. The film followed a light-skinned African American girl returning home to the South after completing her education in the North. Having tasted equality, she is met with and overcomes racist attitudes.

Fox, a major studio, distributed *Pinky*; *Lost Boundaries*, on the other hand, was an independent production. Louis de Rochemont had established his reputation with the *March of Time* newsreel series and did not shy away from postwar issues such as race relations. Based on a true story (see New Hampshire), *Lost Boundaries* followed a fair-skinned African American doc-

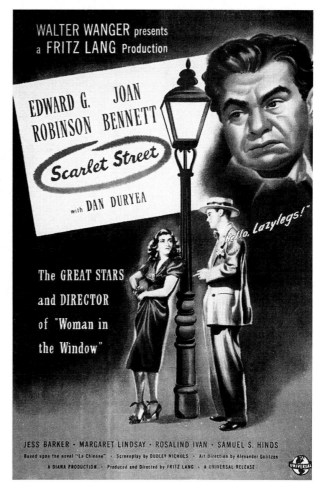

Fritz Lang's unrelentingly dark vision of humanity in *Scarlet Street* (1945) was unwelcome in Atlanta.

tor (Mel Ferrer) unable to find employment. He disguises his true identity and assumes a new life, until his secret is revealed. While Pinky stood up for her race in the face of bigotry, the character in *Lost Boundaries* concealed his ethnicity and was therefore more dangerous to Atlanta's conservative moral authorities.

De Rochemont sued to challenge not just the ban on his film but also censorship in general. His claim was too progressive. Thirty-five years earlier the Supreme Court had ruled motion pictures were not entitled to First Amendment protections. In the *Mutual* case (see Ohio) the High Court saw the projected image as "capable of evil" and in need of regulation.[29] De Rochemont argued that since the 1915 decision, the medium of motion pictures had developed in form and function and was now worthy of constitutional protection. Chief Judge of the Fifth Circuit Joseph C. Hutcheson refused to take that step. Judge Hutcheson found that Atlanta's film censors had acted with legitimate authority to protect the peace, health, morals, and good order of the city.[30] The ban on *Lost Boundaries* stood, but change was in the air. The Supreme Court would shatter their precedent only two years later.

Leaving a trail of broken hearts, Sonny Tufts is no *Swell Guy* (1946) in a film written by Richard Brooks.

The times were changing. In 1955 Christine Smith married Atlanta alderman Ed A. Gilliam, but married life did not mellow the censor.[31] When *The Birth of a Nation* (1915) was rereleased for a fortieth anniversary screening, Christine Smith Gilliam barred the racially provocative epic.[32] Next she targeted the rock-and-roll high school flick *The Blackboard Jungle* (1955). This time Judge Boyd Sloane overturned the ban. Sloane permitted *Blackboard Jungle* and undermined the censor's authority, writing, "There is serious doubt as to the constitutionality of the city [film censorship] ordinance."[33]

Smith Gilliam was losing control. She barred the British film *Room at the Top* (1959), only to discover a Marietta theater defiantly screening the picture despite her prohibition.[34] She objected to the Jules Dassin–directed *Never on Sunday* (1960) because it "presented an objectionable idea," that is, a classical scholar's relationship with a Greek prostitute.[35] *Sunday*'s distributor challenged the Atlanta ordinance, claiming it violated free speech protections. This time the judge agreed, finding the city's censorship laws unconstitutional. It was a major break, but his opinion was overruled on appeal reinstating the ban.[36] Still, the censor's victory was fleeting. The following year two exploitation films came under Smith Gilliam's fire: *Wasted Lives* and *The Birth of Twins* (release dates unknown).[37] Both films were banned. The ban was challenged. Chief Judge William Henry Duckworth of the Georgia Supreme Court never even reached the issue of obscenity. He found the film law unconstitutional on its face. The ordinance was overbroad and went beyond the limited scope needed to uphold the peace, health, morals, and good order of the city. On April 7, 1962, Atlanta's censorship law was thrown out.[38]

Without a censorship law on the books, Smith Gilliam's title was revised to "motion picture reviewer."[39] Her wings were clipped. By 1964 she stepped down, and the era of city censors was over. During her twenty years on the job, Smith Gilliam reviewed over 5,500 films. By 1971 she claimed that her only tie to the industry was reading fan magazines at the hairdresser.[40] There was a sense of resigned bitterness in Smith Gilliam's departure; as she packed up her desk, she recommended that her seat be left vacant—for "it was futile to attempt to protect the public against the impact of obscene movies in light of the recent court decisions," she said.[41]

Even without a film regulation ordinance, censorship continued in Georgia. A Swedish New Wave art film, *I Am Curious (Yellow)* (1967), offered ample nudity of its curvaceous star. It was barred as obscene. The Georgia Supreme Court screened the picture and agreed.[42] A sexploitation confection entitled *Sandra: The Making of a Woman* (1970) was branded obscene. Again, the court agreed.[43]

Albany's authorities challenged the Jack Nicholson, Art Garfunkel, Ann-Margret, and Candice Bergen starrer *Carnal Knowledge* (1971). The Georgia township's council felt the picture's discussion of sex in the seventies was inappropriate. The court agreed: "We hold that the evidence in this record amply supports the verdict of guilty by the showing of the film *Carnal Knowledge* in violation of the definition of distributing obscene materials under our Georgia statutes."[44] This time the United States Supreme Court stepped in to reverse the decision.

After watching *Carnal Knowledge*, the Supreme Court unanimously agreed that Georgia had gone too far. Justice Rehnquist wrote, "We hold that the film could not, as a matter of constitutional law, be found to depict sexual conduct in a patently offensive way, and that it is therefore not outside the protection of the First and Fourteenth Amendments."[45] With this decision SCOTUS drastically limited the state's ability to pursue film-obscenity prosecutions.

The story of film censorship in Georgia began with a bill prohibiting prizefighting pictures in 1897 and ended with *Carnal Knowledge* spilling across screens in the swinging seventies. Unlike the most adamant censors around the country, like Maj. Funkhouser in Chicago and Lloyd T. Binford in Memphis, Atlanta's film expert, Christine Smith Gilliam, seemed to enjoy the movies. When a challenging picture like *Pinky* came before her, she realized the importance movies could play in changing attitudes. Ultimately Smith Gilliam and her fellow film censors retreated to their place on the shelf of history. Still, the threat of censorship waits for the opportunity to silence certain speech. Although laws currently favor free speech, the tension remains. The battle between freedom and control continues.

Hawaii

The crowd was on the edge of their seats as Elsie Adair prepared for her signature move on the roof of Madison Square Garden. The dancer concentrated for a moment before launching into a series of backward aerial somersault twirls. "She is the only lady in the business and the only lady on earth as far as known who can turn the backflip," raved the *New York World*.[1] Adair was an entertainer who played to packed houses along Broadway during the golden era of vaudeville entertainment.

Adair frequently shared the stage bill with two other giants of pop culture: Loie Fuller and Eugen Sandow. Fuller was a modern dancer who innovated whirling, twirling choreography in the Serpentine Dance. Sandow was a specimen of modern masculinity, a pioneering muscle man ripped with incredible definition. In 1894 Florenz Ziegfeld, Jr., signed both Adair and Sandow for a road show. The performers shared the stage to display their marvels of physical fitness.[2] As the tour ended, Sandow returned to Broadway while Adair continued on, bringing her modern dance moves to the Hawaiian Opera House in June 1894 and then on to the Far East.[3]

While Adair was circling the globe, back in New York a new form of entertainment was capturing the public's attention: motion pictures. Sandow was called in to Edison's Black Maria studio to record a series of what would become the earliest commercial films. Meanwhile, Loie Fuller was touring Paris. Her performances captured the attention of Post-Impressionist artists, including Henri de Toulouse-Lautrec and Auguste Rodin, and inspired the Lumière brothers.[4] The *frères* hired an imitator to perform Fuller's Serpentine Dance for their Cinematograph in 1896.

Adair continued to perform until she fell ill in Australia. The dancer's condition was so severe that newspapers announced her imminent death.[5] As she recovered, Elsie was unable to perform her most acrobatic routines. Instead, she added a new act to the show: motion pictures. When Adair returned to Hawaii, her act included the first films to be shown in the paradise islands. At the Honolulu Opera House she entertained audiences with a program of thirty pictures, including *The May Irwin Kiss* (1896), *Stable on Fire* (1896), and *Jumbo, the Horseless Fire-Engine* (1897).[6]

Motion pictures spread across the globe. In 1897 James H. White, chief of Edison's Kinetograph division, left for a round-the-world expedition with cameraman Frederick W. Blechynden.[7] On their return the film crew arrived in Hawaii to shoot such pictures as *Wharf Scene, Honolulu* (1898) and *Honolulu Street Scene* (1898). Before long, Hawaiian audiences were on the filmic front line, as the first to see images of conflict in Asia, from the United States' involvement in the Philippines to the Russo-Japanese War.[8]

As motion pictures grew in popularity so did the call for censorship. In Honolulu all theater owners save one aligned in a policy to steer away from suggestive content. The manager of the Art Theater, Mr. Lawson, stood alone, saying, "The people like pictures that are spicy.... If there are any prudes who don't like the class of pictures I am showing then let them stay away."[9]

By 1914 the territory adopted government-sanctioned censorship. The chamber of commerce appointed a committee of film regulators, with members stationed in Kapaa, Lihue, Koloa, Eleele, and Waimea.[10] These island censors were mostly drawn from academic institutions, demonstrating that the primary focus for film regulators was protecting the welfare of children. Chief censor Henry Walsworth Kinney also served as the territory's superintendent of education; C.B. Morse, a local school principal, held dominion over the screens of Kauai.[11]

The censor's power was largely advisory in Hawaii. When Lois Weber's allegorical art film *Hypocrites* (1915) arrived in Honolulu, the picture's representation of "Truth" as a naked woman skirting across the screen raised eyebrows. The censor board convened but permitted the titillating film.[12] This permissive policy led moral activists to approach territorial governor Wallace Rider Farrington in 1922 to request more rigorous censoring.

The Social Service Association was concerned that "the evils of improperly censored motion pictures upon the people of our island and upon children especially are apparent … promot[ing] immorality and crime in some instances." They petitioned Farrington "to forbid the exhibition of all films … harmful to the morals or the people especially the young."[13]

While censors cracked down, local production picked up in the tropical territory. Henry MacRae was an early director working for Selig Polyscope in California. He collaborated with star Hobart Bosworth on six films in 1913. The following year MacRae transferred to Bison Films and left for Hawaii to shoot a series of exotic island dramas, including *Cast Adrift in the South Seas* (1914), *Isle of Abandoned Hope* (1914), and *A Romance of Hawaii* (1914). Although he returned to Hollywood to churn out his quota of Westerns for Bison, MacRae remained transfixed by the East. By the early 1920s he resumed his eastward journey to direct *Miss Suwanna of Siam* (1923), the first Thai-Hollywood coproduction.

MacRae's films impressed Bosworth. Bosworth left Selig's studio to establish his own production shingle and departed for the tropical territory. In Hawaii Bosworth shot *The Beachcomber* (1915), likely the first picture to feature a Hawaiian actor, known only as Mr. Rahawanaku.

Rahawanaku may have been the first, but the most famous Hawaiian screen star would be the great swimming and surfing champion Duke Kahanamoku. Credited with introducing the flutter kick, Kahanamoku smashed records in the 50, 100, and 220 freestyle events. At the Olympics in 1912 and 1920 he claimed gold medals in the 100-meter freestyle. In 1924 he earned a silver, edged out by Johnny Weissmuller. The following year, while relaxing in Newport Beach, Kahanamoku witnessed a yacht capsize. He rode to the rescue on a surfboard, saving eight people.[14] After planting his longboard in the sand, the Hawaiian hero was quickly cast in Hollywood films. Victor Fleming signed Kahanamoku for *Adventure* (1925), adapted from a Jack London story, and followed up with *Lord Jim* (1925), based on Joseph Conrad's novel. Unfortunately, American

The surfing sequel *Gidget Goes Hawaiian* (1961) saw Deborah Walley stepping into the title role.

audiences were not ready to adopt Kahanamoku as a leading man. For the rest of his film career, the larger-than-life figure was underused as a supporting player in tropical escapist flicks such as *Hula* (1927), *Isle of Sunken Gold* (1927), and *Isle of Escape* (1930).

Pearl Harbor and the postwar years gave Hawaii new significance for American audiences, ranging from chest-thumping patriotism to seductive island pleasures. Howard Hawks's patriotic *Air Force* (1943) was green-lit on the heels of the attack starring John Garfield as an aerial gunner. Fred Zinnemann's *From Here to Eternity* (1953) depicted life on the Honolulu base before the attack; its images of Burt Lancaster and Deborah Kerr locked in an embrace as warm waves wash over their bodies instantly became one of cinema's great icons of uncontainable love. *Eternity* also revitalized Frank Sinatra's career with a win for Best Supporting Actor as the tragic Pvt. Maggio.

As the war receded into memory, Hawaii remerged as a pleasure playground. Elvis Presley returned repeatedly for *Blue Hawaii* (1961), *Girls! Girls! Girls!* (1962), *Paradise Hawaiian Style* (1966), and the concert film *Elvis: Aloha from Hawaii* (1972). Whether tinged with Tiki torch kitsch in *Gidget Goes Hawaiian* (1961) or filled with nail-biting thrill rides in *Jurassic Park* (1993), the crystal waters and golden sunshine of Hawaii beckon to audiences. Since the first film cameras rolled on the Aloha State, the movies have offered a window for audiences to escape into island fantasy.

Idaho

The Rocky Mountains might not be the first place to search for a cinematic sea nymph or a tropical islander, but Esther Williams called Sun Valley her film home in *Duchess of Idaho* (1950). Williams holidayed in the resort town between making her name as MGM's aqua star in extravaganzas like *Neptune's Daughter* (1949) and *Million Dollar Mermaid* (1952). MGM's Nordic ice-skating specialty star Sonja Henie booked a trip to appear in *Sun Valley Serenade* (1941). *Serenade* also notably featured the Glenn Miller Band performing "Chattanooga Choo Choo" in an Academy Award–nominated number, as well as an acrobatic dance by the Nicholas brothers in a rare Hollywood showcase. Marilyn Monroe took a romantic layover in *Bus Stop* (1956), filmed in Idaho, where she sang a sultry version of "That Old Black Magic."

The Million Dollar Mermaid, the ice-skating queen, and the blonde bombshell played strong female characters against the wide-open vistas of the Gem State. But they stood on the shoulders of a giant. Two decades before Williams, Henie, and Monroe arrived, a filmmaker named Nell Shipman established her production company at Priest Lake. In the far northern reaches of the Idaho panhandle Shipman wrote, produced, directed, edited, and starred in a series of outdoor adventures. Far from the soundstages of Hollywood, this bold female filmmaker ventured into the wild to produce movies that celebrated independent women in exciting scenarios. Although Shipman's name may no longer be familiar, she deserves to be remembered as one of cinema's important female pioneers.

Nell Shipman was born in British Columbia and arrived in Southern California by 1912. She found success as a writer—winning both first and second prize in a scriptwriting

Nell Shipman (1892–1970) is a forgotten female film pioneer, a writer-director-star-producer of outdoor adventures.

contest.[1] In the early days of Hollywood before corporate structure was set in place, several women were able to develop behind-the-scenes power. These women achieved a high level of creative control: Anita Loos and Marion Fairfax at Paramount, June Mathis and Frances Marion at MGM, Beta Breuil and Helen Gardner at Vitagraph, and Mary Pickford at United Artists. Universal was the most female-friendly, employing Lois Weber, Ruth Ann Baldwin, Grace Cunard, Cleo Madison, and Ruth Stonehouse above the line.[2] While these women filmmakers earned respect in social message films and costume dramas, Nell Shipman was in a class by herself as a real-life adventure hero.

Shipman could not be confined to the safe space of a studio stage. She earned notice at Vitagraph for her starring role in *God's Country and the Women* (1916), shot in Big Bear, California. The *Moving Picture World* raved the film was "an ideal blending of dramatic story material, beautiful locations and impressive acting."[3] Shipman moved to Universal to make *The Melody of Love* (1916) in Lake Tahoe. Having proven her box office draw, she could focus on independently produced passion projects set in the untamed territory of her youth. The *Moving Picture World* gave *Back to God's Country* (1919) the distinction of "having been made farther north than any other dramatic picture"—in Alberta, Canada.[4] *The Girl from God's Country* (1921) was Shipman's biggest film yet. This north-woods epic pitted the resilient starlet against Mother Nature herself—with fires, earthquakes, and an unrelenting frozen winter. Production proved too much for Shipman's male colleagues. Codirector Bert Van Tuyle suffered a frostbitten foot. Leading man Ronald Byram caught pneumonia on location, dropped out, and died before the film's release.[5]

 The Girl from God's Country hurt Shipman in other ways. The film's budget was too extravagant and put her production company deep in the red.[6] To continue making outdoor films, she relocated to Upper Priest Lake, Idaho, setting up a base of operations at Lionhead Lodge.[7] Along with her crew and the standard movie equipment came Shipman's personal menagerie. This motley supporting cast included bears, beavers, cougars, coyotes, deer, eagles, elk, marmots, muskrats, owls, porcupines, rabbits, raccoons, skunks, and wolves, as well as dogs and cats. Ten buildings were built to house these temperamental costars. Far from Hollywood Central Casting's reserve of character actors, Shipman's critters took on important roles, playing comic relief, heroes, and villains.[8] In one memorable scene in *Back to God's Country*, Shipman skinny-dips in a crisp mountain stream. A pervy prospector ventures closer to take a peek, but as he comes around a boulder a lounging bear scares him away. Nature, nudity, hints of naughtiness, and a funny animal—Shipman had honed a blueprint for popular outdoor adventures.

 From her Idaho base, Shipman starred in, wrote or co-wrote, and directed or co-directed four films between 1923 and 1926. *The Grub-Stake* (1923) promised high drama "where man went mad with the lust for gold and women sold their souls."[9] Reviewers praised Shipman's film, noting, "Few pictures are destined to make a wider appeal."[10] Despite positive notices, *The Grub-Stake* would be her last feature-length

While Dolores was being forced to the wall inside, her father fought the other villain outside the cabin door.

The Clarence Curwood Productions present

Nell Shipman
in
"Back to God's Country"
From the Story, "Wapi, the Walrus" by
James Oliver Curwood
Directed by David M. Hartford
A 'First National Attraction

One girl battles the elements in *Back to God's Country* (1919).

film. Shipman released a series of two-reel outdoor featurettes shot at Priest Lake—*Trail of the North Wind* (1924), *The Light on Lookout Mountain* (1926), and *White Water* (1926)—as her production company went bankrupt.

As Hollywood's studio system solidified in the early 1920s there was less room for a maverick filmmaker making movies on her own terms. By 1925 creditors took over Shipman's Idaho ranch. The bank claimed Shipman's assets but was unable to provide proper care, and her animals starved in their cages. The Kaniksu National Park ranger cried out for aid and donations, and San Diego responded. The city's zoo took in several of the surviving animals.[11] Shipman had achieved success during the pioneering days of moviemaking, but her tale arrived at a sad conclusion.

Nell Shipman's Idaho productions stand as examples of a regional cinema that could exist for but a brief period at a certain point in the development of the American film industry. As Hollywood became the center of production, Los Angeles eclipsed local filmmakers.

While production was centralized in LA, censorship was widespread. Around the country, censors fought against the morally corrupting influence of the movies. During the 1920s, while many states enacted film ordinances, Idaho declined to set up a censor board. By 1934 the *Idaho Falls Post-Register* editorialized against state film regulation, believing the market would correct itself. The paper acknowledged the temptations of the "hotcha flapper" but saw the trend shifting against sinful scenes: "Pictures which show the old style vamp play to empty seats. Youth, romance, clean lives and clean living are having their appeal."[12] The *Post-Register* ran this column the year Joseph Breen assumed control at the Production Code Administration. Breen's position as a centralized censor was intended to rein in inappropriate content and replace regional censoring committees. In the case of Idaho, Breen's strategy was effective.

The issue of state censorship in Idaho simmered on the back burner until 2013. That year the Cannes Film Festival was dominated by a lesbian-themed love story entitled *La vie d'Adèle* (*Blue Is the Warmest Color*, 2013). When a Boise theater and draft house scheduled the art film, it triggered Title 23–614 of the Idaho penal code. Under the code, venues serving alcohol were prohibited from displaying any simulation of sex acts.[13] A strip-club law was turned into film censorship. *Blue* bypassed Boise.[14]

The issue made headlines again in 2016 when *Fifty Shades of Grey* (2015), an erotic feature distributed by Universal Pictures, triggered the same Idaho penal code provision. This time the Idaho chapter of the American Civil Liberties Union (ACLU) filed an action.[15] The law was overreaching, the ACLU complained, and chilled speech that should be protected under the First Amendment. Academy Award–recognized pictures such as *12 Years a Slave* (2013), *The Wolf of Wall Street* (2013), and *American Sniper* (2014), each contained fleeting shots of fondling or simulated sex. "Each of those films could potentially run sideways of the Idaho statute," read the complaint.[16]

While *Blue Is the Warmest Color*, a foreign film, had less sway with regional regulators, Idaho legislators heard the voice of the studios. The code was revised before the case reached a resolution. The schedule of prohibited acts under the alcohol-service license was amended to allow cinemas serving alcohol to screen potentially offensive films.[17]

Free speech triumphed. Wrote the Ninth Circuit, "Content-based regulation of expression by the government, even of indecent expression, is prohibited unless necessary to meet a compelling government interest."[18] Even with this favorable court decision,

Idaho's law demonstrates how vulnerable certain speech remains. Although some may feel the fight against censorship is a chapter for history books, the battle between freedom and control continues.

Illinois

When the Chicago World's Fair opened in 1893, Thomas Edison had recently introduced his peephole Kinetoscope device. The inventor had previously given a private demo at the Brooklyn Institute's Department of Physics in May 1893, but the Columbian Exposition could provide a great opportunity for cinema's commercial launch on a grand stage.[1] Whether the movie machines made it to their Illinois destination is another story.

Anticipation for exciting modern marvels at the Chicago Expo was high. In April 1893 Edison announced the attractions planned for his exhibit, naming his Kinetoscope as the centerpiece.[2] His moving picture machine wasn't unique. Ottomar Anschütz brought his own invention from Germany to the event: the Tachyscope. The Tachyscope created a film-like sequence as images spun around a glass wheel. The device provided about three seconds of entertainment.[3] Anschütz's invention was a step toward the invention of cinema, but his device was far more rudimentary than Edison's peephole projector.

Edison's machine was surely more impressive, but mystery surrounds the question of whether fairgoers could have compared the two devices. Some scholars have argued that the Kinetoscope never made it to the event.[4] Edison had also promoted a Kinetophone, an early talking picture device, which was not completed on time. In the flurry of activity during the run-up to Chicago 1893, the record of exhibits has become shrouded in a historical mist. What remains is the fact that various optical devices captured the imagination of festivalgoers on the cusp of an electronic era.

By 1905 nickelodeons were a booming business, and Chicago emerged as an important hub. Theater owners built movie palaces: Aaron J. Jones established the Orpheum and Bijou in the Loop, and Barney Balaban and Sam Katz laid the foundation for what would become the Paramount-Publix theater chain. Chicago-based film exchanges rented movies out to theaters around the country. These early distribution houses included the Kleine Optical Company, William Swanson & Company, Max Lewis's Chicago Film Exchange, Robert Bachman's 20th Century Optiscope, and the International Projecting and Producing Company.[5]

The Second City also teemed with film production companies. William Selig released his first narrative film in 1896, photographed on location in what would become Rogers Park. Selig set up a Polyscope production plant at 45 E. Randolph, then moved to a larger facility at 3945 N. Western Avenue, with an outdoor "Western" range where WGN-TV stands today. Pioneering producers George K. Spoor and Broncho Billy Anderson used the "S" and the "A" from their last names to create Essanay Film Studio in 1907 and built stages at 1333–1345 W. Argyle, in an impressive stone building that remains standing. In 1910 Samuel Hutchinson established American Film Manufacturing Co., or Flying "A," at 6227 N. Broadway and later became one of the first producers to relocate to California.

On the South Side of Chicago, "race film" studios catering to African American audiences opened their doors by the 1910s. The Micheaux Film Co., owned and operated by the prolific writer-producer-director Oscar Micheaux, centered its operations at 538 S. Dearborn, and William Foster's Foster Photoplay opened at 3312 S. Wabash Avenue.[6]

While Chicago production, distribution, and exhibition took off, the local film industry encountered a new challenge. In 1907 Chicago became the first city in America to pass and enforce a film censorship law.

On April 30, 1907, Chicago police chief George Shippy took to the offensive against the film threat. Mayor Fred Busse gave Shippy the go-ahead to allocate a squad of ten policemen to censor scenes of a morbid or criminal nature. Chief Shippy had been alerted "that in several 5 cent theaters after the regular performances for the night a select crowd would witness moving pictures of the vilest type." Shippy further informed the public that he had "heard and noticed the 'blood and thunder' pictures ... which have a great effect on the boys and girls.... Starting tonight men

Chicago Police Chief George Shippy (1859–1913) was among the first authorities to crack down on inappropriate motion pictures.

will be sent to every 5 cent theater to witness the shows."[7] Shippy's task force found that penny arcades were the worst offenders. One undercover operative reported that he "was attracted to one machine by seeing a boy hardly out of knee trousers looking through the slot, which he could just reach on his tip toes. The pictures were a series of poses by nude women."[8]

There might not have been nudity in *The James Boys in Missouri* (1908) and *The Night Riders* (1908), but these two pictures delivered on the "blood and thunder." Both were ripped-from-the-headlines, crowd-pleasing tales of true-life outlaws. *The James Boys in Missouri* was based on the tale of a group of bandits already popularized in pulp magazine stories. *The Night Riders* centered on a vigilante group active in Kentucky.[9] A Chicago theater owner named Jake Block scheduled the films, knowing they would be popular draws at his box office. He should have anticipated that Chief Shippy would object to the motion pictures glamorizing outlaw activities. As soon as the titles hit Block's marquee, Shippy's men moved in. Block fought back, challenging both the police and the city ordinance. This was the first major film censorship challenge to go before a judge.

In 1909 *Block v. Chicago* came before the Illinois Supreme Court. Chief Judge James Cartwright was skeptical of Block's free speech argument: "It is true that pictures representing the career of the James Boys illustrate experiences connected with the history of the country, but it does not follow that they are not immoral."[10] Block tried to claim First Amendment protections, but the court shut him down. Judge Cartwright was concerned with the possible effects the exciting outlaws might have on young audiences. Not only did the court uphold Chicago's film law but it also applauded Chief Shippy's aggressive enforcement. After a decade of cinema's expansive growth in Chicago, a line was drawn.

After the *Block* decision there was resistance from Chicago's film community. Motion pictures of the "Fight of the Century" pitting Jack Johnson against former heavyweight champion Jim Jeffries looked like sure moneymakers. Aaron Jones and George Spoor lobbied to lift the city's ban on prizefighting pictures. The mayor and the police chief would not be swayed. Jones and Spoor argued that they had already paid $60,000 for exhibition rights in Chicago, but to no avail: there would be no permits. Any fight film shown was confiscated and could land the theater owners in court.[11]

When Chief Shippy died, the city looked for a new censor and found the man who was born for the job: Maj. Metellus Lucullus Cicero Funkhouser. Stepping in as the city's morality czar on March 20, 1913, Maj. Funkhouser embodied his role like a censor sent from Central Casting.[12] With a handlebar mustache, an eye for obscenity, and the iron fist of enforcement, Funkhouser embarked on a crusade to clean the screens of Chicago.

Funkhouser objected to what he called "freak dances," banning films of the tango and the turkey trot: "They will not be permitted in Chicago.... [T]he objection is not based so much upon these pictures in themselves but upon the effect they would have on thousands of young people.... [T]hink of a young girl or young man with two or three drinks down trying these dances."[13] He banned the motion picture *Absinthe* (1913), which depicted an artist's descent into alcoholism. He recalled a permit for the exploitation documentary *Cocaine Traffic* a.k.a. *The Drug Terror* (1914) to ensure that children were excluded from shows.[14] He stopped exhibition of Theda Bara's *The Rose of Blood* (1917). Maj. Funkhouser's opinions were personal, his decisions arbitrary, his rulings final.

In addition to issuing outright bans, Funkhouser employed a team to edit out inappropriate scenes for Chicago's cinemas. They blue-penciled anti–German propaganda in Mary Pickford's *The Littlest American* (1917) and in D.W. Griffith's *Hearts of the World* (1918).[15] For *The Duke's Talisman* (1913), a Gaumont thriller, they excised a sequence of a man stabbed and thrown over a precipice. In Vitagraph's *The Christian* (1914), the censors cut a subtitle where the film's heroine cried, "Robert, to save me from disgrace you must marry me." Even Charlie Chaplin's Little Tramp was not safe. In *A Woman* (1915), Charlie's cross-dressing leads to comic confusion. It entertained audiences, but drag was serious business to Funkhouser. He cut multiple scenes from the film but interestingly left in a male-on-male kiss.[16]

Funkhouser may have cleaned the city's screens of immoral and indecent pictures, but he didn't make many friends doing it. The Major came under fire in 1918 when the city council voted to pink-slip the overly enthusiastic censor. He had crossed the line on a visit to the Art Institute of Chicago. While escorting his family into the museum he spotted a towering bronze sculpture of a male nude that he found improper. Albin Polasek's *The Sower* had stood outside the Pan-American Exposition in San Francisco before finding a permanent home at the Art Institute. Offended by the brazen nudity Funkhouser ordered it removed. When the massive sculpture couldn't be budged, he ordered it draped. A film industry trade paper reported, "In the eyes of Chicago censorship, as many picture producers have found, art counts for little."[17] Within a week Funkhouser's position was up for review.

"The proposal to eliminate Maj. Funkhouser is prompted by the belief that he is not qualified to pass judgment on moving pictures," wrote the *Chicago Daily Tribune*. "It is a conviction based on the cumulating evidence that Maj. Funkhouser is temperamentally

and intellectually unfitted for the position."[18] After six years on the job, the city put the Major out to pasture, ordering him into retirement.

There was more drama on the horizon for the film community in the Land of Lincoln. In 1915 Governor Edward Fitzsimmons Dunne vetoed a bill that would have provided a state film censorship agency.[19] The proposal came up again as Governor Frank Lowden took office. The new bill died in the state legislature on June 18, 1919.[20] While the state had backed down, Chicago continued censoring its screens. Real-life train robber and convicted criminal Al Jennings parlayed his notoriety in the newspapers into movie-marquee semi-stardom. He appeared

Top: **Major Metellus Lucullus Cicero Funkhouser (1864–1926) took over the job of Chicago's chief moral guardian in 1913, banning all films that personally offended him.** *Right:* **Bohemian artists in Paris found inspiration in a bottle in** *Absinthe* **(1914)— the film was banned in Chicago and is now lost.**

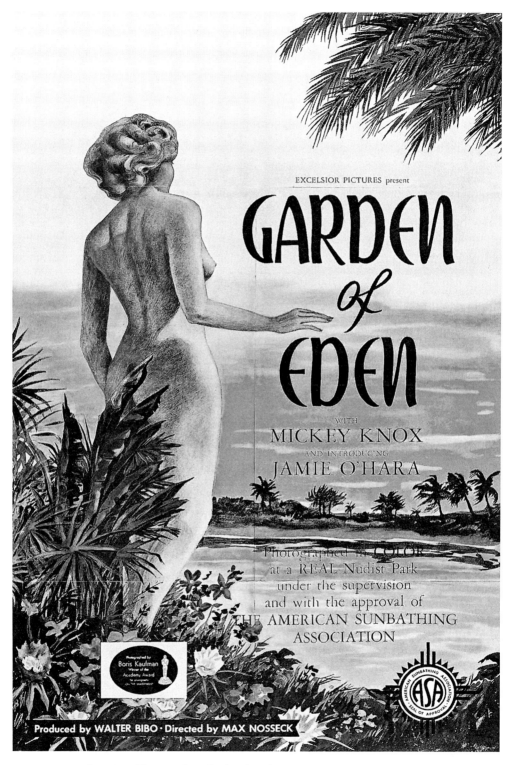

Pioneering exploitation film *Garden of Eden* (1954) was approved by the American Sunbathing Association but ran into trouble with censors across the United States.

in *The Lady of the Dugout* (1918). Claiming that the picture glorified crime and criminals, Chicago barred *Dugout*.[21]

Four decades later Chicago was still a battleground for the fight for freedom of the screen. Columbia Pictures cried foul when the city barred Otto Preminger's *Anatomy of a Murder* (1959) based on the use of the words "rape" and "contraceptive."[22] Paramount Pictures protested an adults-only rating for *Desire under the Elms* (1958) starring Sophia Loren and Anthony Perkins.[23] The major studios eventually backed down, but a smaller distributor put up the biggest fight.

Times Film Corp. imported a French film entitled *Le blé en herbe* (*The Game of Love*, 1954) but saw it banned in Chicago. The company sued. The court watched the coming-of-age tale with displeasure: "In the introductory scenes a flying start is made when a 16-year old boy is shown completely nude on a bathing beach in the presence of a group of younger girls. On that plane the narrative proceeds to reveal the seduction of this boy by a physically attractive woman old enough to be his mother.... The erotic thread of the story is carried, without deviation toward any wholesome idea, through scene after scene."[24] Times Film lost the case.

A few years later the distributor was back in court with the German-language film *Don Juan* (1955), a picture based on Mozart's opera *Don Giovanni*. There was no doubt this film was acceptable, but Times tested the law and refused to submit the picture for approval. They argued the First Amendment should protect their picture on principle—that content was irrelevant to the concept of free speech. It was a bold move. They lost, appealed, and lost again before the Seventh Circuit.[25] Free speech was not absolute.

A decade later Universal Pictures led a charge to have the city's censorship ordinance declared unconstitutional, but even the major studio failed.[26]

Instead of in one fell swoop, the censors would die a death of a thousand cuts. It was not the major studios but independent filmmakers that brought down the regulators. An exploitation movie named *Mom and Dad* (1950) demonstrated before the court that images of birth were not indecent.[27] *Garden of Eden* (1954), an eyewinking "documentary" on sunbathing, confirmed that nudity by itself was not obscene.[28] Finally, when the censors summarily banned Louis Malle's *Les amants* (*The Lovers*, 1958) without providing a reason, the Seventh Circuit stepped in to overrule the film board. The court found that the film's importer, Zenith International, had been deprived of its constitutional right to a fair hearing; that there were no standards and no safeguards to prevent arbitrary rulings; and that Zenith had not been given any indication as to why the city found the film to be obscene and immoral.[29]

The final verdict on film regulation in Chicago arrived in 1966, when a local lawyer named Elmer Gertz put the nail in the coffin of censorship. Gertz had been a longtime civil rights advocate, unafraid to take on unpopular clients. He represented Jack Ruby and secured parole for Nathan Leopold, infamous for the Leopold-Loeb thrill killing. But it was Gertz's work to overturn state censorship that established his legacy. Teaming with attorney Edward de Grazia, Gertz cleared the path for Henry Miller's *Tropic of Cancer* to be published in the United States. Three years after his literary *Cancer* victory, Gertz was fighting for *Body of a Female* (1964).

Located on Michigan Avenue, the World Playhouse Theater had screened art films since the 1930s. In the sixties the World suffered hard times and rebranded itself as a grind house showing adult movies.[30] When the theater scheduled an S&M-tinged slasher flick called *Body of a Female*, the city's last remaining cinema censor objected. The Illinois court sided with Chicago's censor, finding the law was valid and the film obscene.[31] The Supreme Court disagreed—not only with *Body of a Female*'s alleged obscenity but also with the validity of the state law. Finding the Illinois film censorship statute unconstitutional, SCOTUS overturned the state court's decision. Gertz prevailed.[32]

Several obscenity prosecutions lingered through the mid–1970s, but with *Body of a Female* the Chicago censor board had been dealt a deathblow.

Shippy, Funkhouser, and their corps of Chicago censors had believed it was their mission to protect the city's youth from visions of crime, sex, and dance steps that might be difficult when drunk, but there was a bigger issue to consider: whether the government should be authorized to prevent citizens from reading certain books and seeing certain films. The First Amendment permits a broad range of topics, but even disagreeable opinions and bad movies should be able to find their audience. Advocates like Elmer Gertz helped to liberate speech from the authority of administrators. From the first censorship law to the demise of regulators, Chicago played an important role in the development of civil liberties.

Indiana

Indiana is the undisputed champion of sports films. No state has hosted as many cinematic wins on the court, field, or road. In first place is *Hoosiers* (1986). *Hoosiers* starred Gene Hackman as the hotheaded, curmudgeonly coach of a high school basketball team. Against the odds Hackman leads his underdogs to the state championship. Hackman was recognized with an Academy Award nomination for his performance.

The Indiana native David Anspaugh directed *Hoosiers*. Anspaugh captured lightning in a bottle for a second time with *Rudy* (1993). *Rudy* followed the true story of teen who yearns to play football but lacks good grades and money. When his buddy is killed in an accident, Rudy (Sean Astin) is moved to action, overcoming obstacles to fight for his dream. *Rudy* became a fan favorite and was recognized by ESPN as one of the greatest sports films.

Anspaugh's pictures are but two achievements in a celebrated string of films focusing on Indiana athletics. Talkies were still new when audiences were jolted by the roar of racing motors in *Speedway* (1929). Directed by Harry Beaumont, who would win an Academy Award that same year for *The Broadway Melody* (1929), *Speedway* focused on the Indianapolis 500. A checkered flag waved again in *The Crowd Roars* (1932), with James Cagney in the driver's seat and Howard Hawks behind the camera. *The Crowd Roars* was so popular it was remade with added sex appeal, starring "Oomph Girl" Ann Sheridan in *Indianapolis Speedway* (1939).

Lloyd Bacon directed *Indianapolis Speedway*, and he focused his camera on another Indiana icon the next year. *Knute Rockne, All American* (1940) was a biopic based on the famed Notre Dame football coach. The film may have starred Pat O'Brien, but a twenty-nine-year-old actor named Ronald Reagan became the picture's standout. Reagan played the talented but tragic halfback George Gipp. Confined to a hospital bed, Reagan's character delivered one of sports film's most memorable lines: "Ask them to go in there with all they got and win just one for the Gipper."

Fast cars, beautiful women, and heartbreaking football icons were box office attractions, but Indiana's bench went deeper. Harness horse racing was the subject in *Home in Indiana* (1944), road bike racing in *Breaking Away* (1979), and speedboating on the Ohio River in *Madison* (2001).

Indiana may be the champion of cinema sports, but the state is also a contender for the title of "Birthplace of the Censors." In the land of the free, two of America's most powerful censors hailed from the Hoosier State: Will Hays and Byron Price. Hays, brought up in Sullivan, served as the first president of the Motion Picture Producers and Distributors Association. From his office came the infamous Production Code, which regulated racy movie content and forced filmmakers to convey naughty moments using suggestive scenes. Lesser known but equally influential was Byron Price, a Topeka native appointed by President Franklin Roosevelt to lead the U.S. Office of Censorship during World War II.

Harness racing in the Hoosier State in *Home in Indiana* (1944).

Even before Hays and Price, Indiana authorities were concerned about the influence of movies. As early as 1910 Indianapolis police superintendent Martin J. Hyland cracked down on local nickelodeons. Hyland worried that the release of the popular Jack Johnson–Jim Jeffries fight film would cause racial unrest. The controversial loops showed Johnson, a towering African American boxer, in the act of knocking down the former—white—champion Jeffries. When Hyland heard that reels of the film were arriving in Indianapolis, he met the shipment at the train station. "If anyone attempts to show these pictures they will be arrested," he said. The distributor argued the films weren't actual fights—they were reenacted amusements. The ploy didn't sway Hyland. The police superintendent commented, "It does not make a difference if the films are not the genuine article."[1] Hyland's intimidation was successful. The distributor never unsealed the crates and instead caught the next train out of town. Superintendent Hyland's strong-armed censorship kept the peace.

Fight films weren't the only pictures that fired up the Indianapolis police superintendent. Hyland blamed the movies for an uptick in delinquency. Only two weeks after the "Fight of the Century" was sent packing, the *Indianapolis Star* reported that Hyland was "convinced that moving picture films showing murders, holdups, robberies, thefts, and other kinds of crime are causing a general increase in juvenile crime.[2]

Soon calls for censorship crisscrossed Indiana. After *The Birth of a Nation* (1915) opened in Lafayette, sixty miles northwest of Indianapolis, one disturbed audience member left the theater and shot an African American teenager.[3] In Evansville, 175 miles south of Indianapolis, Mayor Benjamin Bosse considered a ban on *Damaged Goods* (1914).[4] The picture, which told the story of a young man ravaged by VD, sat at the bottom half of a double feature with the equally controversial *The Miracle of Life* (1915). In *The Miracle of Life* a woman has an abortion and is haunted by a visitation of "the-child-that-might-have-been."[5] Meanwhile, forty-five miles northeast of Indianapolis, in Anderson, Mayor J.H. Millett called for a censorship ordinance, concerned that certain films could be "demoralizing to children."[6]

Five years later in 1921, Representative Julia Nelson, the first female member of the Indiana legislature, authored a statewide film censorship measure.[7] Her proposal would bar movies that incited crime or were deemed immoral, indecent, or obscene, as well as ban prizefighting and bullfighting pictures. The bill passed in the House but failed in the state Senate.[8] The *Fort Wayne Sentinel* editorialized that a law was not needed because the market would self-correct and discourage inappropriate content. "A picture which is suggestive, salacious, or immoral may 'go over big' once," reasoned the *Sentinel*, "but inevitably there is a revulsion…. The American people [are] pure at heart."[9] Virtuous midwestern moral fiber would carry the day. Censorship was dead in Indiana. Or was it?

Nine months after Nelson's bill was defeated, Will Hays was appointed president of the Motion Picture Producers and Distributors Association (MPPDA).[10] Born just west of Bloomfield, Hays would hold moral dominion over the film industry, monitoring movies for forbidden actions. The Hays Office guided Hollywood for over three decades. Hays's dictums evolved from a list of "Don'ts and Be Carefuls"—for instance, don't include profanity or nudity in films, and be careful of depicting crime and cruelty to children—to a more formal code. For a full generation, on-screen married couples never slept in the same bed, never kissed for longer than three seconds, and never used a toilet—all forbidden activities. The MPPDA's sanctions were intended to soothe state censors around the country while allowing filmmakers limited creative freedom. Some people have argued that the Hays Code stunted filmmaking in Hollywood, but his guidelines also contributed to the golden age of movies.

Just as the Hays era was closing, another son of Indiana moved onto the national stage: Byron Price. Ten days after the attack on Pearl Harbor in December 1941, President Franklin Roosevelt appointed Price as the nation's director of censorship. The wartime post was charged with balancing national security and freedom of the press. Roosevelt explained that "all Americans abhor censorship, just as they abhor war. But … some degree of censorship is essential in wartime."[11] Price found himself in a thankless position, upholding national security while curbing constitutional protections. He described censorship "as a military weapon that was 'a necessary evil' in a time of total war."[12]

Confusion reigned in Hollywood. Producers were led to believe that war pictures showing military defeat were forbidden. Several films, including *Mrs. Miniver* (1942) and *Wake Island* (1942), were prohibited from export. When studio bosses from MGM, Paramount, and Columbia objected, the U.S. Office of Censorship clarified that their order "applied only to newsreels and not to entertainment pictures, although the text had failed to say so."[13]

Despite turbulence at the censor's post, in 1944 Price was awarded a Pulitzer Special Award.[14] The following year Price closed his office.[15] By December 1945, only two months after Will Hays's retirement, the MPPDA hired Price as vice president of the Motion Picture Producers Group.[16] From government censor to Hollywood insider, Byron Price's journey was unique.

In postwar America institutional regulation came under scrutiny. As state censorship was becoming less tolerated, films were becoming more provocative. Elia Kazan's *Baby Doll* (1956) raised eyebrows with images of a girl-child in lingerie and a revenge-rape plotline. The picture was informally banned in Hammond-area theaters but played without incident in Indianapolis.[17]

Movies kept pushing the limits. At a Fort Wayne drive-in, projected images of bare breasts and buttocks attracted attention. When saucy scenes of a sexploitation flick could be seen by passersby the city brought suit. But times had changed, and the Seventh Circuit struck Fort Wayne's ordinance as overreaching. Banning all nudity was unenforceable; the law might extend to artworks and anthropological films, as well as to babies' bottoms and innocent glimpses of bare flesh. Judge William Campbell understood the importance of protecting children from inappropriate material but found the ordinance at issue was broader than permissible.[18]

A similar issue came up in 2001 when an Indianapolis law attempted to limit children's access to violent video games. Once again, the Seventh Circuit righted the boat. Judge Richard Posner separated violence from obscenity and favored broad free speech rights. While Posner did not entirely rule out regulation of violent media for minors, he made clear that such laws needed to be narrowly tailored, respecting First Amendment protections.[19]

Indiana played an important role in the development of film and free speech. When other states were enacting censorship laws, Indiana lawmakers voted theirs down. On the other hand, America's two most powerful censors both hailed from the Hoosier State. Playing both ends against the middle, morality regulators and freedom fighters vied for the hearts, minds, and eyes of Indiana audiences for close to one hundred years. In the end, the First Amendment's guarantee to protect all forms of speech gave filmmakers the winning edge.

Iowa

Eunice Goodrich was born in Chicago in 1861, the daughter of an industrialist who had cornered the market on sewing machine manufacture in the Second City. She married British-born, Chicago-educated William Pottle, Jr., and together they hit the midwestern vaudeville theater circuit in 1882.[1] The Goodrich Comedy Company successfully road-showed their routines around Illinois, Iowa, and Kansas, later adding a juvenile act called "Pottle's Baby." When their daughter's cute act grew tiresome, Goodrich and Pottle added a new gimmick: the Vivrescope. The Vivrescope was an early motion picture device. It was rudimentary but still proved a successful draw to attract crowds on an 1896–1897 tour through Iowa.[2]

Goodrich and Pottle were itinerant show people and among the first to introduce moving pictures to Iowa audiences. Their programs consisted of various scenes cobbled together from Edison releases, such as *The Blacksmith Shop* (1895) and *Leigh Sister's Famous Umbrella Dance* (1895), and from Lumière actualities, such as *The Arrival of a Train* (1896) and *Washing Day in Switzerland* (1896). Despite the couple's secondhand titles, one commentator enjoyed the scenes from the Vivrescope viewing system, finding the image quality offered "less vibration so that the pictures are not so trying to the eyes as those produced by other machines."[3]

The early Hawkeye State audiences also enjoyed action pictures. As the Spanish-American War heated up in newspapers, images came to life on screen with views of *The Wreck of the Battleship Maine* (1898). Rousing patriotic fare fired up nationalistic feelings in *Capture of Spanish Fort Near Santiago* (1896), *Battle of Guantanamo* (1898), *Hoisting of the American Flag at Cavite* (1898), and *Execution of the Spanish Spy* (1898).[4] Another source of pride came from regional productions, like *Building the Greatest Dam in the World* (1912). Shot on location at the Keokuk Dam in southern Iowa, this documentary focused on the largest public-works project commissioned prior to the Panama Canal.

With the growing popularity of the movies came calls for censorship. Iowa's legislature considered a film law in 1913. The proposed Burt Bill prohibited films deemed "sacrilegious, obscene, or indecent."[5] There was special concern for children, who might sneak a peek at pictures that were suggestive or immoral.[6] When a more robust ordinance to establish a statewide film agency came up for debate, resistance came from the most unlikely place. J.W. Binder, an executive at the National Board of Censorship based in New York, made a trip to Des Moines. Binder explained that the National Board was a private, nongovernmental organization supported in part by film industry leaders. It reviewed ninety-six percent of pictures produced in the United States, so a state censor would be unnecessary, redundant, and possibly unconstitutional. Binder's position may seem counterintuitive. He said, "I believe the state has no more right to censor moving pictures than it has to censor speech or the press."[7] Why would the leader of an established censorship board protest state censorship? The answer was personal: if local laws were passed, Binder's job was on the line. With his own livelihood vulnerable, Binder made a convincing argument. The proposed law was killed.[8]

Even without a formal regulation, local watchdogs kept a sharp eye on inappropriate movies. Only four months after the state declined to enact a film law, *The Americano* (1916) arrived in Des Moines. The picture was a political thriller, with Douglas Fairbanks rescuing the deposed leader of a Central American country for the love of the leader's daughter. The National Board of Censorship passed the picture, but Binder's agency missed a scene that struck a chord among Iowa audiences. In a controversial sequence the American flag was torn down and trampled. Des Moines watchdogs branded the film "unfit for the eyes of impressionable boys and girls."[9] An even greater challenge was on the horizon.

The Birth of a Nation (1915) sparked nationwide controversy. While the motion picture invigorated the American film industry, its racist content infuriated many audiences.

Cities like Minneapolis moved to ban *Birth*, and Boston did its best to contain racially motivated violence in the streets. As the picture moved through Mason City, a township in north-central Iowa, locals sabotaged screenings. Six of the film's twelve reels were stolen and destroyed.[10] Citizens of Keokuk in the southeastern corner of the state also protested the picture, concerned it would "engender race strife and hatred, and would disturb if not destroy the friendly relations" between the races.[11] *Birth* was briefly banned in Des Moines. Davenport attempted to abort screenings, while the epic attracted crowds in Cedar Rapids. Eventually Des Moines gave in and permitted the picture. *The Birth of a Nation* played for over a month at the Berchel Theater, charging the top-tier price of one dollar a ticket.[12] It was the same stage on which Eunice Goodrich and Pottle's Baby had entertained audiences with their Vivrescope only twenty years earlier.

The movies had changed, but the need to control content had not. Theda Bara's bosom-baring version of *Salome* (1918) was a top draw in Mason City, raising eyebrows and the need for a morality czar.[13] Scheduled for Des Moines, an edu-exploitation film entitled *Some Wild Oats* (1919) dealt with the "evil effects" of syphilis. With the sheriff, the Federation of Women's Clubs, the YMCA, and various other groups behind him, Des Moines police chief Roscoe Saunders applied to Judge Lester Johnson of the Iowa district court for a temporary restraining order to stop the "suggestive photoplay." Judge Johnson signed the TRO.[14]

Despite this court order, *Oats* opened for an audience of three hundred the next day. Chief Saunders stormed the theater and arrested its manager, Charles O'Connell. O'Connell was freed on twenty-five-dollars bail but challenged the arrest. An expedited trial was scheduled, and a media circus surrounded the courthouse.[15] This time Judge T.L. Sellers viewed the picture and found it was not immoral, indecent, or obscene. The film, declared Judge Sellers, "appear[ed] to teach a lesson that ought to be learned by everyone."[16] *Some Wild Oats* was cleared for exhibition.

Despite this victory, the battle to wipe inappropriate content from Iowa screens continued. Fifty years later *Deep Throat* (1972) emerged from the underground stag film circuit to become a mainstream blockbuster. Anticipating a solid box office, owners of a Marion grind house applied for a court order to prevent police from interfering with their skin-flick exhibition. In a complicated sequence of rulings, the federal court declined to issue an injunction while the state court deemed the film obscene and banned public showings. Only Chief Judge Edward Joseph McManus dissented, supporting the theater owner's right to be free from state interference.[17]

Judge McManus's vote did not carry the day, but his opinion demonstrated movement toward more progressive policies. Some speech may be disagreeable, disrespectful, or downright distasteful; still, the un-politically-correct content of *Birth of a Nation*, the sex education of *Wild Oats*, and the amorous acrobatics of *Deep Throat* should not be vulnerable to knee-jerk suppression by state authorities.

Motion pictures are the most provocative medium of mass communication. In 2004 R.L. Fridley, owner of the Des Moines–based Fridley Theatres refused to show Michael Moore's politically charged documentary *Fahrenheit 9/11* (2004). Fridley claimed the film "incite[d] terrorism."[18] Since Fridley was a private businessman and not a state agent, he was free to ban the film from his theater.

Rather than keeping a film out of the public eye, another scenario saw a movie pushed into open debate. Aiming to incite controversy during the 2016 Iowa caucuses, Donald Trump rented out a Des Moines movie theater. He offered free round-the-clock screenings of *13 Hours* (2016), a film on the Benghazi fracas.[19] Trump's intent was to use the film as a political weapon, aiming to call attention to the foreign policies of his soon-to-be opponent Hillary Clinton. Whether the Trump stunt changed hearts and minds is difficult to know, but Iowans at least enjoyed an afternoon at the movies as respite from tiresome campaigning.

Kansas

Kansas is America's heartland, but in the movies the midwestern state can become the portal to another world. Dorothy whirlwinded over the rainbow to a Technicolor land in *The Wizard of Oz* (1939). Adaptations of L. Frank Baum's classic fantasy novel were produced as early as 1910 and as recently as 2017, but it was MGM's 1939 version that gave the cinema one of its most memorable one-liners: "Toto, I've a feeling we're not in Kansas anymore." While Dorothy yearned to return to the family farm, another famous character arrived in Kansas from his destroyed home planet. A Kryptonian baby crash-landed in a cornfield to become Clark Kent a.k.a. Superman. The Man of Steel appeared in animated shorts in 1941, in a live-action low-budget B-movie in 1948, and in a television series in 1958. The 1978 blockbuster film starring Christopher Reeves revived the super-hero for a new generation.[1] Whether the characters were homesick for the homestead or seeking out a new home world, the comforts of Kansas greeted them when they landed.

The Sunflower State became an on-screen safe space for Dorothy and Clark, but it could be a troublesome region for filmmakers. As early as 1911, censorship surfaced in Wichita.

When a Western adventure yarn entitled *The James Boys in Missouri* (1908) opened, young audiences flocked to nickelodeon theaters. On-screen horses galloped and excitement grew, and then at a critical moment just as Jesse James aimed his six-shooter at an opponent, a blur obscured the scene. The blur covered the action again when Robert Ford prepared to fire on the film's antihero. A local newspaper reported that the projectionist "was carefully obliterating the censored scenes by putting his hand over his machine" lens, under the direction of C.R. Reeves, who was acting as the city's authorized censor.[2] Feeling cheated, the crowd grew ornery. Having paid their nickels, they wanted to see blood flowing. Frustrated, they began menacing the theater manager. According to reports, that's "when Reeves got an inspiration…. [P]ulling out his marshal's star, dusting it and pinning it on his breast where everybody could see it," he placed the theater manager under protective arrest.[3]

Not long after the *James Boys* incident, Kansas became one of the first states to pass a film censorship law. By 1915 the Rev. Festus Foster and Miss Carrie Simpson were appointed motion pictures inspectors.[4] Together they logged nearly ten hours of film a day, and they didn't like a lot of what they saw.

The first film they banned was *The Heart Punch* (1915). *The Heart Punch* starred prizefighter Jess Willard. Willard shot to stardom when he floored Jack Johnson, the first African American heavyweight boxing champion. Claiming the title belt, Willard was labeled "the Great White Hope," a hero to many boxing fans. *The Heart Punch* wasn't a fight film per se; rather, it showed Willard in training. Nevertheless, it was barred from Kansas—not for violence in the ring but for a scene set in a barroom.[5] Saloon scenes were tabooed in the state that launched Prohibition. Carl Laemmle, who produced *The Heart Punch* through IMP, contested the censors' decision. Governor Arthur Capper, along with his secretary of state and the attorney general, convened and considered the challenge. In the end Capper sided with the censors.[6] *The Heart Punch* was KO'd in Kansas.

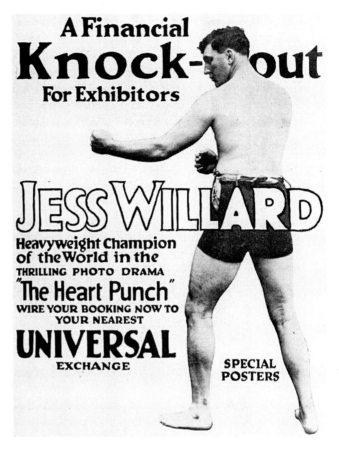

Heavyweight champion Jess Willard (1881–1968) demonstrated the struggles of a prizefighter in and out of the ring in *The Heart Punch* (1915).

Forbidding Jess Willard's fight film was just the beginning of Kansas's campaign to clean the screen. Theda Bara's *Sin* (1915) was banned for images of "murder, seduction, and general immorality."[7] *The Kiss* (1914) updated the Cinderella story with sexy spooning after a boy kisses a girl at a masquerade. When she runs away he tries to locate her by kissing all the girls around to test for the right lips. The Reverend Foster was unfazed by the necking, remarking, "I never could see harm in kissing a pretty girl."[8] Instead it was a gambling scene in *The Kiss* that proved objectionable. Foster witnessed even worse when *Purity* (1916) arrived in Topeka. *Purity* featured Audrey Munson, dubbed "America's First Supermodel," in nude scenes.[9] As Munson disrobed, Foster burst out, "Has that woman no soul?"[10] The picture was rejected. Miss Simpson had other triggers. Upholding Kansas's reputation as the Prohibition State, Simpson had no tolerance for drinking on film. On her first day on the job she demanded cuts to any scene where characters imbibed alcohol, whether in a bar or from a cabaret dancer's shoe.[11] "Even movies must be absolutely dry," rang headlines. "Kansas censors will not permit scenes of drunkenness."[12]

Within her first six months, Simpson formed very clear ideas about what would pass on-screen muster. She explained to reporters that in "her ideal motion picture the hero must wear his hair cut featheredge. She detests the long haired, dress suit models.... There will be no drinking scenes in Miss Simpson's ideal scenario—they are absolutely barred [but] to smoking she has no objection."[13] Simpson welcomed a little on-screen smooching. "If kissing and hugging were eliminated from a play it would be insipid," she said.[14]

Kansas's censors banned the newsreels distributed by Mutual Films, and with a companion case from Ohio, the challenge rose to the U.S. Supreme Court. It was a case of first impression: the first time the issue of whether film was protected speech under the First Amendment would be considered in the Halls of Justice. In its unanimous decision the High Court took a low opinion of the movies. SCOTUS found that film censorship was a valid exercise of the state's police power and it did not interfere with interstate commerce or conflict with the First Amendment.[15] The Court upheld Foster and Simpson's authority to safeguard morals from the corruption of Hollywood.

The Birth of a Nation (1915) was a rousing success across America, but Kansas censors denied the film a permit to play locally. *Birth* was rejected as vicious and immoral.[16] *The Easiest Way* (1918) met with the same hard line. Featuring silent star Clara Kimball Young, *The Easiest Way* told the story of a girl struggling to become an actress. She strives to work her way up but finds the casting couch to be an attractive alternative—the easiest way. The immoral fruits of her decision lead her down a dark path. The film was banned, and its producers appealed. Presuming the censors acted in good faith, Judge C.J. Johnson rubber-stamped their power to cut as they saw fit.[17]

Given the green light to excise inappropriate scenes, Kansas censors took full advantage. Once reels crossed the state line, movies were purged of scenes of men drinking, women smoking, criminals safecracking, and young people shimmy dancing.[18] Charlie Chaplin's *The Pilgrim* (1923) was edited. Greta Garbo's on-screen smooching in *Flesh and the Devil* (1926) was tamed. Even the Academy Award–winning *All Quiet on the Western Front* (1929) was not safe. Censors demanded deletion of a scene showing a boy paddled by his teacher.[19]

Off-color comedy, kissing, paddling, and even choreography were closely inspected. A theater manager protested the cutting of a scene of girls doing an early version of Hula-Hooping, saying, "They only shake a little." "That's right," the censor retorted, "they shake a little too much."[20]

Change came in the 1950s when the Supreme Court extended First Amendment rights to motion pictures after watching an Italian film called *The Miracle* (1959). Before *The Miracle*, the *Mutual* court decision had guided censoring powers. Movies were viewed as an attraction like a circus or an amusement ride—"a business pure and simple"—and subject to regulation.[21] After *The Miracle*, the Supreme Court accepted movies as a legitimate medium of communication.

A year after the *Miracle* decision (see New York) brought movies under the protection of the First Amendment, one Hollywood director set out to challenge the Kansas film code: Otto Preminger. His film *The Moon Is Blue* (1953) followed the flirtations of two bachelors (William Holden and David Niven) as they competed for the attention of a girl. Though innocent by today's standards, *Moon* was controversial in its time for the on-screen uttering of several previously forbidden words, such as "pregnant," "seduce," and "virgin." The censor board's disapproval rested on "sex theme throughout, too frank bedroom dialogue: many sexy words."[22] Preminger didn't back down. In a decision that shocked no one, the state court sided with Kansas's censors. *Moon* was banned in Kansas. Preminger lost the first battle, but he was not defeated.

A decade later Preminger returned to Kansas with *Bunny Lake Is Missing* (1965). There was little raunch in this picture; *Bunny* was a psychological thriller. After a mother reports her daughter missing, a police detective (Laurence Olivier) investigates, only to find that the daughter's disappearance is not what it seems. There was nothing controversial here, no virgins or seductions or pregnancies. The director merely refused to submit *Bunny* for approval on principle. He claimed the code infringed free speech. Preminger and the censors headed to court. This time the studio challenged the censorship law itself. And this time, in a surprising reversal, the Kansas Supreme Court sided with the film-maker: the code was deemed unconstitutional.[23] Otto Preminger prevailed.

While Preminger's triumph was a victory for freedom of the screen, the ruling also had unintended consequences. Six years after *Bunny Lake* was cleared, explicit sex bumped and grinded on-screen in blue-movie blockbusters such as *Deep Throat* (1972) and *The Devil in Miss Jones* (1973). Kansas tried to clamp down on obscenity by raiding several adult grind houses in Wichita. The authorities arrested patrons and confiscated films with such titillating titles as *Youthful Lust*, *Lady Freaks*, and *Little Angel Puss* (release dates unknown). The court reluctantly supported the adult businesses, positioning the police action as "an impermissible prior restraint of rights preserved under the First Amendment."[24] Once the movies were given full

Although Otto Preminger's *The Moon Is Blue* (1953) was banned in Kansas and condemned by the Legion of Decency, it was still a hit.

First Amendment protections, they became difficult to control.

Kansas would forever be home for Dorothy and Superman, but the overprotective policies of the Reverend Foster and Miss Simpson were not compatible with the First

Amendment. Maverick filmmakers like Otto Preminger helped to ensure free speech would remain the rule in America's heartland.

Kentucky

In 1808 a child was born in Fairview, 150 miles southwest of Louisville. A year later another baby boy was born, in Hodgenville, fifty miles south of Louisville. These two children would play important roles in American history. The child of Hodgenville grew up to become President Abraham Lincoln, while his neighbor from Fairview would become Confederate President Jefferson Davis. A third son of Kentucky, born in 1875 just outside Louisville, would also have a significant influence on American culture. He was D.W. Griffith, the country's first major motion picture director.[1]

The Civil War was essential to Griffith's worldview. Whether or not his father, "Thundering Jake" Griffith, played a significant role on the battlefield has never been answered, but the filmmaker fabricated his own family history. He remembered a childhood of rural poverty where his favorite toys were "the aiguillettes and epaulets of a Confederate Brigadier General."[2] One month after his fortieth birthday, Griffith released his controversial Civil War epic, *The Birth of a Nation* (1915). America's first blockbuster film was a pop-culture phenomenon that marked the fiftieth anniversary of the end of the Civil War. Adding to the pomp and circumstance, Griffith arranged for veterans to attend screenings in full uniform in certain locations, including New York and Houston.[3]

Championed by some, reviled by others, there can be no doubt that *The Birth of a Nation* changed film history and laid the foundation for the modern entertainment industry.

Griffith has been credited as the first major American filmmaker, but he may have been inspired by an event in Louisville in October 1894. A traveling showman named Alexander Black arrived in town to present a feature-length magic lantern slide show. While Thomas Edison and his competitors had been working on a technology for moving pictures, Black used an older apparatus. Dissolving between two projected images, Black's technique created a pre-motion-picture attraction. His device was less mechanically revolutionary than others, but the illuminated storytelling was an innovation on the path to feature filmmaking.[4] The timing was right for a seminal moment in film history. Griffith had left his

From struggling stage writer to America's first blockbuster director, D.W. Griffith was immensely successful and controversial.

family homestead and was working in Louisville when Black arrived.[5] In the right place at the right time, the future film director may have attended Black's pioneering picture show. Watching Black's detective drama *Miss Jerry* (1894), Griffith could have been motivated for a career change.

Black's show was a pre-cinema attraction, a spoken narrative over projected slides. Moving pictures proper arrived in Louisville by 1904. The Dreamland Theater opened on April 6, 1904. Other venues followed, including the Bijou and the Marvel. The Princess attempted to show talking pictures with a phonographic attachment before 1916. That experiment failed. Derby City's first movie palace, the Majestic, with a seating capacity of 1,200, opened its doors in 1908.[6] Playhouses were also popping up around the state, including the Hippodrome in Lexington and the Elite in Bowling Green.[7]

Although popular, the flickering pictures also proved controversial. Louisville passed a film censorship ordinance in 1909. A twelve-member board was charged with reviewing and banning movies that were lewd, lascivious, indecent, suggestive of crime, or dangerous to the morals of children.[8] Lexington followed, enacting its own statute in 1915, and Owensboro enacted a law in 1921.[9] Another level of regulation came into play when Kentucky's legislature passed a censorship bill in 1922, prohibiting "indecent films or films not worth while [*sic*]."[10] The law declared that "only such films as are in the judgment of the board of a moral, educational or amusing and harmless character shall be passed … for exhibition in the State of Kentucky."[11]

The films of Roscoe "Fatty" Arbuckle were definitely not amusing to Kentucky's censors. They set their sights on the corpulent comedian. Arbuckle had been a Keystone Cop since 1913, helping to mentor both Charlie Chaplin and Buster Keaton. Although plump, Arbuckle was graceful and unafraid to dress in drag or take a pie in the face. He was the toast of the industry in 1920, signing a $1 million dollar contract with Paramount.[12] Less than a year later Fatty found himself at the center of a celebrity scandal. The details were salacious, telling of a liquor-soaked, Prohibition-era, swinging San Francisco party that ended with the accidental death of a starlet. Although Fatty was acquitted of all charges, his career was finished.[13] Kentucky, along with many other states, banned his films based on the taint of an immoral lifestyle offscreen.

By 1921 film censorship in Louisville was in the hands of two policewomen. Alice Dunlop was the city's first female officer. Mayme Oldham signed on to the force later that year.[14] Charged with administering the no-smut cinema rule, the officers had a mandate: "We do not intend to allow Louisville to be the dumping ground for filthy shows other cities will not permit."[15] As Dunlop and Oldham were cleaning the screens, a grassroots group rose up with outspoken opinions. Beginning in 1934 the Better Films Council of Louisville tried to guide audiences toward morally uplifting films. It was a difficult project. In its first year Mrs. Emmet Horine, the president of the Better Films Council as well as of the Louisville Council of Churchwomen, admitted that "some of the best clean pictures have met with poor success in Louisville, while those depicting crime, delinquency, and other objectionable features have crowded our theaters."[16]

Despite difficulties in regulating film content, attempts to steer popular taste continued. Three decades later, moral authorities in Kentucky used the courts to enforce their opinions. When a Middlesboro theater screened a risqué art film, the police closed in. The film, *The Female: Seventy Times Seven* (1962), had been Argentina's entry into the Cannes Film Festival. The film's American distributor added fuel to the looming controversy by inserting additional sex scenes.[17] The picture's ad campaign didn't help its cause. Posters screamed, "*The Female* makes *I, A Woman* look like Mary Poppins." The film was banned. Its distributor, Cambist Films, challenged the censors but was denied relief. Kentucky's district court found the censorship statute valid and the film obscene.[18]

Shortly after *The Female*, another European picture arrived in Kentucky: *I, A Woman* (1965). This film featured Swedish sexploitation star Essy Persson as a young nurse striving to break free from her repressed upbringing. The film was erotic but not explicit. The opening scene offered hints of incestuous desires: Essy lay nude in bed, caressing herself as her father bowed his violin in the next room. *I, A Woman* pushed the envelope as it explored female sexuality on screen. The Kentucky Court of Appeals banned the film but was reversed by the Supreme Court.[19] Even though the film played on, there was disagreement on the bench. Chief Justice Warren Burger filed a dissent, supporting the states' authority to adopt their own standards for community values. Glossing over the majority decision and siding with Burger's dissent, Kentucky's courts maintained their course, banning a picture called *How to Succeed with Sex* (1970) the following year.

How to Succeed with Sex was a low-grade, raunchy romp directed by Bert I. Gordon. Gordon was the forgotten director of such B-movies as *The Amazing Colossal Man* (1957), *Attack of the Puppet People* (1958), and *Picture Mommy Dead* (1966). *How to Succeed* was a step up for Gordon. The *New York Times* filed a positive review: "Principally one will wish to see this movie for its women, who are lovely. But one may also listen to its dialogue, which is ironic, literate, and occasionally funny."[20] Pulaski County's sheriff, Gilmore Phelps, felt differently. Phelps deemed the movie obscene and stormed the drive-in where *How to Succeed* was playing. Stopping the show, he arrested the theater manager and projectionist. The Kentucky court affirmed his actions.[21]

Only months later, the Pulaski County drive-in was back in the news. This time the film was *Cindy and Donna* (1970), a soft-core confection

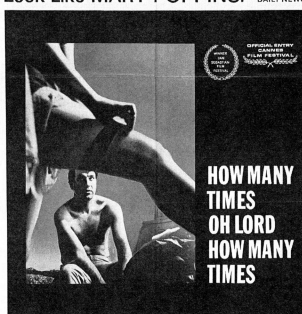

Memoirs of a South American prostitute in *The Female: Seventy Times Seven* (1962).

about the sexual awakening of two teenage girls. Cindy smokes pot, experiments with lesbianism, and seduces her sister's boyfriend. Catching the couple in flagrante delicto, Donna runs away into the street, where she is hit by a car and killed. Once again Sheriff Phelps and his men descended on the drive-in to arrest theater manager Harry Roaden and seize the film. Predictably, the Kentucky Court of Appeals upheld the sheriff. Once again the decision was appealed to the Supreme Court, and once again the decision was reversed. Chief Justice Burger penned the majority opinion, finding the sheriff's actions unacceptable. For Burger it was not an issue of obscenity but of appropriate legal procedure: warrantless seizure of the film could not be permitted.[22]

Even with repeated setbacks, local authorities continued to fight blue films in the Bluegrass State. In 1999 Lexington city council members railed against the screening of *Disco Dolls in Hot Skin* (1978). Obscenity charges were raised but just as quickly dropped.[23] The era of state-supported morality enforcement in Kentucky was drawing to a close as electronic media was emerging along with new challenges.

Louisiana

"Pop" Rock was the man who brought the movies to New Orleans. William T. Rock immigrated to America from Birmingham, England. By the 1890s, after trying his luck running a circus, a hotel, and an electric light company, Rock became interested in motion pictures.[1]

At that time the industry was in a chaotic state, with numerous inventors taking credit for motion picture technology and suing each other for patent infringement. Thomas Armat was among Thomas Edison's earliest and most significant competitors (see Georgia). While Edison's engineers still struggled to perfect their technology, Armat's camera-projector, the Vitascope, threw a clear image onto the screen. What Edison couldn't invent he acquired, and he quickly made an offer on Armat's device. Edison's manufacturing partner believed the product would sell better branded as the "Edison Vitascope," so Armat's name disappeared into history. But before Armat sold out, he licensed "Pop" Rock the right to distribute the Vitascope in Louisiana.[2]

Rock arrived in New Orleans before July 1896 and set up the Vitascope Hall Theater at 623 Canal Street. Before long "Prof. Rock" was a Crescent City celebrity, showing titillating titles such as *The May Irwin Kiss* (1896) and *Skirt Dance* (release date unknown) and manly movies such as *The Blacksmith Shop* (1895) and *The Cockfight at Babylon, Long Island* (release date unknown).[3] In 1898 he returned to New York, where competition in the film business was heating up. Two former stage magicians smitten with the movies, J. Stuart Blackton and Alfred E. Smith, were launching their own production shingle and offered Rock a seat in the C-suite to run the Vitagraph Company. With Blackton's creativity, Smith's corporate management, and Rock's practical experience, Vitagraph emerged as a film industry leader. Interestingly, each one of the three pillars of this pioneering American studio was from England, with Blackton hailing from Sheffield and Smith from Kent. Rock led the company through the early days of filmmaking and saw the movies spread across America to wide audiences before he died in 1916.

William "Pop" Rock (left) built Vitagraph from a pioneering film distributor to a powerhouse studio with Albert E. Smith (center) and J. Stuart Blackton.

Just behind Pop Rock on the way to the Bayou State were other early film producers. American Mutoscope and Biograph used an IMAX-like film format to record local scenes, releasing *Marti Gras Carnival* (1898) and *Loading a Mississippi Steamboat* (1898). Selig Polyscope shot *Panoramic View of the French Market* (1902).

Filmmakers recorded the unique ambience of New Orleans but made their own bizarre contributions as well. A controversial morality tale/exploitation movie entitled *The Inside of the White Slave Traffic* (1913) was shot partially on location in Storyville. The picture captured New Orleans's infamous red-light district before it disappeared.[4] On the other hand, the movies could deliver a dose of surrealism. In August 1917 a railroad caravan containing monkeys and lions rolled into Morgan City, ninety miles west of New Orleans. Dispatched by the National Film Corp. of America, a crew was on location to shoot the first screen version of Edgar Rice Burroughs's *Tarzan of the Apes*. Elmo Lincoln played the noble savage, with Louisiana's swamplands standing in for Africa's jungles, and African American locals hired as tribal extras. "I was supposed to be a Zulu, a wild man," Dudley Solomon remembered. "The studio man on the set said, 'Now we are going to set a trap for you, and you run.' The guy threw a rope on me. I did all I could to get away, because those wild animals sure did look real."[5] According to local legend, to save on transport costs after production wrapped, the crew let monkeys loose into the bayous rather than pay for a return trip to LA. For years it was said that Morgan City residents could hear hollering from the swampland outside town.[6]

As movies became more popular, Louisiana's authorities moved to establish local censor boards. In 1912 Shreveport's city council established a film commission.[7] The New Orleans city council sent a bill to Mayor Martin Behrman requesting he appoint a panel of three men and two women to assist the police inspector in film review.[8] The following year a series of movies were halted, with one censor commenting, "If *September Morn* [1914] needs a bathrobe, *The Miracle* [1913] wants a curtain to hide it entirely."[9] In Baton Rouge a group of fifty women petitioned Mayor Alex Grouchy, Jr., to protest *The Garden of Knowledge* (1916) as "lewd, vulgar, and immoral."[10] In an interesting career switch, Marguerite Clark moved from Paramount Pictures starlet to New Orleans motion picture censor.

For a time, Marguerite Clark rivaled Mary Pickford as America's screen sweetheart. Signed by Adolph Zukor in 1915, Clark starred in, among other titles, the version of *Snow*

The exposé of young women lured into a life of prostitution was scandalous and very popular with *The Inside of the White Slave Traffic* (1913).

White (1916) said to have inspired Walt Disney's first animated feature. In 1918 Clark married Harry Williams, a Louisiana sugar plantation owner and aviation adventurer. She retired from the screen in 1921, commenting, "I knew enough to go home when the party was over and the guests were gone."[11] But by 1935 she was back in the game—on the other side. Clark was appointed by then senator Huey Long to the Motion Picture Censorship Board of Louisiana.[12] While Marguerite Clark's tenure on the censor board was largely symbolic, the Louisiana morality police became more serious in the coming years.

Beginning in the 1960s, as mainstream motion pictures turned more explicit, the Bayou State's film censors became more active. Edward Dmytryk's *Walk on the Wild Side* (1962) recreated the Depression-era French Quarter, with sexually charged action taking place in the lushly appointed rooms of the neighborhood's bordellos.[13] The film starred Laurence Harvey, Jane Fonda, and Barbara Stanwyck and opened with a feline-friendly credit sequence by Saul Bass. Although *Walk* was shot on location, when it came time

Walk on the Wild Side (1962) featured Jane Fonda in a risqué picture set in the bordello district of the French Quarter.

for the premiere the film was persona non grata in New Orleans. The screening was canceled and the picture pulled from the state when the president of the Citizens for Decent Literature, Mrs. Harold R. Ainsworth, petitioned the Crescent City council to "please do all you can to cancel the world premiere…. [I]t will bring shameful publicity to our city."[14]

　　Filmmakers fought back. When a West German motion picture entitled *The Tech-*

nique of Physical Love (1968) was moving through the Port of New Orleans it was seized by U.S. Customs as obscene. The movie made a fetish out of clinical anatomy, opening with a lab-coated moderator, tongue depressor in hand, pointing out the sex organs of nude models and discussing various erogenous zones. Positions of coitus were discussed but never shown. Live models assumed suggestive positions but never engaged in actual or simulated sex. The district court of New Orleans found the film not obscene and ordered Customs to release it.[15]

The following year *The Stewardesses* (1969), a swinging 3-D sexploitation flick, opened in Shreveport. Local authorities moved to shut the exhibiting theater down, claiming that the grind house was a public nuisance. On first pass the court found the film obscene. The filmmakers kept fighting. On appeal the film's producers managed to bypass the issue of obscenity and attack the Louisiana law as unconstitutional. It was a winning strategy. The Louisiana Supreme Court reversed their decision, and *The Stewardesses* was cleared for takeoff.[16] Shreveport police next attempted to censor *Last Tango in Paris* (1972) but met with the same result.[17] Marlon Brando brought the butter to the bayou cinema, and the censors stood by, like his costar, helpless to stop him.

Moral authorities strived to contain and control provocative movies for decades. But a century after the first scenes flickered to life in Pop Rock's theater, a darker issue took center stage. The question was, could a movie incite viewers to commit violent acts, and should the studio or filmmaker be held responsible?

In March 1995, Sarah Edmondson and her boyfriend Benjamin Darrus left their home in Oklahoma, bound for a Grateful Dead concert in Memphis. The night before leaving they had dropped acid (LSD) and watched *Natural Born Killers* (1994) "several times."[18] *Natural Born Killers* is a powerful film based on a screenplay by Quentin Tarantino. The story follows two charismatic murderers, Mickey and Mallory, whose horrific acts are glorified by the media. Starring pitch-perfect Woody Harrelson and Juliette Lewis as the sociopathic lovers and directed by Oliver Stone, *NBK* teems with kinetic editing, brisk dialogue, and memorable imagery.

Several days after watching the film, Edmondson and Darrus drove through Ponchatoula, Louisiana, where they robbed a Time Saver convenience store. Before making a getaway Edmondson shot the clerk, Patsy Ann Byers, rendering her paraplegic. In July 1995 Byers filed suit for damages sustained as a result of the armed robbery and shooting.[19] Byers also filed a supplemental claim naming the film's producer, Warner Bros., and its director, Oliver Stone, as additional defendants. These allegations asserted Edmondson and Darrus went on a crime spree that culminated in the shooting and permanent injury to Byers as a result of seeing *NBK*. Byers argued that all the Hollywood defendants should be liable for distributing a film that they knew or should have known would inspire viewers to commit copycat crimes.[20]

While the First Amendment provides broad protection for free expression, the constitutional guarantee of free speech is not absolute. Speech intended to incite imminent lawless action—and which is likely to produce such action—is not protected. This idea of excluding speech that creates "a clear and present danger" from First Amendment protections dates to 1919. Justice Oliver Wendell Holmes, Jr., famously said that a speaker who falsely shouts fire in a crowded theater cannot claim the words are protected by free speech.[21] Similarly, Patsy Ann Byers argued that *NBK* was a dangerous movie that fell outside the First Amendment as incitement to imminent lawless activity.

After viewing the film Judge Burrell J. Carter Jr., saw nothing in *NBK* that he determined could incite unlawful action. The picture was permeated with glorified and glamorized violent imagery to be sure, but, Carter wrote, "We cannot say that *Natural Born Killers* exhorts, urges, entreats, solicits, or overtly advocates or encourages unlawful or violent activity on the part of viewers."[22] The First Amendment shielded *NBK*. Warner Bros. and Oliver Stone would not be held responsible for violent acts committed by unbalanced spectators.

While *Natural Born Killers* was protected, an important question remains unanswered. Can a movie influence its audience to commit extreme and unlawful actions? Can the moving image take hypnotic control of a viewer? Is there a way to control the medium's potentially powerful and persuasive ability without infringing on the constitutional protections of the First Amendment?

Maine

Although boxing films were incredibly popular during the first decade of filmmaking (see Nevada), projected scenes of pugilists pummeling each other were controversial. The state of Maine was the first to take legislative action. In March 1897, the exhibition of prizefighting motion pictures was prohibited: "Whoever publically exhibits any photographic or other reproduction of a prize fight shall be punished by a fine not exceeding $500."[1] In the northernmost corner of New England, a film history landmark was achieved. This anti-boxing-film law was the first time film censorship was authorized in America.

Even with a law on the books in Maine, boxing movies slipped through the cracks. Scenes of heavyweight champion John L. Sullivan were screened in Bangor on "Edison's latest improved picture machine."[2] Writing in the *Bangor Daily Whig and Courier*, an amusement reviewer's chief complaint about boxing films was the audience's behavior. The reviewer much preferred panoramic vistas, slight comedies, and scenes of trains arriving at stations. After attending a film of a title bout, the reviewer commented, "These biograph pictures of [Jim] Jeffries and [Tom] Sharkey have called out of social recesses human fish new to this theater.... They laugh grimly, they applaud little by the customary expression of hand clapping but declare their approval of a particularly telling punch administered by one gladiator to the other with vigorous satisfaction."[3] The hoots and hollers and jeering shouts aggravated this reviewer. Aggressive spectators had taken over the once-refined experience: "Gone are lovely ladies of light as well as dignified quality that used to make this auditorium seem like a parterre of flowers.... [G]one are the lovers of mirth and melody." Instead the playhouse could have an ominous quality: "There was terror in the air on Wednesday when the picture machine suddenly stopped. If that accident had not been promptly remedied, like as not the house would have been torn to pieces."[4]

Boxing pictures not only changed the film experience, they also changed the law. Although copyright law was embedded in the U.S. Constitution (art. I, § 8, cl. 8), filmmakers discovered that it was difficult to square the law with their developing medium. When the first motion pictures were released, the Copyright Act of 1831 was in place.

This Act provided limited protection for photographic images but was silent on the topic of motion pictures.[5] As Thomas Edison was chasing down rivals who offered comparable devices—the hardware—with aggressive patent litigation, another film pioneer, Siegmund Lubin, found he could earn a living by pirating content—the software.

Lubin duped his competitors' most popular titles, especially boxing pictures. When the Veriscope Company released the enormously successful *The Corbett-Fitzsimmons Fight* (1897), Lubin was not far behind with his *Reproduction of Corbett-Fitzsimmons Fight* (1897). When the American Mutoscope and Biograph Company produced the epic twenty-five-round *Jeffries-Sharkey Contest* (1899), Lubin swiped a portion of the potential box office with his *Reproduction of the Jeffries and Sharkey Fight* (1899). After Edison Manufacturing Co. came out with *The Fitzsimmons-Jeffries Fight* (1899), Lubin rolled on his own *Reproduction of the Jeffries-Fitzsimmons Fight in Eleven Rounds Showing the Knockout* (1899). Edison took his nuisance of a rival to court and obtained the decision that he needed: "celluloid film for a moving picture machine was held to be a photograph" for the purposes of copyright.[6] Taking this defeat in stride, Lubin joined forces with Edison as one of the charter members of the Motion Picture Patent Company, an industry cartel formed to freeze out independent filmmakers.

Protection for motion pictures was shoehorned into the Copyright Act of 1831. The Act also provided an expanded term of copyright protection. The Copyright Act of 1790 had allowed for an initial term of protection, giving the author exclusive rights to his or her work for fourteen years. At the end of the first term living authors could renew their exclusive rights for an additional fourteen years. If the rights were not renewed, the work would fall into the Public Domain (PD) and be free to use for all. The 1831 Act extended the initial term of protection to twenty-eight years plus a fourteen-year renewal period; still, even if properly renewed the work would still fall into the PD forty-two years after publication. While the Framers of the Constitution felt that it was important to give authors an exclusive right to control their own work, the Public Domain was also seen as a valuable resource, a cultural asset necessary for communal creativity.[7]

The Copyright Act of 1831 was in effect during the decades that motion pictures emerged. By 1903 Edison could be sure that his films had some coverage, but the industry was still confused about certain practical issues. Could a motion picture be copyrighted as one single work? Was a film a single unit, despite the repetition of hundreds of images that flickered by from eighteen to forty frames per second to create the illusion of motion? Or must each and every one of those incrementally different frames be copyrighted as a unique work? Edison was not taking any chances; his company created rolls of paper prints from the reels of negative celluloid to deposit at the U.S. Copyright Office to ensure the fullest protection.[8] This "belts and suspenders" policy of protecting both the complete motion picture as well as each individual frame within it was likely conceived by Edison lawyer Frank L. Dyer. Dyer's approach had an unforeseen benefit. As the flammable nitrate film stock of these early motion pictures was worn, scattered, or destroyed, the paper-based prints were archived. It is through these copyright records preserved on paper that much of early motion picture history has survived.

By 1909 a new federal copyright act was ratified, which extended the renewal term to twenty-eight-years (viz. twenty-eight year initial term plus twenty-eight year renewal). Next, Congress recognized the growth of the film business and passed the Townsend Amendment in 1912. "The occasion for this proposed amendment is the fact that the production of motion pictures photoplays ... has become a business of vast proportions," declared the House of Representatives. "The money therein invested is so great and the property rights so valuable that the committee is of the opinion that the copyright law ought to be so amended as to give to them distinct and definite recognition and protection."[9] Under the Townsend Amendment a motion picture properly registered and timely renewed could claim copyright protection for a fifty-six-year term.

The Townsend Amendment took effect August 4, 1912. Edison was first in line to register his paper prints of motion picture film. The first film to receive a certificate was *The Charge of the Light Brigade* (1912), directed by J. Searle Dawley.[10] Under the law, Dawley's picture received twenty-eight years of copyright protection, until 1940. A timely renewal would have secured an additional term of twenty-eight years.

By 1940 the Edison Manufacturing Co. was a primordial relic of the film industry. While Edison was defunct and unable to renew protections, a rightful successor-in-interest could file a copyright renewal. So who held rights to Edison's films? By the late 1910s, the first wave of film pioneers phased out as Vitagraph swallowed up rights, films, and personnel. Vitagraph formed a composite company called V-S-L-E with the remnants of Selig, Lubin, and Essanay Studios. Edison's assets followed a complicated chain to title, sold several times before being folded into V-S-L-E.[11]

Vitagraph housed their conglomerate studio on a sprawling Burbank back lot not far from Universal City. A decade later, as Warner Bros. prepared for a talkie revolution, Warner acquired Vitagraph, its studio, and its assets. The successor in interest to Dawley's *Charge of the Light Brigade* may have been Warner when the renewal date came up in 1940. Warner may have had the right to renew, but the creaky old film was probably viewed as of little value. If anyone wanted to see the Tennyson poem on screen, Errol Flynn's big-budget version had been released by Warner Bros. four years earlier in 1936. Even if renewed, the 1912 picture would have "termed out" in 1968 and fallen into the public domain.

Bangor, Maine, resident Al Taylor loved old movies. In 1969 when Taylor was twenty years old, films of an earlier era weren't seen as classic movies. They were just old movies. Unwanted in theaters, many Hollywood gems of the 1940s and 1950s were downgraded to late-night programming on second-rate television channels. Taylor hosted one of those programs, *Series Classic Showcase*. A few years later Taylor had the idea of taking the programming to a wider audience by using the new medium of home video. In 1973 he created Classic Film Museum Inc. Classic Film Museum monetized the old movies that no one seemed to care about anymore.

No one cared until they started throwing off money again.[12]

In 1974 Summa Corp., the successor in interest to the rights to several Howard Hughes films, cried foul. Taylor's Classic Film Museum had been distributing two Hughes films, *Hells Angels* (1930) and *Scarface: The Shame of a Nation* (1932). Summa charged that Taylor was pirating the pictures and filed a lawsuit.[13] Classic Film fought valiantly, even subpoenaing Hughes from his Las Vegas hotel room to testify. The millionaire recluse did not appear before the court and Classic Film settled.[14]

When Taylor received another claim later that year, he was willing to fight harder. Warner Bros. charged that Classic Film was infringing on the studio's rights to the original version of *A Star Is Born* (1937). *A Star Is Born* is a Technicolor classic that chronicles the highs and lows of life in Hollywood. Janet Gaynor played Esther Blodgett, a midwestern farm girl who dreams of film fame. As a struggling actress, she meets a famous actor named Norman Maine (Fredric March). He is soon sucked into a downward spiral

A Star Is Born (1937) **peeks behind the scenes at the inner struggles of actors on the way up and the way down.**

of alcoholism as her star rises. The film was praised and nominated for six Academy Awards, with Gaynor claiming the trophy for Best Actress.

Warner Bros. admitted that copyright on the film had lapsed but argued the picture was derived from a screenplay—and that work was unpublished. Unpublished works could be protected by a "common law copyright." It was an esoteric plan cooked up by lawyers. They attempted to bootstrap protection by claiming elements of the film were still under copyright. But both Judge Edward Thaxter Gignoux of the Maine district court and the three-judge panel of the First Circuit agreed: no to Warner Bros. The decision affirmed that "the owner of a common-law copyright in the underlying work cannot expand the statutorily created monopoly.... This is the price to be paid by the copyright holder in exchange for the exclusive statutory monopoly he enjoyed."[15] Classic Film Museum paved the way for other independent distributors to exploit PD works.

In 1978 copyright duration was extended to a period of time seventy years after the death of the creator. In the case of "works for hire," like Hollywood studio films, copyright would hold for 120 years after creation or 95 years after publication, whichever is shorter. With international conventions influencing U.S. copyright law, the legal landscape can be confusing. But the lesson of Classic Film Museum is that once a work falls into the public domain, there (generally) it stays.

Maine may have been the first state to enact a film censorship law, but it was also the state that cleared the way for PD films to be freely exploited. Film studios still challenge the term of copyright protection because so much money rides on their exclusive rights. Once Mickey Mouse—who first appeared in *Steamboat Willie* (1928)—falls into the PD (currently pegged at 2023), a rippling effect will be felt within the multi-billion-

SHARKEY HOPES TO WIN
WITHIN FIFTEEN ROUNDS

Sailor Pugilist Predicts That He Will Defeat Jeffries in
That Time, but the Heavy Weight Champion
Also Says He Is Sure of Victory.

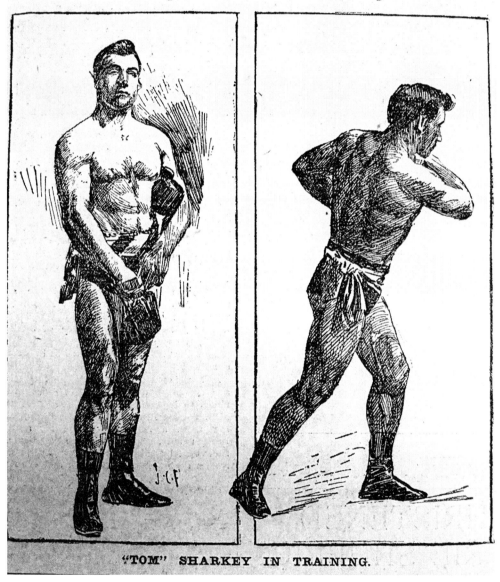

"TOM" SHARKEY IN TRAINING.

Appearing in many prizefighting pictures, "Sailor Tom" Sharkey (1873–1953) battled heavyweight champions Bob Fitzsimmons, Jim Jeffries, and "Gentleman Jim" Corbett.

dollar company. There is a delicate balance between granting authors exclusive rights to their work and allowing for the inevitable time when works must come to be owned by all as a cultural heritage.

Maryland

Although its southern neighbor claims to be "for lovers," Maryland has been a prime location for movie romance.

It's easy to remember Tom Hanks's home base in *Sleepless in Seattle* (1993), but it takes a real movie buff to remember that his love interest, Meg Ryan, was based in Baltimore. While the starry-eyed lovers of *Sleepless* crisscrossed the country into each other's arms, another popular Bay State couple featured a more reluctant fiancée. Julia Roberts acted the title role in the *Runaway Bride* (1999). In *Bride*, Richard Gere played a reporter who travels to Maryland to profile Roberts's nervous nuptials. Instead he finds himself replacing the groom at the altar. Garry Marshall, director of *Bride*, and Nora Ephron, director of *Sleepless*, proved themselves to be modern masters of romantic comedy set against the Maryland background.

Maryland has been the setting for several improbable relationships. In *The Mating Game* (1959), Debbie Reynolds found her one-hundred-year-old family farm under investigation by the IRS. Only in Hollywood could amorous attraction develop with an auditor. Playing the taxman, Tony Randall finds a financial solution and gets the girl. Even more unexpected were the sparks between party-boy divorce mediators Owen Wilson and Vince Vaughn and blue-blooded good girls Rachel McAdams and Isla Fisher in *Wedding Crashers* (2005). Self-invited to a power wedding, the couples discover love during a reception at the stately Inn at Perry Cabin in Saint Michaels.

While audiences welcomed these romantic pairings, moving pictures originally received a less welcoming reception in Maryland. The film industry was in transition when Maryland established a board of censors in 1916. The nickelodeon boom was ending and the studio era was on the rise. Wary of the new mass media, Maryland's legislature enacted a film censorship law, becoming one of the first states to take action. A three-person review board was charged with previewing movies to determine whether they were "moral and proper."[1]

One of the first films banned in Maryland was a pacifistic picture with a daring message called *War Brides* (1916). In the film, a king orders his soldiers to impregnate townsfolk to build up his army. One protesting woman (Alla Nazimova) cries out, "If you will not give us women the right to vote for or against war, I shall not bear a child for such a country!" She kills herself, her body landing at the king's feet. The progressive picture was released during World War I, four years before women were given the right to vote in the United States. Maryland's censors felt *War Brides*, with its anti-authority message, had to be silenced. The board banned the picture as "unpatriotic, immoral, and [having] a tendency to hamper recruiting." The film's producer, Lewis J. Selznick, appealed the decision. The state court found that although the film "was not immoral in the narrower sense … it might obstruct the recruiting and enlisting service of the United States."[2] The ban remained.

The struggles of love and war were seen in the film debut of Russian star Alla Nazimova's *War Bride* (1916).

Censoring a political picture was rare. Maryland's movie militia was mostly concerned with suggestive scenes, titillating images, and illicit passions. Drinking, gambling, and glorified criminal action were red-flagged and blue-penciled. But the board had difficulty keeping up with the quantity of films flooding their office, stating in their annual report of 1920 that it was impossible "to apply the same yardstick of standards to every film." Instead they developed rules of thumb, rejecting "stories built on illicit love, over-passionate love scenes, attempted criminal assaults upon women, nakedness and indecent costumes ... men and women living together in adultery and without marriage, drinking and gambling scenes made attractive ... materialization of the figure of Christ ... and chloroforming victims for criminal purposes."[3] Among the problematic pictures cited by the board were *Old Wives for New* (1918), *The Unchastened Woman* (1918), and *A Sister to Salome* (1920).[4]

By the 1940s Helen Tingley, one of Baltimore's most colorful censors, felt that the real trouble with motion pictures wasn't immorality. In her words, "It was stupidity." Viewing eight films a day, she became jaded by bottom-of-the-bill B-movies. She confessed in an interview, "I'd like to scream after a whole day of B pictures ... and I frequently do. Since taking this job I've become nearsighted and I get raging headaches, but I'm crazy about it. I've never done anything that's more fun." After watching Shirley Temple in *Honeymoon* (1947), a late-career stinker, Tingley remarked, "We can reject pictures that are sacrilegious, obscene, indecent, immoral.... [T]oo bad we can't bar this little gem for inhumanity to the audience."[5]

Tingley had a sense of humor, but the subject of censorship was deadly serious. Motion picture regulators used their authority to maintain conservative values in a rapidly changing world.

A turning point came when Otto Preminger released *The Man with the Golden Arm* (1955). In the picture Frank Sinatra played a recovering drug addict. Released from a recovery program, he is tempted down a dark path. In one scene a pusher prepares a hypodermic needle while Sinatra rolls up his sleeve and wraps a necktie around his arm. The actual injection is not shown, but the effects are clear as Sinatra twitches before settling into a stupor. Following their review, Maryland's censors issued an order to cut the scene. The studio refused and challenged the censorship law as an unconstitutional limitation on the First Amendment. The censors prevailed in the lower court, but on appeal, United Artists won the day. The appeals court felt the censored scene did not "advocate or teach the use of ... narcotics. On the contrary," wrote Judge Edward Delaplaine, "the evidence is strong and convincing that the picture is likely to have a beneficial effect as a deterrent from the use of narcotics."[6] The censors were still powerful, but the courts were beginning to weigh the censors' moral authority against free speech protections.

In 1960 Governor J. Millard Tawes appointed a larger-than-life figure to the film censor board: Mary Avara. Dubbed "the X-Rated Grandma," Avara enthusiastically exercised her authority to cut, edit, and ban films. "I made up my own ratings," she announced during a guest spot on *The Johnny Carson Show*. "G for garbage and R for rotten. How else could you describe such filth?"[7] For over two decades Avara reviewed as many as 450 films a year at a time when barriers were breaking down and morals were loosening. "We do have people who like this garbage, but I say let these sickies go down on The Block (Baltimore's adult sex show area) and watch them."[8]

And yet, under Avara's watch, the censor's power diminished. A documentary called *Naked Amazon* (1954) focused on tribal life in the South American rainforest. It was

Native nudity was too titillating for Maryland's censors when seen in *Naked Amazon* (1955).

banned for nudity but overruled by Maryland's Court of Appeals. After watching the ethnographic study on Kamayura Indians, Judge Hall Hammond commented that except to the most excitable and imaginative viewer, the film could not trigger lustful ideas.[9]

Next, a naturalist travelogue, *Have Figure—Will Travel* (1963), followed three girls along the intracoastal waterway to a nudist resort. The censors found the picture's nakedness improper. Once again Judge Hammond was on the case, this time appreciating the cinematic sites: "The photography was very good, the dialogue was unobjectionable, and the picture had artistic value." The board of review had a very specific complaint: "If the picture contained only scenes of nudity within the nudist camps it would have been licensed without deletions, but … while nudity in the camps was not obscene, it was on the boat because in that locale it was not a normal way of life."[10] Nautical nudity was not normal. On the other hand, it was perfectly normal to be naked at the nudist resort. This was an interesting theory of appropriate nudity, but Judge Hammond rejected it. *Have Figure* was cleared to play in Maryland.

Avara was no prude. In one interview—and she loved giving interviews—she commented on her own experience outside the screening room: "Let me tell you, when you've had a full-blooded Italian man, believe me, you know all about sex. You don't need nobody to show you anything on the screen."[11] Day in and day out, Avara was faced with naked flesh on display.

When Russ Meyer's *Lorna* (1964) came to town, the king of the nudie-cuties found his film blocked by Avara. Meyer convinced the court his exploitation flick was not obscene.[12] On the other hand, *This Picture Is Censored* (1965) was censored.[13] The Danish drama *A Stranger Knocks* (1959) was denied a permit.[14] A rogue's gallery of offensive titles queued up at the Annapolis courthouse. The decisions came down fast and furious. Soft-core auteur Radley Metzger stood by as *The Dirty Girls* (1965) was barred.[15] Swedish sensation *I Am Curious (Yellow)* (1967) was banned, along with *The Wicked Die Slow* (1968) and *Alimony Lovers* (1969).[16] The court did not even view these grind house loops, prompting Judge Hammond to sigh, "Our relief at this is great and joy fills our hearts."[17] The bizarre S&M debauchery of *Odd Tastes* (1968) was blocked.[18] Nazi sexploitation in *Love*

Vigilante veterans of the Civil War set out on a mission of vengeance in *The Wicked Die Slow* (1968).

Camp 7 (1969) was halted.[19] Unnamed 16 mm sex loops seized from peep-show playhouses in Baltimore's tenderloin district were deemed obscene, along with the most popular porno of all time, *Deep Throat* (1972).[20]

Maryland witnessed a frenzy of film censorship. In 1976 a bill was introduced to the state senate to outlaw snuff films and put a stop to pornographic movies that portrayed the killing and dismemberment of women. The legislators conceded, "[We] aren't really sure the films actually exist ... [but we're] not taking any chances."[21]

A watershed moment occurred in 1965 when the Supreme Court declared Maryland's film law unconstitutional. This decision did not turn on the issue of free speech; rather, the High Court found that the commission's complicated administrative procedure deprived filmmakers of due process.[22] This Baltimore case was a turning point in film history that sounded a death knell for motion picture censor boards around the country.

By the 1970s Baltimore's film scene was energized by John Waters, a director who reveled in the tawdry with films like *Pink Flamingos* (1972). Avara was no fan. "Waters! I don't even want to discuss him," she told the *Baltimore Sun*. "Makes my mouth feel dirty."[23] The feeling was mutual. The director recalled his dealings with the censor in his book *Shock Value*: "I looked at her crooked wig hat and polyester pants suit and realized there was no point in arguing style."[24]

Avara hung on long after her position became an anachronism, out of step with the times. After twenty years of enthusiastic censorship, she stood by helplessly as her post was defunded in 1981. Among the final performances she reviewed were James Bond in *For Your Eyes Only* (1981) and Kermit the Frog in *The Great Muppet Caper* (1981).[25]

Maryland played an important role in the development of First Amendment rights. The state was among the first to organize an agency to monitor the movies. Nearly fifty years later a court decision coming from Maryland helped to end the era of institutional censorship.

Massachusetts

The most famous film seen by the fewest people must be *Titicut Follies* (1967). Directed by Boston born and bred, Harvard-educated Frederick Wiseman, *Titicut* was a documentary that illustrated life at a Massachusetts correctional facility. Wiseman wanted to shed light on the state-run institution for the criminally insane, but with his directorial debut he opened a Pandora's box of problems.

The project began in 1965, when Wiseman contacted the prison department for permission to make a documentary on Bridgewater State Hospital. The filmmaker explained that his picture would illustrate various services performed at the facility and show a slice of life inside a hospital for the criminally insane. Wiseman's request was granted, provided the rights of the inmates were fully protected and releases were signed for each subject that appeared in the picture.[1]

But when Wiseman walked through the threshold, he found a chamber of horrors. For twenty-nine days he documented bedlam, capturing scenes that would haunt any viewer. Richard Schickel's review of the film for *Life* magazine observed that the "atmosphere is one of aimless hopelessness punctuated by outbursts of unthinking, almost ritualized violence. A psychiatrist turns an interview with an inmate into a sadistic baiting, or, with malicious cheerfulness force-feeds a dying old man, while we wonder whether the ash from the doctor's carelessly dangling cigarette is really going to fall into the glop being funneled into the convulsively shuddering throat."[2] When the superintendent saw the finished film he objected—to the excessive nudity. He told Wiseman the film was an invasion of inmates' privacy and that the releases were invalid due to the inmates' mental incapacity.[3]

Schickel, on the other hand, came out the other side of the film with a positive perspective on the grueling scenes: "A society's treatment of the least of its citizens … is perhaps the best measure of its civilization…. When a work achieves this kind of power, it must be regarded as art."[4] Despite rumors the picture was banned, *Titicut* was given a special screening after the New York Film Festival in October 1967.[5] Roger Ebert commented that the film "is one of the most despairing documentaries I have ever seen.... *Titicut Follies* will dismay and disgust many of those who see it. Few of us have the slightest idea of conditions in the nation's mental prison-hospitals."[6] While critics applauded Wiseman's critique of the harsh conditions of institutional state confinement, Massachusetts authorities were outraged at the exposé.

On October 17, 1967, the Massachusetts legislature gathered in the sub-basement of the statehouse to watch the film.[7] Both for and against Wiseman's film, opinions were intense. Some objected to the conditions inmates endured; others objected to Wiseman shedding light on them. By the end of the year, Massachusetts attorney general Elliot Richardson obtained an injunction against exhibition of the film.[8] *Titicut Follies* presented an important legal question, pitting two fundamental rights against each other: free speech and the right to privacy.

The Massachusetts Supreme Court tried to have it both ways. Because the subjects were mentally incapacitated, their consents—even if Wiseman had received consents—would not be valid. But Wiseman had produced a scathing indictment of an institutional mechanism, precisely what the First Amendment was intended to protect. Judge R. Ammi Cutter upheld the injunction barring the film from wide audiences but modified the order to allow showings to specialized professional audiences.[9] With his investigative reporting, Wiseman had touched a raw nerve. He discovered the difficulties of exposing scenes the government would rather remain hidden—a theme just as relevant and shocking a quarter century later in 2003, when photographs of abuse at the Abu Ghraib prison in Iraq came to light.

Wiseman emerged as a leading voice in American documentary filmmaking, fascinated with digging below the surfaces of institutional apparatuses in *High School* (1968), *Hospital* (1970), and *Public Housing* (1997). In 1991 Massachusetts finally lifted its ban on *Titicut Follies*. Commented Wiseman, "It reaffirms the importance of the First Amendment in protecting filmmakers' rights to freedom of expression."[10]

Titicut Follies was not the first film to expose the tension between free expression and the state's efforts to control content. When *The Birth of a Nation* (1915) was released, Bay State legislators were moved to action. D.W. Griffith's film tapped into a groundswell of popularity with audiences, but Massachusetts representatives found the picture's unreconstructed view of the Civil War objectionable.

In February 1915 protesters surrounded the statehouse, petitioning for a film censorship bill.[11] By April the crowd numbered over 1,500.[12] "This is a matter of emergency and exigency," stated Judge Thomas Dowd as he made plans to screen the film.[13] Booker T. Washington submitted an amicus brief: "Best thing would be to stop [*The Birth of a Nation*] as it can result in nothing but stirring up race prejudice."[14] On the other side, theater owners engaged in a campaign to kill any proposed regulation. An editorial in the *Boston Daily Globe* stated that "if enacted into law [film censorship] will assassinate dramatic art in the State of Massachusetts."[15]

Into this tinderbox, Judge Dowd submitted his decision. He called for a single scene to be cut: the sequence in which Gus, a former slave, pursues Flora (Mae Marsh) with intentions to sexually assault her.[16] She flees and throws herself off a cliff while the Ku Klux Klan rides to avenge her. Without this volatile sequence the film lacked a climax, but so it played in Massachusetts theaters. Audiences flooded box offices, generating huge receipts. The success of *Birth* helped establish the career of future movie mogul Louis B. Mayer, who held the film's distribution rights for New England.[17]

The Supreme Picture of All Time

The BIRTH OF A NATION

Endlessly controversial, *The Birth of a Nation* (1915) is a problematic picture, but it undeniably took the American film industry to a new level.

Following the *Birth of a Nation* brouhaha, Massachusetts swiftly ratified what became known as the "Birth of a Nation Bill" to censor controversial movies. The bill was passed in May 1915.[18] Titillating titles such as *Is Any Girl Safe?* (1916) and *Where Are My Children?* (1916) hit snags with the state censor's office.[19] When *Birth of a Nation* returned for an encore in 1921, Boston censors stopped the show. Despite sold-out ticket sales, the film was forbidden and the theater's license suspended.[20] The law was short lived. In a 1922 referendum the "Birth of a Nation Bill" was rejected by popular vote.[21]

Film censorship was dead in Massachusetts. Or was it? Even without a formal film commission, unwanted viewpoints could be silenced. In *Blockade* (1938), Henry Fonda played a farmer caught up in the Spanish Civil War. The picture was charged with "taking a side with Communistic aims" and banned in Sommerville.[22] Joan Crawford and Clark Gable appeared in *Strange Cargo* (1940), but Boston audiences missed out due to the film's controversial religious overtones.[23] Even the great Greta Garbo ran afoul of the state's speech police. *Two Faced Woman* (1941) was banned in the cradle of liberty.[24] Worcester cut Alfred Hitchcock's *Rope* (1948). The local newspaper reported that Worcester's police chief, William F. Finneran, didn't even disclose what he objected to in the film.[25]

Gradually the laws began to loosen. When the Brattle Theater in Harvard Square scheduled *Miss Julie* (1951), they were denied a license for Sunday showings. *Miss Julie* was a motion picture adaptation of August Strindberg's modernist play. Anita Björk played a Swedish countess who dares to have a relationship with one of her servants. Strindberg's play critiqued the old social structure as it collided with a modern woman. *Miss Julie* was awarded the Grand Prix du Festival at Cannes.[26] In Massachusetts, the problem was not with the picture but rather with when the theater wanted to show it.

Miss Julie played the Brattle throughout the week without incident. When the theater applied for a Sunday screening license they were denied. Massachusetts had maintained blue laws prohibiting certain activities on Sundays since colonial days. In 1908 the statute was amended to regulate proper entertainment on the Lord's day. Brattle challenged the law, claiming that it violated their First Amendment rights. The Massachusetts Supreme Court agreed: "It is unthinkable that there is a power absent as to secular days, to require the submission to advance scrutiny by governmental authority."[27] Free speech prevailed as the blue laws were red-flagged.

Henry Fonda played a peasant farmer with Socialistic leanings during the Spanish Civil War in *Blockade* (1938).

By the end of the decade naked bodies could prance across Massachusetts screens—even on Sundays. After reviewing an exploitation pseudo-documentary on life in a nudist colony entitled *Garden of Eden* (1954), the state's high court held that nonsexual nudity was not obscene. Judge Arthur Whittemore commented, "The fundamental freedoms of speech and press have contributed greatly to the development and well-being of our free society and are indispensable to its continued growth." He further warned, "The door barring federal and state intrusion into this area [of censorship] … must be kept tightly closed."[28]

That door was opened wider as the 1970s approached and old values were challenged by a more progressive culture. *I Am Curious (Yellow)* (1967) was a Swedish New Wave film that focused on a free-living, free-loving college coed. As soon as it unspooled on Suffolk County screens it was hit with charges.

One of the First Amendment's greatest legal advocates stepped up to defend the picture. Attorney Edward de Grazia fought for classic books, including Henry Miller's *Tropic of Cancer* and William S. Burroughs's *Naked Lunch*.[29] Here he defended the movies. On appeal Alan Dershowitz joined the cause. Still, the Supreme Court remanded the case due to a procedural issue. *Yellow* remained banned in Boston.[30]

Top: Gable and Crawford simmered in the tropics in *Strange Cargo* (1950), proving too hot for Massachusetts' censors. *Bottom:* Alf Sjöberg's Swedish film adaptation of *Miss Julie* (1951) came under fire for Sunday showings in Boston.

Free speech remains vulnerable. Outside Boston, Dedham's board of selectmen pressured a local theater to cancel showings of *Henry and June*, the first NC-17-rated film.[31] The Massachusetts Bay Transit Authority cracked down on advertising it deemed too saucy for the subway. The T pulled down posters for Adam Sandler's *Big Daddy* (1999) and a remake of *Psycho* (1998), as well as the Jerry O'Connell–Shannon Elizabeth teen comedy *Tomcats* (2001). The *Tomcats* ad featured the legs and stomach of a woman in boxer shorts, with a slogan above her crotch reading, "The last man standing gets the kitty." Denying these promos a place on the rapid-transit walls, Robert Prince, then general manager of the MBTA, commented, "Young ladies and children ride our system, and I didn't think they should be subjected to [the] ad[s]."[32]

Massachusetts has wrestled with defining permissible and inappropriate content. Frederick Wiseman walked the line between critical expression and intrusion into privacy. D.W. Griffith riled audiences with racial dog whistles but also pushed the film industry to new heights. Even the idea of protecting impressionable eyes from sexually themed ads is a double-edged sword. The challenge of balancing free speech with proper conduct is a continuing and continually changing effort.

Michigan

Cars and movies are two key ingredients of the American experience. Both the car and the cinema developed around the same time, products of the technological revolution. In 1891 Thomas Edison applied for a patent on his motion-picture device, while a young engineer named Henry Ford was hired at the Edison Illuminating Company.[1] A dozen years later in 1903, Ford's prototype horseless carriage was on the road, while Edison Film released its first commercial hit, *The Great Train Robbery*.[2]

Early on Henry Ford felt the need for speed. He built a race car nicknamed "999" that driver Barney Oldfield rocketed to a record mile a minute on June 15, 1903.[3] Almost twenty-five years after he set that record, Oldfield starred in *The First Auto* (1927). This first fast-and-furious film included moments of sync sound—in a racing sequence viewers could hear the cry "Go!" Released in June 1927, *The First Auto* beat *The Jazz Singer* to theaters by four months.[4] While Al Jolson entertained audiences with ad-libbed improv and jazzy songs, *The First Auto*'s soundtrack was mainly filled with racing engines and roaring crowds, making it less attractive for history books.

Aside from fast cars, the built-in drama between labor and capital became an important element of Detroit's on-screen image. In *Black Legion* (1937) Humphrey Bogart played a Motor City machinist passed over for a promotion, losing out to an immigrant. In retaliation he joins a secret society, the Black Legion of the film's title. The film drew attention to a real-life hate group making headlines at the time of release.[5]

Inspired by the bio of United Auto Workers president Walter Reuther, Pat O'Brien exposed corruption in the Motor City in *Inside Detroit* (1956).[6] In motion pictures, representations of car industry characters could range from engineering visionaries in Francis Ford Coppola's *Tucker: The Man and His Dream* (1988) to corporate villains in Michael Moore's *Roger & Me* (1989).

Audiences heard the roar of racecars in *The First Auto* (1927), a sound film that opened one month before *The Jazz Singer.*

Because of the close relationship between manufacturing and movie moguls, it should not be surprising that motion pictures arrived early in Detroit. In December 1895, Edison's early competitors the Latham brothers (see West Virginia) introduced their Eidoloscope at the Wonderland Theater, projecting images of horse races, boxing bouts, wrestling matches, and cockfights.[7] Edward Amet followed with his Magniscope, setting up a makeshift screening room in Pennewell, Cowan & Coe's general store. Amet's program included films of the state militia shot on location in Michigan.[8] Even local churches were getting in on the screening game, with Detroit's Our Lady of the Rosary presenting a Passion Play to its parishioners in 1901.[9]

For a moment in time Detroit filmmakers established a network of studios. The American Motion Pictures Company of Detroit dared to challenge the Motion Picture Patent Company, asking for congressional intervention in busting the film trust.[10] The Atlas Motion Picture Company was one of the first businesses to use the "Made in the USA" label. In their single year of existence, Atlas released several auto-humor shorts, including *The Jitney Submarine* (1915) and *The Parson Slips a Cog* (1915).

But all was not well in Michigan's motion picture community. In 1913 state senator W.A. Rosenkrans introduced a film censorship bill.[11] The proposal died in committee. Instead censors were installed on a municipal level. Pontiac considered regulation. Benton Harbor installed a film czar.[12] Detroit caused the biggest stir when patrolman Lester

Potter and Lieutenant Royal A. Baker were elevated to police censors. Charged with barring films suggestive of crime or immorality, these two had little patience for "scenes that depict[ed] hold-ups, crimes, etc.," which they believed could affect "the minds of the young boy who is easily tempted."[13]

For a hard-boiled cop who had previously made newspaper headlines for chasing down criminals and dodging live fire on the streets of Motor City, Officer Potter developed a coy side when it came to on-screen sex.[14] When Potter viewed Moral Feature Film Co.'s forced-prostitution-themed thriller *The Inside of the White Slave Traffic* (1913), reporters noticed the picture "brought a blush to his cheek."[15] Notwithstanding Potter's prudishness, the picture was passed.

In his downtime from his duties as censor, Lt. Baker penned several screenplays, including a police procedural, *The Girl Deputy* (1912). But Baker, too, had his limits. After Roscoe "Fatty" Arbuckle's indictment for rape and murder charges, Baker barred the comedian from Michigan's screens. Fatty's fast-living friend and on-screen partner, Mabel Normand, also found herself involved in a murder case. Lt. Baker pulled her films from city theaters as well.[16]

"I'm takin' over this town...again!

I'm gonna throw Detroit wide open! Dice, dames, the horses, the numbers—the works! And no one better get in my way!"

The story of Mobdom's attempt to take over America's Auto Capital!

INSIDE DETROIT

starring

DENNIS O'KEEFE · PAT O'BRIEN

co-starring TINA CARVER · MARGARET FIELD

Written for the Screen by ROBERT E. KENT and JAMES B. GORDON

Produced by SAM KATZMAN · Directed by FRED F. SEARS · A CLOVER PRODUCTION · A COLUMBIA PICTURE

Pat O'Brien exposed corruption in the UAW in the controversial *Inside Detroit* (1956).

By 1933 police inspector Charles W. Snyder took over censorship duties in Detroit. He handled his film duties solo, often puffing on a cigar in a screening room, he recalled, but never missing a word or scene. Snyder's methods could be informal. Raiding a stag film showing, he hauled the entire audience down to the station and told them, "I'm not taking you to court. But there's a phone over there and I've got plenty of nickels. You're not going home until you call up your wives and they come and get you."[17]

It wasn't only misbehaving performers and blue movies that aroused Inspector Snyder. Under his watch top stars were not immune to Michigan's morality police. Clark Gable appeared as an ex-convict and Joan Crawford as a saloon girl in *Strange Cargo* (1940). The film was banned. The Ginger Rogers vehicle *Primrose Path* (1940) was barred as indecent.[18] There were some treats for Michiganders. Howard Hughes's

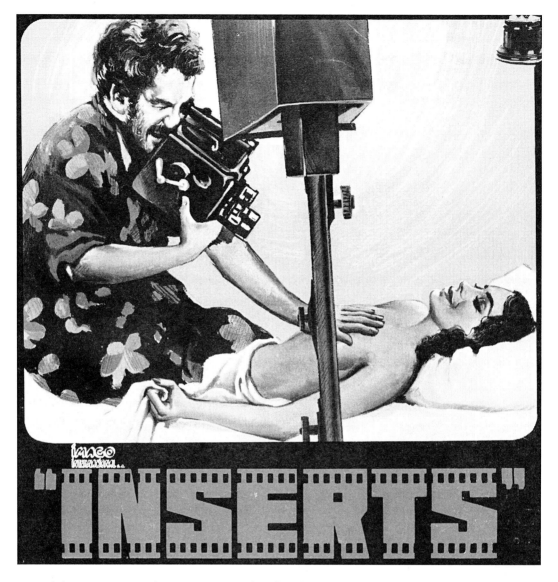

While not a pornographic picture, *Inserts* (1975) with Richard Dreyfuss was too racy for a campus screening.

The Outlaw (1943) was outlawed across the country. On a test run the mogul purchased a Detroit theater to show his film uncut for Motor City audiences so they could witness Jane Russell in unabridged voluptuousness, all cleavage and pout.[19]

Hughes's theater offered a titillating glimpse to paying patrons. Other Michigan theaters ran into trouble. In Paris Township a drive-in was shuttered for projecting "a display of pictures not fit for children to see onto places within their view on public streets, on residential properties and in private homes, without the consent of the property owners and the parents."[20] In Detroit an adult grind house came under fire. Motor City moral authorities attempted to zone the unwanted business out of existence, but the Sixth Circuit reversed the order, finding the zoning ordinance defectively vague. The city's effort to control urban blight overstepped First Amendment protections.[21] A year later in 1969 Detroit again tried to shutter adult theaters. This time the case rose to the Supreme Court.

From the High Court an important ruling came down: dirty movies were branded as a lower quality of speech. Free speech was not the same for all speech. The Court determined that Michigan's zoning ordinance limiting adult films did not offend constitutional protections: "We hold that the zoning ordinances requiring that adult motion picture theaters not be located within 1,000 feet of two other regulated uses does not violate the Equal Protection Clause of the Fourteenth Amendment."[22] Under the ruling, adult theaters could be subject to laws intended to prevent urban blight. Zoning turned out to be an effective end run around the First Amendment, able to evict inappropriate and unwanted speech from main street venues.

Grand Valley College in western Michigan courted controversy when its student activities committee programmed an X-rated movie for campus entertainment. The picture *Inserts* (1975) featured Richard Dreyfuss in the tale of Hollywood's early sound era. Set in the 1930s the film centered on the life of a fictional silent film director. With the onset of talkies, the demand for silent films evaporates and the former power player is reduced to turning out stag loops. The *New York Times* noted that *Inserts* was not pornographic even though it had received an X-rating for nudity.[23] The movie's rating was later reduced to a hard R; still, it was racy enough to have a day in court.

In the *Inserts* case, Michigan's court overruled the college's ban, viewing free speech as a "natural right." In a wildly progressive moment, Judge Douglas Hillman wrote, "Only by the free flow of ideas does society become enriched. Only by the back and forth of controversy do we gain that capacity for critical analysis which tends to correct errors."[24]

Hillman's comment remains relevant. As the United States hardens into uncompromising ideologies, this Michigan holding is a reminder that from the clash of ideas, new solutions emerge. Movies may be an amusement, but they may also help to begin valuable discussions.

Minnesota

There is something about the winter winds whistling through the Land of Ten Thousand Lakes that generates a distinctive Minnesota character. The region that formed part of the original Northwest Territory has given Hollywood film history some of its quirkiest eccentrics.

For many audiences, the Coen brothers' *Fargo* (1996) put Minnesota on the cinematic map. This darkly comic crime thriller follows a pregnant police chief (Frances McDormand) as she tracks down murder suspects. It might not sound funny on paper when a hapless car salesman (William H. Macy) hires a bumbling hit man (Steve Buscemi) to kidnap his wife and extort a ransom from his wealthy father-in-law. A bad plan leads to worse results as bodies pile up … leading to the infamous wood-chipper scene. *Fargo* was widely praised, nominated for eight Academy Awards and winning Best Actress for McDormand and Best Original Screenplay for the Coens. With bleak snowy scenes, cumbersome parkas, and lilting accents, *Fargo* was a love song to the Star of the North.

Everyone remembers the snow, the accents, and the wood chipper, but the cast members of *Fargo* were not the only movie Minnesotans to make an impression. Reprising their odd-couple association a quarter century later, Jack Lemmon and Walter Matthau bickered on screen in *Grumpy Old Men* (1993). The setting: Wabasha, Minnesota. Two numbskulls (Billy Bob Thornton and Bill Paxton) find a treasure trove of stolen loot in *A Simple Plan* (1998), but greed and distrust lead to catastrophe. In *Juno* (2007), a pregnant teen searches the pennysaver for potential adoptive parents. Finding humor and warmth in a potentially devastating situation, *Juno* became an indie-film darling, winning an Academy Award for writer Diablo Cody and recognition for geek-chic star Ellen Page.

One of film history's overlooked quirky characters helped introduce cinema to the state. The *New York Times* called Burton Holmes the "Father of the Travelogue."[1] Born

The Father of the Travelogue, Burton Holmes (1870–1958) traveled the globe returning with wit and wisdom for film audiences.

into wealth, Holmes left on a grand tour of Europe with his grandmother in 1886 when he was sixteen years old. He photographed scenes of his travels with a box camera. Returning home, he found his local camera club in financial straits. He agreed to raise funds by showing his pictures and narrating tales of his journey. The modern travelogue was born. Holmes's wanderlust was insatiable. He voyaged through the Far East, the Maghreb, and Polynesia. Returning with photographic images and exotic stories, Holmes fascinated American audiences with his colorful performances. He had a flair for showmanship, performing in elaborate costumes—a Japanese silk kimono, Arabian robes, a reindeer-fur hat acquired in an indigenous Scandinavian village. By the early 1890s, Holmes began incorporating motion pictures into his lectures.

Holmes arrived at the Saint Paul Metropolitan Opera House in March 1898 with a new program boasting "scenes which the eye of no white man before has ever rested upon."[2] Promoting his installment on Japan, the *Saint Paul Globe* wrote, "Mr. Holmes' lectures are beautifully illustrated in colors, in addition to which he has included this season a series of motion pictures, taken by himself and Mr. Oscar Bennett Depue, his assistant."[3] Cinema was new, and Burton Holmes's travelogues transported spectators on fantastic voyages across the globe. Subsequent shows focused on the Passion Play at Oberammergau, Germany, in 1901; the Russian landscape from Saint Petersburg across the Trans-Siberian Railroad in 1902; and the crystalline fjords of Norway in 1903.[4]

Not everyone loved the picture shows. Two hundred concerned citizens packed Minneapolis City Hall in 1911, declaring the need to protect the morals of young people from the influence of cinema.[5] Authorities began to take a stricter approach to film content in 1913. A bill introduced in the state senate focused on controlling crime on film: "All poisoning scenes are [to be] eliminated because of the ease and insidiousness of this crime. The crime of arson may not be depicted. Drunkenness in women and children is under the ban."[6] The first test of censorship came two years later when *The Birth of a Nation* (1915) was released.

The Birth of a Nation was scheduled to play Minneapolis in 1915. Mayor Wallace Nye stepped in to ban the controversial film, fearing it would trigger race riots.[7] Theater manager Alexander "Buzz" Bainbridge challenged the order. At court the ban was upheld, and *Birth* bypassed Minneapolis for the time being. While this legal drama was unfolding, a playhouse in Saint Paul opened D.W. Griffith's epic without incident.[8] Even with a ban in place the blockbuster proved unstoppable, returning to Minneapolis and playing to sold-out auditoriums on both sides of the river.[9] Buzz Bainbridge's story doesn't end there. The Mill City impresario decided that he would make a better mayor than Nye. He announced his candidacy on a Friday the thirteenth, standing under a ladder, holding an open umbrella, with his fingers crossed. Two decades after Nye canceled his showing of *Birth*, Buzz Bainbridge reported for work at the mayor's office.[10]

Mayor Nye and his censor board were more lenient with risqué reels. In June 1916 *Damaged Goods* (1914), a VD-prevention thriller, arrived in Minneapolis. The mayor scrutinized the film but allowed it to pass.[11] The next month, *Inspiration* (1916), an art film featuring vintage supermodel Audrey Munson posing in nude scenes as a painter's muse was scheduled at a local theater. Upon hearing that the artist's inspiration wasn't wearing enough clothes, the mayor declared, "That's an odd state of affairs…. Guess I had better take a look for myself."[12] He passed the picture. *Is Any Girl Safe?* (1916) and *The Little Girl Next Door* (1916), were both anti-prostitution pictures. Both passed.[13] Only

A shop girl falls for a rich playboy in *The Evil Thereof* (1916). Minneapolis banned the picture.

Paramount's *The Evil Thereof* (1916) was tagged as "absolutely unfit for presentations before the Minneapolis public."[14]

One of the most controversial mainstream releases arrived when Howard Hughes completed *The Outlaw* (1941). The filmmaking mogul focused his camera on Jane Russell's curvaceous figure, with lingering shots of low necklines and tough-love hayloft tussles.

Deborah Kerr and Jean Simmons played nomadic nuns in the Himalayas, still *Black Narcissus* (1947) was too sensuous for many censors.

The Outlaw earned a notorious reputation. It was condemned by the Catholic Legion of Decency and banned across the country.[15] The film briefly played Minneapolis in 1946 but was promptly pulled from screens. A year later it opened at the Lyceum Theater. Mayor Hubert Humphrey prescreened the film. Coyly calling it a "Class Z picture," Humphrey found no reason to ban it, and *The Outlaw* played on.[16]

The following year an equally startling film unspooled in Minnesota. Imported from the United Kingdom, *Black Narcissus* (1947) centered on Anglican nuns and was set in the Himalayas. The film featured Deborah Kerr and Jean Simmons in a story simmering with erotic fantasy and exotic locations. Even though it earned a "C" rating, condemned by the Legion of Decency, one young Minneapolis exhibitor took a chance on the film. Ted Mann booked *Black Narcissus* and found that it was a crowd pleaser. This racy film helped launch Mann's career as one of America's greatest theater emcees.

From a Minnesota single-screen theater Mann built a cinema empire. He acquired the 276-screen National General Theater chain. Staking his claim in Hollywood, Mann purchased the historic Grauman Chinese Theater, and dropping the first syllable and adding an "N," he relaunched it as Mann's Theater. Ted Mann's success grew from his gamble on an import that no one wanted to touch because of the trouble it caused with censors.[17]

The battle between free speech and censorship is not locked away in history but still very much alive. In 2014 the Frozen River Film Festival located in Winona iced out *FrackNation* (2013), a pro-fracking documentary. Splitting the difference between screening the picture and silencing its controversial content, festival organizers cancelled the screening but recognized *FrackNation* with a newly created award category: Officially Censored by the Frozen River Film Festival.[18]

From *Birth of a Nation* to *FrackNation*, Minnesota authorities have long been wary of the power of the cinema to influence opinions and behavior, from crime and racism to environmental policy.

Mississippi

Unholy bargains can be made anywhere, but the best locations to get the Devil's attention are in dark forests, in graveyards, or at the crux of a crossroads. These places are said to lie on the threshold to another world, where the spiritual realm and our own reality can overlap.

In the fertile farmland along the Mississippi Delta, the power of the crossroads is at its strongest. The blood, sweat, and toil of plantation slaves provided the right environment for dark legends to take hold. Along with their physical bodies bound in chains, the stories of African folklore were transplanted to the New World. From Nigeria, Yoruba beliefs invoked a trickster god named Eshu Elegbara. Eshu embodied communication, sexuality, fun, and lawlessness. A world away, in the dense humidity of the Deep South, these elements transformed into the music of the blues.

Where is the exact boundary between this world and the next? Some would say along the dusty highways where Routes 61 and 49 meet outside Clarksdale, Mississippi. The most famous local legend surrounds the bluesman Robert Johnson's guitar-playing skill. According to the myth, one evening at the stroke of midnight, Johnson went down to the crossroads to make a deal. He summoned the Devil and traded his immortal soul in return for otherworldly musical ability. Johnson's music reflected his demonic bargain, moaning and wailing, longing for Judgment Day in songs like "Me and the Devil Blues," "Hellhound on My Trail," and his most famous—and perhaps autobiographical—song, "Crossroad Blues."

That wasn't the way it happened at all, according to one of Johnson's colleagues and contemporaries, the bluesman Son House. House recalled Johnson as a god-awful guitar player: "Folks they come and say, 'Why don't you go out and make that boy put that thing down? He running us crazy.'… Finally he left. He run off … and went over in Arkansas some place or other."[1] When Johnson returned, his fingers flew across the fret board. In six months he'd mastered the guitar. This was where the myth came from, according to House. But House, a Baptist preacher who rasped out such songs as "Preachin' the Blues" and "John the Revelator," couldn't or wouldn't believe his friend would make the diabolical deal.

Johnson's Mississippi mythology has never been adequately recorded on film, despite an effort in *Crossroads* (1986). Still, the Devil is no stranger to motion pictures. French fantasy director Georges Méliès frequently dressed up as the fiend, appearing with forked beard in films such as *The House of the Devil* (1896), *The Devil's Castle* (1897), *The Devil's Laboratory* (1897), and *The Infernal Cake-Walk* (1903). Satan was a potbellied Danish man in Benjamin Christensen's *Häxan: Witchcraft through the Ages* (1922); and Mephistopheles, a barrel-chested German in F.W. Murnau's *Faust* (1926). Walter Huston brought impish humor to *The Devil and Daniel Webster* (1941); and Rex Ingram, burlesque clowning in *Cabin in the Sky* (1943). Robert De Niro and Al Pacino portrayed the Prince of Darkness as intense, creepy, and explosive—a character who could easily be your closest confidant—in *Angel Heart* (1987) and *The Devil's Advocate* (1997), respectively.

The Devil was not the problem in Mississippi movie theaters, but rather, demonic possession. This was perhaps a reasonable fear. Against the Devil, we are helpless. But evil influences can be stalled or prevented by prayer and spiritual upkeep. *The Exorcist*

(1973) shocked audiences like very few films had before it. The picture opened with Father Lankester Merrin uncovering a cursed amulet at an archaeological site in Iraq. Max von Sydow played Merrin; giving the character credibility, von Sydow had battled Death a decade and a half earlier in *The Seventh Seal* (1957). In *The Exorcist* von Sydow's Merrin is called upon to help a young girl stricken with unexplainable symptoms: abusive language, uncanny strength, explosive green vomit, and a head that revolves 360 degrees. Doctors are no help, so her mother calls a priest. When the priest arrives, the illness is properly diagnosed as satanic possession.

Around the country *The Exorcist* sickened and thrilled audiences. The *New York Times* reported, "The longlonglonglonglong [*sic*] movie line, was carried to new lengths in recent weeks.... [T]his time, people stood like sheep in the rain, cold, and sleet for up to four hours to see the chilling film about a 12-year old girl going to the devil."[2] But when Academy Award time came, *The Exorcist* was overlooked. The popular film was dismissed by an

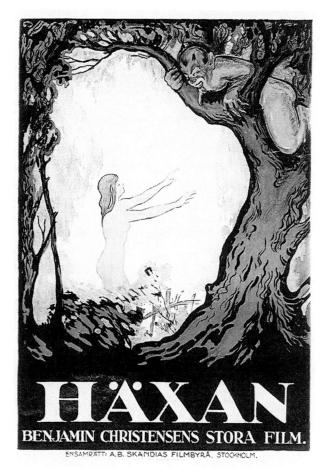

Director Benjamin Christensen summoned cinematic demons and portrayed the devil himself in *Häxan: Witchcraft through the Ages* (1922).

industry that chose "safe entertainment [and] wholesome fun over wicked horror-show titillation."[3]

The state of Mississippi also attempted to exorcise *The Exorcist*. When the picture opened in Hattiesburg, local authorities pounced. Several police officers, a justice of the peace, and Hattiesburg's district attorney attended a showing. After the credits rolled, affidavits were filed, warrants were issued, film prints were seized, and the theater manager and projectionist were arrested. Charges were dismissed against the luckless projectionist, but the theater was put on trial for publicly exhibiting an obscene, indecent, and immoral motion picture in violation of the Mississippi code, Section 97-29-33.[4] The Mississippi Supreme Court found the code overbroad since it could infringe on speech protected by the First Amendment. There were guidelines to judge obscene materials, but indecency and immorality were too vague to be permitted. *The Exorcist* was invited back to Mississippi screens and the film censorship ordinance thrown out.

Motion pictures arrived in Mississippi in 1904, introduced in Vicksburg by a showman named Archie L. Shepard. Movies were at that time seen as a low brow amusement,

German master director F.W. Murnau brought epic creepiness to his version of *Faust* (1926) starring Emil Jannings.

but Shepard brought a feature-length show of "the finest and most elaborate moving pictures that science and artistic skill can produce."[5] Charging twenty-five cents per ticket, Shepard promoted the movies as high-class entertainment "patronized by the elite" and viewed by churchmen, artists, and scholars.[6]

Shepard was one of the earliest and most successful motion picture men to road-show films across the country. He has been credited as the first exhibitor to realize that audiences would attend the theater for two hours to see motion pictures alone—without a vaudeville billing.[7] By 1905, Vicksburg was on Shepard's yearly orbit. Unlike other itinerant film exhibitors, Shepard concentrated on dramatic films, not actualities.[8] His programming prefigured the medium's future as an evening of escapist entertainment. Like a cinema laboratory, Shepard refined his program in theaters and opera houses around the state.

It was shortly after Shepard retired from his yearly visits that Mississippi's moral authorities began to consider movie censorship. Jackson journalists advocated control over "the loathsome, suggestive, and vulgar pictures." Their concern was protecting innocent minds from objectionable content, including "bar-room scenes, murders, enticements flaunted in the faces of children!"[9] The *Jackson Mississippi News* assumed that "people go to moving picture shows to be amused not to be nauseated."[10]

In 1914 a gathering of ministers from Hattiesburg pushed for a censorship ordinance, but the proposal was shot down. The town's commissioners had no budget for a film board.[11] That same year, on the floor of the state senate, a film regulation plan was debated. Scenes of "hugging and kissing unless to show love or tenderness between relatives or to illustrate a true love affair" were to be banned. The proposed law "was also designed to exclude pictures of the Wild West type and those depicting gambling, drinking, smoking cigarettes, and vulgar dances such as the tango." Like the ministers attempting to save Hattiesburg's cineastes, Mississippi's moralistic state senators saw their bill soundly defeated.[12]

Still, the issue of film censorship would not go away. In 1940 the Mississippi legislature finally had the votes to enact motion picture regulations. Under the new bill, the governor was empowered to appoint a three-person review committee charged with approving movies of "a moral, educational or amusing and harmless character" for exhibition within the state.[13]

With Hollywood's Production Code firmly in place and the Legion of Decency and various women's groups monitoring the movies, Mississippi's censors had little to do—until Elia Kazan adapted a Tennessee Williams play set in the Delta State. *Baby Doll* (1956) was shot on location in Benoit, population 444.[14] When it was released the film sounded censorship alarms around the country. *Baby Doll* revolved around a nubile girl child who sucks her thumb, sleeps in a crib, and slinks around in a revealing negligee. Her slow-witted and possibly impotent middle-aged husband eagerly awaits the day he can deflower her. A conflict starts with a neighboring cotton farmer, who seduces and revenge-rapes Baby Doll while her husband is out. Brilliantly acted by Carroll Baker, Karl Malden, and Eli Wallach, *Baby Doll* hit many

As if racial issues weren't controversial enough, *The Defiant Ones* (1958) handcuffed Sidney Poitier to Tony Curtis.

nerves. It was banned in Jackson but played on the screens of Greenville, Indianola, Benoit, and other Mississippi towns.[15]

In the coming years state censors would forbid several other films. The Frank Sinatra–Natalie Wood–Tony Curtis vehicle *Kings Go Forth* (1958) was halted because it contained a romance between a white man and a "mulatto" woman. *The Defiant Ones* (1958) handcuffed Sidney Poitier to Tony Curtis, but it wouldn't be touched by Mississippi theaters.[16] Racial prejudices controlled what content would be permitted on the Southern state's screens, but it wasn't until the Devil came down to Mississippi in the form of a blockbuster horror flick that change would occur and the censorship laws would be thrown away.

Missouri

The St. Louis World's Fair was the biggest entertainment event in American history to that point. When the Louisiana Purchase Exposition opened in 1904, it was larger than the prior expos in Chicago, Paris, and Buffalo—combined.[1] Sprawled out over 1,200 acres in St. Louis's newly designed Forest Park were palaces dedicated to agriculture, machinery, and the arts.

Each of the previous American World's Fairs marked key moments in film history. At the Columbian Exposition in Chicago in 1893, photographic pioneer Eadweard Muybridge demonstrated his Zoopraxiscope, the final technological step before actual motion pictures were invented. Muybridge's device went unnoticed and was replaced by a painted panorama of Pompeii.[2] At the Pan-American Exposition in Buffalo in 1901 cameras rolled as President William McKinley was assassinated; moviemakers manufactured the first mass-media breaking-news event.[3] When the St. Louis Fair opened, filmmaking had developed past one-shot amusements. By 1904 movies told stories: *The Great Train Robbery*, *Uncle Tom's Cabin*, and *What Happened in the Tunnel*, all directed by Edwin S. Porter in 1903, presented audiences with action-adventure, literary adaptation, and sex comedy. Movies had become part of leisure life in America.

As the fair opened William Selig captured *Pres. Roosevelt at the Dedication Ceremonies* (1903). Brazilian filmmakers produced several shorts, including *Pavilhão brasileiro na exposição de St. Louis* (*Brazilian Pavilion at St. Louis Exposition*, 1904). Biograph was on-site to record *Opening Ceremonies, St. Louis Exposition* (1904), as well as *Sec'y Taft's Address & Panorama* (1904) and *West Point Cadets Escorting Liberty Bell* (1904). Biograph also shot a series of industrial films for Westinghouse, including *Steam Hammer* (1904), which captured a massive hydraulic mallet pounding heated steel from a furnace into shape. This may be the first instance of branded content, a concept one hundred years ahead of its time. While these featurettes are interesting historical records, the true cinema testament to Louisiana Purchase Exposition came in a film released forty years later by MGM: *Meet Me in St. Louis* (1944).

Set on the eve of the expo, *Meet Me in St. Louis* celebrated a slice of Americana. The film is an ode to premodern small-town life, with unforgettable musical numbers destined to become standards, including "Have Yourself a Merry Little Christmas" and Judy Garland's version of "Meet Me in St. Louis, Louis." Successful upon release, *Meet Me in St. Louis* was nominated for Academy Awards for its screenplay, cinematography, score, and original song ("The Trolley Song"). Shining in several scenes, seven-year-old Margaret O'Brien was handed a special trophy for Outstanding Child Actress.

Another young St. Louis resident was equally struck by the opulent exposition. Edward V.P. Schneiderhahn devoted pages of his diary to the fair, writing, "Its beauty indescribable ... the Colonnades and end wings and colossal fountains all on the so-called Art Hill. The combination was simply overpowering. When the cascades were in operation and the fountains played one could fancy himself transported to fairy land."[4]

Six years after the fair closed, Schneiderhahn won a seat on the city council.[5] He loved technological marvels but had little regard for moviemaking. Schneiderhahn drafted a film censorship bill, making it the duty of the police chief to censor all films shown in

St. Louis. The bill died in the house of delegates.[6] Still, Schneiderhahn remained a harsh critic, seeking to ban pictures on the basis of his prudish personal opinions. He protested images that he admitted "may not have been indecent but I think [are] improper.... The only rule that governs me in deciding what is an objectionable picture is this: I think of my mother and my sister and ask whether I should care to see either of them expose her person in public [in such a manner]."[7] This was not a legal standard to be sure, but rather, the very definition of arbitrary.

A censorship bill was back in play by 1912. St. Louis delegate Nathan H. Hall opposed pictures showing violent crimes and nominated the city's superintendent of public schools, Ben Blewett, to chair the censor board.[8] With the support of women's groups the bill passed, and for a temporary term at least, motion pictures were subject to censorship in St. Louis.[9]

While a concern over juvenile delinquency was weighing heavily on St. Louis authorities, a more serious issue was unfolding two hundred miles south near Springfield. A vigilante group called the Bald Knobbers had been active in the Ozarks since the 1880s.[10] The backwoods rivalry between the mask-wearing Knobbers and their adversaries was made for the movies. Gus Bennert, the former manager of the Springfield Cubs, a minor-league baseball franchise, transformed himself into a film producer and promoter.[11] Bennert believed the outlaws would make a thrilling crowd-pleasing picture.[12] Mayor George W. Culler felt differently and banned the Knobber films. Springfield authorities sprang into action in 1913 when Bennert's series of violent thrillers were scheduled at a local theater.[13] Bennert conceded his pictures "may be a bit red-blooded" but denied the city's charges that they would have a degrading influence by portraying robbing, beating, and assorted lawlessness.[14] He remained defiant, saying, "I'm going to run the Bald Knobber pictures again if it breaks me.... And I shall get the crowds believe me."[15] Neither the mayor nor the filmmaker would back down, and the case headed to court.[16] In a turnabout, the circuit court judge, Guy Kirby, sided with Bennert, and the action-packed show played on.[17] Unfortunately, Bennert's films are now lost.

In 1918, Henry Goldman took over as Kansas City's censor. Goldman was a different kind of regulator, openly stumping for films he enjoyed—and that were scheduled at the playhouses he managed. His praise for *Lying Lips* (1921) ran on page one of the *Neosho Daily News*.[18] But Goldman could be a taskmaster as well, boasting of one Paramount picture he'd cut so severely that "all that was left of the picture when I got thru trimming … was the box that it came in!"[19] By April 26, 1922, Goldman was discharged from his duties. In keeping with his aggressive style he sued the city. The court found Goldman had no entitlement to his position, and the censor was silenced.[20]

Over the next two decades, independently and internationally produced motion pictures pushed the limits of acceptable speech. An exploitation flick entitled *Mom and Dad* (1950) brought sex education to St. Louis screens. When the Sky Line, a St. Louis drive-in, scheduled the film, local law enforcement moved in, threatening to arrest the theater staff. At trial, the film's titillating content was described by witnesses: "They show the actual birth of a baby, that is in the picture, the private parts of this woman is shown, open and coming apart. That is in a natural birth. Then you see the baby's head coming through the private parts of this woman, and then you see the doctor's hands go in and tug and pull to get the baby out. It is certainly very ugly. Then you go on down to where you see the caesarean operation."[21] Could birth be obscene? The Eighth Circuit thought so. The ban on *Mom and Dad* was upheld. Although the film was controversial at its time

PACIFIC DRIVE-IN THEATRES

SHOW STARTS AT 7 P.M. CHILDREN FREE

SEE! ACTUAL BIRTH OF A BABY!... BOTH NORMAL AND CAESAREAN!... The UNCENSORED, UNCUT VERSION!...

'MOM and DAD'

PLUS 2nd BIG HIT! MOTHER WAS RIGHT! "SHE SHOULDA SAID 'NO!'"

Mom and Dad (1945) discussed the birds and the bees onscreen and has been hailed one of the most successful exploitation films by the Library of Congress.

of release, fifty-five years later the Library of Congress inducted *Mom and Dad* into the National Film Registry.

When a French film teasingly titled *Night of Lust* (1963) unspooled at another drive-in, St. Louis authorities again stepped up to stop the show. This film, set in the underworld of Parisian gangs and cut to a Chet Baker soundtrack, presented a sensuous feast of cool jazz and abundant cleavage. The Supreme Court of Missouri found the picture obscene. This time the case rose to the U.S. Supreme Court, and in 1971 the Missouri ruling was reversed.[22] Risqué pictures were free to screen in St. Louis.

Missouri authorities continued to pressure grind houses that played racy movies. In 1974 *Bride's Delight* and *Stag 20* (release dates unknown) were banned from a Kansas City adult theater and the bans upheld by the court.[23] But free speech had gained an upper hand. The power to control media shapes public opinion and steers cultural direction. Censors like Schneiderhahn and Goldman believed in their mission to protect Missouri's minors from on-screen dangers, but silencing films based on personal bias only chills discussion and silences voices in the marketplace of ideas.

Montana

Movie lovers take spoilers seriously ... especially in Montana. When a friend's Facebook posting revealed details about a subplot of *Star Wars: The Force Awakens* (2015), Arthur Charles Roy of Helena threatened to shoot the boy for oversharing.[1] Roy sent a picture of himself with a firearm—which later turned out to be a BB gun—and the message that he would come to the victim's school to shoot him. This social media correspondence led to a school lockdown and Roy's arrest on a felony charge of assault with a weapon.[2] Roy would probably have fared better, both legally and dramatically, if he had threatened the plot-spoiling Facebook poster with a light saber or a proton torpedo.

Movies arrived in Montana in the late 1890s. Thomas Edison sent a crew to the Big Sky Country to record actualities such as *Tourist Train Leaving Livingston* (1897). A short Edison film entitled *The Overland Express Arriving In Helena* (1900) duplicated the action of the Lumière brothers' famous *Arrival of a Train* (1895). There are subtle differences: the French film reveals well-dressed families preparing to embark, while in the Montana version, the train station teems with workers busily loading wooden crates. *Overland Express* showed America at work taming the Wild West.

Local moviemakers captured daily life outside Butte in *See Montana First* (c. 1911), produced by the Industrial Motion Picture Manufacturing Company of Anaconda. The company invited all Anaconda residents to appear on-screen. "You cannot dodge the camera no matter how fast you travel," they warned. "It is only the 'standstillers' that will not be seen."[3] The town of Butte was featured in panoramas produced by the Forsythe-Gills-Parker Moving Picture Company. In one film, the cameraman was rolling near the fire station when an alarm sounded; he continued cranking his machine to catch the action.[4] Pathé Frères opted for more tranquil landscapes in *Blazing a New Trail in Glacier National Park, Montana* (1913).

By the 1920s local production in Montana captured a rapidly changing world as the industrial era took over. The Library of Congress has preserved several films commissioned by George Kleine, one of the earliest motion picture distributors in America. Kleine's *A Vanishing Race* (1917) documented daily life on the Blackfeet Indian Reservation in northwestern Montana at a time when age-old traditions were dying out.[5] As a contrast to the traditional ways, the Northern Pacific Railway hired Jack Ellis Haynes to capture work on the transcontinental train line. In addition to industrial films, Haynes also took scenic shots of Yellowstone on his western odyssey.[6]

As the projected images grew more influential and financially successful, Montana considered a film ordinance. State Senator Edward Donlan of Missoula County spearheaded the drive for film regulation. Donlan was a colorful figure in local politics. He organized the Thompson Falls Light and Power Company, supplying the region with hydroelectric energy.[7] Donlan's political alliances could also put him in hot water. In a board meeting with A.C. Thomas, chairman of the state's Republican Party, Donlan sat ringside as a reporter named Edith Colby burst in and shot Thomas dead.[8] Not long after witnessing this scene, Donlan sponsored a bill to ban films that depicted crimes such as train robberies, burglaries, and holdups.[9] He was powerful enough to push the proposal through committee, but when his censorship bill arrived in the statehouse in 1921 it was voted down.[10]

With censors on the sidelines, Montana took its place as a magnificent backdrop for motion pictures. Produced by Universal, King Baggot's *Perch of the Devil* (1927) was set around a struggle for control of Montana's copper industry. *Perch* pictured the corruption of industrialists as miners waged a war against unfair employment practices.[11] Fox Film's *Red Skies of Montana* (1952) told a story of fearless heroism, focusing on the parachuting firefighters of the Forest Services Corps. Based on the Mann Gulch fire of 1949 that killed a battalion of smoke jumpers, *Red Skies* was shot on location with Richard Widmark and Jeffrey Hunter.[12]

Barbara Stanwyck starred as Sierra Nevada Jones in *Cattle Queen of Montana* (1954), an RKO picture. Stanwyck's Cattle Queen was no shrinking violet, holstering six-shooters

THE "SMOKE JUMPERS" HIT THE SCREEN IN

RED SKIES of MONTANA

TECHNICOLOR

starring RICHARD CONSTANCE JEFFREY
WIDMARK · SMITH HUNTER

with RICHARD BOONE · WARREN STEVENS · JAMES GRFFITH · JOE SAWYER · Based on a Story by ART COHN

Produced by   Directed by   Screen Play by
SAMUEL G. ENGEL · JOSEPH M. NEWMAN · HARRY KLEINER 20th CENTURY-FOX

Richard Widmark led a battalion of fire fighting smokejumpers in *Red Skies of Montana* (1952) shot on location in Montana.

astride her palomino. When her rancher father dies, Jones is tasked with herding ten thousand head of cattle across the country.[13] "A woman standing alone in a sin hole of lawlessness challenging the evil tongues of prejudice and jealousy," proclaimed the film's trailer. The value of Jones's cattle attracts suitors seeking sex and easy wealth, including one played by Ronald Reagan. The future president sat comfortably on horseback in one of his final film appearances.

Montana also saw a steady stream of A-list talents that were notable if not particularly successful at the box office: Dustin Hoffman in *Little Big Man* (1970), Clint Eastwood and Jeff Bridges in *Thunderbolt and Lightfoot* (1974), and Marlon Brando and Jack Nicholson in *The Missouri Breaks* (1976). The Big Sky Country served as the setting for comedies, such as John Belushi's *Continental Divide* (1981), as well as sci-fi, serving as filming location for *The Thing from Another World* (1951). Robert Redford relied on the untouched wilderness in *A River Runs Through It* (1992) and *The Horse Whisperer* (1996).[14]

The most cinematically stunning sequence capturing Montana's landscape is the opening of Stanley Kubrick's *The Shining* (1980). The film begins with an aerial sequence that follows Going-to-the-Sun Road in Glacier National Park. As Jack Torrence (Jack Nicholson) drives his family toward a chilly catastrophe, Kubrick's camera swoops high above the winding road with shots that show off both the verdant countryside as well as the psychological isolation that awaits the Overlook Hotel's winter watchman.

Barbara Stanwyck and Ronald Reagan lived life on the range in *Cattle Queen of Montana* (1954).

Equally picturesque—and equally ominous for the studio that released the picture—Michael Cimino's big-budget Western *Heaven's Gate* (1980) was produced on location in Glacier National Park and Kalispell. On a quest for authenticity, *Heaven's Gate* meticulously re-created the days of yore but at great expense. The film was a magnificent failure that ended the director's career and played a part in the demise of United Artists. The *New York Times* called *Heaven's Gate* "a $44 million object lesson in directorial ego and executive incompetence."[15]

Film censorship remains a current issue in the wide-open spaces of the Treasure State. Even without a censorship law on the books, certain films have courted trouble. A comedic documentary entitled *The Muslims Are Coming* (2013) was scheduled to play at Hellgate High School in Missoula. Organizers hoped to use the picture as an educational tool to discuss stereotypes about Islam, but all did not go as planned. Protesters assembled outside the school. School administrators stood firm. Despite the angry mob, the picture played on, followed by a discussion.[16] This was a win for the freedom of the screen in the face of outside pressures. Screening controversial movies can have the power to open doors on difficult conversations, to defuse deep-set opinions, and potentially to lead to broader worldviews.

Nebraska

If Hollywood is the dream factory for its industrial output of motion pictures, then Nebraska must be the field of dreams. The Cornhusker State provided an open setting for the nostalgic baseball fantasy *Field of Dreams* (1989) starring Kevin Costner, Ray Liotta, James Earl Jones, and, in his final American film, Burt Lancaster. But Nebraska's pastures of plenty went even further. The midwestern state cultivated some of history's most important and successful movie talents, both in front of the camera and behind the scenes.

Harold Lloyd rivaled Chaplin and Keaton as one of the silent screen's great comedians. The acrobatic entertainer—most famous for hanging perilously from a clock in *Safety Last* (1923)—hailed from Burchard, Nebraska. Cowboy star Hoot Gibson learned to ride in Tekamah and made his movie debut in 1910 in *Pride of the Range*. Leaving Wahoo, Darryl F. Zanuck became a screenwriter at Warner Bros. In 1924 Zanuck penned Rin Tin Tin adventure tales before rising to the position of the studio's president of production. Zanuck left Warner to lead Fox from 1934 to 1941. He stepped down for eighteen months to serve in World War II and returned to Fox from 1943 to 1956. After leaving again to produce films independently, Zanuck was called back for a third term of duty at Fox from 1963 to 1971. Many of the brightest stars had roots in Nebraska. Fred Astaire, Marlon Brando, Montgomery Clift, Nick Nolte, and Gabrielle Union all called Omaha home. A number of Academy Award winners hail from Nebraska: Henry Fonda from Grand Island, James Coburn from Laurel, and Hilary Swank from Lincoln.

From the early flickers of film, Nebraskans loved the movies. Governor John Mickey felt his state should have a strong presence at the St. Louis World's Fair in 1904. At Nebraska's booth in the agriculture pavilion, a movie theater was planned.[1] The booth featured a series of films showcasing scenes of cattle branding, bucking broncos, agricultural production, and modern farming methods.[2]

A decade later Nebraska experienced a brief period of vibrant local film production. The Black Hills Feature Film Company of Chadron produced a Western thriller entitled *Wild Bill and Calamity Jane in the Days of '75 and '76* (1916). The film presented scenes of life on the plains, with wagon trains, stagecoaches, cowboys, Indians, and even Commander George Custer and his troops bivouacking on the eve of their destruction. Freeda Hartzell Romine, a performer who had previously worked as a stunt shooter in Buffalo Bill's Wild West Show, starred in the film.[3] With vigilante murder and scenes of battle, *Wild Bill and Calamity Jane* provided a homegrown draw for local theaters.

The Winnebago Indian Reservation south of Sioux City also nurtured a noteworthy contribution to film history. In 1906, James Young Deer married Red Wing (born Lillian Margaret St. Cyr). Together, Deer and Wing became the first Native American film actors known by name on-screen. Young Deer directed his wife in at least twenty-five films, including *White Fawn's Devotion: A Play Acted by a Tribe of Red Indians in America* (1910), *An Up-to-Date Squaw* (1911), and *The Unwilling Bride* (1912). Red Wing came to the attention of Cecil B. DeMille, who featured the authentic actress in his directorial debut, *The Squaw Man* (1914). Red Wing was not an Indian extra but rather cast in a key role; her character is saved by the film's star Dustin Farnum and repays the debt by rescuing him in return.

In later film histories Young Deer presented a problem: reservation rolls did not preserve his name. Film scholar Angela Aleiss traced Young Deer's identity to James Young Johnson, born outside Washington, D.C. Johnson's ancestry stemmed from a forgotten folk called "the Moors of Delaware," an enclave of people of mixed white, African American, and Native American heritage. The community of "Moors" had incorporated the local Nanticoke Indian tribe, so Young Deer could indeed boast indigenous lineage, just not a direct tie to the better known Winnebagos.[4]

Both the Black Hills Feature Film Company and James Young Deer provide an interesting but short-lived sideshow to Nebraska film history. A more significant contribution came from two brothers based in Lincoln. George and Noble Johnson were not the first African American filmmakers, but they had a drive to produce that had not been seen before in the genre of race movies. Race movies developed in the 1910s as an alternative to the mainstream industry. These niche films were tailored to the African American experience with black actors and stories that appealed to audiences of color. In 1916 the Johnson brothers incorporated the Lincoln Motion Picture Company and began work on a featurette entitled *The Realization of a Negro's Ambition* (1916).[5] The Johnsons saw a brief golden era, releasing films such as *A Trooper of Company K* (1917). *Trooper* was a war picture that purportedly featured actual Buffalo Soldier veterans of the all-black Tenth Cavalry Regiment that fought in the Battle of Carrizal against Mexico. The Johnsons followed up *Trooper* with *A Man's Duty* (1919) and *By Right of Birth* (1921) before their operation folded. In addition to establishing a place in history as pioneering African American filmmakers, the Johnsons inspired other minority artists, such as Oscar Micheaux (see South Dakota), to enter the industry. The brothers experimented with niche marketing and financing techniques that pre-dated "crowd funding" by a century.

By 1921 the Johnsons closed their production shingle. George retired to record an alternative history of film from an African American perspective, while Noble took a steady job at Universal Pictures. Noble Johnson became an all-purpose in-house "exotic" actor, appearing as the Prince of the Indies in *The Thief of Bagdad* (1924) with Douglas Fairbanks, as the Maori harpooner Queequeg in *Moby Dick* (1931) with John Barrymore, and as the tribal chief in *King Kong* (1933). He played many other memorable, if not politically correct, roles over the course of his career, which lasted until 1950.

Even as Nebraska's industry came alive with Black Hills Co., James Young Deer, and Lincoln Co., state authorities were considering how to control the medium. In 1912 Omaha appointed police lieutenant Thomas Hayes to monitor movie theaters. Lt. Hayes was ordered to visit all playhouses and ensure that no objectionable or suggestive scenes were being presented. His orders were to prevent unnecessary noises as well. The Omaha PD assured the city's music-loving citizens, "This does not mean we will prohibit pianos … but they will be allowed to run only during certain hours and with the soft pedal on."[6] In Lincoln informal censorship committees convened when a particularly sordid picture was scheduled for a tour of the region.[7]

Over the next two decades a continual fight raged in the statehouse over the issue of film censorship. Lawmakers introduced an ordinance in 1913, but it became lost in committee. The bill returned in 1919, and the *Moving Picture World* lamented, "The Nebraska bill is so stringent that it will mean practically the elimination of the film business in the smaller cities."[8] Exhibitors fought the law and it was defeated. The *Moving Picture World* breathed a sigh of relief: "Nebraska is safe for at least two years from the fear of state censorship."[9] Sure enough, the topic returned two years later in 1921, and this time both houses passed the censorship ordinance. Governor Samuel Roy McKelvie, the former publisher and editor of the *Nebraska Farmer* had personal feelings against state censorship and vetoed the bill.[10] Still, censorship in Nebraska would not die. By the end of the decade a new proposal was discussed that would position the governor as the state's movie morality czar. The plan was debated as late as 1931. Despite a loyal following among church groups, civic associations, and the Better Film Council, Nebraska's pro-censorship representatives failed to gather enough votes.[11]

Even without a formal censor committee in place, Nebraskans found that films could still be cut and banned. An independently produced Czechoslovakian film entitled *Ecstasy* (1933) raised eyebrows across the United States with scenes of a nude actress named Hedwig Kiesler frolicking in the Bohemian countryside. The picture was stopped at U.S. Customs (see Louisiana), but news of the actress's assets lit up the film industry. Louis B. Mayer signed Kiesler in 1937 and changed her name. As Hedy Lamarr she became one of MGM's great glamour girls of the 1940s. The mayor of Omaha, Dan Bernard Butler, prevented his city from experiencing *Ecstasy*, while the film—with two spicy scenes cut—played in Lincoln without protest.[12] Mayor Butler also disapproved of *Lady of Burlesque* (1943), starring Barbara Stanwyck. *Burlesque* was based on a novel by celebrity stripper Gypsy Rose Lee. Despite Butler's objections, his censoring committee only found the film, which played in the United Kingdom under the titillating title *The G-String Murders*, "rather crude with some double talk" but permissible.[13]

The American Committee on Maternal Welfare coproduced an educational documentary explaining *The Birth of a Baby* (1938). At the time, showing an expectant mother on-screen or even mentioning the word "pregnant" was enough to cause alarm. This film demystified the birthing process with diagrams and descriptions of pre- and postnatal care. Actual delivery was even presented on film, albeit with the mother so concealed that the baby's head seemed to emerge from the parting of drapes. *Life* magazine ran a five-page photo spread hailing *Birth of a Baby* as a valuable tool to reduce maternal and infant mortality rates.[14] Despite the clinical approach, Mayor Butler was still offended by the private act made public. He banned *Birth*, but this time the city welfare board overruled the mayor and allowed the film play.[15]

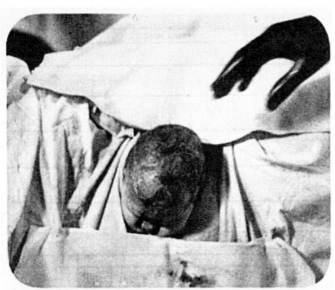

24 Repeated contraction of the uterus pushes the baby down the birth canal. Its head emerges first. The bones are sufficiently soft to conform to shape of opening, thus facilitating delivery.

The Birth of a Baby (1938), a mid-century film version of what to expect when you're expecting, was seen as indecent by many censors.

As times changed, Nebraska's authorities were reluctant to. When Omaha's Pussy Cat Theatre arranged screenings of *Deep Throat* (1972) for seven dollars a couple, the state police threw cold water on the show. Theater owners claimed their constitutional free speech rights had been violated, but after the judge watched the popular porno flick, he concluded the picture was obscene.[16] The First Amendment does not protect obscenity so state authorities were permitted to shut the show down.

State censorship in America was a losing battle in the long run as media became easily accessible and adult materials more commonplace. The days of moral authorities like Mayor Butler, who sought to protect his community from Hollywood's influence, were history. Across the country, new independent producers—similar in their aspirations to Black Hills Film Co. and Lincoln Motion Picture Co.—began working on microbudgets to make movies tailored to targeted audiences. These indies would see a golden age in the coming years.

Nevada

The phrase "motion picture censorship" can conjure images of depraved and demented scenes from fringe films available only to bottom-feeders on the black market: snuff films, sexual fetishes, animal cruelty, abuse of children—lewd, immoral, unsafe, and improper all. Although film regulation generally targets obscene, lewd, immoral, blasphemous, inhuman, and improper images, this is not where the story of film censorship begins.

Film censorship started in part as a reaction to on-screen prizefights. From the earliest days, when overworked engineers played around with filming test scenes, they turned to fisticuffs. One of the first motion pictures recorded in Edison's laboratory showed inventor W.K.L. Dickson sparring with his assistant, William Heise, in *Men Boxing* (1891) (see New Jersey). As Edison's film manufacturing company began to develop a slate of titles, boxing scenes appeared on the first release schedule. The films featured both professional pugilists, as in *Corbett and Courtney Before the Kinetograph* (1894), *The Leonard-Cushing Fight* (1894), and *The Hornbacker-Murphy Fight* (1894), as well as proto-viral-video animals, such as *Prof. Welton's Boxing Cats* (1894) and *Alleni's Boxing Monkeys* (1894).

Boxing loops were well suited to the developing medium of motion picture technology. In a boxing bout all action occurred within the squared-off ring, which made for a practical camera setup. Two-minute rounds of action complemented the limits of the film medium, which in the early days could only accommodate a single reel in the viewing apparatus. When Edison's Kinetoscopes became commercially available in amusement parlors, the multi-round entertainment had patrons lining up to plug their nickels into the addictive motion picture machines. Early film fans, generally working-class individuals, immigrants, and children, would cheer on the exciting scenes. Female audiences were afforded a glimpse of toned, oiled, nearly naked men, a rare and rousing vision in an era still bound by Victorian concepts of decorum.

Boxing was a controversial sport. Even before the fistic loops were produced, many states had already outlawed prizefighting.[1] Where boxing was prohibited there was a legal loophole. The sport itself was taboo, but it was unclear whether *motion picture scenes* of the sport violated the letter of the law. In 1897 the state of Maine closed this loophole, passing anti-boxing-film legislation. This was the first official act of state censorship in America—a full decade before Chicago ratified more inclusive film regulation.

The popularity of boxing infuriated moral authorities of the day. James J. "Gentleman Jim" Corbett was a precursor to the modern-day celebrity. In 1892 Gentleman Jim claimed the heavyweight championship belt, and unlike previous pugilists, he used his fame as a revenue source. He appeared at public events, made speeches, sparred onstage, and in 1896 signed a contract with the Kinetoscope Exhibiting Co. for exclusive motion picture rights to his matches.[2] Gentleman Jim was a pop-culture sports star, so it was predictable that boxing promoters would want to cash in on his biggest bout ever, pairing him with a British challenger, Robert "Lanky Bob" Fitzsimmons. Fitzsimmons was gunning for a title bout; Gentleman Jim, enjoying the luxury of fame, was less excited about the prospect. That fact that Fitz had recently landed a pile-driving blow to Cornelius "Con" Riordan that killed him and earned Fitzsimmons charges for manslaughter was one more reason for Corbett to delay the contest.[3]

Corbett was reluctant to sign on, and laws around the country did not favor the bout. These odds didn't discourage Dallas-based gambler and aspiring boxing promoter Dan Stuart. Stuart envisioned substantial sums of money from the exhibition of a Corbett-Fitzsimmons matchup.[4] On October 12, 1894, Stuart announced the event, and cities and states scrambled to prevent it. Chicago, Florida, Texas, Arkansas, and the Indian Territories slammed their doors shut to the bout. By the end of 1895 the situation looked grim. Stuart considered taking the event to Mexico. The *New York Times* lamented, "Not likely that Fitzsimmons and Corbett will meet anywhere."[5] Corbett was still reluctant to commit. Fitzsimmons was demanding money up front.[6] The enterprise faced failure until Stuart fixed his sights on the state of Nevada.

Nevada's economy was struggling. Between 1890 and 1900 the population fell from 47,000 to 42,000. Mines had dried up, the economy was depressed, and the desert conditions created a bleak landscape that did little to encourage industry.[7] The state was ripe for Stuart's proposal. It took a solid year to negotiate, but in January 1897 Governor Reinhold Sadler signed a bill that permitted Nevada to host the fight. "An Act to restrict and license glove contests, or exhibitions between man and man, and to repeal all other Acts in conflict therewith" gave Stuart the green light. Two months later the boxers faced off in Carson City for the "Fight of the Century."[8]

The Corbett-Fitzsimmons Fight (1897) was photographed on a wide-screen format developed by the Veriscope Company that allowed for a crisp, clear image. The event picture brought film technology to new highs. *Corbett-Fitzsimmons* captured fourteen rounds, ending with Fitzsimmon's punishing blow to Corbett's solar plexus. The wide-gauge, IMAX-like show was projected, rather than viewed through a peephole device, so the audience could feed off the fight crowd's rowdy energy. This picture was also the longest film ever presented up to that point. Running for eighty to one hundred minutes, much of it now lost, *Corbett-Fitzsimmons* paved the way for future feature-length films. Despite several states quickly revising their antiboxing laws to ban boxing pictures, Stuart's fight film was a financial success. Waves of prizefighting pictures followed: *The Fitzsimmons-Jeffries Fight* (1899), *Jeffries-Sharkey Contest* (1899), *The Gans-McGovern Fight* (1901), and the *Gans-Nelson Contest in Goldfield Nevada* (1906). These fistic photoplays entertained audiences and infuriated moralists around the country.

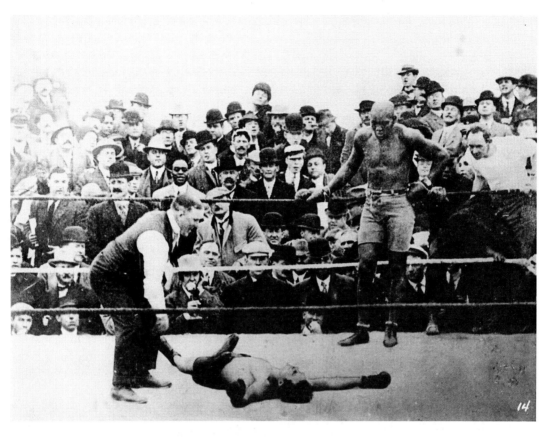

Jack Johnson was the first African American heavyweight boxing champion, but his record of wins triggered racial unrest across America.

A new prizefighting controversy was on the horizon. Rising up through boxing's ranks was a towering pugilist named Jack Johnson. Johnson seemed to be unstoppable. He was also African American. Around the country the "Galveston Giant" struck fear into the hearts of competitors and spectators alike when he clobbered every opponent and declared himself the black heavyweight champion. Johnson KO'd Fitzsimmons in two rounds: "Johnson picked [Fitzsimmons] up bodily and threw him to the floor.... Johnson returned with two right hand uppercuts, one landing under the Cornishman's heart, while the other opened a gash on his left cheek bone. Fitz went down [and] rolled over on his back."[9] Johnson next set his eyes on the reigning world champion: Jim Jeffries.

Jeffries was no longer at the top of his game, having retired undefeated in 1905.[10] Still, mainstream America called for a "Great White Hope" to defeat Johnson. Once the bout was scheduled, it was clear this pairing was not merely a sparring contest between two champions of sport, but also a proxy battle between the races in the ring. The "Fight of the Century" redux was scheduled for Independence Day, 1910, in Reno. Twenty-five thousand spectators gathered at the venue, including hundreds of women.[11] Vitagraph's cameras were in place for a film that would be released under the title *Jeffries-Johnson World's Championship Boxing Contest, Held at Reno, Nevada, July 4, 1910* (1910).

The boxers headed into the ring. Fifteen rounds later, "James J. Jeffries ... winner of twenty-two championship fights, the man who was never brought to his knees before by a blow, to-night passed into history as a broken idol. He met utter defeat at the hands of the black champion."[12] After Johnson knocked Jeffries down twice, the fight was called to prevent a TKO, and the "Great White Hope" was led from the ring bleeding from the nose and mouth, one eye swollen shut. Johnson had a slight abrasion on one lip. Race riots erupted around the country, in Atlanta, Baltimore, Cincinnati, Little Rock, Louisville, New Orleans, Omaha, Philadelphia, and Washington. In Houston a white man slashed a black man's throat on a trolley. In St. Joseph, Missouri, a mob attacked a white man. Police mobilized in New York's Hell's Kitchen, Harlem, and San Juan Hill to control unrest.[13]

The race-based violence moved the federal government to take action. In 1912 Congress passed "An Act to Prohibit the Importation and the Interstate Transportation of Films or other Pictorial Representations of Prize Fights."[14] Fight films could no longer be distributed: acting as a super censor, the state effectively killed a popular genre. When a promoter named Lawrence Weber attempted to import films of a fight staged in Havana, Cuba, officials halted his crates at Customs and confiscated the contents.

Weber challenged the seizure and argued his case up to the Supreme Court. There, in a unanimous decision passed down in 1915, the High Court denied Weber. The ruling: Congress had broad powers to prohibit imported films.[15] Weber's import was a matchup between Jack Johnson and Jess Willard. In that fight Willard, a white boxer, KO'd Johnson in the twenty-sixth round to regain the heavyweight belt. Here was an ironic footnote: the federal law that was passed to quell the race riots provoked by Johnson's win over Jeffries prevented audiences from witnessing the Galveston Giant's fall.

In Havana, Cuba on April 5, 1915, Jack Johnson lost his heavyweight boxing title to Jess Willard. Films of the fight were embargoed from entering the United States.

Nevada has served as the setting for a wide range of favorite films. *Ocean's 11* (1960) assembled Frank Sinatra, Dean Martin, Sammy Davis, Jr., and friends in a buddy heist film. *The Misfits* (1961) teamed Clark Gable, Montgomery Cliff, and Marilyn Monroe against a stark landscape in the twilight of Hollywood's golden age. Elvis Presley delivered hip-swinging glitz to *Viva Las Vegas* (1964), and Nicolas Cage, existential angst to *Leaving Las Vegas* (1995). Sin City was the background for a mind-blowing psychedelic trip in *Fear and Loathing in Las Vegas* (1998) and the comedic capers of what-the-heck-happened-last-night in *The Hangover* (2009). But Nevada's place in film history is even more significant. The Silver State broke down barriers when it permitted boxing films and unleashed violence when it riled up the country with an interracial matchup that revealed an ugly side of America. What happens in Vegas doesn't stay in Vegas—it can affect the whole nation.

New Hampshire

It was a trial for the ages. The fantastical jury was a rogues' gallery of American villains: "Captain Kidd, he killed men for gold. Simon Girty, the renegade; he burned men for gold. Governor [Thomas] Dale, he broke men on the wheel. Asa the Black Monk, he choked them to death. Floyd Ireson and Stede Bonnet, the fiendish butchers. Walter Butler, the king of the [Cherry Valley] Massacre, Big and Little Harpe [Joshua and Wiley Harper], robbers and murderers. [Edward] Teach [a.k.a. Blackbeard], the cutthroat. [Thomas] Morton, the vicious lawyer. And General Benedict Arnold.... A jury of the damned. Dastards, liars, traitors, knaves."[1]

Based on Stephen Vincent Benét's short story, the motion picture adaptation *The Devil and Daniel Webster* (1941) was an all-American gothic folktale. After a New Hampshire farmer named Jabez Stone finds himself in dire straits, he murmurs that he would sell his soul to escape the situation. In the blink of an eye Walter Huston, all smiles and sinister kindness, appears and introduces himself as "Mr. Scratch." Mr. Scratch offers a treasure trove of Hessian gold and seven years of bountiful prosperity for the price of Stone's soul. It seems like a good deal at first. When the stunning enchantress Belle (Simone Simon) shows up, the bargain looks even sweeter. But as happens with all deals with the Devil, the closer Stone comes to reckoning day, the more regret he feels. Before Mr. Scratch can claim his eternal soul, Stone, being an upright American, demands a fair trial.

That is where the crooked jury comes in. Each of these historical scoundrels had been seduced by the Devil's favors. They were indeed a jury of Stone's peers.

To represent his defense, Jabez Stone engages New England's greatest statesman and orator, Daniel Webster. Born in Salisbury, New Hampshire, a graduate of Phillips Exeter Academy, the state's prestigious secondary school, and an alumnus of Dartmouth College, an institute of higher education that pre-dated the Revolutionary War, the real-life Daniel Webster was a New Hampshire man to the core. Played by Edward Arnold in the film, Daniel Webster presents a stunning argument: the statesman appeals to the rogues' sense of national pride—Jabez Stone's soul does not belong to him alone but to his country. In a

Walter Huston played a charismatic demon who tempts a New Hampshire farmer to sell his soul in *Devil and Daniel Webster* (1941).

resonant baritone, Webster concludes his closing argument, saying, "Don't let the country go to the Devil"—words as powerful then as now.

The historical bad guys make an about-face, voting to restore Jabez Stone's soul. Infuriated, Mr. Scratch vows his vengeance on Webster. He pledges to prevent Webster from ever becoming the president of the United States, the lawyer's lifelong ambition. Indeed, the real-life Daniel Webster was passed over for his party's presidential nomination three times. Perhaps Mr. Scratch did have influence with the electorate.

The Devil and Daniel Webster combines the power of a folktale with the favorite American genre of the courtroom drama. The greatest legal films—including *12 Angry Men* (1957), *Inherit the Wind* (1960), and *To Kill a Mockingbird* (1962)—each pushed past legal procedure to reach core human truths, including notions of justice, faith, and equality. *The Devil and Daniel Webster* does just that, crafting a timeless allegory with homegrown American archetypes.

The first motion pictures arrived in Portsmouth, New Hampshire, around 1898. The Music Hall Theater announced an Edison-produced program of "sea fights, land battles, boating scenes, express trains running at full speed, firemen fighting a fire, and in fact about everything to thrill and interest the audience."[2] The Granite State took its motto to heart: "Live Free or Die." While other communities became concerned with motion picture content, there is little evidence of film censorship in New Hampshire. In fact the earliest voice crying out for regulation in New Hampshire came from within the industry itself.

Gustave Frohman was a successful stage emcee. With his brothers, Daniel and Charles, Frohman developed Broadway stars and road-showed touring companies in the 1880s.[3] By 1912 the Frohmans enlisted a young Adolph Zukor in their entertainment business. Zukor persuaded the Frohmans to take a chance on motion pictures. Together, Zukor and the Frohmans imported the French picture *Queen Elisabeth* (1912), a *film d'art* with stage star Sarah Bernhardt, before moving into production with *The Prisoner of Zenda* (1913) and *The Count of Monte Cristo* (1913).[4] They formed the Famous Players Film Company, and, as Daniel Frohman explained the division of labor, Zukor headed the business while "I supply the 'art.'"[5] By 1918, shortly after Zukor acquired Paramount Pictures, the Frohmans left the fold.

During these prolific days of stage and screen production, Gustave Frohman spent his summers in Rye Beach, New Hampshire. The local mogul had an interesting perspective on censorship: "Although I am a producer of moving picture films I am firmly convinced that the films and particularly those depicting social problems, should be subjected to a strict censorship law, and in fact make them more drastic. I regret to admit that several producers, if given a free hand, would flood the city with foul, immoral pictures that would demoralize the youth."[6] While state regulators avoided debate on film censorship, Frohman took an unlikely position advocating regulation of content.

Another New Hampshire man produced films that conversely helped broaden free speech and expand First Amendment rights. Louis de Rochemont's ancestors had settled in New Hampshire in the seventeenth century. Three hundred years later de Rochemont developed the *March of Time* series as war heated up in Europe. While de Rochemont's newsreels are fascinating time capsules that supported the war effort, several of his pictures also raised the ire of film censors. *Ramparts We Watch* (1940) incorporated footage from the Nazi propaganda film *Feuertaufe* (*Baptism of Fire*, 1940) showing a blitzkrieg on Poland.[7] Pennsylvania's board of censors ordered the footage deleted, concerned the scenes "would have a terrifying effect on the masses and on young men about to be conscripted for Army service."[8]

Two years later de Rochemont was again in hot water, this time with the Production Code Administration. The censorship division of the Motion Picture Producers and Distributors Association was not pleased with scenes in *We Are the Marines* (1942) that showed soldiers uttering epithets like "hell" and "damn."[9] But it was *Lost Boundaries* (1949) that caused the greatest alarm.

Lost Boundaries was based on a true story and set in the townships of Keene and Gorham, New Hampshire. For over a decade Dr. Albert Johnston and his wife kept a secret from their friends, neighbors, and children: they were part black.[10] At the time, "passing" as white was highly controversial and even a crime in states like Virginia that had strict anti-miscegenation laws on the books. The real-life Dr. Johnson had been unable to find a job at one of the few hospitals that accepted black interns, but the Maine General Hospital in Portland accepted his application without inquiring about his race. So the deception began. Mrs. Johnston later recalled, "We never once intended to pass over as white.... It just happened accidentally."[11]

The family heritage remained hidden until Dr. Johnson enlisted in the navy and became a lieutenant commander. His commission was revoked, an intelligence officer explained: "We understand ... you have colored blood in your veins."[12] De Rochemont took the Johnstons' story and embellished it. In *Lost Boundaries*, once the family is revealed to be of mixed race, they become pariahs in their community.

The racial theme was too provocative for MGM, where the project had been in development.[13] The studio opted for a less inflammatory social-issue film and released *Intruder in the Dust* (1949), in which a white boy stands up for an older black man accused of murder. *Lost Boundaries* was picked up by de Rochemont and produced independently. De Rochemont shot the film on location in New Hampshire and Maine, directing Mel Ferrer, a white actor, in the leading role.

Lost Boundaries was barred in Memphis, where Lloyd T. Binford, chairman of the city censor board, simply commented, "We don't take that kind of picture here."[14] Atlanta's censor, Christine Smith, banned the film as well. In Atlanta, de Rochemont fought back, filing a case with the Georgia court. Looking past the message of racial tolerance, the Fifth Circuit considered whether *Lost Boundaries* in particular or motion pictures in general should be entitled to the constitutional protections of the First Amendment.[15] The court seemed prepared to admit the medium of film had progressed beyond the early days of production. But jurisprudence is bound by precedent. The governing rule, the *Mutual* decision (see Ohio) set down in 1915, positioned motion pictures outside constitutional protections. Under *Mutual*, film was not speech but "a business pure and simple" that could be regulated by the state.[16]

When *Lost Boundaries* was released the idea that motion pictures could be protected speech was on the horizon, but the law hadn't caught up yet. The court declined to "consult crystal ball gazers or diviners or to do the gazing and divining for ourselves in order to base a decision on a prophesy."[17] Under the existing law, Atlanta could ban *Lost Boundaries*. In the name of preserving peace, morals, and good order in the city, *Lost Boundaries* was chilled out from playing in Hotlanta.[18]

Unlike many communities around the nation, New Hampshire stayed true to its state motto, "Live Free or Die." Government-supported film censorship bypassed the Granite State. Louis de Rochemont may not have been able to prevail with his message of racial tolerance in Southern states, but in the long run his work helped to broaden First Amendment rights and led to greater freedom of the screen.

New Jersey

The story of motion pictures—and film censorship—begins in New Jersey. Thomas Edison established himself as the country's greatest inventor with the introduction of the phonograph in 1877 and the electric light in 1878. With income from his patent royalties, Edison established a research and development laboratory in West Orange, New Jersey. In a letter dated 1888, Edison penned his thoughts on an upcoming project: "I am experimenting upon an instrument which does for the eye what the phonograph does for the ear.... [T]his apparatus I call a Kinetoscope."[1]

W.K.L. Dickson worked on the moving picture project, tasked with making Edison's vision a technical reality. By 1889 Dickson and his assistant William Heise had a prototype built, and they began to photograph playful test shots.[2] The earliest of these motion pictures featured the engineers as subjects in *Monkeyshines, No. 1, 2*, and *3* (all 1890); Dickson doffing his hat in *Dickson Greeting* (1891); and Dickson shaking hands with Heise in *A Hand Shake* (1892). Soon more elaborate setups were recorded, such as *Blacksmith Scene* (1893), in which the technicians took turns pounding on an anvil and swigging from a beer bottle. By the end of the year the motion picture project got the green light, and Edison commissioned construction on the first studio dedicated to moviemaking. Dubbed the "Black Maria," the rotating, retractable-roofed, sheet-metal shed was completed on February 1, 1893.[3]

Out of the Black Maria came the earliest films recorded as entertaining amusements. Eugen Sandow, a performer billed as the strongest man in the world, flexed for the camera in *Sandow* (1894). Authentic cowboys and Indians stopped by to perform in a *Buffalo Dance* (1894), and Col. Cody himself posed for *Buffalo Bill* (1894). Boxing films proved to be the most popular subject among early audiences, and Edison Film Manufacturing Co. responded by restaging bouts in their ironclad studio, including *Corbett and Courtney Before the Kinetograph* (1894) and the *Leonard-Cushing Fight* (1894). These pugilistic pictures triggered the first calls for film censorship.

The first film studio, dubbed the Black Maria, was a sheet metal shack with a retractable roof set on a revolving track.

Boxing was illegal in New Jersey, so when news broke of a fistic ballet staged for cameras, municipal authorities paid a visit to Edison's laboratories. "Whether it was a contest of the character prohibited by law or not," the *New York Sun* speculated, "the Kinetoscope may be subpoenaed before a grand jury."[4] The new technology exposed an ambiguity in the law: if boxing was banned, were moving pictures of boxers also banned? The uncertainty would be resolved three years later when the state of Maine revised their laws to prohibit boxing films, thereby putting the first film censorship law on the books (see Maine).

In addition to boxing, dancing films were also extremely popular with early film audiences. Out of the Black Maria came *Annabelle Butterfly Dance* (1894), *Carmencita's Dance* (1894), and *Lola Yberri's Fan Dance* (1895). These pictures offered a glimpse of bare ankles or shaking hips, titillating and sometimes shocking images to a culture still restrained by notions of Victorian propriety and Edwardian etiquette. When Asbury Park's state senator, James A. Bradley, visited a Kinetoscope parlor, the flickering images of *Carmencita* caught his eye, and not in a good way. "Show such a picture to the good people of Asbury Park? No, no; never!" he reacted. "This picture, sir, is barred from your show. I will not permit it."[5] On that day in July 1894, history recorded the first instance of government film censorship in the United States. Not long after the censorship of *Carmencita* in Atlantic City, Mayor Franklin Pierce Stoy directed his police force to raid a parlor on the boardwalk and seize *Dolorita Passion Dance* (1897).[6]

After W.K.L. Dickson left Edison Manufacturing in 1896, other cameramen began to step out of the Black Maria. James H. White assumed the position of Edison's chief creative director, overseeing productions shot on location, such as *Passaic Falls, New Jersey* (1896) and *Bathing at Atlantic City* (1901). When White left on a world tour, Edwin S. Porter took over as creative lead at the Edison studio. Porter brought a sense of narrative

Behind the scenes of pioneering production at the Black Maria. Note the boxing picture being photographed was accompanied by a soundtrack, as evidenced by audio apparatus on the left.

storytelling to the medium. After Porter directed *The Great Train Robbery* (1903) on location in and around Paterson and Milltown, New Jersey, the Black Maria was considered obsolete. Film's first studio was demolished.[7]

A new phase of film history opened in Fort Lee in 1907. An Edison crew arrived at the Palisades overlooking the Hudson River to photograph an adventure film entitled *Rescued from an Eagle's Nest* (1907). Behind the film's hackneyed story and cheesy taxidermied-bird effects, an actor named D.W. Griffith received his on-screen break. The following year Griffith would begin directing, taking the first step on a road that would lead to *The Birth of a Nation* (1915).

Fort Lee became a mecca for film production. Griffith returned to shoot *The Lonely Villa* (1909) and introduce an actress named Mary Pickford. Carl Laemmle dispatched a production unit to make *Hiawatha* (1909), the first film put out by Independent Motion Picture Co. (IMP). Mark Dintenfass, who in several years would become one of Laemmle's partners in forming Universal Pictures, established the Champion Studio in the unincorporated Coytesville section of Fort Lee in 1909.

Before long Fort Lee teemed with moviemakers. The Société Française des Films et Cinématographes Éclair launched Éclair American in 1911, investing in a state-of-the-art glass studio in Fort Lee. Éclair released literary adaptations, such as *Robin Hood* (1912), *The Legend of Sleepy Hollow* (1912), and Edgar Allan Poe's *The Raven* (1912). French filmmakers Alice Guy and her husband, Herbert Blanché, left their positions at Gaumont to open Solax Studios and moved their offices to Fort Lee in 1912.

The American screen's first identifiable star, Florence Lawrence, set up her own production shingle in Fort Lee in 1912, the Victor Film Company. William Fox branched out from his theater business to production, shooting Theda Bara's breakout performance as a dangerously sexy vamp in *A Fool There Was* (1914) in Fort Lee. Other up-and-coming film studios followed, including Louis B. Mayer's Metro Pictures and the Goldwyn Pictures Corp.[8] In nearby Bayonne, David Horsley established the Centaur Film

The first multi-scene narrative film made in America was *The Great Train Robbery* (1903). Extremely popular, the short film set the stage for future hits.

Company.[9] Centaur would be one of the first studios to lead the exodus to California, opening up a West Coast branch in Hollywood called Nestor Studios in 1911. Back in the Garden State, Laemmle engineered a canny corporate maneuver, merging IMP with Champion, Éclair, and Nestor to form the core of Universal Pictures. Universal was based in Fort Lee from 1912 to 1916 before operations moved to California.[10]

New Jersey's heyday as a filmmaking destination dried up as World War I ended. Some studios, like Solax, closed up shop, while Metro, Goldwyn, and Mayer consolidated. Other events were out of the control of industry executives. A postwar coal shortage, along with the coldest winter in decades and an influenza epidemic, had disastrous effects on East Coast film studios. Those that survived made plans to relocate to sunny California. The last remnants of the New Jersey film industry sat locked away in archives. Reels of flammable nitrate film stock stowed in studio vaults were forgotten. When the aged celluloid ignited and burned in the 1920s and 1930s, the legacy of New Jersey's role in film history was all but wiped out.[11]

As production in New Jersey ebbed and flowed, the state's censors began to assert control over film content. The first town to install a censor board was Montclair, which appointed a panel in 1909.[12] Newark followed, putting a stop to *The Birth of a Nation* (1915).[13] Newark's censors were less successful in their attempts to ban Samuel Cummins's racy venereal-disease-themed edutainment piece, *TNT: The Naked Truth* (1924); Kroger Babb's sex education film *Mom and Dad* (1945); and an ethnographic documentary entitled *Latuko* (1952) that depicted nude native Africans. New Jersey's courts overturned the ban on each of these pictures.[14] When Otto Preminger's *The Moon Is Blue* (1953)—a studio film with no nudity or discussion of social disease—arrived in Jersey City, the screwball comedy was red-flagged as "indecent and obscene."[15] These rulings demonstrate the capricious nature of the decisions that came out of the state censor's office.

The first motion pictures emanated from a New Jersey laboratory. These unsteady flickers of vintage dancers and prizefighters moved local administrators to flex their moral authority in the first acts of film censorship. In another series of firsts, the Garden State attracted movie companies to set up studios. Long before Hollywood, New Jersey was the nation's center of cinema production. But over decades the state's film legacy was ignored until it was forgotten and actually obliterated. The story of New Jersey's film industry has been awaiting re-discovery. A screening of movies like *The Great Train Robbery* and *Annabelle Butterfly Dance* can resurrect ghosts of this forgotten world.

New Mexico

In May 1898 the Cardiff Cinegraph Company eagerly awaited the arrival of film equipment. By early June, George M. Cardiff's picture show was a popular draw in Albuquerque. His scenes of the Spanish-American War, including parades of heavy artillery and the smoking remnants of the battleship *Maine*, thrilled New Mexico's first film audiences.[1] Soon crowd-pleasers like heavyweight boxing championships, including *The Fitzsimmons-Jeffries Fight* (1899) and *Nelson-Britt Prize Fight* (1905), as well as thrillers like *The New Train Robbery* (1904), a sequel, remake, or bootlegged version of the classic *The Great Train Robbery* (1903), were entertaining ABQ's growing base of film fans.[2]

Not long after New Mexico's recognition as a state, communities were considering local film censor boards. Santa Fe's city council appointed a nine-member committee to review *The Birth of a Nation* (1915). Residents were concerned by disturbances across the country stirred up by the film's release. The picture was prescreened by Santa Fe's makeshift morality police, approved, and permitted to open at the Elks Theater two days later.[3] By 1921 New Mexico debated a statewide censoring agency to weed out films "cruel, sacrilegious, obscene, indecent, immoral, and such as tend to debase or corrupt morals."[4] The idea was not popular. The *Santa Fe New Mexican* editorialized, "The job of state censor of movies at $3,490 a year … should be projected into the legislative wast[e] basket pronto."[5]

Rather than straightforward censoring, New Mexico would find innovative methods of silencing unpopular motion pictures. In 1947, the film director Herbert Biberman was called before the House Un-American Activities Committee. He was asked the fateful question: "Are you now or have you ever been a member of the Communist Party?" Biberman refused to answer, claiming his political affiliations were protected under the First Amendment's guarantee of free speech and assembly. His argument was rejected. Branded an unfriendly witness and blacklisted as a member of the Hollywood Ten, Biberman served six months in prison for contempt of Congress.[6] Several years later Biberman, along with several other blacklisted colleagues, including producer Paul Jarrico, screenwriter Michael Wilson, composer Sol Kaplan, and actor Will Geer, collaborated on a motion picture entitled *Salt of the Earth* (1954).

Salt of the Earth centered on a labor strike at a New Mexico mining company. Based on true events and shot on location, Biberman's project was not a popular one with local authorities. The film showed the solidarity of unionized labor rising up to defeat corporate interests. Giving voice to the powerless, the main character was a pregnant Mexican immigrant played by Rosaura Revueltas, an award-winning Mexican actress. Unable to stop the production, U.S. authorities went after the filmmakers any way they could. Immigration police arrested Revueltas on location in Silver City and charged her with entering

Shot in New Mexico with a cast and crew of blacklisted artists, *Salt of the Earth* (1954) made a strong political statement not welcome to many authorities.

the country illegally.[7] When that didn't halt the filming, old-fashioned strong-arm techniques were used. Silver City mayor William Upton ordered the film crew to leave town. When production continued, fifty residents attacked the set.[8] The film was completed, but its troubles hadn't ended.

Salt of the Earth was successfully shown to prolabor audiences around the country. However, when distributors were granted a license to screen the film in Chicago, antiunion interests tried to shut the screening down. Members of the Chicago Moving Picture Machine Operators Union Local 110 were instructed to refuse to project the film.[9] The distributors challenged the union and ultimately prevailed. After another difficult battle Chicago would see *Salt*. Despite these troubles, the picture was recognized as a significant contribution to American cinema when the Library of Congress added it to the National Film Registry four decades after its release.[10]

Immigration raids and street fighting were two alternative methods of film censorship. In 2012 Albuquerque used the technique of zoning to run unwanted movies out of town.

The Guild Cinema is an independent theater located near the University of New Mexico. In 2007 the theater scheduled a weekend festival of erotic films called Pornotopia. Attempting to block the event, the city cited zoning laws that prohibited public screenings of adult films outside specified areas.[11] The Guild wouldn't take this lying down. They challenged the law.

Event organizers claimed their programming was artistic and educational despite the display of nude bodies and explicit sex on screen in titles such as *Couch Surfers: Trans Men in Action*. The city countered that they were not regulating speech but rather targeting the negative secondary effects of adult businesses.[12] The theater responded that any possible secondary effects, such as prostitution, crime, or depreciation of property values, should not be an issue for a festival occurring once a year.[13] The New Mexico Supreme Court ultimately favored the annual festival. With the law on their side, Pornotopia promoters pushed the boundaries and scheduled harder and more shocking fare: *Teach Me, Beat Me* and *Rock Hard Gay Love* in 2013, *Fistbump!* and *Lesbians of Enchantment* in 2014, and *Love Hard* in 2015.[14] Zoning could be useful in some cases, but the laws were limited. The Guild demonstrated that an annual festival could not be reined in as a nuisance based on secondary effects alone. But could a monthly festival? A weekly festival? These questions remain unanswered in the precarious balance between speech and regulation.

The Pornotopia case took place outside the gates of the University of New Mexico. But New Mexico has also seen First Amendment film challenges inside the halls of academia.

In the spring semester of 2012, Monica Pompeo signed up for a course in UNM's Cinematic Arts Department. The class, Images of (Wo)men: From Icons to Iconoclasts, was taught by Professor Caroline Hinkley. Hinkley aimed to discuss the portrayals of women in film as well as issues of race, class, sexuality, and gender. Her syllabus alerted students to the possibility of "incendiary class discussions" and informed students that the course "might not make you comfortable."[15]

Pompeo submitted several papers on admirable female characters in film. One essay focused on the movie *Christopher Strong* (1933), starring Katharine Hepburn and directed by Dorothy Arzner, one of the few female filmmakers working in Hollywood at the time. Another essay analyzed *The Women* (1939), which featured an all-star cast of strong women that included Norma Shearer, Joan Crawford, Paulette Goddard, and Joan Fontaine. A third essay looked at Marilyn Monroe's mercenary use of sexuality in the "Diamonds Are a Girl's Best Friend" number in *Gentlemen Prefer Blondes* (1953). Pompeo received grades of A or A– on each of these written projects. Toward the end of the semester Pompeo was assigned a paper on *Desert Hearts* (1985). Directed by Donna Deitch, *Desert Hearts* was a lesbian-themed romantic drama. The picture was recognized with a Special Jury Prize at the Sundance Film Festival, but Pompeo did not appreciate the explicit sapphic scenes.

Pompeo's essay was critical of the lesbian characters portrayed in the film. She referred to one character as "still sexually vibrant, in spite of her perverse attraction to the same sex" and to the film as "entirely perverse in its desire and attempt to reverse the natural roles of man and woman in addition to championing the barren wombs of these women."[16] Professor Hinkley personally disagreed with her student's viewpoint and stopped grading the paper after two pages. The teacher tagged the essay as hate speech. Pompeo argued that the First Amendment protected her prose. Chief Judge Christina Armijo acknowledged, "The First Amendment violation in this case arises from the irreconcilable conflict between the all-views-are-welcome description of the forum and Hinkley's only-those-views-with-which-I-personally-agree-are-acceptable implementation of the forum."[17] Pompeo argued that despite her critique of lesbian imagery, her analysis fell within the parameters of the class. Does film critique stop when it differs from the teacher's opinion?

It is reasonable to assume the First Amendment might protect Pompeo's speech. On the other hand, the classroom, even in a state school, was positioned as a nonpublic forum. Judge Armijo would allow viewpoint-based restrictions on a student's curricular speech if the restrictions were reasonably related to legitimate pedagogical concerns. The professor quickly amended her account to add that her student's comments were "disruptive and disrespectful."[18] Taking into account the new allegations as well as the opportunity Pompeo was given to rewrite her paper, Judge Armijo ruled in favor of the university. Armijo left open the question of whether "subjective hostility to a student's viewpoint was within the scope of teaching."[19] Arbitrary censorship based on personal distaste was permitted by the system as late as this 2015 decision.

A century ago New Mexico eagerly awaited the first payload of motion picture materials. One hundred years later the state found innovative methods to silence films, or film viewers, that disrupted the status quo. State authorities found that anti-immigration actions, fistfights, zoning ordinances, and academic standards are nontraditional—but very effective—ways to control unwanted, unauthorized, and inappropriate speech.

New York

A beast swats biplanes away from the Empire State Building in *King Kong* (1933). Michael Keaton streaks in his tighty-whities through Times Square in *Birdman* (2014) and Audrey Hepburn window shops in *Breakfast at Tiffany's* (1961). Hoffman crosses a street in *Midnight Cowboy* (1969), De Niro loiters at Columbus Circle in *Taxi Driver* (1976), and Travolta balance-beams on the Verrazano Bridge in *Saturday Night Fever* (1977). These iconic images of New York are an indelible part of movie history. No matter where audiences live, they are familiar with the neighborhoods of New York, from the Financial District in *Wall Street* (1987) to Midtown in *Miracle on 34th Street* (1947), and from Bedford-Stuyvesant in *Do the Right Thing* (1989) to Washington Heights in *West Side Story* (1961).

The Big Apple is more than the most familiar screen location. During the first decade of film history, New York was the incubator and testing ground for the revolutionary new technology. Peep-show parlors opened for business along Broadway. Filmmakers rolled cameras on rooftop studios. Businessmen incorporated and waged legal wars for dominance. While the public adored the cheap amusement, municipal authorities felt their position threatened by the flickering images. They moved to shut down theaters and censor out inappropriate scenes.

New York City emerged as a center of film production, distribution, and corporate organization because of its access to financing, theatrical talent, avenues of distribution, and diverse audiences. Thomas Edison debuted his Kinetoscope, a peephole single-viewer device, in a demonstration for the press in New York in March 1894.[1] Two years later, on April 23, 1896, using technology adapted from Thomas Armat and Charles Francis Jenkins (see Georgia), Edison publically introduced a projection system called the Edison Vitascope at Koster & Bial's Music Hall on Thirty-Fourth and Broadway.[2]

Edison had not been the only inventor developing a moving picture device. The Lumière brothers had a projecting Cinématographe in France; the Skladanowsky brothers, a Bioskop in Germany; and R.W. Paul, G.A. Smith, Birt Acres, and William Friese-Greene were each working on comparable projects in the United Kingdom. But what concerned Edison was his American competition. American Mutoscope and Biograph poached

Outgrowing the Black Maria, Edison studios first moved to Manhattan and then expanded to a spacious facility in the Bronx.

Edison's key engineer W.K.L. Dickson to develop their own system. The Lathams' Lambda Co. had valuable proprietary technology, as did Armat and Jenkins, as well as Edward Amet and Herman Casler.[3] Edison systemically filed patent-infringement suits, taking his competitors to court. He would control the new medium by innovation or intimidation.

Over the next decade, from 1896 to 1907, Edison used New York's courts as a weapon to control the industry. The result was a deluge of lawsuits that drove international competitors, like the Lumières, out of America and devastated others, like the Lathams and Jenkins. In the end two major film manufacturers were left standing: Edison and Biograph. Edison sued Biograph for patent infringement. He prevailed in 1899, but New York's Second Circuit reversed the decision in 1902.[4] Rather than continue competing, Edison and Biograph formed an alliance, the bedrock that would become the Motion Picture Patents Company. They were joined by a secondary group that had allied themselves with the majors: Essanay, George Kleine, Kalem, Lubin, Pathé, Selig, Star-Film and Vitagraph. Together this New York–based cartel monopolized the medium, freezing out emerging filmmakers from competing for screen time.

As the Motion Picture Patents Company members took control of the film industry, they expanded their base of operations in New York. In 1896 Biograph constructed a rooftop studio at 841 Broadway, adjacent to Thirteenth Street and Union Square in Manhattan. Vitagraph opened a plant near City Hall at Nassau and Beekman in 1897. Edison branched out from its Black Maria lab in New Jersey in 1901 and moved to a building near Gramercy Park at 41 East Twenty-First Street. Needing more space, these studios soon moved to the outer boroughs. Biograph relocated to 807 East 175th Street in the Bronx, and Edison to Decatur Avenue and Oliver Place near the Botanical Gardens. Vitagraph opted for a Brooklyn address, building on a lot at East Fourteenth Street and Locust Avenue near Avenue M.[5]

By 1910, film studios were operating in all five boroughs. In addition to Vitagraph in Brooklyn and Biograph and Edison in the Bronx, Gaumont operated out of Flushing and Thanhouser, out of New Rochelle. The Fred Scott Movie Ranch in Staten Island offered outdoor locations that doubled for the Wild West and lawless steppes in *The Life of an American Cowboy* (1909) and *Russia, the Land of Oppression* (1910).[6] While production thrived and movie parlors exhibited to packed houses, not everyone was pleased with the new technological craze.

Theodore A. Bingham became New York City's police commissioner on January 1, 1906, just as the nickelodeon boom began. Unregulated storefront theaters presented a host of problems. These unregulated theaters ran film loops constantly, not even stopping on Sunday. The dark, poorly ventilated screening rooms were firetraps, and the nitrate film stock was highly flammable. Furthermore, movie content presented scenes that openly defied proper etiquette—intruding on a private moment in *The Kiss* (1896), reveling in violence and anarchy in *The Great Train Robbery* (1903), and lampooning author-

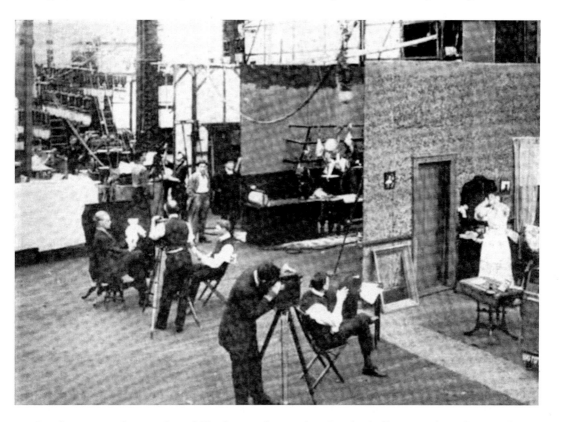

Edison's Bronx studio was a literal film factory that produced multiple films, seen here shot simultaneously and separated only by thin plywood barriers.

ity in *The Policemen's Little Run* (1907). Offscreen, authorities feared an equally alarming moral menace: audiences of women and children mingled un-chaperoned with working-class rabble and unrefined immigrants. On top of all that, theater owners making money on this lowbrow entertainment—men like Marcus Loew, William Fox, and Adolph Zukor—were Jews. To Commissioner Bingham, the last element was the worst of all. The city teemed with foreigners, the police chief wrote, and "Hebrews, mostly Russian," accounted for half the city's criminal population.[7] The guardians of moral authority felt uneasy that this demographic had taken control of motion pictures and popular culture.

Bingham took action in December 1907, demanding that all vaudeville entertainment venues close on Sunday. The owner of nine nickelodeons, William Fox, convinced the court that film shows should be excluded from Bingham's ban, and the police chief was enjoined from interfering with the city's five hundred movie theaters. Many of New York's remaining vaudeville theaters promptly switched over to filmed entertainment.[8] Bingham's actions drove New York's leisure industry further toward moving pictures, precisely the result he didn't want.

But Bingham wasn't beaten. A year later on Christmas Eve 1908, the police chief persuaded Mayor George McClellan Jr., to issue an order closing all theaters in the city. Safety was the issue this time. "I feel personally responsible for the safety and lives of [New York's] citizens," the mayor announced, "[and] therefore order each and every license issued by me for a moving-picture show ... revoked and annulled." This time a coterie of moving pictures men organized, including Fox, Loew, and the president of Vitagraph, William T. Rock. They petitioned Judge Abel Blackmar to stay the executive order. By the first week of 1909 Blackmar reached a decision: the mayor could not close all odeons with a sweeping order.[9] The reels kept running. To strengthen their position, film industry leaders allied themselves with the recently established National Board of Censorship, a nongovernmental organization. The board provided a measure of self-regulation in the hopes this would keep municipal authorities at bay.

Bingham resigned from his post in 1909, but the fight to regulate movies was not over. In December 1912, under pressure from the Tammany Hall political machine, the city's aldermen passed a film ordinance. The proposal focused on inspecting theaters to provide for safe and sanitary conditions, proper ventilation, and clear fire exits, but on the eve of a vote, an amendment was slipped in to enhance "moral safeguards." On January 1, 1913, Mayor William Gaynor vetoed the bill. Gaynor had a progressive view of the First Amendment: "No censorship can be established by law to decide in advance what may or may not be lawfully printed or published. Ours is a government of free speech and a free press."[10]

In 1914, NYC authorities tried a different strategy, directly targeting the content of inappropriate movies. Frank Beal was a director for Selig Polyscope who focused on morality photoplays, producing such pictures as *In the Serpent's Power* (1910), *The Devil, the Servant, and the Man* (1912), and his most famous film, *The Inside of the White Slave Traffic* (1913). *Slave Traffic* was an education/exploitation drama detailing how young women were abducted and procured for prostitution. The picture riveted audiences and riled state censors. Filmmakers and theater owners were hauled into court on charges of immoral exhibition. The *New York Sun* wrote, "For the first time in the history of criminal procedure a moving picture was made part of a criminal trial last night."[11] The jury deliberated for thirty-five minutes before reaching a verdict: the film was unfit for public exhibition, and its exhibitors were guilty of a misdemeanor.[12]

After attempts to control the motion picture industry on a local level in 1906, 1913, and 1914, the state legislature moved to establish a formal film censorship board. Governor Nathan Miller signed the bill on May 14, 1921, to create the New York State Motion Picture Commission.[13] This agency would remain active for forty-four years, from 1921 to 1965.

The first film commissioner was James Wingate, formerly the lead truant officer for the schools of Schenectady County.[14] Wingate banned an Austrian black comedy, *Die Stadt ohne Juden* (*City without Jews*, 1924); a Soviet propaganda piece, *The End of St. Petersburg* (1927); and even ruled out a pro-evolution documentary narrated by Clarence Darrow entitled *The Mystery of Life* (1930). In Wingate's view, "the mating of snails, spiders, and microscopic one-celled animals has no proper place on the … screen."[15] By 1931 Wingate's board boasted of reviewing over 1,500 miles of film and blue-penciling over 3,000 scenes. Censorship was not only morally righteous—it was highly lucrative. Collecting licensing fees and imposing fines, Wingate's agency collected over $1 million each year, according to the agency's reports for 1931 and 1932.[16] In 1932 Wingate was poached by Will Hays's Motion Picture Producers and Distributors Association and became Hollywood's censor for a brief term.[17]

Replacing Wingate in 1932 came Irwin Esmond. Under Esmond's watch, films such as *The Pace That Kills* (1935), *Child Marriage* (1936), and *Assassin of Youth* (1937) were tabooed. The Warner Bros. film *Yes, My Darling Daughter* (1939) was red-flagged, but once the studio cut a scene of a young couple engaging in a weekend "trial marriage," the picture was passed. Similarly, *The Birth of a Baby* (1938) was permitted after the distributor eliminated certain sequences. This would not be the case for Howard Hughes's fetish Western, *The Outlaw* (1943). Hughes refused to cut anything and the board's ban remained in place.[18]

After Esmond's retirement in 1945 came Irwin Conroe. Conroe broke with tradition when he agreed to sit with the *New York Times* and shed light on "the long-standing policy of silence through which the New York State movie censor board has kept its operations a deep, dark secret."[19] Conroe said that his primary aim was to protect the morals of New York's youth, but that he was open to edgy content and frisky language. "I am not one who gets unduly excited over a hell or a damn on the screen, depending on how it is used," he commented.[20]

Following Conroe came New York's most enlightened censor, a man born with a name for the job: Hugh Flick. Dr. Flick held the office from 1950 to 1955. He recalled the Italian import *Riz amaro* (*Bitter Rice*, 1949) as "improper and objectionable" and held back Disney's documentary

Adventurous teens turn on to cocaine and find that white lines lead to *The Pace That Kills* (1935).

The Vanishing Prairie (1954) based on footage of a live bison birth.[21] Still, Flick's regime would be the most important era for the freedom of the screen.

On December 12, 1950, at the Paris Theatre at Fifty-Eighth Street in Manhattan, a foreign film entitled *L'amore* (*Ways of Love*, 1948) opened. Imported by Joseph Burstyn, *L'amore* contained three featurettes. One of these, directed by Roberto Rossellini and entitled *The Miracle*, created a stir. This segment told the story of a simpleminded peasant woman who becomes impregnated by a stranger whom she believes to be Saint Francis. She gives birth in an abandoned chapel and experiences a mother's love for her newborn child. Rossellini's theme was love: sacred and profane. Produced in Europe, the picture bypassed the Motion Picture Producers and Distributors office and Joseph Breen's oversight. *L'amore* won praise at the Venice Film Festival and was approved by the Italian censors. Even New York State's film board granted a license to the film. *L'amore* received positive reviews from the *New York Times*. Indeed, the paper raved, "judged by the highest standards, on either its parts or the whole, [the film] emerges as fully the most rewarding foreign-language entertainment of the year."[22]

It took three weeks for news of the film playing at the Paris to travel seven blocks south to St. Patrick's Cathedral. When Cardinal Francis Spellman heard about Rossellini's featurette, he was furious. Branding *The Miracle* blasphemy, Spellman advised parishioners to boycott the picture, Catholics to picket the theater, and the state board to rescind the film's exhibition permit.[23] Under pressure, the censors issued a new order and the film was banned.

When a young girl gets involved with dope smokers she discovers that street drugs are the *Assassin of Youth* (1937).

The film's distributor, Joseph Burstyn, challenged the order. Hiring an untested First Amendment attorney named Ephraim London, Burstyn went up against the system. He lost.[24] They appealed and Burstyn lost again.[25] Finally, in a last ditch effort, Burstyn and London were granted certiorari by the Supreme Court. Before the highest court in the land, they prevailed. The *New York Times* headlines rang out, "The Miracle Happens," and, "The Supreme Court Proclaims Freedom of the Screen."[26]

The *Miracle* decision did not end censorship. The holding was a narrow one: "We hold only that under the First and Fourteenth Amendments a state may not ban a film on the basis of a censor's conclusion that it is 'sacrilegious.'"[27] This was a crack in the armor of state censorship. Since the *Mutual* decision of 1915 (see Ohio), which had given state censors the upper hand, film-makers had been on the defense. Thirty-seven years later, the *Miracle* decision shifted the balance of power. The days of arbitrary and capricious censorship based on personal disapproval would be numbered.

The next chapter in the story of film censorship would feature an unraveling of the code—a peeling off of permissible reasons for censorship. Under the New York code passed in 1921, regents were empowered to ban films they considered "obscene, indecent, immoral, inhuman, sacrilegious, or of such a character that its exhibition

A featurette directed by Roberto Rossellini entitled *The Miracle* (1948) was the tipping point that finally brought film under the protection of the First Amendment.

would tend to corrupt morals or incite to crime."[28] The *Miracle* decision did away with sacrilegious.

Next on the block were immorality and the tendency to corrupt morals. Directed by Max Ophüls, *La ronde* (1950) dealt with the decadence of belle époque Vienna. According to the court, "The film from beginning to end deals with promiscuity, adultery, fornication and seduction. It portrays ten episodes, with a narrator. Except for the husband and wife episode, each deals with an illicit amorous adventure between two persons, one of the two partners becoming the principal in the next."[29] A prostitute sleeps with a soldier, who beds a maid, who seduces her employer's son, who sexes a married woman, who makes love to her husband, who has his way with a young girl, who fools around with a poet, who lies with an actress, who copulates with a count, who, finally, pays the prostitute for a quick screw. Banned in New York, *La ronde* rose to the Supreme Court, where the Justices screened the picture. They overturned the lower courts without decision.[30] Immorality was OK.

Garden of Eden (1954), an eye-winking pseudo-documentary on sunbathing—and nudism—was halted on grounds of indecency. This time the New York Court of Appeals overruled the state censors.[31]

With sacrilege, immorality, and indecency cut from the censors' playbook, regulators were left with one remaining cause of action: obscenity. With the influx of foreign films and the beginnings of mainstream hard-core pornography, obscenity would become a nagging issue. But it was not an issue the censors would handle. In 1965, the Supreme Court mandated procedural changes to the appeals process of all state film boards. New York's legislature failed to comply and on September 30, 1965, the board of regents decommissioned the motion picture division.[32] With no fanfare the government-sanctioned censorship system was gone from the Empire State.

Motion pictures could still be banned, and New York's court system still teemed with film-related issues, from copyright to idea theft and right of publicity, to trademark dilution and antitrust. The porno chic drove an ugly wormhole into the heart of the Big Apple, transforming Times Square into a den of sleaze and disease for decades. But the state's official system of content approval had reached its conclusion. Freedom of the screen was proclaimed.

North Carolina

Nature can take on a sinister power along the Outer Banks of North Carolina. Off the coast of Hatteras, so many ships have sunk that the region has been called "the Grave-yard of the Atlantic."[1] In 1587 the British colonial village of Roanoke disappeared. The mystery of the outpost has never been conclusively determined; it seems to have been swallowed back into the surrounding wilderness. The movies have shown audiences that revenge can be an unstoppable force of nature, and the epicenter of that storm is the North Carolina location of Cape Fear.

Gregory Peck starred in and produced *Cape Fear* (1962), which was based on a book called *The Executioners*. He claims that looking for a new title, he ran his finger along the Eastern Seaboard and chose Cape Fear based on the location's evocative name. It fit. The film, a black-and-white thriller, saw two men revert to their barbaric animal nature. Peck played an attorney; Robert Mitchum, a recently released criminal named Max Cady. Cady blames his imprisonment on his counsel and returns to wreak havoc. Mitchum's slit-eyed and slow menacing delivery brings a tension that pushes Peck to his limits. As the embodiment of evil, Cady is a sexual predator. One woman is drawn into his ominous orbit, declaring, "You're an animal. Coarse, lustful, barbaric." While shooting the film in Savannah, Georgia, Mitchum was on edge. As a young man he had been arrested for vagrancy and sentenced to work on a Georgia chain gang.[2] Returning to the scene of the crime thirty years later put the actor ill at ease, which worked for the film, recalled the film's director, J. Lee Thompson.[3]

As aggressive as *Cape Fear* was, the film was toned down by the censors of the day. The head of the Production Code Administration, Geoffrey Shurlock, advised Thompson that the film walked a fine line: "There must be no suggestion that Cady is out to rape the girl. You must be careful of violence to women, violence in any form." In one scene, Mitchum eyeballs his nemesis's young daughter scrubbing a rowboat. Shurlock flagged the scene, commenting the actor "looks too lasciviously at the girl."[4]

Cape Fear is a film about a psychotic rapist in which the word "rape" is never uttered. Because of the Production Code, Cady's crimes could only be referred to vaguely and ambiguously. The film also represents another important moment in American cinema. In *Cape Fear*, audiences sided with an everyman moved toward vigilante violence to pro-tect the safety of his family. The vigilante thriller would become a popular genre in the coming years with *Dirty Harry* (1971), *Billy Jack* (1971), and *Death Wish* (1974), but *Cape Fear* stands at the beginning of this violent lineage.

Twenty-nine years later, Martin Scorsese revisited the windblown peninsula in his remake of *Cape Fear* (1991). Scorsese took the underlying insinuation and made it explicit, with Robert De Niro stepping into Mitchum's role. In Scorsese's version, Cady threatens the budding sexuality of his enemy's daughter, literally becoming the Big Bad Wolf on a high school stage. De Niro's Cady borrows from another Mitchum character, the born-again killer in *The Night of the Hunter* (1955). De Niro ripples with muscle and prison tattoos; he tears into willing sexual partners and manhandles the unwilling. Scorsese's *Cape Fear* builds to an apocalyptic scene off the Eastern Seaboard as two men wrestle in a muddy primordial landscape. The biblical battle between good and evil was captured on film.

The biblical testament had long served as a foundation of information and entertainment for North Carolina audiences. One of the first motion pictures that attracted attention in the state was *The Passion Play of Oberammergau* (1898). *The Passion Play* has been considered the first film version of the New Testament.[5] When the Rev. W.H. Stubblebine ascended to the pulpit of a Newton, North Carolina, church in 1901, the first thing he did was make arrangements to purchase a pipe organ.[6] The second thing the Reverend Stubblebine did was acquire a copy of *The Passion Play of Oberammergau*. He used the near-feature-length film to preach the gospel in Lexington, Charlotte, and tabernacles in other communities around the state.[7]

By 1903, a tent-show revival performer named Jethro Almond took up the task of

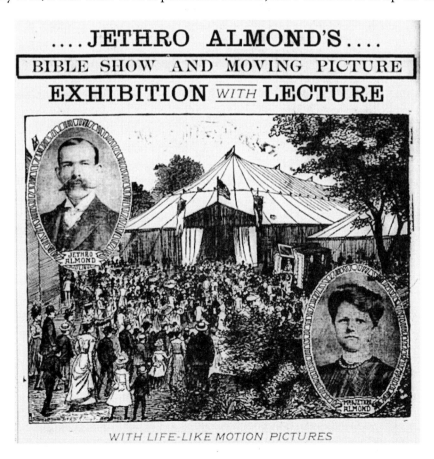

Jethro Almond ran a traveling tent show that offered fire and brimstone sermons along with risqué pictures.

spreading the good word with moving pictures. Based in Albemarle, Almond mounted an elaborate program that included live and filmed elements.[8] For the next decade Almond took his show on the road, the program growing more elaborate with each yearly installment. Almond and his troupe were soon traveling by private railway car with a slate of morally uplifting films that added to *The Passion Play* with provocative titles such as *Ten Nights in a Barroom* (1910).[9]

KEEP THEM OFF! KEEP THEM OFF!
OH HORROR! HORROR!

Technically an anti-alcohol picture, *Ten Nights in a Barroom* offered titillating thrills and shocking scenes.

These morally uplifting message films could cut both ways. Pictures like *Ten Nights in a Barroom* could teach a lesson about the dangers of alcohol and vice, but they also presented titillating and edgy scenes. How to regulate these films was the topic when Charlotte's lawmakers congregated in April 1914 to discuss a film censorship ordinance. One representative, Dr. W.M. Vines, claimed he enjoyed movies but worried about the "bad influence" they might have on local audiences.[10] Charlotte's concerned citizens couldn't agree on a plan of action. Asheville, on the other hand, appointed a film censor. Former newspaperman D. Hiden Ramsey was given the power to deny an exhibition permit to any film that he felt posed a risk to public safety.[11]

In 1921 all eyes were on Raleigh when Senator Ike Meekins proposed a statewide film censorship ordinance. Meekins proclaimed the benefits of a movie-morality law similar to the bills recently passed in Pennsylvania, Ohio, and Kansas. In a rousing statehouse debate, Meekins defended his pro-censorship position by explaining that he didn't know anything about robbing banks but "his eight-year old daughter knows it all. She has learned it at the movies."[12] The Meekins bill passed the senate but

Stark Love (1927) was a hillbilly elegy shot on location in the Great Smoky Mountains of North Carolina.

was ultimately a dead letter.[13] The push for cleaner films would be enforced on a local level. Although Meekins lost the moral movie battle, he was elevated to the federal district court bench in 1924.[14]

With state censorship under control, North Carolina took its place as a Hollywood shooting location. Paramount Pictures sent stars to Asheville to shoot *The Conquest of Canaan* (1921), and to the Great Smoky Mountains for *Stark Love* (1927). In addition to mainstream movies, North Carolina became a production center for race films. Race movies were made by African American filmmakers and tailored to black audiences. Winston-Salem–based William Scales established North State Films and produced *A Giant of His Race* (1921) and *The Devil's Match* (1923).[15] In Greenville, John Warner released the jazz soundie *Pitch a Boogie Woogie* (1947). The greatest and most prolific of the race movie directors, Oscar Micheaux (see South Dakota), died in Charlotte in 1951. The early 1950s saw the twilight of this oft-forgotten fringe film industry, but race movies remain an important area of American culture that deserves further research and recognition.

North Carolina's relationship with Hollywood became rocky again in the 1960s, when the high sheriff of Rutherford County, Damon Huskey, took film censorship into his own hands. Huskey disapproved of the movies playing on local drive-in screens. When he saw *A Piece of Her Action* (1968) and *The Ramrodder* (1969)—the latter a soft-core

The Ramrodder (1969), a sexploitation fetish western, was notable for several Manson family members who appeared in the cast.

sex–Western with the dubious distinction of featuring two members of the Manson family in the cast—lit up on the marquee, Huskey went into action. His deputies stormed the projection booth and confiscated the films—no warrant, no hearing, only the fury of a righteous man going rogue like a virtuous vigilante.

Sheriff Huskey also threatened to shutter two nearby theaters that were showing films that didn't meet with his approval. One screen was playing the Clint Eastwood–Richard Burton World War II actioner *Where Eagles Dare* (1968), the other a sexploitation adaptation of Voltaire's *Candide* called *Candy* (1968). *Candy* was an all-star fiasco featuring Marlon Brando, Ringo Starr, Richard Burton, James Coburn, and John Huston. None of these films were obscene—forgettable films to be sure, but morally corrosive? Unlikely. The lawman's campaign to ban adult movies in his district was an aggressive approach to film regulation. The Fourth Circuit shut the sheriff down, reminding him that the First Amendment protected speech, the Fourth Amendment unreasonable police seizures, and the Fifth due process. Sex and violence could play on despite Huskey's outrage.[16]

When a cinema confection called *Supervixens* (1975) arrived in Raleigh in 1975, billboards went up advertising the picture. The director, Russ Meyer, a self-proclaimed "King Leer," made movies that boasted the most curvaceous models. Meyer's chesty starlets painted on a fifty-foot billboard rubbed Raleigh's moral authorities the wrong way. The posters were ordered brought down. Industry trade papers reported, "Buxom Beauty in Bikini Banned from Billboards."[17]

Voltaire's enlightenment-era novella *Candide* was re-envisioned as a sexy softcore flick with A-list Hollywood actors in *Candy* (1968).

The battle continues. In 2006 a film shot at North Carolina's famed Wilmington production facility sparked outrage. *Hounddog* (2007) was directed by Deborah Kampmeier and starred Dakota Fanning, who was twelve years old at the time of production. Set in the 1950s rural South, *Hounddog* focused on a young girl named Lewellen who is obsessed with Elvis Presley. Rock-and-roll music is her sole pleasure in a life filled with sickness and poverty. Lewellen is promised a ticket to an Elvis concert and lured into an abandoned shed. There she is persuaded to undress and sing, "You ain't nothing but a hound dog." She is raped in a disturbing but nonexplicit seventy-second sequence—Lewellen's hand splashing into the muddy ground; a close up of Fanning's face in shocked distress; a gaping hole in the shed's roof. The rape of a preteen character on-screen who is played by an adolescent girl was overwhelming for many viewers. Although prosecutors in Brunswick County, where *Hounddog* was filmed, found the film did not violate state child sexual exploitation statutes, the controversy was hard to contain.[18] Authorities decided the on-screen depiction of a juvenile rape did not meet the legal requirement to prosecute the filmmakers for child endangerment.

Hounddog's choreographed scene was mistaken for reality, which raised an important point. The protection of children is a paramount responsibility of the state, but can the depiction of an assault cross the line? Should such scenes of sexual abuse be permitted, or is the very idea toxic? How can we educate and warn if we cannot discuss? Kampmeier's film illuminates the issue of a young girl's vulnerability, but it walked too close to the fire. Censoring authorities in North Carolina have for one hundred years sought to protect the moral well-being of the state's citizens, but finding the fine line between a legitimate message and forbidden content remains challenging.

North Dakota

There are many stories about the beginning of movies in America, but North Dakota played an important role in ending the dominance of major film studios.

The first films shown in North Dakota unspooled at a festival held at Devil's Lake on July 1–16, 1899. Among the featured attractions, along with speakers, singers, and musicians, was a new device called a Projectoscope.[1] By the end of the year Turner's Warscope Co. arrived in Bismarck to show thrilling movies of the Spanish-American War, including "the celebrated naval battle between the Oregon and Iowa and the Viscaya, charge of Roosevelt's Rough Riders at San Juan, repulse of Spanish Troops at Santiago, [and] Dewey's fleet at Manila."[2] The moving picture device was a hit with audiences. Local filmmakers planned to produce scenes of wheat farming from seeding to harvest for exhibition at the 1901 Pan-American Exposition in Buffalo.[3]

The following year in 1902, movies became a steady attraction in Bismarck. The earliest exhibitors in town were the Beaty brothers. The Beatys had begun their careers as traveling entertainers. With a makeshift motion picture projector they worked the northern states, visiting small towns like Red Lodge, Montana, and setting their expectations on "raking in enough silver to hold them awhile," as they told a local journalist.[4] The Beatys stayed in the game, and within two years they were industry veterans. The *Bismarck Tribune* recognized them as the "kings of the picture business."[5] They were "the acknowledged leaders in the line of moving picture exhibitions" on the northern Great Plains.[6] The Beatys boasted a unique device fitted with a specially commissioned diamond lens. The "patented lens [will] do away with all that quiver and blur that make the ordinary exhibition … difficult to watch without tiring the eyes," they claimed.[7]

The Beaty brothers didn't produce their own shots, but they were omnivorous in their programming. They offered topical scenes, such as *The Assassination of President McKinley* (1901), *Carrie Nation Smashing a Kansas Saloon* (1901), and *Coronation of Edward VII* (1902); comedies, such as *A Tramp's Dream* and *A Rube's Visit to a Studio* (both 1902); and even an epic ten-scene color version of *Jack and the Beanstalk* (release date unknown). Among their perks to encourage early movie buffs, the Beatys offered a money-back guarantee for unsatisfied customers.

By 1906 pioneering picture men like the Beaty brothers had moved on, giving way to a new generation of showmen. Ernest "Ves" Vesperman, the manager of Bismarck's Atheneum Theater, was likely present at one of the Beatys' film performances. By 1907 Ves stepped in to run the Bijou Theater. He found box office success when he scheduled *Ben-Hur* (1907), the first film version of the rousing biblical epic.[8] Ves continued to program fan favorites, with cartoons like *Mutt and Jeff* (1912), thrillers like Thanhouser's *Robin Hood* (1913), and star vehicles like Mary Pickford's *Less Than Dust* (1916).[9]

Ves remained a top exhibitor in Bismarck through the 1920s, long enough to watch movies develop from a revolutionary amusement to a technology that authorities regarded with skepticism. In 1915 state representative Peder L. Hjelmstad proposed a law that would have created a state-run board of film censors based in Fargo. After debate the Hjelmstad bill was set aside, indefinitely postponed.[10] Five years later the discussion resumed. In 1921 the state house of representatives approved a three-member censor board to "prevent showing of any film … immoral or improper." The senate, on the other hand, argued that movies should be censored at the federal level.[11] North Dakota never ratified a film censorship law. Instead regulation occurred on a municipal level, with townships such as Valley City appointing their own committees to monitor the movies.[12]

North Dakota played an important role in breaking the monopoly that major studios held over the film industry. U.S. antitrust laws had been enacted to prevent any single corporation, combination of corporations, or cartel from dominating a specific market. The idea of these laws was to promote fair competition, which would ultimately benefit consumers. Antitrust laws were invoked against sugar manufacturing conglomerates in 1895, railroad barons in 1904, the meatpacking industry in 1905, and the tobacco trust and Standard Oil in 1911.[13] As Hollywood's dream factory coalesced into vertically integrated businesses dominating production, distribution, and exhibition, it was only a matter of time before the Federal Trade Commission (FTC) closed in on the anticompetitive behavior.

The first step to break the "film trust" was taken in 1921. The studio at the center of the government's complaint was Adolph Zukor's powerful consolidation of Famous Players (production division), Paramount Pictures (distribution division), and the Stanley Booking Company (theatrical exhibition division). The FTC alleged that the company now recognized as Paramount "combined and conspired to secure control and monopolize the motion picture industry, and restrain, restrict and suppress competition in interstate commerce in motion picture films."[14] Hearings on the studio's potentially unfair trade practices began in April 1923 and aired the company's darkest secrets.[15] Paramount's former president, W.W. Hodkinson, who had been pushed out by Zukor, testified that the Paramount system was intentionally crafted to prevent independent producers from gaining access to first-class theaters.[16] Independent theater owners confirmed Hodkinson's statements.[17] The situation did not look good for Paramount.

In July 1927 the FTC handed down its ruling. Paramount was cited for conspiracy to monopolize the movie market and ordered to discontinue unfair methods of competition. The FTC gave the studio sixty days to comply with certain orders.[18] The studio did not comply.

In the next phase, the FTC filed a lawsuit. The Second Circuit agreed that Paramount's system of block booking and vertical control violated federal antitrust laws and policies.[19] At that moment history intervened with the stock market crash and the Great Depression. What was a financial tragedy for America was a stroke of luck for Zukor. The adverse decision against Paramount would not be enforced due to the country's economic troubles. In 1932 when the FTC resumed their action, suing the studio for noncompliance with the order, they must have been shocked to read the court's new assessment. Contrary to the prior ruling, the FTC was told that Paramount "has lawfully exercised its right to sell its product to the best advantage and in such quantities and to such persons as it chooses. It neither has a monopoly and apparently [has] not the ability to acquire one."[20] After a decade of litigation and financial hardship, the studio's monopoly of all areas of motion picture production and distribution would survive for the time being. But not in North Dakota.

Where the United States failed, North Dakota did not. As film censorship boards formed around the country, Bismarck's legislators declined to enact content regulation. But the state did enact protection policies for local theater owners. In 1937 they enacted Chapter 165 to the laws of North Dakota: "an act to prohibit the operation of motion picture theaters which are owned, controlled, managed, or operated, in whole or in part, by producers or distributors of motion picture films, or in which such producers or distributors have any interest." This law was aimed specifically at the theaters owned by corporate giants in order to maintain market space for local businesses. Paramount, now on the offensive, sued to challenge the law.

Before a panel of three judges, the North Dakota court recognized that major studios dominated the industry. Their power and the record of anticompetitive behavior spotlighted in earlier cases favored a protective state law. Taking a broad view of how a monopoly could hurt local businesses, the North Dakota court refused to strike down the state law: "After due consideration of the record in this case and of the excellent arguments and briefs of counsel, we are of the opinion that [Paramount is] not entitled to a declaration that Chapter 165 of the Laws of North Dakota for 1937 is violative of any provision of the Constitution of the United States."[21] North Dakota theater owners stood up to the powers of Hollywood and prevailed.

The federal government resumed its antitrust battle against the studios, ultimately winning the day in 1948.[22] That landmark decision, known as "the Paramount consent decree, " ordered major studios to dismantle their integrated holdings in theatrical exhibition and heralded the end of the golden age of Hollywood. But a decade before the federal government was finally able to secure that outcome, the state of North Dakota had stood up to the corporate powers and fought the studios' unfair trade practices.

North Dakota provided a haven of film freedom where audiences could experience movies uncut by censors and where local showmen were liberated from the monopoly of the industry's big businesses.

Ohio

Ohio was ground zero for the test case that would determine whether free speech was the rule or censors held the power to silence inappropriate or unwanted viewpoints. The Buckeye State was not the first to enact a film censorship bureau, but when the Mutual Film Corp. challenged the state's right to cut, edit, and ban films, the resulting decision was significant. In the *Mutual* case of 1915, the U.S. Supreme Court considered whether constitutional protections extended to the cinema. The result would have a lasting influence on film and the right to free expression for the next thirty-seven years.

The first moving pictures arrived in Ohio as early as 1895 as part of an Edison touring attraction. In May 1895 F.E. Harman's store in Lima hosted Kinetoscope machines showing popular films, including *Blacksmith Scene* (1893), *Bucking Bronco* (1894), and *Imperial Japanese Dance* (1894).[1] By the end of the century movies drew in bigger crowds with popular titles like *The Corbett-Fitzsimmons Fight* (1897), and theaters could charge as much as one dollar a seat.[2]

The first pleas for censorship in Ohio came from state representative George Reed of Wood County. In 1910, Reed drafted a proposal for a state board of review, citing that "the moving pictures displayed now … are twice as immoral as they were two years ago." Reed's outrage was personal. "I saw a vile and suggestive scene exhibited in a moving picture place last night," he said, but his perspective was also practical: "It would cost too much for the state to have an officer in every moving picture house."[3] Reed's proposal for a centralized state board found little support. Instead regulation began on a municipal level. Cleveland established a city censor in 1912, transforming a holding pen at police headquarters into a screening room. There, alongside interrogation rooms, loops of confiscated movies unspooled throughout the day.[4] Within a month, Mayor Newton Baker appointed R.O. Bartholomew as a full-time film censor in the ongoing campaign against lurid entertainments.[5]

By the next calendar quarter, Representative Thornton R. Snyder introduced a film censor bill to the statehouse. Like the Reed proposal, Snyder's was quickly killed. But this time the newly elected governor, James Cox, stepped in. Responding to political pressure, lawmakers resubmitted the proposal and pushed it through the process.[6] The statewide film censorship ordinance was in effect by November 5, 1913.[7]

A three-member film censorship division was created within the Industrial Commission of Ohio. Unlike the long-term moral authorities of Lloyd T. Binford in Memphis, Christine Smith in Atlanta, and Mary Avara in Baltimore, during the first years of its existence the Ohio board saw a high degree of drama and discord. The first team of film regulators included J.A. Maddox and Harry E. Vestal, both former theater owners, and Maude Murray Miller, a former newspaper journalist.[8] These censors were given office space even less cushy than a holding cell: motion picture projectors were sent to the chapel of the Ohio Penitentiary.[9]

The Ohio state censors got off to a productive start, threatening to ban films that contained scenes of the Wild West, criminal activity, drinking, and immoral love.[10] Maddox announced his intent to strictly supervise images of "women dancing in tights or diaphanous apparel and other vulgarities."[11] But within six weeks Maddox resigned. The reason for his sudden departure was not disclosed, but motion picture men may have made Maddox an offer he couldn't refuse. He left the censor's office and returned to managing a theater in Columbus.[12]

As Maddox stepped down, new issues arose. First the censors' expense accounts came under fire. Vestal and Miller were reprimanded for ordering out too lavishly—one-dollar meals three times a day.[13] While Vestal tightened his belt, Miller fought back, asserting that "she couldn't possibly get breakfast for less than $2."[14] Vestal would find himself in even hotter water the following year. After accepting an all-expense-paid trip to California as a guest of a film company, Vestal came under fire and was pressured to resign in March 1915.[15] Despite catering restrictions, Miller soldiered on, described by industry trade magazine *Motography* as "some regular terror as a censoress."[16]

Even with departmental turmoil and reduced craft services, the business of film censorship continued in Ohio. The alcoholic epic *John Barleycorn* (1914) was abridged, with scenes of carousal and drinking bouts cut.[17] *The Birth of a Nation* (1915) was submitted three times for approval but rejected on each occasion based on the film's incendiary racial content. *Birth* was finally granted Ohio's approval in 1917.[18] Geraldine Farrar's version of *Carmen* (1915) was barred but played unpermitted in Cleveland.[19] While these films were cut, banned, and tabooed, it was the censors' refusal to license a series of newsreels distributed by the Mutual Film Corp. that made the greatest impact.

Mutual was a film exchange headed by Harry Aitken. Film exchanges acted as distribution hubs, renting out motion picture reels on a regional basis. Based in Wisconsin, Aitken opened the Western Film Exchange in 1906. Needing to secure films in his distribution pipeline, he negotiated agreements with production houses and major filmmakers. By 1912 Aitken reorganized his company as Mutual Film Corp. and locked exclusive deals with D.W. Griffith, king of comedy Mack Sennett, and top Western maker Thomas Ince. Theater owners wanting to program prestigious blockbusters, popular comedies, or sagebrush soaps would have to license titles from Mutual. Mutual also offered a newsreel service.

It was the newsreels that became the source of a problem. The films were usually produced in New York, and Aitken needed to transport them to Chicago, which acted as the hub for the rest of the country. Between New York and Chicago lay Ohio. Ohio's film censorship ordinance became an administrative obstacle. Aitken resented paying an additional fee and was incensed by the procedural bottleneck caused by the state's review office. He challenged the Ohio law, claiming that film censorship infringed on his company's First Amendment rights as a prior restraint against its freedom of speech. Losing in the lower courts, Aitken was driven by belief and business sense to fight the system all the way to the Supreme Court.

In the Halls of Justice nine men in black robes solemnly contemplated whether motion picture technology could qualify as speech under the First Amendment of the Constitution. If film was speech it could be shielded from arbitrary government censorship. The result was not what Aitken had anticipated. In a unanimous 9–0 decision all Justices agreed that movies did not qualify as speech. Movies would not be protected under the First Amendment. Rather, Justice McKenna wrote, "The exhibition of moving pictures is a business pure and simple, originated and conducted for profit, like other spectacles." Just like a circus, a carnival, or a street parade, the movies could be subject to regulation. But McKenna went further. The movies were so vivid, so attractive, and so entertaining that unlike written expression, the medium of motion pictures was uniquely "capable of evil."[20] Not only *could* movies be regulated—they *should* be.

Mutual v. Ohio was a significant setback for the film industry. This precedent would guide regulation for thirty-seven years, putting filmmakers at a disadvantage against censors across the United States.

With the law on their side, Ohio's movie police flexed their muscle. Boxing films were banned in 1919—the Jess Willard–Jack Dempsey fight film was rejected in toto. The board's new chief censor, Maurice S. Hague, "would not permit boys and girls to see such human butchery."[21] *Fate* (1921), a movie starring Clara Smith Hamon, a pre–reality-TV star who shot to fleeting fame when she was acquitted of murder charges, was banned in Ohio (see Oklahoma).[22] Several unlikely films were passed by the board. Maude Murray Miller personally praised Theda Bara's *Cleopatra* (1917), a titillating title held back in other areas. Grisly newsreel footage of the *Eastland* boat disaster was quarantined in many states but green-lit in Ohio. The state board even permitted *The Toll of Justice* (1916), a Ku Klux Klan recruitment picture.[23]

During the 1930s both studio films and edgy exploitation flicks could equally feel the sting of the censor's cuts. MGM's Academy Award–winning Wallace Beery prison

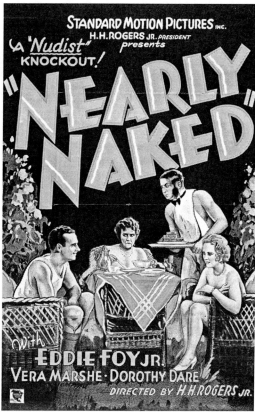

Left: With a racy title but little else *Back to Nature* (1932) lured audiences with the promise of bare flesh. *Right:* Raunchy humor in a nudist colony was barely covered in *Nearly Naked* (1933).

picture, *The Big House* (1930), was stopped due to a prison riot scene. *Baby Face* (1933), a Warner Bros. film starring Barbara Stanwyck as a sexually ravenous secretary working her way up the corporate ladder with alluring charms, was seen as indecent and barred.[24] On the independent side, state censors threw cold water on a string of nudist films, including *Back to Nature* (1932), *Nearly Naked* (1933), and *Elysia (Valley of the Nude)* (1933).

Dr. Clyde Hissong took over as head of Ohio's film board in 1945; it was during his regime that censors began to lose the upper hand. Within his first year on the job, Hissong faced down Howard Hughes's *The Outlaw* (1943). This film, which showcased "the open spaces of the wild west and buxom Jane Russell," was a source of commotion in many states. Hissong quickly banned it from Ohio.[25] The board passed Roberto Rossellini's *Stromboli* (1950) with Ingrid Bergman, but when news of the director and the star's adulterous relationship reached Columbus, a recall was discussed. The private lives of stars could bring their films into question. The censors called an emergency meeting to review the issue of Bergman and Rita Hayworth, who had also made headlines with adulterous behavior.[26] Hissong's ability to ban Hollywood's biggest stars based on their offscreen infidelities marked the height of the censors' strength. Their power had peaked, and for the remainder of the decade the censors saw their powers diminish.

Ohio became an important battleground state on the issue of film and free speech.

SPECTACULAR THRILLS: the bombardment of an army with explosive globes of Greek Fire!

Featuring stripper Lily St. Cyr—the "anatomic bomb"—*Son of Sinbad* (1955) was one of Howard Hughes' most titillating pictures.

When a low-budget film noir remake of Fritz Lang's *M* (1951) crossed the border, Ohio censors became concerned that the tale of a child snatcher "could lead to a serious increase in immorality and crime."[27] In a four-word decision the Supreme Court disagreed: "The judgments are reversed."[28] Two years later, Howard Hughes released two sexy bombshells, *The French Line* (1954) and *Son of Sinbad* (1955). Both films featured legs and cleavage in full-color, wide-screen splendor. The mogul's favorite actress, Jane Russell, was again on display, wrapped in a flimsy plot as an oil heiress in *French Line*. *Sinbad* offered up platinum-blonde beauty Lili St. Cyr, nicknamed the "Anatomic Bomb" for her mind-boggling, eyebrow-raising burlesque striptease shows. Both films were banned for indecency. This time it was the Ohio Supreme Court that reversed the censors' decisions.[29]

The court's judgment sounded a death knell for the state board. Bans were lifted on films previously forbidden, both exploitation films like Kroger Babb's sex-education primer *Mom and Dad* (1945), as well as studio productions such as James Cagney's *Kiss Tomorrow Goodbye* (1950) and Otto Preminger's *The Moon Is Blue* (1953).[30] By 1954 Susannah Warfield, who had served on the film commission since 1922, resigned her post, shut off the lights, and closed the door on an era of censorship.[31]

As the 1960s dawned, old-fashioned etiquette fell away and a new normal emerged that had far less scruples. Pop culture was on the verge of the porno chic, a brief moment in America when almost anything was permitted on mainstream screens. There were few things left that a censor could legitimately cut, but one cause of action remained: obscenity.

Obscenity presented courts with a thorny issue. Where is the line that divides indecent from illicit? Once again, it was an Ohio case that defined the landscape. French filmmaker Louis Malle, previously best known as Jacques Cousteau's cameraman, changed locations from under the sea to beneath the bedsheets in *Les amants* (*The Lovers*, 1958). Malle's sensuous picture was banned as obscene. The ruling was challenged and the case rose to the Supreme Court. From this 1964 decision comes the best one-liner in all of legal history. After viewing *The Lovers*, Justice Potter Stewart considered how he could define pornography. "I know it when I see it," he concluded, but "the motion picture involved in this case is not that."[32]

A decade later the battle was over. The fight for freedom of the screen, which had commenced in 1915 with the unfavorable *Mutual* decision, ended six decades later. In 1974 United Artists petitioned the Ohio court to prevent the sheriff of Erie County from confiscating *Last Tango in Paris* (1972). Judge Don Young favored free expression over government oversight. He saw the danger a state official could pose to vulnerable rights. The sheriff, wrote Judge Young, "by virtue of the power of his office, is able to

French director Louis Malle's *Les amants* (*The Lovers*, 1958) moved one Supreme Court justice to define pornography by declaring, "I know it when I see it."

deny the plaintiff its right to exhibit, and the public its right to see, a controversial motion picture."[33] That right to produce, distribute, and exhibit controversial content must be protected.

Fifty-nine years after the *Mutual* decision sent the message that the state had the power—even the duty—to protect its citizens from the moral corruption, decadence, and depravity seen in Hollywood movies, Ohio's censorship law lapsed. The state toyed with other ways of controlling content—zoning adult theaters into industrial areas or declaring an unwanted theater a nuisance and shutting it down. Even with these alternative methods, the tide had turned against the moral authorities as adult content became more prolific and profanity more commonplace.

Oklahoma

There's a wide spot in the road one hour south of Oklahoma City where Old State Highways 29 and 74 meet. There lies the town of Elmore City (pop. 653 in 1980). Weathered barns lead toward a four-block commercial strip stretching from the Dollar General Store on North Street to City Hall on East E Street. You might not notice it on a quick drive through, but there are no bars, movie theaters, or nightclubs. Kids looking for a little excitement would have to drive twenty-five miles to the nearest bowling alley or sneak out to an abandoned oil rig called "the Slab" for forbidden make-out sessions.[1]

Elmore City began as a wagon-wheel repair shop in 1861, when the area was surrounded by Indian Territory. James Oliver Elmore was a righteous man—you needed faith in that lawless country—and he laid down laws that would keep peace and maintain order. One of those laws was a prohibition on public dancing. The Rev. F.R. Johnson, a Pentecostal preacher in nearby Hennepin, praised Elmore's law: "No good has ever come from a dance.... If you have a dance somebody will crash it and they'll be looking for only two things—women and booze.... You can believe what you want, but one thing leads to another."[2] Elmore City remained a town without rhythm for nearly 120 years.

Then in the late 1970s two Elmore City high schoolers, Leonard Coffee and Rex Kennedy, saw *Saturday Night Fever* (1977). They knew they had to cut loose. They led the Class of '81 to petition for a prom and divided the small town. The younger folk stood together to fight for their right to party, while community elders at the Baptist church and the Church of Christ feared the event "would lead to dancing in the streets."[3] Coffee and Kennedy organized fund-raising events, raising $2,000 in bake sale proceeds, and in a moment of inspiration invited Lester Elmore, the eighty-six-year-old grandson of the town's founder, to be the grand marshal of the homecoming parade. Elmore accepted but was too tuckered out by the procession to attend the party. He commented, "Dancing can be made wicked like anything else.... But I've been dancing ever since I can remember and there's nothing wrong with a good sociable dance. Of course, I don't jitterbug much anymore. I'm down to waltz time now." Perhaps in a nod to the students' zealous opponents, the theme of the prom was "Stairway to Heaven," and the Led Zeppelin anthem rang out as the opening dance.[4] Despite some awkward disco moves, the prom succeeded beautifully; Elmore City was no longer a town without cheer.

Half a country away in Los Angeles, composer Dean Pitchford was admiring his Academy Award for cowriting the theme song to *Fame* (1980). He was considering his follow-up when he read news of the Elmore City prom. The story was perfect. In his script, Pitchford omitted references to Oklahoma because he felt the story was universal. It was the tale of idealistic youth rebelling against older authority. The picture became *Footloose* (1984), a crowd-pleaser that launched Kevin Bacon to stardom. *Footloose* featured stellar supporting characters, from John Lithgow as the fire-and-brimstone preacher to Chris Penn and Sarah Jessica Parker as dancing-deficient best friends. Both the film's theme song and "Let's Hear It for the Boy" charted at number one, and a third single, "Almost Paradise," peaked at number seven. *Footloose* hit a popular nerve, favoring expressive freedom over outdated rules.

Motion pictures arrived in Oklahoma as a traveling attraction. Three showmen packed up their exhibit from the 1901 Texas State Fair and took their reels on the road. They passed through several small towns, including Ardmore, Purcell, and El Reno, on their way to Oklahoma City.[5]

Within a decade the flickering images were feared a menace to society. While Jack Johnson–Jim Jeffries prizefighting pictures proved popular draws with audiences across the nation, the Lyric Theater, Tulsa's oldest movie house, refused to show the films. "A more disgusting revolting spectacle has never been flashed on any screen," said the theater's manager. But fans of the fistic ballet could watch the fight across town at the Empire Theater for the premium price of fifty cents. Beyond Tulsa, the mayors of Muskogee and Sayre also banned the racially provocative fight film.[6]

By 1914 Frank Wooden, the mayor of Tulsa, appointed a city censor. In 1915 Oklahoma City considered a movie censorship ordinance to bar films showing bank robberies, nudity or suggestive poses, and obscene, indecent, licentious, or immoral subjects.[7] The bill didn't pass, but police were still called out on reports of inappropriate movies. Elinor Glyn's torrid romance *Three Weeks* (1914) was a precursor to the steamy erotic thriller *9½ Weeks* (1986). When news that *Three Weeks* had caused a ruckus in Muscogee reached Oklahoma City, local ministers banded together to call for a film ban.[8] Next, *Inspiration* (1915)

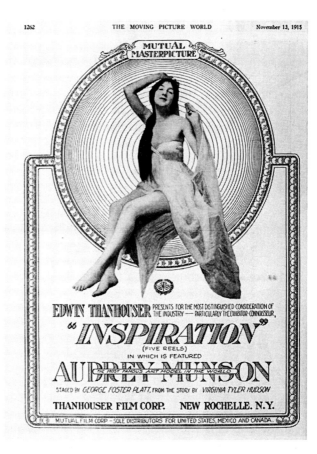

A sculptor searches for the perfect model and finds *Inspiration* (1916) in a nude Audrey Munson.

featured Audrey Munson in nude scenes as an artist's model. When the picture was scheduled in OK City, city officials responded by enacting an emergency film censorship law—"opinion of the Mayor is [the] final criterion."[9]

It was not sex but on-screen crime that united lawmakers with theater owners.

Jacob Louis Hamon was a vastly wealthy political powerhouse in Oklahoma. As chairman of the Republican Territorial Committee in 1909, he had learned the ways of the Washington lobbyist. Partnering with circus magnate John Ringling, Hamon laid down railroads throughout the state. He speculated on oil and land and even built the temporary boomtown of Jakehamon in 1919. In 1920 he became Oklahoma's representative on the Republican National Committee.[10] Then disaster struck. In November 1920 he was shot dead by Clara Smith Hamon, his secretary and mistress and the wife of his son. Clara fled to Mexico, surrendering a month later in Juárez. The lurid details of the ensuing trial made headlines around the country for the case's combination of sex, violence, and politics. Although Clara admitted to the killing, she pleaded self-defense. She had indeed aimed the .25 caliber pistol, but it had only discharged when Hamon struck her with a chair.[11]

Clara was acquitted. Immediately signed by an opportunistic independent filmmaker, she appeared in a picture entitled *Fate* (1921) to capitalize on her newsworthy notoriety. Movie audiences paid their admission for a peek at the femme fatale, but Clara Smith Hamon's *Fate* was not wanted in Oklahoma. Jacob Hamon's adopted hometown of Ardmore convened a censor board to ban immoral, criminal, and indecent pictures. The law was specifically aimed at Clara, prohibiting any actor to appear on-screen "who has been convicted of a crime, or any ex-convict, desperado, bandit, train robber, bank robber, murderer or outlaw."[12]

Independently, theater owners in Oklahoma City banded together with a similar purpose. Without government intervention, local film exhibitors pledged to avoid movies that depicted or glorified crime. They specifically embargoed a popular subgenre of films featuring reality stars who had once lived lawlessly and now reaped the profits in motion pictures. Besides murderess Clara Smith Hamon, trail robber Al Jennings, bank robber Henry Starr, and lawmen turned robbers "Grat" Bob and Emmett Dalton were personae non grata in OK theaters.[13] Oklahoma audiences reluctantly accepted the screening policy and grew accustomed to wholesome, nonviolent, and only slightly sexy screen entertainments.

The Sooner State's movie morality police were back in the news seventy-five years later.

After apprenticing with French filmmakers of the Nouvelle Vague, including Louis Malle, Alain Resnais, and Jean-Pierre Melville, the West German director Volker Schlöndorff prepared his first feature. *Young Törless* (1966) focused on sadistic and homoerotic behavior at an all-boys military academy. The film was nominated for a Palme d'Or at the Cannes Film Festival. Schlöndorff claimed the coveted award when he directed *Die Blechtrommel* (*The Tin Drum*, 1979) a dozen years later.

The Tin Drum, based on the novel by Günter Grass, focused on a boy who resisted the Nazis with bizarre powers. Disgusted with Hitler's henchmen, three-year-old Oskar Matzerath decides to stop physically growing. Armed with a child's snare drum and a glass-shattering shriek, the mature-minded character becomes a miniature anarchy machine. Later, the young man, still in a child's body, begins a relationship with a sixteen-year-old girl. Their love scene would become controversial. David Bennett, a twelve-

The Tin Drum (1979), a Palme d'Or–winning art film based on a Nobel Prize–winning author's novel, was branded child porn in Oklahoma.

year-old actor, played Oskar on-screen as he performed a simulated, nonexplicit sexual act on a twenty-five-year-old actress portraying a sixteen-year-old character. While slightly risqué, the scene didn't raise any eyebrows for nearly two decades.

The Tin Drum was celebrated as an artistic achievement at film festivals around the world. In addition to the Cannes prize, the film won an Academy Award for Best Foreign Language Film as well as honors in Germany, Japan, and Sweden. The Los Angeles Film Critics Association recognized *The Tin Drum* as a cinematic achievement, as did the Kansas City Film Critics Circle. But not Oklahoma.

Michael D. Camfield was an Oklahoma City–based fan of foreign films and an ACLU operative.[14] In June 1997 a concerned citizen informed the Oklahoma City Police Department that *The Tin Drum* might violate the state's child pornography laws. When Camfield was notified of the investigation, he visited a Blockbuster store and rented a cassette copy of the film. Not long after Camfield was out the door, police confiscated all nine remaining copies of the movie in the city. They were missing one copy. The force descended on Camfield's house. Camfield and the Video Dealers Association filed a lawsuit to stop the state from interfering with the picture, claiming that First Amendment rights were being violated and that child pornography in the film was nonexistent.

Around the country *The Tin Drum* was transformed from an art film to the ultimate taboo movie. In California four Blockbuster stores ripped the title off their shelves, only to meekly restore them a week later.[15]

The stage was set for a battle royal pitting free expression against child pornography. But before the Oklahoma court turned to the claims, the judges considered the police

behavior. Rather than approaching the issue systematically with a fair hearing, the authorities had unilaterally confiscated the allegedly obscene materials. Even worse, the police
record reflected that the city did not intend to pursue criminal sanctions but rather acted
solely to remove the film from public access.[16] This was an example of state censorship
at its worst: arbitrary, unfair, aggressive, and one-sided.

Presiding over the case, Judge Ralph Thompson considered the police action against
an internationally celebrated film that had been shown on television and was widely
available on home video. The answer was self-evident, without even reaching the issue
of obscenity, immorality, or indecency. The police had acted inappropriately and constitutional guarantees must be protected.

From dancing to crime to art films that walk the line, Oklahoma authorities have
kept a close watch on the limits of acceptable entertainment. Even faced with aggressive
moral authorities, the First Amendment remains a powerful sentinel safeguarding free
expression.

Oregon

The snap of a twig, the rustle of leaves, inhuman prints left in the mud. These are
the telltale signs of Bigfoot. Also known as Sasquatch, this mythical hairy humanoid
creature is said to prowl the Pacific Northwest. Bigfoot is one of the "big three" in cryp-
tozoology, keeping company with Nessie the Loch Ness Monster and the Himalayan Yeti.
Cryptozoological creatures stalk many states—the Mothman of West Virginia, the Ozark
Howler of Missouri, the Hodag of Wisconsin, the Fouke Monster of Arkansas, not to
mention various Wampus cats, jackalopes, and thunderbirds wandering the back roads
of rural America. What differentiates Bigfoot from these other bogeymen is that it has
been captured on film. Bigfoot's home state could well be Oregon.

On October 20, 1967, Robert Patterson and Bob Gimlin were hiking through the
countryside along the Oregon-California border. They heard a sudden noise. They
smelled a fetid odor. Then they spotted a strange creature. Gimlin was paralyzed with
fear while his partner had the presence of mind to record the scene on his 16 mm Bolex
camera.[1] The 59.5-second shot has become known as the *Patterson-Gimlin Film* (1967),
and is perhaps the most intensely studied strip of celluloid after the *Zapruder Film*'s
images of the John F. Kennedy assassination. Nearly fifty years later, the *Patterson-Gimlin
Film* still stuns open-minded audiences. The grainy images have never been conclusively
debunked, withstanding the scrutiny of scientists, forensic analysts, special effects experts,
and costume designers.[2] Despite modern technology, GPS, and deforestation, the legend
of Bigfoot remains a reality for many. As recently as August 2016, a dog fitted with a
GoPro camera was let loose in Oregon and picked up footage of an apelike biped shuffling
off into the greenery.[3]

The *Patterson-Gimlin Film* was incorporated into *The Legend of Bigfoot* (1975), also
shot in Oregon, to create one of the earliest found-footage pseudo-documentaries. The
genre would become infamous and controversial with release of *Cannibal Holocaust*
(1980) and vastly profitable with *The Blair Witch Project* (1999). But *The Legend of Bigfoot*

In a famous clip, the *Patterson-Gimlin Film* (1967) purportedly captured Bigfoot in his or her natural habitat.

and *Patterson-Gimlin Film* mark the roots of this provocative hyperrealistic style of film-making.

Even in the days before Bigfoot was caught on tape, filmmakers were drawn to the untamed countryside of Oregon. William Selig was one of the first to produce locally shot films. He recorded such titles as *Fish Traps Columbia River* (1904), *Panoramic View of the Columbia* (1904), and *Panoramic View of Multnomah Falls* (1904). A feature-length picture focusing on life on the range was shot during a roundup at Pendleton and released as *Where Cowboy Is King* (1915).[4]

Portland emerged as a regional film hub, but an undercurrent of discontent with motion pictures simmered. A censoring committee was organized in January 1915, prompting a warning that "immoral films are doomed."[5] By March, Portland mayor H. Russell Albee appointed Mrs. A.C. Newill as chairperson and Mrs. E.B. Colwell as secretary of the board of city censors. Newill and Colwell each had an assistant, forming a four-person, all-female board.[6] Newill explained their mission as "the prevention of immoral, obscene, indecent or grewsome [*sic*] … motion pictures."[7]

Oregon's first forbidden films were torn from the headlines. *Sontag and Evans in the Follies of Crime* (1915) focused on the adventures of an outlaw gang. John Sontag and Chris Evans were Oregon's answer to Butch Cassidy and the Sundance Kid. Train robbing, murder, and general mayhem were their calling cards. After a particularly rich haul the two desperados planned to head for Mexico, but Evans insisted on saying goodbye to his wife and daughter. That's when the outlaws were caught. After a standoff and shoot-out,

Sontag died of his wounds.[8] Evans served fifteen years. Paroled, he left prison for a quiet life in Portland. Evans was closing out his twilight years when *The Follies of Crime* was released. Mary Jane Evans, his faithful wife who had stood by his side during the long prison term, petitioned the Portland film board to stop the picture. Evans was a reformed man, she argued, his outlaw days behind him. Portland's censors obliged, banning the picture.[9] Two years later Evans died.

Another true-life tragedy met with the censors' disapproval. When a newsreel depicting a passenger boat catastrophe on the Chicago River called *The Eastland Disaster* (1915) was released, it was banned on arrival in Oregon. "I do not believe in commercializing such an unfortunate occurrence," Mrs. Colwell stated.[10] Colwell and her colleagues disapproved of scenes in other actualities "showing horses being required to hurtle barricades or go down steep hillsides … on the ground that they showed brutality."[11] Newsworthy stories could be cut for sheer "awfulness." It was a far cry from modern-day news cycles that emphasize shootings, stabbings, and salacious events.

Outlaws and disasters were one thing, but the pictures that most rankled the all-female board of Oregon censors were bodice rippers. Bathing beauties were cut from Mack Sennett's *Stolen Magic* (1915), with regulators citing "the sinuous movements of a young woman dancer."[12] The screen's first sex symbol, Theda Bara, was a lightning rod. Her first major film role as a voracious vamp, in *A Fool There Was* (1915), was scrutinized but passed.[13] Not so for Bara's *The Kreutzer Sonata* (1915) and *The Serpent* (1916), both Russian-themed tales of murder, betrayal, adultery, and debauchery. Both were found unfit to play in Portland.[14] European sex symbol Pola Negri was banned in *Forbidden Paradise* (1924).[15] Even Marlene Dietrich was prohibited for being too suggestive in *The Room Upstairs* (1950).[16]

One problem with Oregon's morality police was their arbitrary and unpredictable decisions. After condemning one of his pictures as "vulgar and unfit to be seen by the Portland public," the manager of a film exchange asked Colwell what was specifically objectionable. She admitted there was nothing particularly offensive but had suggested "some cuts be made in a scene showing a plumbing shop with bathroom fixtures on display."[17] Toilets were a no-no on Stumptown screens.

Other films were tagged for similarly capricious reasons. *Fools First* (1922), a Richard Dix–Claire Windsor vehicle was banned for demonstrating criminal techniques.[18] Cecil B. DeMille's *The King of Kings* (1927) was stopped. Censors "requested the film be cut so that persons of the Jewish race would not be offended."[19] A Dwain Esper–produced exploitation picture entitled *Narcotic* (1933) was halted for portraying drug use.[20] A German import, *S.A.-Mann Brand* (1933), told the story of a truck driver falling on hard times. His life is changed when he begins listening to Adolf Hitler. *S.A.-Mann Brand* was banned.[21] City censors tried to mute the internationally acclaimed Italian film *The Bicycle Thief* (1948) based on a nonexplicit two-minute scene set in a brothel. This time the court overruled the censors and allowed the Academy Award–recognized picture to play local theaters.[22]

Strict regulation of film remained in place until 1961. When theater manager Nancy Welch programmed a Louis Malle film at her art house, she triggered a major change in the state law. *Les amants* (*The Lovers*, 1958) featured Jeanne Moreau in the typically French scenario of a woman finding satisfaction in an adulterous affair. Welch submitted the film for an exhibition permit. The censors took issue with a scene set in a bathroom where Moreau and her paramour slip into a tub.[23] Welch declined to edit the film and the two parties headed to court. But times had changed. Oregon's high court respected the Supreme Court's recent ruling that recognized motion pictures as protected speech. Oregon's *Lovers* decision not only overruled the Portland censors but also declared the film ordinance unconstitutional.[24] The censors had only succeeded in providing Welch with the best promotion for her film. After *The Lovers* was cleared, it unspooled before packed crowds. Over four thousand ticket holders lined up for a glimpse of the nearly forbidden French film.[25]

Film had achieved free speech rights, but there were still limits. Grind house theater manager Sol D. Maizels discovered this when he booked two edgy imported films very different from the sophisticated fare of Louis Malle. Kôji Wakamatsu's *The Love Robots* (1966) was a Japanese fetish film, and Gilbert Wolmark's *Little Girls* (1966), a lurid take of forced prostitution. Both pictures were soft-core sexploitation flicks. Both films were seized from the theater. This time the Oregon Supreme Court stepped back, allowing the prosecution to proceed.[26] Maizels settled and moved on to less provocative programming. An Oregon drive-in was cited for showing *Southern Comforts* (1971), a Bethel Buckalew-directed Z-grade flick teeming with hillbilly honeys dropping their Daisy Dukes. Visible from outside the venue, the film's scenes distracted motorists and bothered at least one resident who found it difficult to keep her "children from looking out the window at the allegedly deviant conduct being shown."[27] *Southern Comforts* was banned.

Despite these setbacks, the progression toward broad free speech rights was unstoppable. Oregon's courts soon supported a wide-ranging marketplace of ideas, protecting communications that many would find objectionable. By 1987 the Oregon Supreme Court unanimously threw out the state's law criminalizing obscenity, writing, "In this state any person can write, print, read, say, show or sell anything to a consenting adult even though that expression may be generally or universally considered 'obscene.'"[28]

With this decision Oregon became the first state to abolish the offense of obscenity.[29]

Pennsylvania

Imagine the discovery of long-lost motion picture footage of Abraham Lincoln delivering the Gettysburg Address. Or moving picture images of Union soldiers marching off to fight in one of the bloodiest battles of the Civil War, on Pennsylvania's green hillsides. Such a discovery sounds far-fetched, but it might not be, courtesy of Coleman Sellers.

Coleman Sellers was a successful and well-known mechanical engineer and inventor who came from a long line of Pennsylvanians. In February 1861 Sellers filed a patent for his Kinematoscope.[1] He beat Edison and the Lumière brothers to the punch by three decades. Sellers pre-dated the pioneering picture makers Eadweard Muybridge, Étienne-Jules Marey, and William Friese-Greene by ten years.

For his Kinematoscope, Sellers took a series of photographs and mounted them in a drum. By turning a handle and looking through a slot, the illusion of motion sprang to life. This motion picture maker had innovation in his genes. His grandfather, Nathan Sellers, had been a Revolutionary War patriot, so skilled in mechanical engineering that he was summoned by the Continental Congress to refine the design of early American firearms.[2] Based on this heritage, the details of the Kinematoscope invention, and the precisely right timing, it is possible that Sellers was able to produce a motion picture on location at Gettysburg in 1863. From his Philadelphia home, Coleman Sellers was only a day's journey from the historic battle. Sellers is a forgotten pioneer in film history. Might he have captured such priceless footage?

Less speculative is Pennsylvania's role in the early development of the motion picture industry. A German-Jewish immigrant who arrived in Philadelphia in 1876 became the first American movie mogul: Siegmund Lubin. Lubin was Thomas Edison's earliest motion picture making competitor, promoting the Lubin Cineograph and Projectoscope in 1897–1898 with pirated reproductions of famous boxing bouts and scenes of bullfights, cockfights, and war.[3] By 1904 Lubin allied with Edison and moved to the inner circle as a charter member of the Motion Picture Patent Company, which attempted to freeze out independent filmmakers by charging a fee for use of various technical patents.[4] While other filmmakers of the era were cranking out scenes on rooftop studios, Lubin established a sprawling 340-acre studio complex in North Philadelphia that he dubbed "Lubinville."[5] Lubin led the industry's expansion, opening production stages first in Florida and then in California. For nearly two decades Lubin was an industry leader, but by 1915 Philadelphia's film mogul was out of the picture.

Across the state, Pittsburgh has its own claim to film history fame. John P. Harris and his brother-in-law, Harry Davis, converted a storefront into a ninety-six-seat moving picture showroom. Opening their doors in June 1905 for around-the-clock showings of *The Great Train Robbery* (1903) at five cents admission, Harris and Davis have been credited as the creators of the first nickelodeon.[6] Inspired by the heaps of coins, the Warner brothers, Harry, Albert, Sam and Jack, pooled their savings to purchase a projector and rent space in nearby New Castle. The brothers, who would later incorporate as Warner Bros., opened their first venture, the Cascade Picture Palace, on February 2, 1907.[7]

Pennsylvania film pioneers recorded early pictures, built the first major studio, and opened the first nickelodeon theater. They also established the first statewide film censorship board of review.

A bill for government-supported film censorship was proposed in the Pennsylvania House of Representatives in April 1911. While several cities, such as Chicago, had enacted motion picture regulation laws, Pennsylvania was the first state to consider a statewide plan.[8] By June 1911, Governor John Kinley Tener signed the bill, and state censorship became official.[9] The office of film examiner was charged with blocking all films "tending to debase or corrupt morals."[10] But there was a problem. The bill had no provision for the censors' salaries. The budgeting issue lingered until 1914, when Tener finally funded his movie morality task force. J. Louis Breitinger, an attorney for the exhibitors' league of Pennsylvania, became chief censor, supported with assistance from Mrs. E. Cyrus Niver.[11]

Theaters owners pounced, calling the censor committee the "curse of the ages" that would "rob movies of all their thrills."[12] The board fired back, announcing its standards and the elimination of scenes that "would tend to debase or inflame the mind to improper adventures." Barrooms, drinking, and drunkenness were out, as were prolonged and passionate lovemaking, insufficient clothing, objectionable dances, underworld scenes, and opium dens. Breitinger felt a woman shouldn't smoke cigarettes.[13] Niver believed "one yard of film is long enough for any kiss."[14]

Pennsylvania censor Mrs. E. Cyrus Niver believed that "one yard of film is long enough for any kiss."

While exhibitors opposed the censors—one calling Breitinger "drunk with power"— they mostly abided by the rules.[15] Siegmund Lubin was one of the few to openly defy the board. The regional mogul claimed his *Cocaine Traffic, or the Drug Terror* (1914) contained a strong moral message. Although the censors challenged Lubin, Judge Robert Umbel agreed with him and the film played on.[16]

The issue of film censorship took on even greater importance as *The Birth of a Nation* (1915) barnstormed across the state. Philadelphia saw anti–*Birth* riots.[17] The mayor of Pittsburgh banned the film.[18] Still, the picture played in both cities. Mutual Film Corp. rose up to challenge the state's authority and the film law as unconstitutional but the company's argument couldn't convince the Pennsylvania Supreme Court. In an important decision that added to Mutual's mounting legal losses (see Ohio), the Keystone State court supported the state's broad police powers. The ruling saw the need to protect the morals, manners, and public health of the commonwealth.[19]

The *Birth of a Nation* decision was followed by a sweeping display of authority by the state censors. Scenes of safecrackers were snipped.[20] Babies tied to train tracks were cut.[21] Saucy subtitles such as "How in Hell Did You Get into Town?" were rejected. Even Mack Sennett's slapstick comedies were scrutinized. In *My Valet* (1915), objections were raised when Mabel Normand and two men "bump each other in not quite the most decorous manner." A fat man punched in the stomach, a child stealing an apple, a tramp pilfering a watch—all ended up on the cutting-room floor.[22] The banned pictures were piling up: *Damaged Goods* (1914), *Race Suicide* (1916), *The Price He Paid* (1916), *Enlighten Thy Daughter* (1917), and *The Girl Who Didn't Think* (1917).[23] Even William S. Hart's "red blooded" Westerns were butchered.[24]

The state's courts consistently sided with the censors. When scenes from a film called *Virtue* (1915) were edited, the Pennsylvania Supreme Court declared they would only interfere if the censor's ruling was "an arbitrary or oppressive abuse of discretion."[25] The same result occurred when *The Brand* (1919) was banned three years later. An exhibitor of the sex-education and syphilis-themed cautionary tale *The End of the Road* (1919) challenged his film's rejection. The case went unrecorded, but the exhibiting theater's box office only opened the next morning to issue refunds.[26]

Pennsylvania film men had been gunning for Breitinger's head since he was appointed. The chief censor was finally dismissed in 1920. His replacement was a more philosophical and thoughtful administrator: Dr. Ellis Paxson Oberholtzer.[27] Oberholtzer's system of review was less arbitrary and more methodical. He authored a book, *The Morals of the Movies*, that provides a valuable glimpse into how state censors approached motion pictures in the late 1910s, as Victorian morality was falling away and the roaring twenties were gathering momentum. *Morals of the Movies* pleaded that "censors, social reformers, school men, neurologists, criminologists, and the intelligent, self-respecting and responsible element in the industry come together like bond brothers to accomplish ends which are obviously so desirable and necessary that the screen may be rid of what now amounts to a scandalous public offense."[28] Oberholtzer realized that movies had the power to teach and inspire as well as to dement and pervert.

While Oberholtzer's ideals were lofty, political pressures drove him to cut scenes that entertained a new generation of movie buffs. Flapper Colleen Moore found her films tabooed. Oberholtzer even cut Chaplin's Little Tramp, seeing the celebrated comedian's pictures as "illegitimate amusement."[29] While Oberholtzer intended to guide motion pictures to moral uplift, he was fighting an impossible battle. Like Breitinger before him, Oberholtzer's censoring put a target on his back. He was removed from the review board by the early 1920s.[30]

The state board of film review would experience rapid turnover during the next two decades while announcing its most overtly political roster of changes. Pennsylvania's censors banned *Spanish Earth* (1937), an anti–Francoist documentary written by Ernest Hemingway and narrated by Orson Welles.[31] After the acting head of the censor commission, Margaret F. Palmer, issued an embargo on the Russian film *Baltic Deputy* (1937), she received death threats. An assailant threw acid at her, burning her clothing.[32] Equally controversial was a docudrama directed by Louis de Rochemont that incorporated scenes from a Nazi propaganda film. De Rochemont had created the *March of Time* series, an important news source for America's involvement in World War II. Despite this pedigree, *The Ramparts We Watch* (1940) was ruled unreleasable in Pennsylvania.[33]

For four decades, Pennsylvania's morality militia held the high ground, but after the war they found themselves under attack. At theaters across the state it was action, adventure, skimpy bikinis, and exciting exploitation films that audiences raced out to see.

Returning from the Nuremberg trials, Pennsylvania judge Michael Angelo Musmanno set out to clean the screens of his home state's movie theaters. He found the Nazis easier to silence.

A prolific director of quickie-cheapies, Sam Newfield released *Wild Weed* a.k.a. *She Shoulda Said No!* (1949). The picture starred sloe-eyed Lila Leeds, an actress more famous for her arrest on marijuana possession with Robert Mitchum than for her walk-on screen roles.[34] Rocketed to reality stardom by her drug bust, Leeds played a girl in *She Shoulda Said No!* who becomes mixed up with drugs, sex, and school debt in a *Reefer Madness*–style exploitation flick. The censors banned the film. The court overturned the decision. Justice Musmanno dissented. Perhaps still reeling from the fog of war, Musmanno explained his objection: "The Pennsylvania Motion Picture Censorship Act is a fortress, armed originally with five cannon to protect the welfare of the people from the forces of immorality and intemperate greed.... History has never shown in America a surrender, while artillery of this formidableness was fighting on the side of the right.[35]

Next up, a grind house smoker called *Undercover Girls* (release date unknown) was banned as indecent and immoral. The exhibitor appealed, and this time the Keystone court not only overruled the film board but also invalidated the film law. Once again, Musmanno cried foul: "Now, there is nothing ... to save clean-minded, clean-thinking men, women and children of this State from the vulgarities, obscenities and indecencies which some moving picture producers are determined to inflict on the public for the sake of a greed-soaked dollar."[36]

A revised film law was quickly passed and just as quickly challenged. Brigitte Bardot's eyebrow-raising bikini in *...And God Created Woman* (1956) was racy but permitted. Mus-

CENSOR MENACED

Mrs. Margaret F. Palmer, chairman of Pennsylvania's board of motion pictures, is being guarded by state troopers following an acid attack and her report that numerous threats to "knock her off" had been received after her board had banned the Soviet-made film, "Baltic Deputy." She is the widow of the late Attorney General A. Mitchell Palmer.

After banning the Soviet film *Baltic Deputy* (1937), Pennsylvania censor Margaret Palmer received death threats.

manno again dissented. Without temperance and moral purity, he cried, "[We] may well be on the way to a cinematic Gomorrah."[37] In 1961 the film law was killed again, with Musmanno lamenting for "the flood of cinematic filth always pounding at the borders of our Commonwealth."[38] The zombielike film censorship bill was resurrected before the state legislature in 1965. Musmanno, a vocal supporter, claimed the law was necessary to

She Shoulda Said No! (1949) featured Lila Leeds, a B-level actress most famous for getting busted for marijuana with Robert Mitchum than her acting ability.

"drain off the moral sewage running through many of the motion pictures screens.... [T]he manner in which illegal and illicit behavior is being treated in many movies is weakening the moral fiber of youthful and immature minds."[39]

In his strenuous efforts to clean the state's screens of filth, Musmanno was fighting an unwinnable war. When the soft-core sapphic sex romp *Thérèse and Isabelle* (1968) came up for review, the Pennsylvania Supreme Court rubber-stamped it as "not obscene."[40] Musmanno had died the year before the decision came down.

Judge Musmanno may have savored the melodrama of seeing himself as the last guardian of values. It is interesting to note that Musmanno was not only a distinguished jurist but also had a notable screen credit. The judge had authored a story that was picked up by Warner Bros. and produced as *Black Fury* (1935). In the film Paul Muni played a striking Pennsylvania coal miner who is beaten by company thugs. Maryland refused to permit the provocative film. Chicago banned *Black Fury* on grounds that it could spur the public to social unrest.[41] During the time Musmanno railed in favor of film censorship, he had firsthand knowledge that political forces could squelch significant speech. Despite the sting of censorship to his own story, Musmanno still supported the state's power to suppress unwelcome voices.

Rhode Island

As the motion picture industry developed past its pioneering stage during the first decade of the twentieth century, regional film producers began to stage their own productions. These local moviemakers thrived for a brief period from approximately 1910 to 1920. Once the industry centralized, with production in Hollywood and financing in New York, these local industries receded into history and were mostly forgotten. While details have become obscure a century later, provincial picture makers remain an interesting and overlooked area of film history.

During this period, several early filmmakers set up studios in and around Rhode

Island. New Jersey–based Solax Film Co. produced the first feature in state, *Ben Bolt* (1913). Philadelphia's Lubin Manufacturing Co. set up a satellite studio in Newport to shoot military-themed pictures in preparation for America's involvement in World War I; the films included *The Nation's Peril* (1915) and *A Man's Making* (1915).[1] Vitagraph sent crews to the Ocean State to shoot *The Christian* (1914) and *The Hero of Submarine D-2* (1916). Douglas Fairbanks introduced his son Douglas Fairbanks, Jr., on-screen in *American Aristocracy* (1916), filmed in and around Watch Hill.[2] Other fleeting filmmakers of the period who have long since vanished include the Coronet Film Corp., the Commonwealth Photoplay Corp., and the What Cheer Film Co., all based in Providence; the M&M Picture Co. in Westerly; and the Western Film Co. in Warren.[3]

Taking a page out of D.W. Griffith's playbook, a successful Broadway playwright and actor named Joseph Byron Totten made the switch to filmed entertainment in 1915. Totten purchased a farmhouse on the Rhode Island–Connecticut border and transformed it into a movie studio.[4] From that base of operations Totten wrote and directed *The Call of the Sea* (1915) on Block Island, *The Lighthouse by the Sea* (1915) in Newport, and *Hearts and Roses* (1915) in Westerly.[5] During his productive three-year stint in Rhode Island, Totten completed over twelve pictures for Essanay Film Mfg. Co. before moving to Vitagraph's Brooklyn-based studio and eventually returning to the stage.[6]

The most successful local studio was the Eastern Film Co. of Providence. Three aspiring film producers, Frederick S. Peck, Benjamin L. Cook, and Elwood F. Bostwick, acquired the industrial workspace of the defunct Eagle Brewery in 1915.[7] Peck, the president of Eastern, was one of the wealthiest men in New England. Cook had financial connections as the manager of an investment banking and brokerage firm.[8] Bostwick took charge as Eastern's general manager and creative director. Arriving in the film world from theater, Bostwick quickly mounted several productions. Within its first twelve months of production, Eastern announced a slate of comedies, including *The Red Petticoat* (1915), as well as a maritime drama, *Cap'n Eri* (1915), and a crime thriller, *Diamonds* (1915).[9]

Following in the steps of D.W. Griffith, Joseph Byron Totten went from stage to screen setting up a New England studio.

Bostwick set his sights on high-class entertainment. This lofty perfectionist goal would lead Eastern into financial trouble. By the third quarter of 1915 Bostwick claimed to have finished forty-eight pictures but explained, "We discarded thirty because they fell below the standard set for our product."[10] With this financially reckless policy, Bostwick ensured his production shingle would not be around for long.

Several of Eastern's "releasable" pictures were the work of Beta Breuil. Breuil was a notable woman in the film industry of the 1910s. She began her career at Vitagraph as an entry-level assistant but within four months had moved up the ranks to become the head of the studio's scenario department.[11] Eastern gave her the opportunity to write and perhaps even produce and direct her original stories. At Eastern, Breuil penned a series of flower-themed titles: *Daisies* (1915), *Wisteria* (1915), *Violets* (1916), and *My Lady of the Lilacs* (c. 1916–1919).[12]

Although Elwood Bostwick was an equal-opportunity employer willing to entrust women with key responsibilities, his perfectionist production policies led to his removal by the end of 1915. Into his position stepped Frank Tichenor. Tichenor had a far more business-oriented outlook as compared to the obsessive Bostwick. Tichenor, formerly the manager of the Photo Play Production Co. in New York, ran the Rhode Island facility from offices in Times Square.[13] He diversified Eastern by acquiring a stage in Jacksonville. The Florida plant was purchased from Vim Comedy, a small studio beset by legal issues.[14] The southern soundstage was branded Amber Star Film Corp., with a comedy division called Jaxon that came with a slate of performers poached from Vim. Three more production teams were put in place to churn out Sparkle Comedies, Pokes and Jabs Comedies, and Finn and Haddie Comedies.[15]

Despite this burst of production, by the end of 1917 Tichenor recalled Eastern employees to Providence and sold off the southern branch. His decision would prove ill-fated. On August 23, 1917, a fire swept through the Rhode Island facility, effectively putting an end to Eastern's output.[16] Jaxon comedies continued to

Elwood F. Bostwick, president of Production for the Eastern Film Co. of Providence. His perfectionism led to his demise.

be released through 1918. Tichenor attempted to revive the studio as a producer of industrial and educational content, releasing titles such as *The Reward of Courage* (1921), a cancer-awareness film.[17] But the regional producer could not recover from the catastrophic fire, and as Hollywood consolidated in California, Eastern faded into history.

Motion pictures unspooled across Rhode Island as early as 1899. American Mutoscope and Biograph had film crews on hand to photograph *Parade in Providence* (1899), *Market Square, Providence* (1899), and *Arrival of Boat, Providence* (1899). Edison Manufacturing was only slightly behind Biograph, focusing on exciting subjects such as *Military Scenes at Newport* (1900), *Exploding a Whitehead Torpedo* (1900), and *Torpedo Boats Racing off Newport* (1902). Despite film's popularity with audiences, there were cries for regulation. In 1903 the *Newport Mercury* recorded that "a moving picture exhibition was scheduled to take place at the Opera House last Sunday evening, but the police commission declined to allow it as no license had been issued and it was not for the benefit of a church."[18] By the mid–1910s police lieutenant Richard Gamble was assigned to oversee theatrical productions and films as censor until his death in 1922.[19]

After Lt. Gamble's regime, the film censor position was left vacant; still, certain subjects were personae non grata in Providence. *Professor Mamlock* (1938) was produced in Russia as anti–Nazi propaganda. Rhode Island's police refused a permit on grounds it was Communist propaganda.[20] As values began to change after World War II, Providence refused to budge on censorship. Both *Lady Chatterley's Lover* (1955) and *...And God Created Woman* (1956) represented a challenge to traditional values. Both ran into trouble when they were scheduled to play at the Avon Theater. *Lady Chatterley* focused on a woman who pursued sexual satisfaction independent from her impotent husband. The film was based on D.H. Lawrence's book, which was also banned from publication in the United States until 1959.[21] In *...And God Created Woman*, director Roger Vadim established his wife Brigitte Bardot as an international sex symbol. Bardot played a liberated woman not afraid to dance barefoot to bongo music and pursue her own passions.

A rare female writer-director, Beta Breuil (1876– ?) was given creative control at the Eastern Film Co. of Rhode Island.

The laws of Rhode Island prohibited exhibition of any film without a license. Kingsley International dutifully submitted *Lady Chatterley* and *...And God Created Woman*. The Providence amusement inspector screened the pictures and informed Kingsley "he would under no circumstances approve" the films.[22] Kingsley protested but the court dismissed the claim. One judge, Calvert McGruder, dissented. He recognized that while the Supreme Court had recently embraced film within the First Amendment it had not struck down all censorship.[23] McGruder understood that the "area of permissible prior restraint in this field remains somewhat cloudy."[24] Although McGruder felt the issue worthy of discussion, he was in the minority. The French art films would not play in Providence.

A decade later an even more racy European film was cleared for Rhode Island screenings. The Danish film *Uden en trævl* (*Without a Stitch*, 1968) focused on a girl's sexual coming of age. Her diary records amorous encounters that range from sapphic romance to sadistic spankings, all seen on-screen. The court turned to the current legal measure of obscenity. At the time, the *Roth-Memoirs* test directed the court to consider three factors: (1) whether a work's dominant theme taken as a whole appealed to prurient interests in sex; (2) whether the work offended contemporary community standards; and (3) whether the work was utterly without *any* redeeming social value.[25] Despite the picture's explicit sexual content, Rhode Island's court was unable to pin down whether *Without a Stitch* was legally obscene. The censor's ban was overruled and the picture played on.

Shortly after the *Without a Stitch* decision, a group of Providence theater operators petitioned the U.S. Supreme Court to review Rhode Island's censorship laws. They hoped the High Court would consider the regulations unconstitutional, but the panel declined to review their claim. Only Justice Hugo Black and Justice William O. Douglas, both free speech purists, voted in favor of granting certiorari.[26] Even without a formal declaration from the Court, Rhode Island's film censorship law quietly gave way to the changing times, and motion picture regulators followed the state's once vibrant film studio system into obscurity.

South Carolina

It seemed like any other day on the campus of the University of South Carolina in Columbia. A tall, mustachioed stranger in a gray suit approached Chi Psi on fraternity row and knocked on the door. A camera crew kept their distance. In broken English the stranger explained that he was a journalist from the former Soviet republic of Kazakhstan and he was in America making a documentary. The journalist was looking for interview subjects. He indicated that the documentary would not be released in the United States or disclose the names of interviewees, the fraternity, or the university, according to a complaint later filed by two participants.[1]

To prepare for the interview segment, the journalist, who identified himself as "Borat," and his crew took three fraternity brothers to a nearby bar "to loosen up." The students were plied with alcohol even though at least one was underage. After several rounds a "Standard Consent Agreement" was brought out.[2] The drunken teens signed. The stranger was not an international journalist but rather the British comedian Sacha Baron Cohen. Cohen's brand of comedy was improvisational and character driven. He created ludicrously stereotypical characters—a white Brit pretending to be a hip-hop B-boy, a gay Austrian fashionista—in order to elicit reaction from unknowing participants. That response, whether it was revulsion or support, could put Baron Cohen's participants in an embarrassing position. Baron Cohen was passing through South Carolina on production for his first major studio motion picture: *Borat: Cultural Learnings of America for Make Benefit Glorious Nation of Kazakhstan* (2006).

The frat brothers were loaded into an RV for an interview on the road. How the segment went would later depend on who was asked. Sasha Baron Cohen must have been delighted by the reactions of the Southern students. Over the course of an inebriated tirade, the unwitting interviewees laughingly spewed racist comments. One wished he could own a slave. Another indicated how easy life was for minorities in America. It was true candid-camera material, which perhaps struck directly at the heart of lingering Southern prejudices. The victims didn't find the stunt enjoyable or enlightening. They filed suit to enjoin the film, or at least to cut these segments from the home-video version.

In their complaint, two frat brothers claimed that but for alcohol and encouragement, they "engaged in behavior that they otherwise would not have engaged in."[3] The resulting film was not only released in America, contrary to Baron Cohen/Borat's alleged representations, but it brought in box office numbers that reached $128 million within two months of release.[4] The plaintiffs claimed to have suffered mental anguish, loss of reputation, and emotional and physical distress.[5] They sued Baron Cohen and the picture's distributor, 20th Century Fox, for fraud, defamation, false light, and invasion of privacy, among other claims. The case made headlines—one unintended consequence of suing the studio was that it obliterated the students' hopes to remain anonymous—and raised several interesting issues in the balance between First Amendment protections and privacy rights.

The First Amendment protects the right of content producers, writers, artists, and filmmakers to engage in free expression. But the right to privacy protects an individual from unwanted intrusion into personal space or unauthorized access to privileged documents in a situation where the subject would have a reasonable expectation of privacy. Journalists can generally record subjects in public view without their permission—here the First Amendment prevails. But once the conversation is no longer in public, a talent release based on a full understanding of the recording to be used is usually the proper course of action (but see the case of *Titicut Follies* in Massachusetts). Is a release valid if it is based on intentional fraud (e.g., the statement that the film will not be released in the United States)? Is a release valid if the signer is intoxicated?

Perhaps a different result would have been reached if the case had been tried in South Carolina, but the lawsuit was relocated to Los Angeles. Perhaps in the Palmetto State privacy rights would have prevailed. In LA, Judge Joseph Biderman ruled for the studio, finding the students had failed to show a reasonable probability of success on the merits of their case or that money damages alone would be insufficient to resolve their claims.[6] The frat brothers' comments would not be South Carolina's finest moment on film.

Some of the earliest screenings of movies in South Carolina took place at the courthouse. Motion pictures were an exciting new technology when the Rev. Frederick W. Wey demonstrated his Kinetoscope at the Greenville courthouse in 1901.[7] Within a few years, movies delivered amusements like *The Great Train Robbery* (1903) to the state's eager audiences. The *Greenville News* raved, "The best notion one could possibly get of a train robbery is suggested in [this] series of pictures. Men climb on an express train … kill the express messenger, [and] dynamite the strong box." The reviewer went on, "I sat by a man who has lived in the West, who has seen outlaws fight and die, and he says the pictures were true to life."[8]

By 1914 Columbia-based filmmaker W.L. Blanchard began filming life in South Carolina. He recorded footage of the controversial governor, Coleman L. Blease, at home and at work.[9] One morning on his way to the governor's office, Blanchard passed the Columbia statehouse and spied H.H. Gardner, the Virginia Daredevil, preparing to scale the stately building. Blanchard's camera was rolling when the daredevil tumbled off the slick marble façade.[10] Next, Blanchard shot scenes of military exercises and enlisted life on location at Camp Moore, a nearby National Guard base.[11] The city of Greenville invited Blanchard to capture their local color on film. Over a three-day period, the movie man filmed a parade, street scenes, and coeds at Lander College. The local newspaper proudly boasted, "Greenwood is going to star in moving pictures!"[12] Sadly, these records of life in small-town South Carolina circa 1916 have been lost.

While popular with audiences, movies weren't beloved in all corners of the state. The topic of film censorship was raised in 1916 when Greenville's city attorney sent a note to the police commissioner, W.T. Bull.[13] No action was taken. The issue returned four years later when Governor Robert Cooper proposed a board of censors in his State of the State address.[14] A bill went up for debate that would "mak[e] it an offense to exhibit indecent, lude [sic], or immoral pictures."[15] Defying Gov. Cooper, the state senate unanimously voted the bill down, finding it "impractical."[16] The issue still didn't go away. Film censorship was floated again in 1938, aimed at "deleting drinking, murder, and divorce scenes from movies shown in South Carolina."[17] It too was lost in committee.

Official censorship was not going to work in South Carolina, but a chilling wind still blew when inappropriate materials were scheduled to screen in the state. *Monty Python's Life of Brian* (1979) was intended as a religious satire by the British comic troupe. Set in biblical times, the film follows a Jewish boy born in a manger neighboring Jesus's own. Ecclesiastical confusion ensues. This film was borderline blasphemy for many. *Life of Brian* was banned in parts of England, Ireland, Scotland, and Norway and protested in New Jersey.[18] South Carolina relied on political coercion to control the film. When the Rev. William Solomon learned that *Brian* was scheduled to play in South Carolina, he went on the offensive: "I was upset by three things.... The film held up to deliberate ridicule my faith in Jesus Christ and made fun of His suffering. Secondly, the movie is definitely Anti-Semitic and heavy on derogatory terms applied to Jewish people. Finally, it was not art. It was cruel and sarcastic, but it was not art."[19] The Reverend Solomon contacted Senator Strom Thurmond. Thurmond applied pressure, calling the General Cinema Corp. with a message that South Carolinians "take their religion very seriously."[20] This suggestion persuaded the theater to suspend showings. In response to the unofficial ban, 150 protesters convened outside the theater with signs that read, "Resurrect *Brian*, Crucify Censors," and, "Strom Doesn't Pay for My Movie Ticket."[21]

Even though state censorship never passed in South Carolina, alternative means of controlling inappropriate movies developed. Political pressure can be powerfully persuasive in the short term, as Sen. Thurmond demonstrated, but targeted lawsuits can be more troublesome. The un-politically correct SC students may have had a point that Baron Cohen's film delivered a punch line by duping them into spouting racist off-the-cuff comments.

The bigger issue pitting free speech against privacy rights is still in flux. The fraternity brothers lost their claim; but in a 2016 privacy/disclosure case, the wrestling icon Hulk Hogan prevailed against the scandal website Gawker.[22] Free speech and privacy remain in continual tension, open for debate on a case-by-case basis.

South Dakota

The climactic sequence in *North by Northwest* (1959)—as Cary Grant and Eva Marie Saint flee the clutches of Martin Landau atop Mount Rushmore—may be one of the most famous scenes in cinema history. But it wasn't easy to get permission to shoot on the national monument. Alfred Hitchcock had long wanted to use the iconic South Dakota location. While the director had featured the Statue of Liberty in *Saboteur* (1942), studio effects were used for the scene's dramatic highlight. When Hitch requested access to Rushmore, the National Park Service was skeptical. Even if the bulk of the filming occurred on an MGM soundstage, would the Master of Suspense desecrate the shrine of democracy?

Permission was granted on the condition that no violence would be staged on the

To get clearance to shoot on location, Alfred Hitchcock promised the National Park Service there would be no deaths on Mt. Rushmore in *North by Northwest* (1959). He lied.

monument. They obviously hadn't liked seeing saboteur Norman Lloyd falling to his death from the pinnacle of the statue's torch platform. MGM's production lawyers assured park officials that Hitchcock would treat the site respectfully, and "none of our characters would tread upon the faces or heads of the sculpture."[1] When Hitch mentioned he envisioned a race across the faces, with Grant—the actor, not the president—ducking for cover inside an immense stone nostril of Abraham Lincoln, the park rangers limited the film crew's access to below the chin and above the forehead.[2] There would be no man in Lincoln's nose. Still, Hitch had the last laugh. As Cary Grant hangs from the monument's precipice by one hand, grasping Eva Marie Saint with the other, Landau sadistically steps on the hero's knuckles. With a single gunshot, the evil spy tumbles off the rock face and the stars are saved. It was nearly the same as *Saboteur*'s objectionable scene, but *North by Northwest*'s imagery was so memorable that it proved unstoppable.

South Dakota's rugged scenery provided unforgettable images. A gnarled tree stands against a bleak landscape in Terrence Malick's directorial feature debut *Badlands* (1973), capturing the isolation of the film's murderous couple, played by Martin Sheen and Sissy Spacek. *Badlands* ignited the New York Film Festival, a rural companion piece to Scorsese's *Mean Streets* (1973), which screened the week before. The *New York Times* found Sheen and Spacek "splendid as the self-absorbed cruel, possibly psychotic children of our time."[3] Twenty years later the Dakota prairie took on another meaning, attesting to one man's resilience against all odds and merciless nature in *Dances with Wolves* (1990). Kevin Costner's re-envisioning of the West, shot partially on location in South Dakota, claimed seven Academy Awards, including Best Picture, Director, Adapted Screenplay, Cinematography, Editing, and Film Score.

It's not only the harsh landscape of South Dakota that has been featured on film but also the region's colorful characters, especially Deadwood's finest: Wild Bill Hickok and

Calamity Jane. Although their on-film lives have often been embellished from their actual bios, the exploits of Wild Bill and Calamity Jane have captured imaginations for close to one hundred years. Cowboy star William S. Hart played the unlucky gambler, murdered with the "dead man's hand" of two aces and two eights, in *Wild Bill Hickok* (1923). Gary Cooper took on the role in *The Plainsman* (1936), with Jean Arthur as Calamity Jane. *Badlands of Dakota* (1941) featured Richard Dix and Frances Farmer as the frontier couple, and Doris Day and Howard Keel gave the tale a musical adaptation in *Calamity Jane* (1953).

South Dakota was also the setting for the story of one of history's most imaginative characters behind the scenes: Oscar Micheaux. Micheaux was a pioneering African American writer-director-producer and the strongest voice in the genre of race films. Race films featured African American actors in stories tailored to African American audiences at a time when minorities were excluded from Hollywood and segregated in theaters. Micheaux captured powerful performances by Paul Robeson in *Body and Soul* (1925) and created an alternative star sys-

William S. Hart played Deadwood's finest in *Wild Bill Hickok* (1923).

tem with the "Black Valentino," Lorenzo Tucker; the "Sepia Mae West," Bee Freeman; Ethel Moses, the "Negro Harlow"; and Alfred "Slick" Chester, the "Colored Cagney."[4] Micheaux wasn't the first black filmmaker; William D. Foster had begun producing short comedies in Chicago in 1912, and the Nebraska-based Lincoln Photoplay Co., led by George and Noble Johnson, had focused on uplifting message films since 1916. Still, it was Micheaux who would become the movement's most prolific and exciting figure.

Micheaux rose from humble beginnings. The son of former slaves, he became a Pullman porter before purchasing a homestead near Gregory, South Dakota, in 1905. When a 1909 drought parched the plains lands, Micheaux moved to Sioux City.[5] There he wrote and self-published an autobiographical novel: *The Conquest: The Story of a*

Negro Pioneer (1913). The story celebrated self-reliance and the uncompromising will to succeed. This inspiring story attracted the Johnson brothers. George and Noble wanted to adapt the novel as a film, but Micheaux insisted that he direct.[6] The negotiations failed, and like his self-reliant fictional character, Micheaux was inspired do it on his own.

Retitled *The Homesteader* (1918), Micheaux's first production courted controversy. In addition to the drama of a hardscrabble farmer battling natural elements, he injected an interracial love story. The farmer becomes successful and falls in love with a white neighbor's daughter—scandalous. Order is restored when the girl is revealed to be a light-skinned African American; still, hints of racial equality challenged notions of proper behavior. Micheaux frequently addressed progressive and challenging plot points in his movies. *Within Our Gates* (1918) adapted a story similar to the ripped-from-the-headlines Leo Frank lynching in Atlanta to the race film format. *Symbol of the Unconquered* (1920), *The House Behind the Cedars* (1927), and *Veiled Aristocracy* (1932) focused on light-skinned African Americans passing as white. Micheaux criticized the hypocrisy of self-righteous churchmen in *Deceit* (1923) and *Body and Soul* (1925). While this makes Micheaux a fascinating figure from a modern perspective, at the time his views often landed him in hot water. An ongoing battle with the Virginia censor Evan Chesterman delayed Micheaux's films along the important Southern circuit of segregated theaters.

Micheaux's films could present disruptive ideas for the audiences of his era. His shoestring budgets and low-fidelity production values can be difficult for modern audiences to watch. Still, the legend of Oscar Micheaux is larger than life. He wrote his own stories, raised his own funds, and produced his films seemingly on willpower alone. He distributed films to audiences that were excluded from the mainstream media of Hollywood. In this, Micheaux, who made his final film in 1948, paved the way for socially conscious filmmakers and later African American directors, from Spike Lee to John Singleton and Julie Dash to Ava DuVernay.

Micheaux faced pushback from censors in the Southern states, but from the earliest days of motion pictures South Dakota steered clear of regulating on-screen content.

When the movies first arrived in South Dakota, they were a saloon diversion. The Bodega Saloon in Deadwood began showing canned entertainment in 1899.[7] The Deadwood Theater opened in 1905 and was soon being managed by Melvin Clare "M.C." Kellogg.[8] Kellogg attracted audiences with popular titles such as Broncho Billy's *The Flower of the Prairie* (1910) and the Gaumont tearjerker *The Unwritten Letter* (1909).[9] Kellogg had retired by the time a film censorship bill was introduced to the South Dakota legislature in 1921. The ordinance would have banned all films "sacrilegious, obscene, indecent, immoral or such as tend, in the judgment of the board, to debase or corrupt public morals or tend to incite the commission of crimes."[10] The proposal was approved in the statehouse but seems to have gotten lost on the way to the governor.[11] There are no records of South Dakota ever censoring a picture or even convening a review board.

That record stood for nearly one hundred years. In 2015 the state made news with censorship of a documentary. When the University of South Dakota in Vermillion scheduled *Honor Diaries* (2013) the screening was suspiciously canceled.

Honor Diaries focused on nine women opposing gender inequality and human rights abuses against women in majority–Muslim nations.[12] The film intended to give a voice to the powerless and invisible members of society. At USD *Honor Diaries* caused a rift in academia. A professor of media and journalism named Miglena Sternadori supported the screening, saying the documentary depicted issues relevant to women's, feminist, and gender studies. A critic of the film, Ibrahim Hooper, spoke for the Council on American-Islamic Relations, calling the film Islamophobic.[13]

In their first skirmish, Hooper convinced the university to stop the screening. The discussion on women's rights was silenced in what the documentary's supporters called "stealth repression."[14] In the end, champions of free speech prevailed. Despite the controversy *Honor Diaries* was rescheduled, with a discussion to follow the screening.[15]

At a time when confronting racial issues could trigger a tinderbox ready to explode, Oscar Micheaux did not shy away from raising difficult discussions. What his motion pictures lacked in technical quality they made up for in social importance, asking viewers to consider significant topics. Micheaux was able to use the medium of motion pictures as a catalyst for social change. A century later, *Honor Diaries* demonstrates this mission is still relevant. Movies have the power to not only entertain but also to begin dialogues on important issues, as long as audiences remain open to alternative and sometimes-uncomfortable viewpoints.

Tennessee

During the final months of his twenty-eight-year tenure as the municipal film censor of Memphis, eighty-eight-year-old Lloyd T. Binford explained his passion for scissoring sin from his city's movie screens: "There's a certain amount of the devil in all of us.... [H]e's trying to get us and plants wrong thoughts in our minds. Many movies stimulate those wrong thoughts."[1]

Although Binford was appointed by Mayor Edward Hull "Boss" Crump, he saw his position as more than a political office. Binford saw censorship as a cosmic responsibility, saving the souls of Tennessee residents from the evil, corruptive, and even demonic influence of Hollywood.

State authorities in Tennessee had censored certain motion pictures long before Binford arrived on the scene. In 1911 as Boss Crump was consolidating his political machine in Memphis, he claimed the moral high ground by forbidding provocative pictures. Boxing films were banned, as well as any film, newsreel, or narrative based on the recent Beulah Binford incident.[2]

The Beulah Binford incident was making headlines. When one of Richmond's wealthiest citizens murdered his wife and claimed a bizarre alibi—a bearded stranger had leaped out of the woods and fired at point-blank range—tabloids showcased the scandal. Police investigators were led to a Lolita-like thirteen-year-old named Beulah Binford, who "had a reputation as a hellcat, known to take money from anyone, for anything."[3] Miss Binford had seduced the Virginia gentleman and persuaded him to commit the horrific act. Two months after her wayward lover's murder conviction, filmmakers flocked to Miss Binford with hopes of parlaying her notoriety into box office lucre. Boss Crump was not alone in his disapproval; along with Memphis, Philadelphia, and Providence banned the killer coquette from stage and screen.[4]

Meanwhile, across the state in Nashville, Mayor Hilary E. Howse empaneled his own five-person film censor board in 1914.[5] A local lumber miller named Hamilton Love rose to the position of Music City's chief censor. Love declared it his mission to ban "indecent, morbid and degrading and exceedingly depressing" motion pictures.[6] He blue-penciled lurid dramas that exploited themes of birth control and prostitution, such as *Twilight Sleep* (1915) and *Where Are the Unborn?* (1916).[7] Films with risqué topics, if produced on better budgets by more reputable studios, might pass muster: Universal's birth-control advisory *Where Are My Children?* (1916) was passed, as was Essanay's prostitution cautionary tale *The Little Girl Next Door* (1916).[8]

As his health deteriorated, Love's passion for film—and censorship—did not. When the film maven became bedridden, eight reels of Rudolph Valentino's breakout film *The Sheik* (1921) were delivered to his home. The picture unspooled on a makeshift screen set up beside Love's sickbed. The censor declared it was "one of the most wonderful productions he had witnessed in years."[9] Three months later, on May 3, 1922, Hamilton Love died.[10]

Nashville quickly replaced its city censor, naming Vivian Tupper to the post.[11] Her passion for film and love for cinema could not match that of her aptly named predecessor. There are few records of censorship under her regime.

For the next three decades, the epicenter of Tennessee film censorship would reside in Memphis, where Lloyd T. Binford held court. Heading toward retirement, Binford fondly recalled his reign of terror and proudly called himself the "most notorious censor in the world."[12]

Binford, the son of a Confederate colonel, rose from humble beginnings. He was born in 1867 in the backwater town of Duck Hill, Mississippi, shortly after the Civil War. By 1917 he was a prominent Mississippi businessman, winning friends by handing out Binford-branded souvenirs that ranged from square pencils to fifty-dollar watches. Binford opened an insurance business in a log cabin and within a decade built the twenty-two-story Columbia Mutual Tower in Memphis.[13] The tower still stands at 62 N. Main Street. In the late 1920s Binford shifted his focus from insurance coverage to film censorship. Boss Crump handed Binford a tin badge that he brandished with pride and power as he stormed the city's cinemas.[14]

Unlike Hamilton Love, who reserved his cuts for racy midnight movies or controversial issues, from the beginning Binford could find objectionable material in the most mainstream fare. When Cecil B. DeMille's *The King of Kings* (1927) was scheduled to play Memphis, Binford sat in judgment. Claiming he had received letters from Christians stating that Hollywood's biblical exegesis was incorrect and from Jews who felt the picture would arouse anti–Semitic prejudice, Binford demanded cuts.[15] The case went to court. Ruling in favor of the board and finding that film censorship was "well within the police power of the State," the *King of Kings* decision cemented Binford's power.[16] He quickly became known as the nation's busiest and most controversial movie censor.[17]

Binford banned hard-boiled film noirs, including *Dead End* (1937) with Humphrey Bogart and *Dillinger* (1945) with Lawrence Tierney. He claimed these were not "proper picture[s] to show before the youth of today.… We think it would encourage crime and there is no need of showing a picture that might influence boys to be gangsters."[18] Violent Westerns didn't fare much better. *Jesse James* (1939) with Tyrone Power and *The Return of Frank James* (1940) with Henry Fonda were barred for the "glamorizing of criminals who rob and murder ruthlessly."[19] Neither James Stewart's *Destry Rides Again* (1939) nor Randolph Scott's *When the Daltons Rode* (1940) was permitted, "on grounds that excessive gunplay might contribute to juvenile delinquency."[20] Howard Hughes's titillating *The*

Censors tussled with Russell, banning Howard Hughes' *The Outlaw* (1943) in many states around the country.

Outlaw (1943) featuring Jane Russell was banned in Memphis, but not for the two reasons that got the film in trouble in other states. Overlooking Russell's cleavage, Binford found the film had "too much shooting in it to be a good example for boys and girls."[21] Binford similarly tabooed David O. Selznick's paean to the fit figure of his own paramour Jennifer Jones, *Duel in the Sun* (1946). The censor called it "the most repellant movie seen this year."[22]

An actor's offscreen behavior could provoke Binford to clip on-screen performances. By the mid–1940s Charlie Chaplin's star was fading. The comedian was also under attack for left-leaning politics, rumors of a sex scandal, nonpayment of taxes, and his relationship with Oona O'Neill, a woman thirty-six years his junior. When Chaplin released *Monsieur Verdoux* (1947), his first film in seven years, Binford promptly banished it. The censor's rationale was "Chaplin's reputation." He added a more substantive reason for his rejection: "Murder is not a joke."[23] This ire did not calm over time. When a revival of *City Lights* (1931) was planned, Binford put the kibosh on the show, commenting that the star was "an enemy of godliness in all its forms ... a traitor to the Christian way of life and an enemy of decency, virtue, and marriage."[24]

If Chaplin was a menace, Ingrid Bergman was a monster. Bergman endeared herself to movie audiences as the lovelorn Ilsa in *Casablanca* (1942). She claimed the moral high ground with Academy Award–nominated performances as a nun in *The Bells of St. Mary's*

(1945) and a martyr in *Joan of Arc* (1948). Then on the set of *Stromboli* (1950) she indulged in an adulterous relationship with director Roberto Rossellini that filled gossip columns and outraged fans. Binford announced Bergman would be persona non grata on Memphis screens "because of her conduct not because of the pictures."[25]

Gun-toting hombres and morally challenged movie stars may have stirred the pot, but Lloyd T. Binford reserved special antipathy for racially integrated films. The frequently remade scenario in *Brewster's Millions* centered on a young man who stands to inherit $7 million—but only if he can blow $1 million. Four filmed adaptations had already been produced before Allan Dwan's 1945 version.[26] Dwan added an African American character played by Eddie Anderson as the inheritor's butler and confidant. This infuriated Binford, who prohibited the picture in Memphis, citing that "it presented too much familiarity between the races" and was "inimical to the public welfare ... [because] the picture presents too much social equality and racial mixture."[27]

The situation became worse when a Hal Roach–produced kiddie comedy came to town. Roach was famous for assembling the cast of Little Rascals for the *Our Gang* series. After sixteen years of churning out shorts, Roach sold the franchise to MGM in 1938. A decade later he tried to reboot the concept with a movie called *Curley* (1947). *Curley* presented a very similar lineup as the original cast; the plot even followed an *Our Gang* episode closely. There was one problem. The mixed-race cast was seen in school together. An integrated classroom in 1940s Memphis could not be tolerated. The Memphis board of censors sent a letter to the film's distributor, United Artists, stating, "I am sorry to have to inform you that [we are] unable to approve your *Curley* picture with the little negroes as the south does not permit negroes in white school nor recognize social equality between the races even in children. Yours truly /s/ Lloyd T. Binford Chairman."[28] The studio brought the city censors to court. Two decades after the *King of Kings* case, the legitimacy and authority of the Memphis censor board was again challenged. Once again Binford's board prevailed.

While the *Curley* case was still under review by the Tennessee court, Binford turned his attention to a musical picture called *A Song Is Born* (1948). The movie was director Howard Hawks's Technicolor remake of his own screwball comedy *Ball of Fire* (1941). The new film starred Danny Kaye and an ensemble that included jazzmen Louis Armstrong, Tommy Dorsey, Benny Goodman, and Lionel Hampton. Predictably unhip, Binford found it a "rough, bawdy, noisy picture. What's more," he said, the movie was not "right for Memphians to see on the screen [because] the film has no segregation."[29] When a revival of *Imitation of Life* (1934) rolled into town, Binford chided the film as "one of the most disgusting cases of racial equality I have ever seen."[30] Lena Horne's showcase number "Love" in MGM's *Ziegfeld Follies* (1946) was ordered cut out.[31]

The tenor of popular culture began to change in 1949 with the release of a series of high-profile social-issue films. *Home of the Brave* (1949), released by United Artists, considered race in the military. MGM's *Intruder in the Dust* (1949) looked at race relations in a small Southern town. Against all odds, Lloyd Binford approved both films.[32] Fox Films released *Pinky* (1949), the story of a light-skinned African American girl passing as white in the North and coming to terms with her identity after returning home to the South. Binford permitted *Pinky*; however, when a similarly themed "passing" picture called *Lost Boundaries* (1949) crossed his desk, he issued a rejection.[33] Perhaps *Lost Boundaries* was treated differently because it was based on the true-life tale of a family hiding their heritage (see New Hampshire). Perhaps the film was more vulnerable because it was an independent production or because it was already the focus of censorship litigation in Atlanta.[34] Facing pressure to reevaluate his decision, Binford reluctantly stated that movies with racial themes would no longer be banned in Memphis: "We'll just have to pass these pictures."[35]

Violent films and socially relevant pictures were but two of the topics that riled Binford's sense of moral authority. In the postwar world, audiences yearned for more titillating shows, and Hollywood delivered the goods. Dorothy Lamour played a sexy good-time barroom girl in *Lulu Belle* (1948). The film was banned for a sensual performance that "cater[ed] to the lowest impulses of its audiences."[36] When Gwen Verdon, wearing midriff-baring crimson scarves and golden leggings, gave a hip-shaking shimmy dance to liven up the stolid biblical epic *David and Bathsheba* (1951), Binford charged that the film had "misused and abused the Holy Bible."[37] He prayed for cuts to the "vulgar dance."[38] Cold water was thrown on suggestive pictures, including Jane Russell's *The French Line* (1953), Rita Hayworth's *Sadie Thompson* (1953), and Jan Sterling's striptease sequence in *The Human Jungle* (1954).[39]

In his final year on the job, the eighty-nine-year-old Binford blue-penciled popular films with the energy of a man half his age. He flagged *The Wild One* (1953), *The Blackboard Jungle* (1955), *Night of the Hunter* (1955), and *I Am a Camera* (1955).[40] Following this burst of activity, Binford handed in his tin movie police badge. After twenty-seven years of censoring services, he conceded, "They need a younger man."[41] Eleven months later Binford was dead.[42] An era had ended.

Or had it? Even without Binford in the censor's seat, movies were still on uncertain ground in Memphis. Despite one round of cuts to the film, the reconfigured censor board demanded *Lady Chatterley's Lover* (1955) carry an "adults only" demarcation. Elia Kazan's *Baby Doll* (1956) was banned as immoral.[43] When soft-core films featuring bare flesh began hitting local screens as midnight movies, Memphis censors issued bans to halt such nudie-cuties as *Nudist Paradise* (1959) and *Hideout in the Sun* (1960).[44]

One Memphis film buff named Bill Kendall opened an art-house theater in the 1960s to showcase European films. He came under fire when he programmed *The L-Shaped Room* (1962). *Room* featured Leslie Caron as a young girl who is French, pregnant, and unmarried—scandalous. Kendall

The Human Jungle (1954) had it all: juvenile delinquency, murder, mobsters, and Jan Sterling as a menacing moll.

fought the indictment and prevailed.[45] Next, the less arty but more spicy *Women of the World* (1963) came under review. The board banned; the distributor sued. This time the result was decisive: the Tennessee district court found the state's film censorship ordinance unconstitutional as a prior restraint on the First Amendment and freedom of speech.[46] The epoch of film censorship that began in 1911 with Boss Crump's decree came to a close on July 9, 1965. The Tennessee censor board was disbanded.

While Kendall's program of art films elevated the film medium, a darker undercurrent of seamier cinema was seeping into mainstream culture. By the late 1960s grind houses began openly screening hard-core films. Films that crossed the line as obscene could still be shuttered, but the balance of power had shifted to favor free expression. State authorities could no longer bar a film with a wave of their hand or a flash of a badge.[47]

Texas

The Lone Star State's legendary fortress has been the focus of films from John Wayne's *The Alamo* (1960) to *Pee-wee's Big Adventure* (1985). The doomed citadel first appeared on-screen in the Gaston Méliès–produced *The Immortal Alamo* (1911). The story of film in Texas begins a dozen years before Gaston invited audiences to remember the Alamo.

Seeing that staged fighting films were a draw for early film audiences, the Texas-based boxing promoter Dan Stuart believed that an authentic bout could pull in real returns. He began negotiating a filmed matchup between Robert "Lanky Bob" Fitzsimmons and the Irishman Peter Maher.[1] A movie man named Enoch Rector took notice. Rector was an inventor and marketing professional. After working with Thomas Edison's motion picture division he left to team with the Latham brothers on a competing device (see West Virginia). When that partnership soured Rector struck out on his own.

In the early months of 1896 Rector and Stuart discussed filming the Fitzsimmons-Maher bout. This was the first time content was developed from a purely economic standpoint—not to demonstrate the medium's picture-making capability but to fill theaters with paying spectators. The first obstacle was that boxing was outlawed in Texas. This problem was solved when Judge Roy Bean offered Stuart and Rector a venue for their fistic ballet: a sandbar on the Mexican side of the Rio Grande sat just outside Bean's jurisdiction of Langtry. On this no-man's-land a makeshift canvas circle was squared. The fight was on, planned for February 21, 1896.[2]

One minute and thirty-five seconds into the first round, Fitzsimmons landed a punishing blow to the Irishman's jaw and ended the event with a knockout. Rector's film crew missed the battle. The day was dark and overcast; without enough light to shoot the scene, the first film event went unrecorded.[3] Undeterred by this setback, Rector moved his crew further into Mexico to film a bullfight, the picture later released as *Corrida de toros* (1896). Putting a positive spin on the Texas-Mexico location shoot, Rector told the *Galveston Daily News*, "I was successful in photographing the most bloody and exciting bull fight.... [A]s you know we failed to photograph the fight owing to the cloudy and unfavorable weather. We were all ready and had the Kinetoscope charged for the occasion

On a Rio Grande sandbar "Lanky Bob" Fitzsimmons prepared to fight Peter Maher in the first major film event. The fistic ballet was not caught on film due to inclement weather.

but we could not control the elements."[4] Rector and Stuart reteamed to promote the next title bout, pitting Fitzsimmons against "Gentleman Jim" Corbett. That endeavor would prove more successful. A year later, the Fitzsimmons-Corbett fight was shot in sunny Carson City (see Nevada).

Not long after Rector's experiment, other motion picture teams were dispatched to Texas. As early as January 1897, Magniscopes were entertaining audiences with Edison-

Film pioneer Gaston Méliès (1852–1915) took his production shingle Star Films to San Antonio and then on to the South Seas.

produced titles such as *Haymakers at Work* (1896) and *Mounted Police Charge* (1896).[5] Cameramen were on location to record the aftermath of a hurricane in a series of actualities, including *Galveston Disaster* (1900), *Bird's-Eye View of Dock Front, Galveston* (1900), and *Searching Ruins on Broadway, Galveston for Dead Bodies* (1900).

Despite their popularity and newsworthiness, movies came under fire by the end of the decade. Based on the perceived need to protect juveniles and impressionable viewers, cries for censorship sounded. "Until the pictures cease to depict killings and law breaking, and the interior of bawdy houses and the butchering of animals," warned the *Houston Post*, "the shows of each town should be compelled by an ordinance to support a censor."[6] In December 1909 Fort Worth fast-tracked the creation of a censor's office to regulate immoral films in the market.[7]

Even as censors increased their activity, one of the East Coast's industry leaders moved all operations to San Antonio. Gaston Méliès was one of the founding members of the Motion Picture Patent Company, Thomas Edison's film trust of powerbrokers formed during the first decade of filmmaking. Gaston arrived in New York in 1903, sent by his brother, the trick-film pioneer Georges Méliès. Georges was the mastermind of wildly inventive fantasy films such as *Le voyage dans la lune* (*A Trip to the Moon*, 1902). Unlike his counterparts, who churned out motion pictures on industrial assembly lines, Georges handcrafted pictures that were works of art. He was infuriated when American producers created unauthorized duplicates of his work. These dupes stole his art and cheated him out of his royalties. Within a year of Méliès's most famous and profitable release, Edison, Lubin, Selig, and Vitagraph each offered their own pirated versions of *A Trip to the Moon*.[8] As a response, Georges dispatched his brother to New York with orders to open up a distribution office for their Star-Films and put a stop to the theft of his intellectual property.[9]

Establishing the Méliès brand in New York, Gaston joined forces with the major players of the budding film industry. By 1910 Star-Films began suffering from internal troubles as Georges's trick-film output diminished. Gaston needed movies in his distribution pipeline. He closed the New York office and relocated to San Antonio.

Gaston's move to Texas was drastic. In 1910 the film industry was situated on the East Coast with some offices in Chicago. Apart from a filmmaking oasis in Jacksonville, Florida, very little was located south of the Mason-Dixon Line, and Hollywood production was still years off. Why Gaston relocated and how he chose San Antonio remains a mystery, but once the Star-Film ranch was equipped, the facility was able to produce and release Western films on a furious schedule.[10] Gaston stepped into the director's seat for films such as *Under the Stars and Bars* (1910) and *The Great Heart of the West* (1911). A second unit operated under the direction of William F. Haddock, whom Gaston had poached from Edison. Haddock's company included Francis Ford, the older brother of the future director John Ford. Together Haddock and Ford made nearly fifty films, mostly Westerns, from 1910 to 1911, including *Speed Versus Death* (1910) and *The Immortal Alamo* (1911).

Shot on location, *The Immortal Alamo* (1911) was the earliest film version of the doomed patriots' last stand.

By 1912 Gaston Méliès closed his ranch studio and continued westward. He stopped briefly to shoot several films in California before taking his company off the map. The Méliès crew continued to make films in Australia, New Zealand, and Asia, leaving behind the Westerns featuring cowboys and Indians for eastern-flavored films populated by Maoris, Aborigines, and Polynesians.[11] Méliès's eastward journey is significant because in 2010 a picture shot on the Texas Star-Film ranch was discovered in a New Zealand vault. A thousand miles away from Texas, a time capsule of Lone Star filmmaking lost for one hundred years was opened.[12]

Meanwhile, back on the mainland, film censors were becoming more powerful. In 1913 Houston empaneled a three-person board to crack down on immoral films. Popular sentiment favored regulation, with the *Houston Post* editorializing that "censors must be given full authority to suppress improper films and the police must be given ample authority to close places that flagrantly violate the law."[13] Despite such editorializing, Texas censors never achieved the power that regulators in other states held. The proto-sexploitation flick *The Seventh Commandment* (1915) was tagged but cleared in the courtroom. Houston unanimously approved the often-controversial *The Birth of a Nation* (1915).[14] The Dallas censor board, formed in 1915, was slightly more successful, banning nineteen films, including the sex-education infotainment piece *The Miracle of Life* (1915), during their first year of operation.[15]

Moving into the 1930s and 1940s, certain controversial pictures came under scrutiny. When MGM's *Strange Interlude* (1932) arrived in Abilene, local authorities fretted over the content. Based on a play by Eugene O'Neill, *Interlude* dealt with mature issues, but "the acting was suburb, the story unusual and intriguing and presentation excellent."[16] The censors passed the picture with an adults-only proviso.

A different result was reached when Fox's *Pinky* (1949) reached Marshall, Texas. *Pinky* focused on a light-skinned African American girl who had passed for white in the North at nursing school. Returning home to the South, she confronts racist attitudes while caring for an elderly unreconstructed neighbor. Atlanta's censor passed the film with glowing recommendations. The City Too Busy to Hate saw *Pinky* as a mirror that could reflect Southern attitudes, start conversations, and prompt reconsideration of prejudices. The film could stimulate a call for change. Such change was not welcome in Marshall. Relying on the thirty-seven-year old *Mutual* precedent (see Ohio), the Texas court upheld the censors and banned *Pinky* without even considering the First Amendment or any infringement on free speech.[17] This would be the final time a court could dismiss a free speech claim so effortlessly. The *Pinky* case was appealed to the Supreme Court and overruled with four words: "The judgment is reversed."[18]

Times were changing. The *Miracle* decision (see New York) came down less than a month before *Pinky* arrived on Capitol Hill, and it overruled *Mutual*. Movies could still be censored for certain reasons, but the circle was narrowing. Texas censors, however, remained on the offensive.

When Ingmar Bergman's *The Virgin Spring* (1960) hit the marquee at the Capri Theatre in Fort Worth, cinephiles were happy but censors, less so. Bergman's film is an artful meditation on faith and revenge. Set in medieval Sweden, *Virgin Spring* witnesses the brutal rape and murder of a young girl. Her killers end up inadvertently begging for food and shelter from the girl's parents. Discovering the truth, the mourning family exact revenge. *The Virgin Spring* was recognized with an Academy Award for Best Foreign Film. That honor did not count for much in Fort Worth. Censors demanded cuts to the nonexplicit scene of sexual assault. The Capri refused to comply. Once again the Texas court stood behind its city censors: "We cannot say from this record that the 'Rape Scene,' which we have not viewed, is not indecent and is not obscene."[19] Without even viewing the film, the court upheld the prohibition on *Virgin Spring*.

Three years later Louis Malle's *Viva Maria!* (1965) was halted from playing a Dallas theater. The complaint was the film presented images of "sexual promiscuity" that could corrupt the minds of children. Similar to the *Virgin Spring* case, the Texas court upheld the censors. This time the theater owners appealed the decision to the U.S. Supreme Court. This time a different result was reached. The High Court recognized the need to protect minors from certain materials but maintained that such need for protection could not be seen as a green light for broader suppression. Content regulation must be "narrowly drawn, reasonable and [with] definite standards for the officials to follow."[20] By 1968, as censorship ordinances were falling around the country, Texas also found its film boards disfavored.

Brigitte Bardot (left) and Jeanne Moreau make South American rebellion sexy in *Viva Maria!* (1965).

In 1971, not long after municipal censor agencies were defunded, the Texas Film Commission (TFC) was established. Governor Preston Smith couched the TFC in positive terms, explaining that it was "in the social, economic and educational interest of Texas to encourage the development of the film-communication industry."[21] In time the commission would discover a new method of regulating content.

In 2007 the Texas legislature established the Texas Moving Image Industry Incentive Program, which allowed the TFC to administer grants to films produced in Texas.[22] With this power over purse strings came an insidious system of control. The TFC could deny funds to any project that "portrays Texas or Texans in a negative fashion."[23] Exactly how this "negative portrayal" calibration would be made or standardized was never clarified. Not only could the commission withhold valuable tax incentives from projects they didn't like, but also, even if permission was granted, the commission could revoke approval at any time. This left filmmakers in a lurch—if one scene made one bureaucrat at the TFC bristle, it could send the production into turnaround, effectively killing the project.

In 2010 the producer Emilio Ferrari was developing a film based on the siege of the

Branch Davidian compound in Waco. His $30 million budget hinged on a fifteen percent TFC rebate. The rebate was denied on grounds that the picture showed "Texans in a negative fashion."[24] The TFC commissioner also expressed disapproval based on his feeling that "the script was factually inaccurate."[25] This is an example of censorship imposed at its most arbitrary and capricious level. Under the First Amendment, there is no distinction for factual accuracy in creative content; state approval should not be a factor in whether a film can be made or funded. Ferrari's film was terminated. A pro–TFC advocate could argue that the producers were still free to make the film, just not with Texas tax-incentive funding. However, this view avoids the TFC's very raison d'être: to entice filmmakers to commit to producing locally. The "negative portrayal" provision created a loophole for the TFC, a state-supported bait-and-switch con game.

The "portrayal of Texas or Texans" provision was challenged in 2015. With *Machete* (2010), director Robert Rodriguez created an ode to B-movie exploitation flicks. The film starred Danny Trejo, an actor whose beautifully ravaged face could compress years of agony into a single stony glare. Trejo played a disgraced *federale* on an odyssey of revenge. Rodriguez's film used harsh Texas exteriors to reflect his character's bleak psychological inner landscape. *Machete* raised the critically disregarded genre of the exploitation film to an action-packed art form. Only, the TFC didn't see it that way.

Initially the TFC encouraged Rodriguez's Troublemaker Studios to shoot locally, approving *Machete* for acceptance into the incentive program.[26] The production spent $8 million in Texas and created hundreds of jobs for workers servicing the film. But once the TFC saw a trailer, they reneged on their commitment.[27] In the film, Trejo's character is hired to assassinate a Texas state senator bent on deporting illegal immigrants. Anti-immigrant activists seized on the picture to deluge the state film commission with complaints.[28] There were indications that Governor Rick Perry also applied pressure to encourage the TFC to revoke the incentives.[29] By reneging on promised support, the TFC, a state authority, was censoring content based on personal disapproval. This was a clear violation of First Amendment protections. Rodriguez's production company headed to court.

For Rodriguez, the question was whether the TFC's actions—denying payment on an approved financial rebate and incentive—represented an unconstitutional attempt by the state to influence the speech of movie producers. The complaint alleged that the TFC chilled free speech, impaired economic development, and subverted the state's Moving Image Industry Incentive Program.[30] The court positioned the issue differently, finding the state commission's denial could be appropriate at any stage, be it pre- or post production.[31] This decision stood as a warning to film producers intending to shoot in Texas: present the state positively or risk retaliation. Independent films that proceed with production relying on the TFC's commitment to participate may stand on shaky ground.

While the *Machete* case was a cautionary tale for producers, exhibitors can also find themselves pressured by state authorities. In April 2016 a pseudo-documentary entitled *Vaxxed: From Cover-Up to Catastrophe* (2016) was scheduled to play a Houston international film festival. *Vaxxed* investigated a purported connection between childhood vaccinations and autism. The mayor of Houston, Sylvester Turner, disagreed with the documentary's thesis and pressured the festival, which was heavily funded by city tax dollars, to cancel the screening. The film's producers offered to arrange a private screening for Turner but the mayor declined. The controversial doc was silenced. Mayor Turner's censorship was based on personal feelings and impulsive enforcement.[32]

The Lone Star State has a rich film history. From the earliest days Texas was an attractive venue for the first boxing blockbuster, but inclement weather hampered that production. Still, it was not long before movie men arrived to set up studios and make use of the diverse landscape. Although censorship was never enacted on a statewide level, municipalities set up their own means of film regulation.[33] Abilene, Corsicana, Dallas, Denison, El Paso, Fort Worth, and Houston all organized censor boards; Austin, by contrast, declined to empanel motion picture regulators.[34]

Over time, as censorship boards became disfavored by popular feeling and case law, the Texas Film Commission found an innovative method to rein in unsuitable content. While enticing filmmakers by offering incentives, the commission also wielded power to rescind their offers, an authority that held up in court. The Texas Moving Image Industry Incentive Program and Mayor Turner's actions provide examples of how the tension between free speech and state control still exists. Both film producers and film audiences must be mindful of rights that can all too easily become fettered by regulation.

Utah

The medium of motion pictures and the state of Utah share a birth date. The Salt Lake state joined the Union only four months before the first public exhibition of Edison's Vitascope.

In early films, one of Utah's most defining features, Mormonism, was portrayed as a strange and striking way of life. The Biograph-produced *A Trip to Salt Lake City* (1905) depicted a husband being henpecked—several times over. The one-shot short film is set on a train as a plural-married man puts his wives and mob of children to bed in a sleeper car. When the children ask for a glass of milk, their father rolls out a keg and attaches several straws to it. The humor here is slightly anti–Mormon; subsequent films on the subject quickly became darker. Before the end of the decade movie producers drew on "the Mormon problem" as fodder for films.[1]

A series of films presented horrific visions of the Mormon pioneers. The Danish company Nordisk released *A Victim of the Mormons* (1911), the story of a young girl abducted by a lecherous preacher. Pathé Frères followed with blood-soaked visions of the Western frontier in *An Episode of the Early Mormon Days* (1911) and *The Mountain Meadows Massacre* (1912). These pictures sensationalized a historical tragedy of 1857, depicting Joseph Smith and Brigham Young as leading the charge against wagon trains of settlers moving through the territory.[2] Pathé's polygamy thriller *Marriage or Death* (1912) angered Mormon elders, especially when the state censor board permitted the picture.[3] The disparaging genre continued with *The Mormon* (1912), produced by Flying "A," and *The Danites* (1912), produced by Selig. *The Danites* told the story of a fringe congregation that murders a family of ranchers. A brother and sister escape the massacre and are pursued by a bloodthirsty extremist group pledged to exterminate the trespassers.[4]

After the release of these anti–Mormon pictures, the Church of Jesus Christ of Latter-Day Saints (LDS) decided to take history into their own hands by commissioning movies that told their side of the story. *One Hundred Years of Mormonism* (1913), produced

The DANITES

Written by McKEE RANKIN. Produced by FRANCIS BOGGS

Mormons were portrayed as bloodthirsty, vengeful villains in Selig's *The Danites* (1912).

by the Utah Moving Picture Company, depicted the inspiring tale of the faith's struggle and triumph.[5] Following the success of *Hundred Years*, the LDS elders authorized two brothers, Chet and Shirl Lawson, to adapt the Book of Mormon to film. The Lawsons' aspirations were enormous, aiming to pictorialize the entire tale, from Lehi's exodus to Moroni's gold plates.

The first installment of the Lawsons' Mormon epic was entitled *The Life of Nephi* (1915). Despite a sympathetic audience eager to see the sacred text on-screen, subsequent chapters never came to pass. Like many silent pictures, *Nephi* disappeared into film history, until LDS archivist Brian Sokolowsky discovered forty stills in a weathered suitcase in 2002. Sokolowsky unpacked the stunning hand-painted images and rediscovered a lost chapter from regional film history. Produced the same year as America's first great historical epic film, *The Birth of a Nation* (1915), *Nephi*'s vivid plates are all that remain of a lost passion project.[6]

The golden era of Mormon cinema commenced in 1953 with the work of "Judge" Wetzel O. Whitaker. Judge Whitaker began his career as an animator for Walt Disney in 1939. He cut his teeth on shorts such as *Donald Gets Drafted* (1942) and *Donald's Off Day* (1944) before moving up to features. Whitaker was on the team that animated many of Disney's great classics, including *Cinderella* (1950), *Alice in Wonderland* (1951), and *Peter Pan* (1953).[7] Church apostles took notice of the animator and recalled him to Brigham

Young University (BYU) to start up LDS Motion Picture Studios. By 1963 only two academic institutions in the United States could boast fully operational movie studios: the University of Southern California and BYU—and BYU's was bigger.[8] Whitaker put out a steady stream of LDS-approved featurettes, including 'Til Death Do Us Part (1960), Worth Waiting For (1962), and Marriage: What Kind For You? (1967).

The ambitions of "Mollywood," a Mormon Hollywood based in Utah, were more fully realized by the year 2000. God's Army (2000), a story about missionaries in Los Angeles, was produced on a $300,000 budget and brought in over $2.6 million.[9] The Other Side of Heaven (2001) followed missionaries to Tonga and earned $4.7 million at the box office.[10] The faith-based war film Saints and Soldiers (2003) saw $1.3 million, profitable enough to warrant two sequels that strived to cross over and reach mainstream audiences: Saints and Soldiers: Airborne Creed (2012) and Saints and Soldiers: The Void (2014). Another trilogy, The Work and the Glory (2004), The Work and the Glory: American Zion (2005), and The Work and the Glory III: A House Divided (2006), financed in part by Utah Jazz owner Larry Miller, also demonstrated the hearty box office potential of faith-friendly films.[11]

While Utah's filmmakers were building a wholesome Hollywood that tracked with LDS values, the mainstream film industry was seeing an increase in violence and profanity. Fox's R-rated Deadpool (2016) took this trend to a new height. In Deadpool Ryan Reynolds played a cynical superhero who spews vulgarity and explodes with over-the-top violence. The result of Deadpool's pyrotechnic display was a payday of lucre. The picture took in nearly $350 million in its first six weeks.[12]

Box offices around the country welcomed Deadpool as the picture made up for a disappointing quarter of ticket sales. But not everyone was entertained.

One Friday night in February 2016, three agents of the Utah State Bureau of Investigation conducted a covert operation. Undercover as ordinary movie fans, they drank beers and took in a show.[13] Relaxing in the darkened theater, they watched as Reynolds mugged for the camera and villains were shot, stabbed, battered, and bruised. An extended sex montage, not explicit, in which Deadpool and his lover spend a year in various amorous positions, bothered the agents. And then it happened. In the picture's closing credits, an animated sequence pictured the hero atop a unicorn. The snarky, red-cloaked crusader caressed the animal's horn until it climaxed rainbows. To many who saw it, this was absurd.

To Agent Bradley Bullock, it was obscene. He set down his beer and returned to the office to draft a complaint. Bullock's report triggered an investigation into the violation of a state code that prohibited exhibitions of sexual simulation in a venue that served alcohol. In the past the law had been invoked to run risqué releases, such as The Hangover Part II (2011), Magic Mike XXL (2015) and Ted 2 (2015), out of town.[14] Those films, while raunchy, did not dare to pictorialize the climactic moment. Deadpool edged over the top; the Utah agents could not tolerate a crude cartoon ejaculating rainbows.

In recent years Utah recognized the broad protections of the First Amendment, reluctantly permitting even the most salacious cinema and championing free speech over poor taste. When Salt Lake City authorities attempted to shutter an adult movie grind house in 1980, the court denied them. While Chief Judge Aldon Anderson was sympathetic to the desire to regulate offensive content, he invalidated the city's obscenity ordinance as unconstitutionally overbroad.[15]

Deadpool presented a different situation. Overeager Utah SBI agents retrofitted the state's revised obscenity statute aimed at behavior at bikini bars to apply it to movie houses. This overreach is not consistent with the Constitution's guarantee of personal liberty and on September 1, 2017, the Utah district court struck down the law and ruled for the theater.[16] The strength of the First Amendment is that even the most gratuitous and absurd expression shall not be subject to government approval.

When movie screens became filled with images of hate speech aimed at Mormons, Utah filmmakers were motivated to take control of their own movies. The result is a regional industry that has survived and thrived by catering to a niche audience. While the state's homegrown film industry nurtured faith-based family values, the over-the-top sex and violence seen in mainstream Hollywood fare was not welcomed by Utah authorities. *Deadpool* might be an irreverent popcorn flick, but the lesson of Utah's overreaction is important. Free speech remains a vulnerable right. If we do not remain vigilant and question the motives of speech police, a century of progress that expanded personal liberties can quickly be lost.

Vermont

The green mountains of Vermont seem to be a world away from the hustle and bustle of the megalopolis of the Eastern Seaboard. Manhattan lies just three hundred miles south of Montpelier, but the difference is dramatic.

The towering pines and maples of the Green Mountain State are perfectly suited for a winter wonderland. Perhaps that's why Paramount Pictures set their Yuletide chestnut *White Christmas* (1954) in Vermont. Starring Bing Crosby and Danny Kaye and showcasing Irving Berlin's songs, *White Christmas* was tailor-made to be an evergreen seasonal film. The picture was a companion piece to *Holiday Inn* (1942), released by Paramount a dozen years earlier and set in nearby Connecticut. Frank Capra's Christmas masterpiece *It's a Wonderful Life* (1946) took place in Bedford Falls, a fictional upper New York State town, but the director had paid cinematic homage to Vermont a decade earlier. In *Mr. Deeds Goes to Town* (1936) Gary Cooper played an unassumingly modest man, a resident of Mandrake Falls, a fictional Vermont village. When Deeds inherits $1 million, he finds the money comes with a world of trouble. He ultimately uses his treasure trove to finance a utopia of collective farming for needy Vermonter families—a strangely socialist conclusion for a film by one of midcentury America's most popular directors.[1]

Several of Hollywood's great stars and directors relied on the rustic settings of Vermont to complete their film-scapes. William A. Wellman introduced his screwball damsel in distress Carole Lombard in *Nothing Sacred* (1937) in Warsaw, another fictional Vermont town. As her vision dimmed, Bette Davis's character's last recollection would be of her Vermont garden in *Dark Victory* (1939). Alfred Hitchcock called on Vermont in two pictures. In *Spellbound* (1945), Ingrid Bergman encountered a shady man with no past—played by Gregory Peck—at a Vermont mental hospital. This film also boasted a stylish dream sequence designed by surrealist painter Salvador Dalí. A decade later the Master of Suspense returned to shoot *The Trouble with Harry* (1955). Harry is a dead body; the trouble is what to do with him. While the dark comedy of *Harry* was a rare flop for Hitch upon release, the gag of a bothersome corpse would become a motion picture trope, most notably in *Weekend at Bernie's* (1989), a film better in concept than execution.

D.W. Griffith crafted the most iconic image of Vermont on film in *Way Down East* (1920). The famous ice-floe sequence was shot on location at the White River Junction.[2] In the film Lillian Gish plays a tragic character. After the death of her baby she wanders into an oncoming nor'easter, a blinding blizzard. She loses her way and ends up on an ice floe drifting toward a waterfall and certain doom. This was a Griffith movie, so her last minute rescue was de rigueur. The scene was shot outdoors under merciless winter conditions. According to reports, as icicles formed on Gish's eyelashes, Griffith insisted on shooting her close-ups before allowing the crew to offer her a blanket.[3] With suffering for the sake of art, the scene lives on as a masterpiece.

Not everyone appreciated *Way Down East*. Pennsylvania's board of film regulators objected to the picture's birth sequence. Images of birth, no matter how nonexplicit, were off limits. Childbirth was a topic seen as inappropriate in entertainment, so the scene was censored in the Keystone State.[4] The death of Gish's infant, however, was permitted by Pennsylvania.

Pennsylvania had enacted its film censorship law in 1911; a similar measure was introduced in Vermont in 1917.[5] The Vermont proposal died in committee. In 1921 the issue returned as the topic of motion picture regulation came before the statehouse in a bill to "restrict the showing of pictures which are thought to be corrupting or tending to promote crime."[6] What followed was a hotly debated topic pitting motion picture promoters—with an ally in Vermont native Calvin Coolidge—against an outspoken cadre of pastors and self-proclaimed moralists.[7]

Only months after statewide censorship was voted down in Montpelier, the city of Burlington amended its char-

D.W. Griffith's *Way Down East* (1920) exposed Lillian Gish to the elements, famously trapping her on an icy river heading for doom.

ter in April 1921 to create a moving picture censorship board for the city.[8] While Vermont technically remained a noncensoring state, its largest city had a censor board, which effectively meant regulation for the entire region by default.

Decades later one member of the Vermont establishment spoke up in a bold voice. In 1995 then state representative Matt Dunne founded the Vermont Film Commission. By 2005, while serving as state senator, Dunne penned an insightful article on the motion pictures industry. He considered three recently released films that had courted controversy: *The Passion of the Christ* (2004), Mel Gibson's ultraviolent retelling of the climactic New Testament moment; *The Day After Tomorrow* (2004), a cautionary climate-change natural-disaster film; and *Fahrenheit 9/11* (2004), Michael Moore's documentary lambasting George W. Bush. Whether Dunne agreed with the filmmakers' points of view or not, he found their courage both an inspiration and a signal of the emerging rift in American culture: "While concern over censorship, either political or corporate, is a real issue today, the recent controversy may actually be the harbinger of a renewal of politically and socially charged productions … [which are] redefining the film industry business model to match the new polarized American audience."[9] Dunne rightly foresaw a widening cultural fissure in the nation's fabric. Political leanings were transforming from passions to fashions, from deeply held beliefs to marketing campaigns. The Vermont statesman predicted that filmmakers "may soon have to worry about injecting controversy [into their pictures] in order to make them economically viable."[10]

Writing in 2004, Dunne had faith that filmmakers with a message in mind, the courage to deliver it, and a market that was accepting of diverse opinions would be valuable to the democratic dialogue. A decade later the results appear less positive and more polarizing. Movies could be seen as early symptoms of deep divisions in the body politic. Dunne hoped controversial content could create a market for well-meaning discourse and persuade audiences to think about issues. Instead, the country fractured into factions from which it has not emerged.

State censorship presents a dangerous suppression of free speech. The division of American audiences is equally alarming. The path to the future is clear but not easy, requiring cooperation, collaboration, compassion, patience, and tolerance. Modern mass media has played a role in creating and intensifying this division, but in the hands of thoughtful filmmakers, the media can reach out and repair seemingly unmendable rifts.

Virginia

Lost to memory and buried in film history is a racially charged battle between free speech and censorship. The two opponents were an aging Virginia administrator named Evan R. Chesterman and a firebrand director of race movies, Oscar Micheaux.

Beginning in 1919, Micheaux emerged as a pioneering black filmmaker who wrote, directed, produced, and self-distributed "race movies." His films were made for African American audiences, featured African American actors, and focused on issues tailored to his viewers, such as "passing," mixed-race relationships, and attitudes about skin tone (see South Dakota). Micheaux offered an alternative to Hollywood pictures with titles

Oscar Micheaux directed *God's Step Children* (1938), focusing on race issues a decade before Hollywood discovered socially conscious films.

such as *Within Our Gates* (1920), *The Symbol of the Unconquered* (1920), and *God's Step Children* (1938). To some, he was a filmmaker whose ideas were ahead of his time, but to the Virginia film board, Micheaux was a nuisance. Chesterman, at the helm of the state's film bureau, was the author of a book entitled *Things Mundane*.[1] These two men lived their lives at the opposite ends of the American experience: one a maverick entertainer known for his flair, the other a desk-bound bureaucrat.

Micheaux was an established name, having already released four films, when he was contacted by some potential investors, a group of African American businessmen based in Roanoke. Following the money, Micheaux set up an office in the Gainsboro area of Roanoke in 1922. This would become the director's southern base of operations for his next six films—three years' time, by Micheaux's tireless schedule.[2]

Meanwhile, Chesterman was moving up in Virginia's bureaucratic ranks. In April 1922 he was appointed to a three-year term on the state board of motion picture censors.[3] Chesterman reviewed films for inappropriate content and issued licenses for exhibition within the state. Within five months his commission reported on 150 miles of motion picture film.[4] The two men were headed for a collision.

In February 1924 Micheaux began exhibiting *Birthright* (1924) in Virginia without a license. It is unclear whether he ever submitted his film for approval, but when the board was notified of the unlicensed exhibitions, they sent notices to Lynchburg, Norfolk,

Roanoke, and other cities: "The exhibition of *Birthright* is an audacious and inexcusable violation of the Censorship Act.... We have reason to believe that [the film] bears upon the race question and embodies sub-titles which this board would find most objection-able."[5] Micheaux reached out to Chesterman with a sob story. He would have obtained a license, he claimed, and should have, but somehow the certificate had been overlooked by his film company. The film board fined Micheaux twenty-five dollars and noted that the director admitted to the unpermitted exhibition but "told a somewhat pathetic story of financial difficulties, mismanagement on the part of subordinates, and partial ignorance of the law."[6]

Only a few months later Micheaux was back with a new film, *A Son of Satan* (1924). This time the film was submitted for review. It was promptly rejected: "The central figure in the plot is a mulatto.... [B]y implication at least the audience is led to believe that the criminal tendencies of the man are inherited from his white forefathers. *A Son of Satan*, at best, is unwholesome as it touches unpleasantly on miscegenation .... [and] will prove irritating if not hurtful alike to quadroons, octoroons, half-breeds, and those of pure African descent."[7] Virginia's film censorship bureau feared Micheaux's inflammatory scenes could lead to racial unrest, but they masked this concern in moral trappings: "In all probability [the film] will be offered only to negro theaters where a large proportion of the audience will doubtless be illiterate, or so ignorant as to misinterpret even what is good in the films."[8]

Micheaux produced his third film in Virginia, *The House Behind the Cedars* (1927). Once again the director focused on forbidden subject matter. *Cedars* was a feature-length essay on the temptations of miscegenation, and it was adapted from the true-life headline-making story of Leonard "Kip" Rhinelander and Alice Beatrice Jones. Rhinelander had married the beautiful Jones but sued her for fraud when he discovered post-nuptials that his wife had been hiding her biracial heritage.[9] The story was scandalous, involving race, sex, passing, and a courtroom drama. It was an irresistible scenario to Micheaux. But not to Chesterman. The Virginia film board found *Cedars* inappropriate for motion picture entertainment.

In 1924 the state legislature amended the code of Virginia to more strictly define racial identity. Section 5099(a)(2) of the code, entitled "Preservation of Racial Identity," made it a felony for any person to knowingly falsify their race or birth certificate.[10] Chesterman's board of censors rejected *House Behind the Cedars*, commenting that the picture "indirectly contravenes the spirit of the recently enacted anti-miscegenation law."[11] Chesterman, acting as an agent of the state, used his position as a moral authority to maintain segregation on-screen. His reasoning was paternalistic, arising from the perceived need to protect minority audiences from these unsavory images for their own good.

As the sound era approached, Micheaux was one of the few race filmmakers to survive the transition to talkies. Chesterman's transition was not as successful; he died in 1931.[12] Micheaux, on the other hand, continued to make movies like a force of nature, updating *House Behind the Cedars* as *Veiled Aristocrats* (1932), as well as directing musicals, such as *The Darktown Revue* (1930); gangster pictures, including *The Girl from Chicago* (1933); and mysteries, like *Murder in Harlem* (1935). Shooting on shoestring budgets and unconcerned with technical quality, Micheaux soldiered on until the years caught up with him. He released his final film in 1948—after thirty years of do-it-yourself filmmaking.

Virginia's rich history of filmmaking and film censorship started before the Micheaux-Chesterman saga and continued long after. Virginians became interested in motion pictures as early as 1897.[13] Only the practical realities of a new medium could hinder the film fad—Richmond audiences excited to view a boxing match went home disappointed when the eight-hundred-pound projector fell off a delivery wagon, "busting" the machine.[14]

As movies gained popularity, the flickering images came to the attention of bluenosed members of an older generation. In Richmond, a film ordinance was enacted in 1916 over the objections of Mayor George Ainslie, who called the bill "unnecessary."[15] Two years later the state legislature considered a statewide board of motion picture censors. The proposal moved in and out of committee, weighing moral protection against censorship's drain on state finances.[16] Free speech was never a consideration. By March 15, 1922, a film censorship law was passed, directing a three-member panel to examine motion pictures for content that could be considered obscene, indecent, or inhuman and for themes that would tend to corrupt morals or incite viewers to crime.[17] It was under this law that Chesterman was installed, along with a co-censor, Emma Speed.[18] Prior to her career as a state censor, Speed had authored comedic pulp novels, including *Mammy's White Folks* and *Miss Minerva's Baby*.[19]

During the 1920s films were routinely passed or edited, with little drama aside from the Chesterman-Micheaux sideshow. In fact, by collecting license fees, the board proved to be a moneymaker for the state, allaying concerns that the agency would drain state resources.[20]

By the 1930s, emphasis shifted away from race issues toward other controversial topics. Paramount's jazz-age fable of a fast-living flapper, *Confessions of a Co-Ed* (1931), was rejected as too sexy.[21] *Hitler—The Beast of Berlin* (1939), one of America's earliest antifascist films, was barred in Virginia. *Beast of Berlin* was directed by Sam Newfield, a filmmaker best remembered for his bottom-of-the-bill titles like the all-monkey prison film *The Little Big House* (1930), the all-dwarf Western *The Terror of Tiny Town* (1938), and the ultra-low-budget horror film *The Invisible Killer* (1939). *Beast of Berlin* was equally over the top but also politically risky, released two years before the United States entered World War II. Unwilling to offend the Führer or Virginia's German citizenry, the censors refused to issue *Beast* a release permit on grounds it "would arouse violent resentment against Germany and tend to incite crime."[22]

The following year another important censorship case made Virginia headlines. The American Committee on Maternal Welfare commissioned an educational film on prenatal care. Released as *The Birth of a Baby* (1938), the docudrama was hailed as "important," artistic, and sensitive. Although Virginia's state-run board of censors passed the picture, Lynchburg's authorities threatened to storm the projection booth on opening night. The Dominion Theater convinced the court to issue an order to prevent police interference. The issue turned not on the film's content but on the balance of power—if the *state* censor board had passed the film, the court found, then *city* authorities must abide by that decision.[23] *The Birth of a Baby* played on. Pictures could still be cut and banned, but one level of the bureaucracy was stripped away.

By 1950 a new regime of motion picture authorities took over in Virginia. This administration of all-female film censors was composed of Chairperson Mrs. Russell F. Wagners, Lollie C. Whitehead, and Margaret K. Gregory, "three gentle grandmothers who witness more violence than any other movie-goers in the state."[24] A decade later this

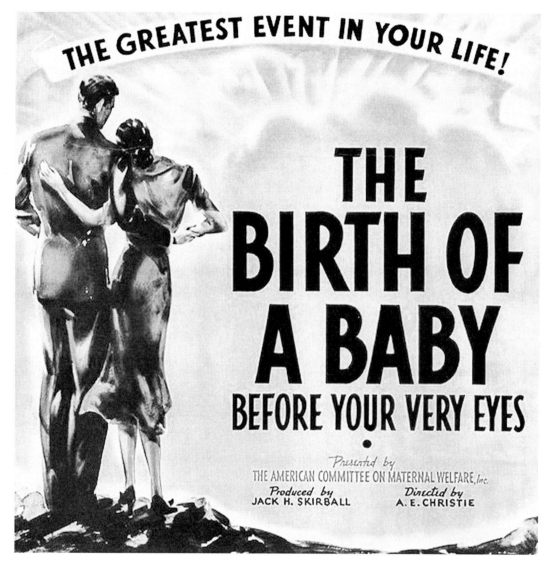

THE GREATEST EVENT IN YOUR LIFE!

THE BIRTH OF A BABY

BEFORE YOUR VERY EYES

•

Presented by
THE AMERICAN COMMITTEE ON MATERNAL WELFARE, *Inc.*
Produced by   *Directed by*
JACK H. SKIRBALL   A. E. CHRISTIE

Intended as a serious documentary, *The Birth of a Baby* (1938) was seen by some as titillating and indecent.

trio was still at work screening films, but they were a dying breed. By that time, in 1963, only four states beside Virginia still funded censor commissions: New York, Kansas, and Maryland.

The end came in an unlikely blaze of sun and sand. A British documentary entitled *Traveling Light* (1961) ogled naturalist sunbathers at a nude beach in Corsica. Mrs. Wagners considered the film obscene. She declared that she would only pass it if the nude scenes were cut out.[25] That would leave the filmmakers with less on than their sunbathers: "except for a few travel scenes, that is the movie," complained the filmmakers.[26] They challenged the censors, and Virginia's forty-year-old censorship ordinance came under scrutiny. Looking at the Supreme Court's recent *Miracle* decision (see New York), the Richmond circuit court judge, John Wingo Knowles, struck down Virginia's movie cen-

Nudism on the sun-kissed island of Corsica became an alluring midnight movie in America as seen in *Traveling Light* (1961).

sorship statute. He held that it was an unconstitutional infringement on the freedom of speech.[27] Without a censorship statute in place, Virginia's board of review would survive for only a few more years. The censors no longer had any teeth. In 1968 the board was disbanded.

Virginia has a rich and varied history of film censorship, but in the end, whether the theme was mixed-race romance or sunbaked bottoms, filmmakers fought for freedom of the screen in the Old Dominion State.

Washington

The vistas of Washington State provide a glimpse of untouched America as it once was, from the mighty Columbia River to the Cascade Range and steaming Mount St. Helens. Dwarfed by vast natural wonders, humans seem small. But when the camera zooms in on a Washington State character ... very often there is something that's off.

Look at Bella Swan (Kristen Stewart) as she moves to a small town on the Olympic Peninsula in *Twilight* (2008). Bella might seem like the typical teenager next door, if perhaps a little more sensitive. Definitely not the type of girl who would get mixed up in a love triangle with a vampire and werewolf. Or consider the fictional town of Twin Peaks. It might appear to be a typical sleepy village, except for the unsolved murder of the beautiful homecoming queen. And several other unsettling details involving backward-speaking dwarves, giants, and demonic predators. The stone-faced federal agent played by Kyle MacLachlan approached these oddities with a business-as-usual flair in the two-season TV series (1990–1991), its motion picture spin-off, *Twin Peaks: Fire Walk with Me* (1992), and a limited revival in 2017.

Other weirdness in Washington State might include a high schooler on the verge of starting all-out nuclear war in *WarGames* (1983), or a cursed videotape that leads to the death of the viewer seven days after watching it. *The Ring* (2002) was adapted from a Japanese psychological horror film, but the landscapes of the Pacific Northwest helped isolate each character, making for an even more eerie thriller. On both sides of the Pacific, *The Ring* threw off sequels and remakes, including *Rings* (2005), *The Ring Two* (2005), and *Rings* (2016), that kept teenaged thrill-seeking audiences on the edge of their seats.

One hundred years earlier, young moviegoers were enjoying scenes that similarly infuriated adult authority figures. Spokane's police began monitoring nickelodeons as early as 1910. By 1913, Mayor Nelson Pratt banned a film teaching tango steps, commenting, "I won't let my daughter do those dances."[1] The film Mayor Pratt was likely referring to was *Motion Picture Dancing Lessons* (1913), in which Wallace "Old Man" McCutcheon demonstrated his smooth moves for the camera. McCutcheon was one of the first directors in the movie business, with work dating back to before 1903. He was over fifty when he performed the tango for the camera—which probably didn't paint the most titillating picture, but it was enough to get him banned in Spokane.

In Seattle, Samuel Glasgow was appointed city commissioner of public works, the organization that oversaw movie regulation in 1914.[2] As Seattle's censor, Glasgow took his job as moral arbiter for the Pacific Northwest very seriously. *War's Women* (1915) was confiscated from theaters.[3] *Smashing the Vice Trust* (1914) was banned.[4] But when the most controversial film of the day arrived—*The Birth of a Nation* (1915)—Glasgow gave it a pass. The censor pooh-poohed the concerns of minority audiences as being overly sensitive about the picture's racist element. Although he dismissed "the unwarranted fear of the results [the film] may have," he did snip one scene.[5] Cutting a close-up of the rapacious ex-slave Gus's face as he pursued Flora to her death made the film more palatable to the censor.

Film morals remained a priority in Seattle, where Bertha Landes became the first female mayor of a major American city. As news of Charlie Chaplin's divorce from Lita Grey made headlines in 1927, Landes directed her censors to consider whether the comedian's films should be barred from exhibition based on his personal immorality.[6]

Following its showings in Seattle, *The Birth of a Nation* also became a trigger in Tacoma. The picture was considered so controversial that city commissioner F.H. Pettit convened a fifteen-member censor board. Mindful of the racial issues at hand, Pettit was vigilant to place minority screeners on the panel.[7] Nevertheless, after viewing the Civil War epic, the panel approved the picture, and it played to packed auditoriums.[8] This was not the same result for *Sapho* (1913) and *Undine* (1916), both films that contained nudity, and a prostitution/police drama entitled *Who's Your Neighbor?* (1917).[9] Each of these racy films was banned from Tacoma cinemas. Tacoma passed a formal censorship ordinance in 1917, banning any picture deemed "immoral, obscene, lewd, lascivious, suggestive, or of any indecent character, or which shall tend to exert a harmful influence upon public morals, or which portrays brutality, or which shall tend to disturb the peace."[10] Pettit organized a morality militia, naming Mrs. Leonard Crassweller, Mrs. Harriett Hazeltine, and the Rev. Lamont Hay as his top officers.[11]

Even with systems of municipal authorities in place watching for off-color entertainment, most films arrived in Washington State preapproved. Various nongovernmental institutions vetted films, from the Motion Picture Producers and Distributors Association to the National Board of Review and the film division of the Catholic Legion of Decency. It wasn't until after World War II that Washington's film regulators made their voices heard with increasing regularity. Spokane put the kibosh on Howard Hughes's cleavage-baring cowboy film *The Outlaw* (1943) in 1946.[12] Seattle cut *Rope* (1948), criticizing the film because "it was not apparent enough that the guilty are punished for their crime and it does not seem to be a proper picture for children and for impressionable adults."[13]

As more explicit content emerged in Washington theaters, authorities sought out new tools to enforce morality in media. The first method was the use of the state's obscenity statute. Radley Metzger was a stylish director, able to walk a fine line by keeping his films suggestive but not descending fully into explicit hard-core content. When Metzger's soft-core adaptation of the Bizet opera *Carmen*, entitled *Carmen, Baby* (1967), played at the Park Y drive-in in Richland, the theater was cited. The director's arty titillation held little sway with Judge Frank Little. Little found the film obscene, further commenting, "It seems to me the major crime involved would be petty larceny for charging people admission to see it."[14]

Metzger appealed to the U.S. Supreme Court. The High Court overturned Judge Little's decision. Little's holding had rested on a recently passed provision of the state's obscenity law tailored specifically for nudity on outdoor movie screens.[15] The theater owner did not have fair notice of the regulation. The case was reversed on procedural grounds—the alleged obscenity of *Carmen, Baby* was beside the point.

Spokane attempted another strategy, invoking one of the state's stranger regulations. The law at issue prohibited materials that could incite lust. Once again SCOTUS struck the law. This time, rather than fair notice, the flaw in the law was an overly broad prohibition: "The word [lust] had come to be understood as referring to a healthy, wholesome, human reaction common to millions of well-adjusted persons in our society, rather than to any shameful or morbid desire."[16] Banning materials that incited lust could too easily conflict with constitutionally protected content.

The town of Renton tested a third strategy to rein in inappropriate content: creative use of zoning laws. Zoning did not explicitly ban the racy content exhibited at adult theaters but rather forbade the grind houses from operating within one thousand feet of residential areas or schools.[17] Playtime Theatres found themselves in that forbidden zone. The theater owners challenged the law, hoping to continue the winning streak of Washington's free speech advocates. This time, however, on appeal to the Supreme Court the zoning law was upheld. The zoning statute was a narrowly tailored and effective method of regulating adult venues. Zoning could condemn inappropriate content to less accessible locations while not silencing undesirable speech.

While it could effectively contain adult-oriented businesses, zoning had other consequences. By labeling certain expression and confining it to specific areas, authorities could chill unorthodox opinions while sidestepping constitutional protections. The city of Renton used zoning as a shield to protect their community; however, zoning can also be used aggressively to corral and silence voices outside of the mainstream current of thought and belief.

In Renton the seeds were sown for "free speech zones" that soon sprouted on college campuses around the nation. Speech zones were intended to enforce civility and respect but could also enable authorities and administrators to suppress expression.[18] On-campus protests could be stifled, and unfavorable opinions could be branded as micro-aggressions. Renton's zoning regulation successfully banished certain films, but the strategy had a consequence, giving new ammunition to censors under a new name. Just like in the picturesque township of Twin Peaks, all might look fine on the surface, but the shadow of suppression can fall cross that landscape.

West Virginia

In the earliest days of motion pictures, the work of four West Virginians took experimental technology to a new level. Maj. Woodville Latham was an inventor; his sons, Otway and Grey Latham, exhibitors; and Enoch J. Rector, a promoter and marketing man. Together these four West Virginians paved the way for the commercial film industry that soon developed.

Their film venture began as an afterthought. Otway Latham left the Appalachian region for New York, where he found work managing a pharmaceutical firm. He saw a prototype of the Kinetoscope in May 1894 and bought in as one of Edison's earliest franchisees. By August, Otway set up the Kinetoscope Exhibition Company with his brother Grey and a classmate from Parkersburg, West Virginia, named Enoch Rector.[1] The Latham brothers and Rector, along with Otway's former boss acting as financier, Samuel J. Tilden, were among the first entrepreneurs to enter the film business.[2]

The following month the Kinetoscope Exhibition Company opened a parlor at 83 Nassau Street in New York City. Their first program offered a film of the Corbett-Courtney boxing bout shot in the Black Maria. News of the film fight set off alarms. In New Jersey a grand jury was convened to determine whether films of the matchup violated the state's anti-prizefighting law. Authorities stormed into Edison's Menlo Park laboratory and paid a visit to the Kinetoscope Company. "I shouldn't be surprised if they tried to pull us all [in]," Rector told the *New York Evening World*. "However, I think it can easily be proven that we have violated no law. The affair was conducted for scientific purposes … and was neither rough nor brutal."[3] No violation was found. Although the actual fistic ballet remained illegal, motion pictures of the event would not be censored (see Maine). In October 1894 Grey Latham negotiated for the Kinetoscope Company's next feature, pitting "Gentleman Jim" Corbett against "Lanky Bob" Fitzsimmons. Although Grey had difficulty finding a location to stage the event, the motion picture was a presold property. Enthusiastic audiences stood ready to plug their nickels into Kinetoscope machines to see the fight.[4]

Having attracted a sizable crowd of customers, the Latham brothers aspired to put on a better show. The Edison Kinetoscope device was a single-viewer system. Patrons queued up to watch their minute of entertainment through a viewfinder. The Lathams dreamed of projecting boxing bouts on a screen. This would have two great advantages. First, operating costs could be lowered because screening rooms would require a single machine instead of a battery of Kinetoscopes. Second, the projected image would transform the medium from a solitary activity into a group event. The question was how to make this aspiration a technological reality.

Perhaps this question dominated the Lathams' Christmas dinner conversation that year. Their father, Maj. Woodville Latham, a veteran of the Confederate Army, had been teaching chemistry at the University of West Virginia. After serving on the battlefield, Woodville found he was not cut out for academic life. At one point university regents investigated Woodville on charges of profanity. Witnesses heard him spout salty talk such as, "Botheration dod burn the d—d thing [sic]."[5] Woodville was acquitted but instructed to find a new career. It didn't seem to take much convincing for Woodville to join his sons in their new venture. The Lambda Company, with Grey as president, Otway as vice president, and Maj. Woodville as secretary and treasurer, was chartered on December 29, 1894. The Lathams intended to devise and manufacture an innovative motion picture device, focusing specifically on projection.[6]

Woodville spearheaded the project and Lambda's secretive research and development lab became a harbor for dissatisfied Edison employees. W.K.L. Dickson had been the chief engineer on Edison's film project but became increasingly unhappy as the great inventor took credit for his contributions. Eugène Lauste, also present at the inception of motion pictures and a fellow Edison malcontent, also joined Lambda.[7] In less than six months the Lambda team built a projecting prototype. "Prof. Woodville Latham yesterday gave a private exhibition of the workings of what he calls a Panopticon," the *New York Times* reported in April 1895. Lambda's device was "precisely like that of a Kinetoscope only that the pictures are much larger and can be seen by a large number of people assembled in the darkened room."[8] Three weeks later Lambda premiered a boxing film on their new format: *Young Griffo v. Battling Charles Barnett* (1895).[9]

The Lathams continued to improve on their device, unveiling an improved version called the Eidoloscope by July 1895.[10] Woodville set his shutter speed at forty frames per second for a crisp image.[11] To allow for longer films, they engineered what came to be known as "the Latham Loop." The Latham Loop was a slackened section of celluloid that reduced pull, eased strain, and alleviated tension on the filmstrip as it moved through the projector's gate. The concept was likely developed by Dickson and Lauste, but the Lathams quickly claimed—and patented—the innovation. The Latham Loop was an important advance for the motion pictures industry, a technical modification that paved the way for feature films. The Loop would also become the subject of a mountain of litigation.

Tasting success, the Lathams and Rector became mired in internal squabbling, legal problems, technical challenges, and increasing debt. Rector and Tilden left the fold to develop the Veriscope Company, which produced a wide-screen IMAX-like format. The Veriscope venture centered on a boxing bout that anticipated high box office returns: the heavyweight championship bout pitting Corbett against Fitzsimmons. After considerable drama surrounding production, the pugilists took to the ring in Carson City, Nevada, on March 17, 1897.[12] *The Corbett-Fitzsimmons Fight* (1897), directed by Rector, has been considered the first feature-length film and the longest made up to that date, covering fourteen rounds of fighting and over one hundred minutes of film (see Nevada).

Unlike Rector, the Lathams did not have a second act. After the collapse of Lambda, their valuable Loop patent was sold to E & H. T. Anthony Co., which passed it to Anthony & Scovill Co. (Ansco), a photographic lab and competitor to Eastman Kodak. The Lathams' intellectual property was transferred from Ansco to Edison's major rival, American Mutoscope and Biograph.[13] Biograph had been acquiring numerous patents, which they used as leverage in legal battles against their arch competitor.[14] Ultimately, Edison and Biograph settled, pooling their patents in the Motion Picture Patent Company and forming a cartel intended to freeze out independent filmmakers. By then the Lathams were already a film industry footnote.

Grey and Otway moved into the real estate business in New York. By August 1906 Otway died, the circumstances unrecorded; seven months later, Grey tumbled off a streetcar near Astor Place in Greenwich Village and died.[15] Maj. Woodville lived to testify in numerous patent suits before he died in 1911.[16] The story of how four sons of West Virginia played a role in the invention of movies had come to an end. But movies in West Virginia were just beginning.

The first motion pictures to screen in the Mountain State arrived in 1894.[17] The issue of censorship arose in Charleston when Mayor George Breece and Police Chief Adam McCown tried to ban *The Birth of a Nation* (1915). The racially provocative content of the film motivated moral authorities around the nation to speak out, but when Mayor Breece and Chief McCown announced their plan to prevent any screenings, the Kanawha Circuit Court stepped in. Judge Sam D. Littlepage approved an injunction to stop any state interference.[18] *Birth* played on in West Virginia.

Unhappy with Littlepage's decision, West Virginia legislators appointed a film censorship council, which convened the following year in 1916.[19] These administrators were prepared when *Birth* returned to the state in 1918, and they promptly banned the film. "The picture is calculated to stir up hatred and prejudice," ruled the regulators. "This would result in a bad effect … and hinder proper co-operation between the races."[20] The state senate approved a more elaborate bill in 1921 that mandated a censor board bar films deemed sacrilegious, obscene, indecent, or immoral.[21] The board remained active through 1960; however, its censoring activities were limited. Since West Virginia generally received prints imported through Ohio, Pennsylvania, Maryland, or Virginia—all states that rigorously regulated films—the West Virginia censors' job was generally handled before films crossed the border.[22]

One of the most famous films set in West Virginia caused alarm to censor boards outside of the state. Charles Laughton's stylish and stylized *The Night of the Hunter* (1955) featured Robert Mitchum posing as a corrupt, murderous preacher hunting two children with a connection to stolen loot. Teeming with suppressed sexuality, homicidal infidelity, immorality, and the menacing pursuit of vulnerable children, it was foreseeable that *Hunter* could raise alarms. Despite the controversial material, the picture was an artistic gem. Four decades after she starred in *The Birth of a Nation* (1915), Lillian Gish played a frail old woman in *Hunter*; the silhouette of her character seated in a rocking chair with shotgun at the ready would become an iconic image in film history. Mitchum contributed his own indelible character, appearing with memorably inked knuckles tattooed "love" and "hate." At the time of the film's release, censors saw *Night of the Hunter* not as art but as a corrupting influence on children. The film was banned in Memphis, as well as in Australia and Sweden.[23] Although domestic and international censors shut down the film as a dangerous and depraved vision, *Hunter* played without incident in West Virginia.

West Virginia was a rare state with a censorship ordinance on the books and a regulatory council sitting in session but finding little to act on. The legacy of West Virginia's visionary inventors stands as the Mountain State's greatest contribution to film history.

Wisconsin

The final scene of *The Way of All Flesh* (1927) takes place on a snowy Wisconsin street corner. A destitute man separated from his family for years glimpses his grown son through a window. The boy he once taught to play violin is now a celebrated virtuoso. The winds howl silently, but the old man is filled with warm joy.

When *The Way of All Flesh* premiered, critics called it Emil Jannings's perfect performance.[1] The *New York Times* named it one of the ten best films of the year.[2] Jannings was feted and awarded with the first Academy Award for Best Actor. But no one alive today has ever seen this film.

Jannings was best known as the leading actor of German cinema, having starred in such international hits as *Madame DuBarry* (1919), *The Last Laugh* (1924), and *Faust* (1926). *The Way of All Flesh* was his Hollywood debut. The story focused on the trusted cashier of a Milwaukee bank. Given a briefcase of bonds to deliver to Chicago, the cashier succumbs to a woman's charms. He wakes from a drunken sleep to discover his valuables gone.[3] *Flesh* follows the character's descent into depression and desperation. "In spite of its extravagant sentimental ending," the *New York Times* wrote, "[*Flesh*] is a film that revealed that Emil Jannings could do as good work in Hollywood as he did in Berlin."[4]

Although Ernst Lubitsch's *The Patriot* (1928) was nominated for four Academy Awards and claimed Best Writing, the film is now considered lost.

Unfortunately, the celebrated picture is now lost. All that exists is an excerpt of the final scene. The following year, Jannings starred in the Russian-set film *The Patriot* (1928). Playing the treacherous Tsar Paul I, Jannings demonstrated his talent as a monstrous menace. *The Patriot* was nominated for an Academy Award, but that film, too, has been lost. These lost films are notable because of the attention they received, but they are not alone. According to the Library of Congress, less than fifteen percent of the estimated eleven thousand silent films released by major studios still exist.[5] Some films resurface, but those are the exceptions. Even films that have not disappeared are at risk. If not properly preserved, nitrate film stock degenerates into goo. Films that don't decompose can burst into flame, as the nitrate film stock is highly flammable. In 1937 Fox Film's entire silent film archive ignited and was destroyed.[6] In 1978 a spark at Universal wiped out another period of film history.[7] Other damage to films of the silent era was intentional. During World War II, many films were stripped of their silver nitrate, which was repurposed in the production of munitions. Other films were intentionally thrown away, seen as valueless relics of a bygone era.

The lesson of Jannings's lost performances is instructive. We must find, save, and preserve our film history, or risk the films dissolving into the mists of memory.

Although Wisconsin was the setting for Emil Jannings's American debut, few people today might mistake the Badger State for Hollywood. Yet in the early years of filmmaking, Milwaukee was a movie hub. Waukesha natives Harry Aitken and his brother Roy established the Western Film Exchange in 1906, which distributed films to regional theaters. At the time, the Motion Picture Patent Company (MPPC) strived to control all production and, through its subsidiary General Film, monopolize distribution. This cartel worked to freeze out independent companies like the Aitkens'.[8]

From their Wisconsin offices, the Aitkens could put some distance between their operations and the MPPC's enforcement brigades. But the Aitkens needed pictures in their pipeline to distribute, so in 1910 they partnered with a Chicago-based production shingle, American Film Manufacturing or Flying 'A' Studios. Securing a new round of financing in 1912, the Aitkens and their partner, John Freuler, a Milwaukee-based realtor, opened a new operation called Mutual Films.[9] Mutual distributed movies and newsreels from their Milwaukee headquarters and Chicago studio.

The future of this midwestern movie factory looked promising until the mayor of Milwaukee appointed a censor board in 1913. The city council authorized Mayor Gerhard Adolph Bading to set up a seven-member film review division. The board included the president of the Milwaukee Bar Association and union representatives, as well as members of Edison's MPPC.[10] Getting films past these administrators could be difficult enough, but Edison operatives saw to it that it would be more difficult for some than for others.

The Milwaukee film censorship commission was charged with reviewing films and cutting inappropriate content. *The Birth of a Nation* (1915) was criticized but permitted.[11] Not so for a prostitution/police procedural starring Lottie Pickford, Mary's little sister, called *The House of Bondage* (1914). *Bondage* was banned.[12] In Madison, a censor board was proposed in 1919. It was up and running a decade later.[13] Mayor—soon to be Governor—Albert Schmedeman led the charge to shut down an edu-exploitation birth-control flick called *No More Children* (1929).[14] Other risqué pictures, including *What Price Glory* (1926) and *Party Girl* (1930), raised eyebrows but were permitted to play.[15]

As film censorship agencies sprang up around the state and around the country, Wisconsin's film mogul Harry Aitken became a free speech activist out of necessity. When his newsreels were held up in Ohio, Aitken challenged the censors all the way to the Supreme Court. In the landmark case of *Mutual v. Ohio*, the High Court handed down a unanimous ruling: motion pictures were *not* considered speech. Aitken suffered a resounding defeat, but the judgment had profound implications for all filmmakers. Not only was the medium not protected under the First Amendment, but Justice Joseph

Mary's Pickford's little sister Lottie starred in *The House of Bondage* (1914), one of many prostitution thrillers popular at the time.

McKenna declared that moving pictures were "capable of evil."[16] The court essentially recommended regulation. McKenna's decision seemed to indicate the state had a duty to protect the morals of its impressionable citizens.

Empowered by the *Mutual* ruling, Wisconsin's movie police scrutinized many of Hollywood's classics. Fritz Lang's film noir *Scarlet Street* (1946) was banned in Milwaukee.[17] Censors objected to a scene showing the commission of a murder. *Blackboard Jungle* (1955) was tagged for its raucous rock-and-roll soundtrack and scenes of juvenile delinquency. Censors OK'd *Rebel Without a Cause* (1955) only after all references to switchblades, stolen cars, and drunk teens were deleted.[18]

Across the state, civic authorities worked to shut down teenage counterculture. The city of Kenosha sued to keep its kids from attending the movie version of *Woodstock* (1970). The motion picture documentary of the festival captured musicians and hippies with psychedelic cinematography, jazzing up the muddy venue with split screens and optical effects to create a musical head trip. The film looked like it might have been staged, wrote Vincent Canby in the *New York Times*, "by a stoned Cecil B. DeMille."[19] This time, a towering figure in Wisconsin politics intervened. Judge John Reynolds, Jr.—the former state attorney general, former governor, and former presidential candidate—chided the censors.

Judge Reynolds heard the case and admonished the Kenosha Sanhedrin for attempting to ban *Woodstock*. "The defendants maintain that they are merely 'classifying' and not 'censoring.' I disagree. A prior restraint on First Amendment rights does not have to be total to be impermissible," Reynolds wrote. "First Amendment rights are sacred and are of paramount importance."[20] Judge Reynolds's progressive view on freedom of the screen sounded a death knell for the film censor commission in Wisconsin.

The boundaries between permissible and inappropriate motion pictures remain in flux. Benjamin Borger was much like any other junior high school student in his Kenosha class. He read his syllabus and was excited for a classroom screening of *Schindler's List* (1993). But when it came time for the lesson unit, the school district stopped the show. A budding First Amendment activist, Borger filed a lawsuit seeking to prevent the district

Left: The mother of four wants *No More Children* (1929) and dies as she undergoes a sterilization procedure. *Above:* Douglas Fairbanks, Jr., played a playboy bachelor caught up with an underground escort service in *Party Girl* (1930)—risqué but permitted in Milwaukee.

from canceling his movie day in school. The school's actions, claimed Borger, violated the students' rights under the First Amendment.[21] Judge Reynolds was back on the case. This time he disagreed. High school students had no right to see an R-rated film as part of a class.[22]

Judge Reynolds's message is an interesting one. From the *Woodstock* case, his view is clear: the First Amendment was intended to protect all forms of speech. Even disagreeable ideas that create controversy, aggravate elders, and stir debate must be safeguarded. However, Reynolds acknowledged that in certain settings, like a classroom or a courtroom, free speech may be reasonably abridged. These spaces should be the exception. Borger's protest remains valid; it is a civic duty to challenge any chilling of First Amendment rights. Sitting silently as authorities encroach on free speech can put at risk hard-won civil liberties.

Wyoming

If Montana claims the big sky, Wyoming can counter its northern neighbor with a landscape tailor-made for wide-screen motion pictures. George Stevens put the scenery to perfect use in *Shane* (1954). In *Shane* a man with a mysterious past appears from nowhere to stand up for defenseless homesteaders. Stevens elevated the genre of the sagebrush soap opera to artistic achievement, winning an Academy Award for the film's cinematography. The film's final scene is an iconic moment: the injured hero (Alan Ladd) rides off into the distance as the Grand Teton Range looms before him and the cries of the young boy behind him—"Shane! Come back!"—echo in the distance.

Wyoming's striking scenery was recorded in documentary-style short films during the late 1910s. The Rothacker Film Mfg. Co. shot *Ranch Life in the Big Horn Mountains* (1917) at the Eaton Ranch in Wolf, Wyoming. Opera and screen diva Geraldine Farrar made headlines for her torrid affairs with Arturo Toscanini, Enrico Caruso, and the ill-fated film star Lou Tellegen. Against a Wyoming backdrop Farrar overflowed with primitive passion in *The Hell Cat* (1918), romancing both a town sheriff as well as an outlaw. *The Hell Cat* delivered crowd-pleasing sex and violence. When Farrar's character ran up against a ranch hand, she experienced "the deepest indignity against womanhood," wrote a contemporary reviewer, before she "burie[d] a dagger in his heart." Filmed around Jackson Hole by Robert C. Bruce, *The Wolf of the Tetons* (1919) focused on a lone wolf as it wanders across the rugged landscape before joining a new pack.[1] For perhaps Wyoming's most memorable film, Steven Spielberg scouted the state to find the perfect location for his alien landing in *Close Encounters of the Third Kind* (1977). The monolithic mesa shape of Devils Tower seemed to have been waiting for eons to host Spielberg's extraterrestrials.

While Wyoming has striking scenery, it lacks population. The 2010 U.S. census ranked Wyoming the least populated state in the Union. Cowboy country's 563,626 residents make Idaho look like a teeming metropolis with over a million. North Dakota and Montana, and even Delaware, the District of Columbia, and Hawaii count far more heads than Wyoming.[2] With such a sparse population, motion picture exhibitors mostly bypassed the state. To make film distribution economically viable in the wide western territory, several states would need to be bundled together.

The first film distributor to recognize this economy of scale was Harry A. Sherman. Establishing the Elliott-Sherman Film Company in Minneapolis in 1915, Sherman acquired distribution rights for *The Birth of a Nation* (1915) in seventeen states: Arizona, Colorado, Idaho, Iowa, Kansas, Montana, Minnesota, Nebraska, Nevada, New Mexico, North Dakota, Oregon, South Dakota, Utah, Washington, Wisconsin, and Wyoming.[3] The investment was vastly successful, earning Sherman over $1 million within ten months.[4]

Next, Sherman picked up distribution rights for a Selig production called *The Crisis* (1916), which capitalized on the Civil War's cinematic popularity after *Birth*.[5] Redirecting his profits into a production shingle, Sherman formed Harry Sherman Productions in 1918 and specialized in modest-budget Westerns that catered to the audience he had come to know well. Between 1935 and 1944 Sherman produced fifty-five Hopalong Cassidy films, with William Boyd in the title role. Sherman's B-movie factory made use of recurring company players, such as George "Gabby" Hayes and George "Superman" Reeves. A young upstart named Bob Mitchum was able to build his acting résumé with Sherman's company, appearing in six "Hoppy" films, including *Bar 20* (1943), *Colt Comrades* (1943), and *False Colors* (1943).

Life in the West could be wild and free, but in the early years of the century, Wyoming authorities tried to rein in improper behavior. By 1912 the Cheyenne city council proposed fines for profanity, considered banning suggestive dances, and flirted with film censorship. The council sent a recommendation to the mayor to appoint a board and inspect all "picture films … and either approve or condemn [them] before they shall be used for show of exhibition purposes."[6] The bill was never signed, and Wyoming remained a land of free speech for the moment.

One hundred years later the specter of state censorship reemerged as environmental activists focused on Wyoming's ecology. Josh Fox brought the impact of hydraulic fracturing or "fracking," the process of using a high-pressure water jet to drill for fossil fuels, to national attention with his documentary *Gasland* (2010). Using memorable footage, such as a scene in which tap water running from a kitchen faucet is set on fire, Fox exposed the environmental damage of fracking in several locations, including Pavillion, Wyoming. In addition to flammable, foul-smelling water, Fox discovered sick people and animals around frack-drilling sites.[7] *Gasland* was celebrated at the Sundance Film Festival and nominated for an Academy Award, but whistle-blowing had consequences. Working on a follow-up, Fox was unable to gain access to congressional hearings on the issue. So he went ahead and set up cameras on Capitol Hill. Although he claimed to be within his First Amendment rights, Fox left the location in handcuffs, arrested by the DC police.[8]

The lines were drawn in the battle between documentary filmmakers and corporate institutions from energy conglomerates to factory farms. In a covert investigation, Humane Society operatives captured footage of farmworkers in Wyoming abusing pigs. This footage led to charges of animal cruelty. Corporate lobbyists responded by pressuring the state to enact laws that criminalized undercover footage. Critics of these laws called them "Ag-Gag" bills. At first the proposals stalled due to opposition from environmentalists and animal rights advocates, including Bob Barker, former host of *The Price Is Right*.[9] But the environmentalists' victory was fleeting. Two years later in March 2015, Governor Matt Mead signed the Data Trespass Bill to criminalize undercover filmmaking that could be used for whistle-blowing purposes.[10]

The Society for the Prevention of Cruelty to Animals and the Center for Food Safety criticized the Data Trespass Bill as "Ag Gag," effectively creating a prior restraint that silences speech that could embarrass, imperil, or otherwise injure big businesses involved in farming or drilling. The law requires researchers and documentary crews to ask permission before entering private land to collect evidence of suspected polluting or illegal activity. Governor Mead attempted to calm these concerns by stating, "The legislation is aimed at protecting and strengthening private property rights and has nothing to do with animals or animal cruelty."[11]

In 2016 the Western Watersheds Project challenged the Data Trespass Bill. During the course of routine testing, the Western Watersheds Project had discovered groundwater tainted with E. coli bacteria. The water flowed from territory controlled by the U.S. Bureau of Land Management, but the contamination was likely a by-product of livestock grazing on the lands. If this contamination stemmed from a violation of the Clean Water Act, local ranchers would face tighter restrictions. However, under the Data Trespass Bill, the Western Watersheds research would be unusable. Judge Scott W. Skavdahl rejected Watersheds' First Amendment claim, finding that constitutional protections did not extend to trespassing on private property to collect data or footage. The charge was positioned as free speech versus privacy.[12] While the Western Watersheds Project focused on gathering data, Wyoming's law can also have severe consequences for documentary filmmakers, shutting down speech intended to expose, protest, and inform the public of environmental violations.

Documentary has a tradition in American cinema that dates from the travelogues of Burton Holmes (see Minnesota) to the films of Robert Flaherty, most famously *Nanook of the North* (1922). Flaherty's late-career project *The Louisiana Story* (1948) documented the construction of an oil rig in bayou country. The rig brought jobs and prosperity to the backwaters, but this was only part of the picture. Standard Oil financed *Louisiana Story*. So Flaherty's documentary was one-sided, presenting its benefactor in the most positive light and avoiding any discussion of the hazards that would one day manifest in incidents like the Deepwater Horizon disaster. Documentary filmmaking serves a valuable purpose that can have real-world effects. *Blackfish* (2013) exposed treatment of SeaWorld's orcas and led to the discontinuation of the theme-park company's orca performances and breeding program. From *Titicut Follies* (1967) and *Harlan County, USA* (1976) to *Jesus Camp* (2006), documentary filmmakers have the ability to bring misconduct and inconvenient truths into the light.

The Wyoming Data Trespass Bill and others like it chill important speech, silencing debate in favor of corporate interests. Laws in Iowa, Kansas, Missouri, Montana, North Dakota, and Utah have also made it illegal for activists to shoot footage undercover in industrial animal operations.[13] This is a disturbing trend of prior restraint in the heartland of America's farming communities. Freedom of speech, freedom of the press, and free expression are central to democracy, and laws that unreasonably confine expression run counter to constitutional protections.

Motion pictures, both reality-based documentary as well as narrative fiction, can provide far more than an evening's entertainment. The medium has the ability to effect social change: to expose, critique, raise issues, and question the status quo. Motion pictures in America can entertain audiences, as with Hopalong Cassidy oaters, as well as educate, as with insightful documentaries like *Gasland*. Free speech may be protected under the First Amendment, but we must recognize that expression that runs counter to powerful economic forces is always at risk.

Conclusion

From coast to coast, movies across America have entertained audiences and agitated moral authorities for over a century. While filmmakers fought to present edgy and exciting subjects, state censors often pushed back, cutting up, editing, abridging, tampering with, and even banning pictures they felt presented a moral threat to impressionable viewers. State-authorized censors set their sights on indecent, immoral, suggestive, blasphemous, explosively violent, and politically unwelcome pictures, from primitively produced dancing loops to suggestive screwball comedies, and from stag films to ultraviolent splatter. Until 1952 government officials had broad powers to suppress certain speech because the medium of motion pictures was not yet recognized under the First Amendment. It may be hard to believe in our current age of electronic media that there was a time in recent history when movies sat outside the realm of constitutionally protected speech.

In my previous book, *Dirty Words and Filthy Pictures: Film and the First Amendment*, I recounted the grinding legal battles that paved the path to the freedom of the screen. During Hollywood's four-decade golden age from the 1920s through the 1950s, the major studios' most accomplished cinematic achievements were vulnerable to interference from government-appointed censors who cared little for the liveliest art. With the censors' power at its height, studio executives mostly steered clear of legal battles on free speech issues, instead remaining focused on the bottom line. Instead of fighting for free speech, the studios' strategy was to embrace self-censorship, charging Will Hays and his taskmaster Joseph Breen with monitoring the movies with the hope this "austerity measure" would hold off regional regulators. But the cuts imposed by Breen, Hays, and the Production Code Administration were not true censorship. These men had no government authority to enforce their decisions.

The true censors were authorized by their individual states. Some of these figures were colorful characters complete with memorable backstories—Funkhouser, Binford, Avara—while others were nameless members of administrative panels, men in gray flannel suits passing judgment on the movies that bothered them. *Film Censorship in America: A State-by-State Guide* hopes to fill out this forgotten history of state-authorized film-censorship bureaus.

Even after motion pictures were embraced as constitutionally protected speech under the First Amendment, free expression remains the most vulnerable right. Students can be silenced in the classroom and corralled into Free Speech Zones on college campuses. Whistleblowers and industry watchdogs are subject to ag-gag laws, and reporters are vulnerable to cracks in state shield laws meant to protect confidential sources.[1] With the suppression of certain speech and the specter of online surveillance, the promising personal freedom of the information age belies a dark reality.

The tension between freedom of expression and control of content remains central to modern life. As we move deeper into the twenty-first century, the means and modes of communication and expression become ever more accessible and the apparatus of surveillance and regulation more commonplace. This is not a new development: *Film Censorship in America: A State-by-State Guide* demonstrates that we are a country in love with movies and media and passionate about telling stories. But *Film Censorship in America* also uncovers an unyielding drive to silence certain voices. By appreciating the history of censorship in America we can remain vigilant to threats against personal liberties in the future.

Chapter Notes

Epigraph

1. "Memphis Bans Chaplin Movie," in *Kingsport News*, June 10, 1947.

Introduction

1. "Prince of Wales in View," *New York Times*, Nov. 18, 1894; inflation calculator at http://www.in2013dollars.com/1891-dollars-in-2016?amount=300.
2. "Edison's Vitascope Cheered," *New York Times*, Apr. 24, 1896.
3. "Went to Picture Show Laughed Till He Died," *Daytona Daily News*, Jan. 10, 1910. The title of the film Holcend watched was not reported.
4. "Never Saw Movie, Named Ohio Censor," *New Castle Herald*, Feb. 11, 1922.
5. "Censorship of Moving Pictures," *Burlington Free Press*, Feb. 19, 1921.
6. "Crime Essential to Movies, Says David Griffith," *Eau Claire Leader*, Dec. 15, 1920.

Alabama

1. Bob Luckie, "About Birmingham: Talking Pictures Show Great Improvement Over Hand-Cranked Variety 35 Years Ago," *Birmingham News*, July 21, 1940.
2. *Ibid.*
3. R. Bruce Brasell, "A Dangerous Experiment to Try: Film Censorship During the Twentieth Century in Mobile, Alabama," *Film History* 15, no. 1 (2003): 82.
4. "Protest Showing of Fight Films," *Salt Lake City Republican*, July 7, 1910; "Court Rules City May Censor Pictures," *Tennessean*, Nov. 8, 1917.
5. *Brooks v. City of Birmingham*, 32 F.2d 274, 274 (N.D. Ala. 1929).
6. "Wallace Reid Dies, Fighting Valiantly Against Dope Evil," *Atlanta Constitution*, Jan. 19, 1923.
7. *Brooks v. City of Birmingham*, 32 F.2d 274, 274 (N.D. Ala. 1929).
8. *Brooks*, 32 F.2d at 275.
9. "Movie Council Declares War on Commission," *Birmingham News*, Jan. 27, 1937.
10. "Movie Counsel Will Carry On," *Birmingham News*, Feb. 9, 1937.
11. R. Bruce Brasell, "A Dangerous Experiment to Try," *Film History* 15, no. 1 (2003): 90–91.
12. *Entertainment Ventures, Inc. v. Brewer*, 306 F. Supp. 802, 806 (M.D. Ala. 1969).
13. *Entertainment Ventures*, 306 F. Supp. at 806.
14. See *United Artists Corp. v. Wright*, 368 F. Supp. 1034 (M.D. Ala. 1974).

15. Ben Flanagan, "Pastor Had Planned Large Scale Effort to Mobilize Protest of Norwegian Film Screening," *Birmingham News*, June 8, 2012.

Alaska

1. Oscar B. Depue, "My Fifty Years in Motion Pictures," in *A Technological History of Motion Pictures and Television*, ed. Raymond Fielding (Berkeley: University of California Press, 1967), 60.
2. Frank Kessler and Sabine Lenk, "The French Connection: Franco-German Film Relations Before World War I," in *A Second Life: German Cinema's First Decades*, ed. Thomas Elsaesser and Michael Wedel (Amsterdam: Amsterdam University Press, 1996), 64.
3. American Film Institute, *The American Film Institute Catalog of Motion Pictures Produced in the United States: Feature Films, 1921–1930* (Berkeley: University of California Press, 1971), 7.
4. Yvonne Dennis, Arlene Hirschfelder, and Shannon Flynn, *Native American Almanac: More than 50,000 Years of the Cultures and Histories of Indigenous Peoples* (Canton, MI: Visible Ink Press, 2016), 404.
5. Laurie Lawlor, *Shadow Catcher: The Life and Work of Edward S. Curtis* (Lincoln: University of Nebraska Press, 1994), 99.
6. "Notes Written on the Screen," *New York Times* (hereafter cited as *NYT*), Dec. 6, 1914.
7. Mordaunt Hall, "An Eskimo Romance," *NYT*, June 29, 1925; American Film Institute, *The American Film Institute Catalog: Within Our Gates: Ethnicity in American Feature Films, 1911–1960* (Berkeley: University of California Press, 1997), 554.
8. American Film Institute, *The American Film Institute Catalog of Motion Pictures Produced in the United States: Feature Films, 1921–1930* (Berkeley: University of California Press, 1971), 469.
9. *Ibid.*, 410.
10. *Ibid.*
11. *Ibid.*, 488.
12. See J. Hoberman, "Fictitious Tales, Actual Odysseys," *NYT*, Oct. 9, 2015.
13. "Top 10 Alaskans: Ray Mala," *Time*, n.d., content.time.com/time/specials/packages/article/0,28804,1869388_1869390_1869471,00.html.
14. "Screen News Here and in Hollywood," *NYT*, Feb. 25, 1941.
15. *United States v. Nuzum*, 5 Alaska 198, 198–199 (D. Alaska 1914).
16. "'Movie' Photos Are Being Made Through Alaska," *Fairbanks Daily Times*, June 29, 1913.

Arizona

1. "Cecil De Mille, 77, Pioneer of Movies, Dead in Hollywood," *NYT*, Jan. 22, 1959.
2. "New Feature Company," *Moving Picture World* (hereafter cited as *MPW*), Dec. 20, 1913, 1417.
3. Robert S. Birchard, *Cecil B. DeMille's Hollywood* (Lexington: University of Kentucky Press, 2004); Lili DeBarbieri, *Location Filming in Arizona* (Charleston, SC: Arcadia, 2014); E. J. Fleming, ed., *The Movieland Directory* (Jefferson, NC: McFarland, 2004).
4. "Lasky Will Make *Brewster's Millions* Picture," *MPW*, Jan. 17, 1914, 298.
5. "The City and the County," *Arizona Weekly Journal-Miner*, Nov. 10, 1897; "To Night," *Flagstaff Sun-Democrat*, Nov. 11, 1897.
6. "The Phoenix Carnival," *Copper Era and Morenci Leader*, Nov. 22, 1900; "Nothing Like It," *Coconino Sun*, Jan. 10, 1903.
7. *The Caballero's Way* was the first screen adaptation of the Cisco Kid, who would become more widely known when Warner Baxter won an Academy Award for the role in *In Old Arizona* (1928) and appeared in four follow-up films. Cesar Romero played Cisco in five films produced 1939–1941, and Gilbert Roland, in six films 1946–1947. Duncan Renaldo would be most associated with the sombrero'd character, appearing in eight films and a TV series that ran 1950–1956.
8. "Ordinance No. 51," *Arizona Republic*, Jan. 23, 1912.
9. "Around the State," *Arizona Daily Star*, Apr. 26, 1918; "Sidney Drew Film and Stage Star Dies," *NYT*, Apr. 10, 1919.
10. *Cactus Corp. v. State ex rel. Murphy*, 14 Ariz. App. 38, 39 (Ariz. Ct. App. 1971).
11. *Cactus Corp.*, 14 Ariz. App. at 40.
12. *BBS Productions v. Purcell*, 360 F. Supp. 801, 804 (D. Ariz. 1973).

Arkansas

1. Bill Becker, "Old Film Cowboy Remembers When," *NYT*, Mar. 27, 1961.
2. "Horse Opera," *Life*, Oct. 28, 1946, 26.
3. "*The Great Train Robbery* as Rehearsed in New Jersey," *NYT*, Mar. 13, 1904.
4. Eleanor Barkhorn and Spencer Kornhaber, "A Cultural History of Pie-ing from *Mr. Flip* to Rupert Murdoch," *Atlantic*, July 19, 2011.
5. "Freeman Harrison Owens (1890–1979)," *The Encyclopedia of Arkansas History and Culture*, n.d., www.encyclopediaofarkansas.net/encyclopedia/entry-detail.aspx?entryID=66.
6. "Invents a Camerascope," *Arkansas Democrat*, Mar. 20, 1910.
7. "May Come to Little Rock," *Arkansas Democrat*, July 14, 1910.
8. "Motion Pictures," *Daily Arkansas Gazette*, July 10, 1910.
9. "Prohibited at Little Rock," *Abilene Semi-Weekly*, July 8, 1910.
10. "Little Rock Now Has a Board of Censors," *Daily Arkansas Gazette*, Mar. 19, 1911.
11. "Old Production That Cost $5,700 Amassed $475,000," *NYT*, May 31, 1925.
12. "*The Traffic in Souls*," *Daily Arkansas Gazette*, Feb. 17, 1914.

13. "Mayor and Censors to View *Purity*," *Daily Arkansas Gazette*, Oct. 29, 1916.
14. "*Purity* Is Shown but in Abbreviated Form," *Daily Arkansas Gazette*, Oct. 31, 1916.
15. Fay Hempstead, *Historical Review of Arkansas: Its Commerce, Industry, and Modern Affairs*, Vol. 2 (Chicago: Lewis Publishing, 1911), 856.
16. "*Enlighten Thy Daughter*," *Daily Arkansas Gazette*, Mar. 18, 1918.
17. "Judge Sees *Cleopatra*," *Daily Arkansas Gazette*, Mar. 26, 1918.
18. "Resigns as Censor," *Daily Arkansas Gazette*, Apr. 16, 1918.
19. "To Draft Ordinance," *Daily Arkansas Gazette*, May 11, 1918.
20. "Storm Rises over Censorship at L.R.," *Hope Star*, Mar. 30, 1933.
21. *United Artists Theatre Circuit v. Thompson*, 316 F. Supp. 815, 816 (W.D. Ark. 1970).
22. "Police, Censors Raid Joy Twin Theater," *El Dorado Times*, Feb. 18, 1971.
23. "Adult Cinema, Little Rock Theater, Sets *Deep Throat*," *Northwest Arkansas Times*, Aug. 28, 1973.
24. *Wild Cinemas of Little Rock v. Bentley*, 499 F. Supp. 655, 658–659 (W.D. Ark. 1980).

California

1. Charles Musser, *The Emergence of Cinema: The American Screen to 1907* (Berkeley: University of California Press, 1990), 81.
2. "Edison's Latest Triumph," *San Francisco Chronicle*, July 29, 1894.
3. *Ibid.*
4. "Ordinances to Regulate the Phonograph and Kinetoscope," *San Francisco Call*, Oct. 27, 1894.
5. "Chicken and Anti-Kinetoscope Ordinances Recommended," *Los Angeles Herald*, July 3, 1897; "Kinetoscope Law," *Los Angeles Times*, July 23, 1897.
6. Nathan Masters, "This 1897 Film Was the First Movie Made in Los Angeles," KCETLink, Oct. 2, 2016, https://www.kcet.org/shows/lost-la/this-1897-film-was-the-first-movie-made-in-los-angeles.
7. Geoffrey Bell, *The Golden Gate and the Silver Screen* (Rutherford, NJ: Fairleigh Dickinson University Press, 1984), 100.
8. Ernest Beyl, "Movie Making in San Francisco," *Marina Times*, Apr. 2015; Library of Congress, "*A Trip Down Market Street Before the Fire*," n.d., https://www.loc.gov/item/00694408.
9. Estelle Lawton Lindsey, "How They Make Movies," *Wichita Beacon*, Sep. 30, 1910; Cecilia Rasmussen, "Movie Industry's Roots in Garden of Edendale," *Los Angeles Times*, Sep. 16, 2001.
10. Marc Wanamaker and Robert W. Nudelman, *Early Hollywood* (Charleston, SC: Arcadia, 2007), 31.
11. Nita Lelyveld, "Relocated Market in Echo Park Salutes Mack Sennett's First Film Studio," *Los Angeles Times*, Feb. 27, 2015.
12. "The Growth of Flying A Company," *Movie*, Dec. 1915; Barney Brantingham, "The Short, Happy Life of Flying A," *Santa Barbara Independent*, Feb. 11, 2010; Santa Barbara Historical Museum, "The Flying A: Silent Film In Santa Barbara," n.d, www.santabarbaramuseum.com/exh-previous-FlyingA.html.
13. "Flying A Silent Film Studio Restored as a Live-Work Beauty," *Los Angeles Times*, 2016, www.latimes.

com/la-hm-silent-film-studio-photos-photogallery.
html.
14. Ernest Beyl, "Movie Making in San Francisco,"
Marina Times, Apr. 2015.
15. Thomas Glaydsz, "Once Lost Film Returns to Bay
Area," *Huffington Post,* Nov. 19, 2012, www.huffingtonpost.
com/thomas-gladysz/salomy-jane-film_b_1893879.html.
16. *Ibid.*
17. See "Film Making and Chaplin," Niles Essanay
Silent Film Museum, n.d., nilesfilmmuseum.org/?tv=
5858133164425216&dtv=6692962964602880&to=51625
64665212928.
18. *Ibid.*
19. "Balboa's Year Eventful," *Movie,* Dec. 1915; Jean-
Jacques Jura and Rodney Norman Bardin II, *Balboa
Films: A History and Filmography of the Silent Film Studio* (Jefferson, NC: McFarland, 1999).
20. Claudine E. Burnett, "Long Beach 100 Years Ago,
Part II," *Long Beach Post,* Dec. 31, 2013.
21. *"The Diamond Thieves," MPW,* Feb. 19, 1916; *"The
Scarlet Chastity," MPW,* Apr. 15, 1916; also see Gregory
L. Williams, "Filming San Diego Hollywood's Backlot,
1898–2002," *Journal of San Diego History* 48, no. 2,
sandiegohistory.org/journal/2002/april/filming/.
22. "To Censor Picture Shows," *Los Angeles Herald,*
July 24, 1909.
23. "Board of Censors for Nickelodeons," *San Francisco Call,* Apr. 13, 1909.
24. "Mayor Would Censor Moving Picture Shows,"
Los Angeles Herald, Jan. 27, 1909; "Pasadena Will Censor
Moving Picture Shows," *Santa Ana Register,* Apr. 1, 1910;
"Berkeley Places Ban on Risque Pictures," *Oakland Tribune,* June 25, 1910; "Board of Censors Is to Be Created,"
San Francisco Call, July 9, 1910.
25. "Measure Passed to Establish Moving Picture
Censorship in the State," *San Francisco Call,* May 9, 1913.
26. "Nickelodeon Proprietor Convicted by Shortall,"
San Francisco Chronicle, June 14, 1911.
27. "For Shame! Charley! His Film Is Banned," *Santa
Ana Register,* July 13, 1915.
28. "Film Censor Board to Be Abolished Is Council's
Decision," *Los Angeles Herald,* Mar. 7, 1916; "Ordinance
to Abolish Board of Censors Appears Likely to Pass,"
San Francisco Chronicle, Sep. 2, 1916.
29. *United States v. Two Tin Boxes,* 79 F.2d 1017 (2d
Cir. 1935).
30. "Russian Film Banned," *Santa Ana Register,* May
13, 1935.
31. "Hays Bans Lewis Novel for Screen," *Oakland
Tribune,* Feb. 16, 1936.
32. "Movie Snuff Gets Snuffed," *Santa Cruz Sentinel,*
Mar. 24, 1976.
33. "Anti-Snuff Film Bill Advances," *Eureka Times
Standard,* June 17, 1977.

Colorado

1. William Jones, "Harry Buckwalter: Pioneer Colorado Filmmaker," *Film History* 4, no. 2 (1990): 89.
2. "Local News," *Colorado Springs Weekly Gazette,*
Dec. 11, 1902.
3. "Stage Coach Held Up Within Mile of City," *Colorado Springs Weekly Gazette,* Oct. 6, 1904.
4. "Buckwalter Will Not Make 'Knock' Picture He
Planned," *Colorado Springs Weekly Gazette,* June 16, 1904.
5. "Buckwalter Films Mitchel," *MPW,* Dec. 13, 1913,
1426.

6. "Board of Censors," *Fort Wayne Daily News,* Sep.
29, 1913.
7. E.C. Day, "Censorship in Colorado," *MPW,* July
1, 1916, 126.
8. "Club of Movie Censor Descends on Boulder,"
Greeley Daily Tribune, Feb. 20, 1919.
9. "Screen Club of Denver Enters Censorship Fight,"
MPW, Feb. 1, 1919, 599.
10. "Bill to Censor 'Movies' Fails through Error,"
Santa Fe New Mexican, Feb. 10, 1921.
11. *Clean Flicks of Colorado v. Soderbergh,* 433 F.
Supp. 2d 1236, 1242 (D. Colo. 2006).
12. *Clean Flicks* 433 F. Supp. 2d at 1242, citing *Campbell v. Acuff-Rose Music,* 510 U.S. 569, 579 (1994).
13. In an interesting coda to the transformative issue
central to the Clean Flicks case, lead plaintiff Steven
Soderbergh made news again in 2015 when he launched
a website offering newly edited versions of classic films.
Soderbergh led the charge to shutter the family-friendly
derivative works, but on his website Extension765.com,
he offered alternative unauthorized versions of *Psycho*
(1960), *Raiders of the Lost Ark* (1981), and *2001: A Space
Odyssey* (1968). In Soderbergh's view, his own artistic
reedits must have satisfied the transformative test, while
the more practical abridgements that could possibly
open up R-rated films to new and younger audiences
were illegitimate. See David Post, "Steven Soderbergh,
Copyright Infringer?" *Washington Post,* Jan. 16, 2015.
14. *Dallas Buyers Club v. Huston,* Civil Action No.
15-cv-00598-WYD-MEH (D. Colo. 2016), 25.
15. Dana Liebelson, "Why It's Getting Harder to Sue
Illegal Movie Downloaders," *Mother Jones,* Feb. 17, 2014.
16. Matthew Sag, "IP Litigation in United States District Courts—2015 Update," paper, Loyola University
Chicago School of Law, Jan. 5, 2016, https://dx.doi.org/
10.2139/ssrn.2711326.
17. Ernesto, *"Dallas Buyers Club* Sues BitTorrent Pirates Citing Oscar Wins," TorrentFreak, Mar. 12, 2014,
https://torrentfreak.com/dallas-buyers-club-sues-bit
torrent-pirates-citing-oscar-wins-140312/.
18. *Dallas Buyers Club v. Huston,* Civil Action No.
15-cv-00598-WYD-MEH (D. Colo. 2016); *Dallas Buyers
Club v. Eldridge,* Civil Action No. 14-cv-01629-WYD-
MEH (D. Colo. 2015); *Dallas Buyers Club v. Cordova,*
Civil Action No. 14-cv-01469-WYD-MEH (D. Colo.
2015).
19. Andy, "People Sued for Piracy in the U.S. Drops
84% Since 2010," TorrentFreak, Jan. 15, 2016, https://tor-
rentfreak.com/people-sued-for-piracy-in-united-states-
drops-84-since-2010-160114/.

Connecticut

1. Richard Schickle, *D.W. Griffith: An American Life*
(New York: Limelight Editions, 1996), 108.
2. Kelly R. Brown, *Florence Lawrence, the Biograph
Girl: America's First Movie Star* (Jefferson, NC: McFarland, 1999), 192–193.
3. "Movie Censorship," *Bridgeport Telegram,* Apr.
21, 1921.
4. "Motion Picture Censor Is Sought for Connecticut," *Bridgeport Telegram,* Jan. 30, 1925.
5. "Theaters to Pay $192,000 in Tax Levies to State,"
Bridgeport Telegram, July 2, 1927.
6. "Film Producers to Withdraw from State if Movie
Tax Bill Stands," *Bridgeport Telegram,* July 2, 1925.
7. *Mutual Film v. Ohio,* 236 U.S. 230, 244–245 (1915).

8. *Fox Film Corp. v. Trumbull*, 7 F.2d 715, 724 (D. Conn. 1925).

9. "Connecticut Tax on Movie Films," *Chicago Daily Tribune*, Aug. 18, 1925.

10. Plan Fund to Pay Movie Tax," *Chicago Daily Tribune*, Sep. 3, 1925; "Theatres to Give Tenth of Receipts for Flood," *Chicago Daily Tribune*, Nov. 9, 1927.

Delaware

1. "Mr. Edison's Latest," *Wilmington Evening Journal*, Mar. 10, 1894.

2. Advertisement for Wonderland Theatre, *Wilmington Evening Journal*, Dec. 7, 1896; Advertisement for Grand Opera House, *Wilmington Morning News*, Nov. 13, 1897.

3. *State v. Morris*, 76 Atl. 479, 480 (Del. 1910).

4. "Took No Action on Fight Films," *Wilmington Morning News*, July 13, 1910.

5. "Plays of To-Day," *Wilmington Morning News*, Jan. 7, 1911.

6. "Suggest Censors for Picture Shows," *Wilmington Evening Journal*, Feb. 5, 1915; "Would Change Sessions of the Legislature," *Wilmington Morning News*, Feb. 2, 1915.

7. "Seven Years in Prison for Men Who Tote Pistols," *Wilmington Evening Journal*, Mar. 9, 1915.

8. "To Avoid Racial Feeling," *Wilmington News Journal*, May 21, 1915.

9. "Movie Censors Provided," *Wilmington News Journal*, June 4, 1915.

10. "Club Women Decide That Moving Picture Censorship Is Not Needed Here," *Wilmington Evening Journal*, Feb. 20, 1917.

11. Lewis D. Black Jr., "Why Corporations Choose Delaware" (Delaware Department of State, Division of Corporations, 2007), corp.delaware.gov/whycorporations_web.pdf.

12. *The Film Daily Year Book of Motion Pictures* (New York: Film Daily, 1962), 1071.

13. Tino Balio, *United Artists, Volume 1: The Company Built by the Stars* (Madison: University of Wisconsin Press, 1996), 29.

14. Steven Bingen, *Warner Bros.: Hollywood's Ultimate Backlot* (Lanham, MD: Taylor Trade, 2014), 10.

15. *In re: The Walt Disney Company Derivative Litigation*, 907 A.2 693, 699–701 (Del. Ch. 2005).

16. *In re: The Walt Disney Company*, 907 A.2 at 703–704.

17. *In re: The Walt Disney Company*, 907 A.2 at 713–723.

18. *In re: The Walt Disney Company Derivative Litigation*, 906 A.2d 27, 35 (Sup. Ct. 2006).

19. *In re: The Walt Disney Company Derivative Litigation*, 907 A.2 693, 746–747 (Del. Ch. 2005).

20. *In re: The Walt Disney Company*, 907 A.2 at 771.

21. Laura M. Holson, "Disney Agrees to Acquire Pixar in a $7.4 Billion Deal," *NYT*, Jan. 25, 2006; Brooks Barnes and Michael Cieply, "Disney Swoops Into Action, Buying Marvel for $4 Billion," *NYT*, Aug. 31, 2009; Michael J. De La Merced, "With Lucasfilm Deal, Disney Spends Big to Land a Lucrative Franchise," *NYT*, Oct. 30, 2012.

Florida

1. Charles Musser, *The Emergence of Cinema* (Berkeley: University of California Press, 1990), 252.

2. C. Scott Combs, *Deathwatch: American Film, Technology, and the End of Life* (New York: Columbia University Press, 2014), 35.

3. David Nolan, "Silent Films in St. Augustine," *St. Augustine Record*, Oct. 27, 2000.

4. "The Sunny South in Motion Pictures," *MPW*, Dec. 19, 1908.

5. Joseph P. Eckhardt, *The King of the Movies: Film Pioneer Siegmund Lubin* (Madison, NJ: Fairleigh Dickinson Press, 1997), 93–138.

6. Q. David Bowers, "Volume 1: Narrative History," in *Thanhouser Films: An Encyclopedia and History*, n. d.,www.thanhouser.org/tcocd/Narrative_files/c5s2.htm.

7. "Dintenfass Gets Loving Cup," *MPW*, Mar. 18, 1916.

8. "Engages Billy Reeves," *Motography*, Apr. 3, 1915.

9. Reeves met an untimely end, succumbing to injuries after an ostrich attack while shooting a film; see "Attack by Ostriches Kills Film Comedian," *Oakland Tribune*, July 7, 1921.

10. "Oliver Hardy of Film Team Dies," *NYT*, Aug. 8, 1957.

11. Barbara Tepa Lupack, *Richard E. Norman and Race Filmmaking* (Bloomington: Indiana University Press, 2014).

12. "At the Bijou Dream Today," *Vicksburg Evening Post*, Apr. 22, 1916.

13. David Nolan, "Silent Film in St. Augustine," *St. Augustine Record*, Oct. 27, 2000; "Theda Bara During Shooting of Film '*A Woman There Was*' in Miami Beach, Florida," Florida Memory, n.d., https://www.floridamemory.com/items/show/25660.

14. Blair Miller, *Almost Hollywood: The Forgotten Story of Jacksonville, Florida* (Lanham, MD: Hamilton Books, 2013), 10.

15. Mark Woods, "One Hundred Years Ago, We Had a Mayoral Race for the Ages," *Jacksonville Florida Times Union*, Mar. 22, 2015.

16. Ron Johnson, "Today in Florida History, Nov. 20," *Jacksonville Florida Times Union*, Nov. 20, 2012.

17. William Sheafe Chase, *Catechism on Motion Pictures in Inter-State Commerce* (New York: New York Civic League, 1922).

18. "Florida Senate Passes Film Act," *Atlanta Constitution*, June 2, 1921; also see 27 Florida Laws, 1921, C. 8523 (p. 317); revised as Fla. Stat. Ann. §521.01 (1943).

19. "*Girls Gone Wild* Founder Joseph Francis Pleads Guilty in Sexual Exploitation Case," DOJ press release, Sep. 26, 2006, https://www.justice.gov/archive/opa/pr/2006/September/06_crm_644.html; "Foreign Operator of Obscene Web Sites Arrested on Federal Obscenity Charges," DOJ press release, Sep. 7, 2006, https://www.justice.gov/archive/opa/pr/2006/September/06_crm_599.html; "Producer Paul Little Indicted on Obscenity Charges," DOJ press release, May 31, 2007, https://www.justice.gov/archive/opa/pr/2007/May/07_crm_393.html.

Georgia

1. "The Atlanta Exposition," *NYT*, Sep. 19, 1895.

2. "Past and Present," *NYT*, Dec. 1, 1918.

3. Charles Francis Jenkins, *Animated Pictures: An Exposition of the Historical Development of Chronophotography* (Washington, DC: H.L. McQueen, 1898), 34.

4. "Past and Present," *NYT*, Dec. 1, 1918; Donald G. Godfrey, *C. Francis Jenkins, Pioneer of Film and Television* (Urbana: University of Illinois Press, 2014), 39.

5. The inventors pressed on separately. The Phantoscope project was abandoned. Armet filed patents on a new device he called the Vitascope and piqued Thomas Edison's interest. Jenkins appealed to Alexander Graham Bell with less success; instead, Jenkins sued his former partner for patent infringement. The case was dismissed in *Jenkins v. Jenkins and Armet*. This case was part of the patent war that divided the film industry in its formative days. See *Official Gazette of the U.S. Patent Office*, vol. 78, no. 12, Mar. 23, 1897; see also "Inventor of Moving Picture Machines," *Washington DC Evening Times*, Nov. 28, 1898.

6. "To Stop the Kinetoscope," *Atlanta Constitution*, Mar. 26, 1897; "She Opposes Fights," *Atlanta Constitution*, Mar. 30, 1897.

7. "Mayors Will Stop It," *Baltimore Sun*, July 7, 1910. Maddox aligned with Southern mayors, including Mayor D.C. Richardson of Richmond, Mayor J.S. Wynn of Raleigh, Mayor Walter G. MacRae of Wilmington, Mayor R.G. Rhett of Charleston, Mayor H.E. Howse of Nashville, Mayor Martin Behrman of New Orleans, and Mayor W.O. Head of Louisville.

8. *Atlanta Enterprises v. Crawford*, 22 F.2d 834 (N.D. Ga. 1927); also see *In re Film and Pictorial Representation of Dempsey-Tunney Fight*, 22 F.2d 837 (N.D. Ga. 1927).

9. "Moving Picture Shows Raided by Police," *Atlanta Constitution*, July 17, 1909; "More Exits Needed in Picture Shows," *Atlanta Constitution*, Jan. 1, 1911.

10. "Hats Off after Six O'Clock P.M." *Atlanta Constitution*, Feb. 25, 1910.

11. See advertisement for *Some Wild Oats* in *Atlanta Constitution*, Apr. 8, 1923.

12. Margaret T. McGehee, "Disturbing the Peace: *Lost Boundaries*, *Pinky*, and Censorship in Atlanta, Georgia, 1949–1952," *Cinema Journal* 46, no. 1 (Autumn 2006): 26.

13. "Atlanta Censors Will Pass Today on *Three Weeks*," *Atlanta Constitution*, May 15, 1915.

14. "Atlanta Censors Stamp Approval on *The Unborn*," *Atlanta Constitution*, Sep. 13, 1916.

15. "In a Serious Vein on a Serious Matter," *Atlanta Constitution*, Aug. 1, 1915.

16. "Leo Frank Films in Court," *Greenwood Daily Journal*, Sep. 16, 1915; "Leo Frank on Films at Princess Theatre To-Day," *Charlotte News*, Aug. 30, 1915.

17. "Leo Frank Drama in 'Movies' May be Prohibited in Atlanta," *Greenwood Daily Journal*, Jan. 20, 1915.

18. "*Ravished Armenia* in Film," *NYT*, Feb. 15, 1919.

19. "*Auction of Souls* Barred in Atlanta by Censor's Board," *NYT*, June 20, 1919.

20. McGehee, "Disturbing the Peace," *Cinema Journal* 46, no. 1 (Autumn 2006).

21. "Atlanta Bans Picture," *NYT*, Feb. 4, 1946.

22. "Wanger Charges Film-Ban Libel," *Huntingdon Daily News*, Feb. 12, 1946; "Wanger Protests Censorship on *Scarlet Street*," *Danville Bee*, Feb. 12, 1946. Five years later Wanger shot Jennings Lang (unrelated to Fritz) in a Beverly Hills parking lot. Jennings was an MCA talent agent whom Wanger believed was having an affair with Bennett. See "Wanger Victim May Be Crippled," *NYT*, Jan. 20, 1952.

23. "Wanger Protests Ban on Movie," *Kingsport Times*, Feb. 14, 1946; "Ban on *Scarlet Street* Upheld," *NYT*, Feb. 15, 1946.

24. "Atlanta Censor Board Bans *Imitation of Life* Revival Because of Racial Angle," *Afro American*, Oct. 13, 1945.

25. "Atlanta Bans *Swell Guy*," *Cumberland Evening Times*, Feb. 19, 1947.

26. Thomas M. Pryor, "Censorship Ties *Rope* in Knots," *NYT*, Nov. 21, 1948.

27. "Suit Filed in Atlanta Challenges Film Censor," *Long Beach Independent*, Nov. 29, 1949.

28. "*Pinky* Paves Way in Atlanta Opening," *Brooklyn Daily Eagle*, Nov. 18, 1949.

29. *Mutual Film Corp. v. Ohio*, 236 U.S. 230, 244 (1915).

30. *RD-DR Corp. v. Smith*, 183 F.2d 562 (5th Cir. 1950); "Freedom of Press Protection Ruled Out for Movies," *St. Petersburg Evening Independent*, Mar. 9, 1950.

31. McGehee, "Disturbing the Peace," *Cinema Journal* 46, no. 1 (Autumn 2006).

32. "Former Movie Censor Against Liberal Films," *Rome News-Tribune*, Feb. 15, 1971.

33. "Judge Permits Movie Showing," *Anniston Star*, July 6, 1955; "Loew's Fights Atlanta Film Ban," *NYT*, June 4, 1955.

34. "Atlanta Censors Face Legal Fight," *NYT*, Sep. 25, 1960.

35. *City of Atlanta v. Lopert Picture Corp.*, 217 Ga. 432, 435 (Ga. 1961); "Atlanta's Woman Censor Faces Another Court Test," *Tucson Daily Citizen*, Mar. 21, 1961.

36. *City of Atlanta v. Lopert Picture Corp.*, 217 Ga. 432, 436 (Ga. 1961).

37. "Movie Censor Laws in Atlanta Upset," *NYT*, Apr. 8, 1962.

38. *K. Gordon Murray Prods. v. Floyd*, 217 Ga. 784, 793 (Ga. 1962).

39. Minnie Hire Moody, "She Saw 5,500 Movies," *Newark Advocate*, Sep. 24, 1971.

40. "Former Movie Censor Against Liberal Films," *Rome News-Tribune*, Feb. 15, 1971.

41. Minnie Hire Moody, "She Saw 5,500 Movies," *Newark Advocate*, Sep. 24, 1971.

42. *Evans Theatre Corp. v. Slaton*, 227 Ga. 377 (Ga. 1971).

43. *1024 Peachtree Corp. d/b/a Metro Theatre v. Slaton*, 228 Ga. 102 (Ga. 1971).

44. *Jenkins v. State*, 230 Ga. 726, 728 (Ga. 1973).

45. *Jenkins v. Georgia*, 418 U.S. 153, 161 (1974).

Hawaii

1. "Turns the Backflip," *New York World*, July 9, 1893.

2. Advertisement, *San Francisco Call*, May 13, 1894.

3. Advertisement, *Hawaii Holomua*, June 30, 1894; "Stage News and Notes," *New York Evening World*, Aug. 22, 1894.

4. Toulouse-Lautrec painted Fuller's performance at the Folies Bergère in a work entitled *At the Music Hall*. Fuller's relationship with Rodin has been documented in Richard Nelson Current and Marcia Ewing Current, *Loie Fuller, Goddess of Light* (Boston: Northeastern University Press, 1997).

5. "Plays and Players," *Rochester Democrat and Chronicle*, Sep. 5, 1897.

6. "Heavy Program," *Daily Pacific Commercial Advertiser*, Apr. 22, 1898.

7. "James H. White," *Who's Who of Victorian Cinema*, n.d., http://www.victorian-cinema.net/white.

8. "The Manila Show Co.," *Honolulu Evening Bulletin*, Mar. 25, 1899; "Moving Picture Exhibition," *Honolulu Evening Bulletin*, June 17, 1904.

9. "Will Censor Their Pictures," *Pacific Commercial Advertiser*, June 30, 1909.

10. "First Report of Picture Censors," *Lihue Garden Island*, Dec. 29, 1914.

11. "Superintendent Kinney Tours Schools of Kauai," *Lihue Garden Island*, May 19, 1914; "First Report of Picture Censors," *Lihue Garden Island*, Dec. 29, 1914.

12. "Dr. Wadman's New Crusade," *Maui News*, July 31, 1915.

13. "Urge Governor to Appoint Movie Censor," *Lihue Garden Island*, Feb. 14, 1922.

14. "Duke Kahanamoku Dies at 77," *NYT*, Jan. 23, 1968.

Idaho

1. "The Egan School of Music, Drama and Fine Arts Awards Prizes for Scenarios," *Los Angeles Times*, Nov. 10, 1912.

2. The Women Film Pioneers Project at the Columbia University Center for Digital Research and Scholarship has compiled an invaluable resource recording the accomplishments of women working within the Hollywood studio system; see https://wfpp.cdrs.columbia.edu/.

3. "*God's Country and the Woman*," *MPW*, May 6, 1916.

4. "Circuit to Release Curwood Film," *MPW*, Sep. 20, 1919.

5. Kay Armatage, *The Girl from God's Country: Nell Shipman and the Silent Cinema* (Toronto: University of Toronto Press, 2003), 111.

6. George Melnyk, *One Hundred Years of Canadian Cinema* (Toronto: University of Toronto Press, 2004), 32.

7. Advertisement, *Shamokin News-Dispatch*, Apr. 4, 1924; "Priest Lake," *Idaho: A Portrait*, n.d., http://idahoptv.org/productions/idahoportrait/tour/priestltour.html.

8. Armatage, *The Girl from God's Country* (Toronto: University of Toronto Press, 2003), 17; "Animal Features with Nell Shipman Make It an Unusual Production," *San Bernardino County Sun*, Dec. 9, 1919.

9. "*Grub-Stake* Nell Shipman's Latest and Best Picture at the Palace," *Bryan TX Eagle*, Apr. 23, 1923.

10. "*The Grub-Stake* Is Nell Shipman's Latest Feature," *Altoona Tribune*, Apr. 9, 1923.

11. "Animals Owned by Movie Actress Are Starving in Cages," *Ogden Standard-Examiner*, June 9, 1925; "Court Attaches Menagerie Owned by Nell Shipman," *Albany Democrat-Herald*, Apr. 10, 1925; Armatage, *The Girl from God's Country* (Toronto: University of Toronto Press, 2003), 302.

12. "Regulating the Pictures," *Idaho Falls Post-Register*, Apr. 16, 1934.

13. See Idaho Code, Title 23 Alcoholic Beverages, Chapter 6 Penal Provisions, 23-614(d) at https://legislature.idaho.gov/statutesrules/idstat/Title23/T23CH6/SECT23-614/.

14. George Prentice, "*Blue Is the Warmest Color*," *Boise Weekly*, Oct. 9, 2013.

15. Harrison Berry, "Idaho State Police Responds to Settlement of VAC/ACLU Lawsuit," *Boise Weekly*, Sep. 30, 2016.

16. George Prentice, "Censorship and Sensibility: Idaho Must Answer for Its Speech-Chilling Statute," *Boise Weekly*, Jan. 27, 2016.

17. Berry, "Idaho State Police Responds to Settlement of VAC/ACLU Lawsuit," *Boise Weekly*, Sep. 30, 2016.

18. *LSO Ltd. v. Stroh*, 205 F.3d 1146, 1158 (9th Cir. 2000).

Illinois

1. Charles Musser, *Before the Nickelodeon: Edwin S. Porter and the Edison Manufacturing Company* (Berkeley: University of California Press, 1991), 35.

2. "Edison's New Marvel," *Indianapolis News*, Apr. 27, 1893.

3. "Chicago Reports Many Variations in Picture Shows," *MPW*, July 15, 1916, 413.

4. "A Chronology of the World's Film Productions and Film Shows before May 1896," *Who's Who in Victorian Cinema*, n.d., http://www.victorian-cinema.net/when_chrono.

5. Musser, *Before the Nickelodeon* (Berkeley: University of California Press, 1991), 155, 328, 444.

6. Michael Corcoran and Arnie Bernstein, *Hollywood on Lake Michigan: 100+ Years of Chicago and the Movies* (Chicago: Chicago Review Press, 2013).

7. "Police to Censor Shows," *Chicago Daily Tribune*, Apr. 30, 1907. The city's film ordinance formally went into effect on Nov. 20, 1907; see "Police Chief Picture Censor," *Chicago Daily Tribune*, Nov. 21, 1907.

8. "Censors Inspect Nickel Theaters," *Chicago Daily Tribune*, May 1, 1907.

9. See "Night Riders Kill Kentucky Farmer," *NYT*, Mar. 22, 1908.

10. *Block v. City of Chicago*, 87 N.E. 1011, 1016 (Ill. 1909).

11. "Try to Lift Ban off Fight Films," *Chicago Daily Tribune*, July 31, 1910.

12. "Funkhouser as Morals Guardian," *Chicago Daily Tribune*, Mar. 21, 1913.

13. "Freak Dances Betold in Moving Pictures," *Chicago Daily Tribune*, Oct. 23, 1913.

14. "Court Upholds Police Censors," *Chicago Daily Tribune*, Jan. 25, 1914; "Funkhouser Recalls Permit for the Drug Terror Film," *Chicago Inter Ocean*, Mar. 27, 1914.

15. "Judge Carpenter to Rule on *Rose of Blood* Film," *Chicago Daily Tribune*, Dec. 15, 1917; "Anti-German Film Rejected by Funkhouser," *Chicago Daily Tribune*, June 30, 1917; "Aldermen Back Major's Griffith Film Cutouts," *Chicago Daily Tribune*, May 1, 1918.

16. "What the Censors Did," *Chicago Daily Tribune*, Mar. 21, 1914; "Censor Cutouts," *Chicago Daily Tribune*, May 14, 1914; Adam Selzer, "Charlie Chaplin Faced Censorship in Chicago 100 Years Ago," *Time Out Chicago*, Dec. 18, 2014.

17. "Latest News of Chicago," *Motography*, May 4, 1918.

18. "Eliminating Maj. Funkhouser," *Chicago Daily Tribune*, May 11, 1918; "The Movie Censorship," *Chicago Eagle*, May 25, 1918.

19. "Censor Bill Vetoed," *Muskogee Times-Democrat*, July 10, 1915.

20. "House Passes Bill for Movie Censor," *Decatur Daily Review*, June 8, 1917; "Film Censor Bill Killed," *Decatur Daily Review*, June 18, 1919.

21. "City Again Bars Film That Glorifies Crime," *Chicago Daily Tribune*, Jan. 18, 1921.

22. *Columbia Pictures Corp. v. City of Chicago*, 184 F. Supp. 817 (N.D. Ill. 1959).

23. *Paramount v. City of Chicago*, 172 F. Supp. 69 (N.D. Ill. 1959).
24. *Times Film Corp. v. City of Chicago*, 244 F.2d 432, 436 (7th Cir. 1957).
25. *Times Film Corp. v. City of Chicago*, 271 F.2d 90 (7th Cir. 1959).
26. *Universal Film Exchanges Inc. v. City of Chicago*, 288 F. Supp. 286 (N.D. Ill. 1968).
27. *Capitol Enterprises v. City of Chicago*, 260 F.2d 670 (7th Cir. 1958).
28. *Excelsior Pictures Corp. v. City of Chicago*, 182 F. Supp. 400 (1960).
29. *Zenith International Film Corp. v. City of Chicago*, 291 F.2d 785, 790 (7th Cir. 1961).
30. Trevor Jensen, "Charles Teitel Dies at 93," *Los Angeles Times*, Apr. 16, 2009.
31. *Cusack v. Teitel*, 38 Ill. 53 (Ill. 1967).
32. *Teitel Film Corp. v. Cusack*, 390 U.S. 139 (1968).

Indiana

1. "Prize Fight Films Here," *Indianapolis Star*, July 18, 1910; see also "Hyland to Censor Prize Fight Films," *Indianapolis Star*, July 10, 1910.
2. "Blames Films for Juvenile Crimes," *Indianapolis Star*, Aug. 1, 1910.
3. "News Brief," *Fort Wayne News*, Apr. 29, 1916.
4. "Mayor to Censor *Damaged Goods*," *Evansville Press*, Oct. 30, 1915.
5. Ad for Majestic Theater, *Evansville Press*, Nov. 1915.
6. "Anderson May Censor Films," *Fort Wayne Journal-Gazette*, Sep. 7, 1916.
7. "Film Curb Bill Wins in Indiana," *Courier-Journal*, Mar. 5, 1921.
8. "No Film Censor," *Fort Wayne Sentinel*, Mar. 8, 1921.
9. "Not Needed," *Fort Wayne Sentinel*, Mar. 1, 1921.
10. "Will H. Hays Signs to Direct Movies," *NYT*, Jan. 19, 1922.
11. Frank L. Kluckhohn, "President Appoints Byron Price to Direct Wartime Censorship," *NYT*, Dec. 17, 1941.
12. Peter B. Flint, "Byron Price, Wartime Chief of U.S. Censorship, Is Dead," *NYT*, Aug. 8, 1981.
13. Thomas F. Brady, "Hollywood Reports," *NYT*, Oct. 25, 1942.
14. See "Byron Price," Pulitzer Prizes website, http://www.pulitzer.org/winners/byron-price-0.
15. "The Censor Shuts Up Shop," *NYT*, Aug. 17, 1945.
16. "Statement Planned on Hays Retirement," *NYT*, Sep. 18, 1945; "Byron Price Named Film Industry Aide," *NYT*, Dec. 5, 1945.
17. "No Showing of *Baby Doll* in Hammond," *Hammond Times*, Jan. 31, 1957; "*Baby Doll* Dull, Drab, Says Censor," *Columbus Republic*, Jan. 30, 1957.
18. *Cinecom Theaters Midwest States Inc. v. City of Fort Wayne*, 473 F.2d 1297, 1302 (7th Cir. 1973).
19. *American Amusement Machine Association v. Kendrick*, 244 F.3d 572, 580 (2001).

Iowa

1. "Guide to the Adelaide Eunice Goodrich Collection circa 1837–1916," University of Chicago Library Special Collections Research Center, 2006, http://www.lib.

uchicago.edu/e/scrc/findingaids/view.php?eadid=ICU.SPCL.GOODRICH; Charles Edward Ellis, *An Authentic History of the Benevolent and Protective Order of the Elks* (Chicago; Charles Edward Ellis, 1910), 212.
2. "Burtis Opera House," *Davenport Daily Leader*, Dec. 29, 1896; "Goodrich Comedy Company," *Carroll Sentinel*, Jan. 11, 1897.
3. "Announcements," *Lincoln Courier*, Jan. 16, 1897.
4. "Will Be War," *Davenport Daily Leader*, Apr. 14, 1898; "Great War Pictures!" *Davenport Daily Leader*, Sep. 4, 1898.
5. "Proposes State Censor for Motion Pictures," *Nevada State Journal*, Jan. 30, 1913; "State Censor for Picture Films," *St. Louis Post-Dispatch*, Jan. 30, 1913.
6. "Hawkeye State News," *Humeston New Era*, Nov. 19, 1913.
7. "Opposes Censorship of Movies by State," *Des Moines Register* (hereafter cited as *DMR*), Mar. 13, 1915.
8. "Movie Censorship Bills Are Killed," *DMR*, Mar. 16, 1915.
9. "Keeping Tab on the Movies," *DMR*, July 29, 1915.
10. "*Birth of a Nation* Film Destroyed by Negros," *Springfield Republican*, Dec. 9, 1915.
11. "Ministerial Body Opposes Picture," *Daily Gate City*, Feb. 15, 1916.
12. "*Birth of Nation* Barred," *Hospers Tribune*, May 5, 1916; "Movie Ban is Planned," *DMR*, Dec. 12, 1915; "Cedar Rapids Boosts for Prohibited Film," *DMR*, Apr. 26, 1916; Advertisement, *DMR*, May 20, 1916.
13. "*Salome* Smashes Records for Western Exhibitors," *MPW*, May 10, 1919, 922.
14. "Judge Enjoins Plan to Block *Wild Oats* Film," *DMR*, Sep. 18, 1921.
15. "Saunders Closes *Wild Oats* Show," *DMR*, Sep. 19, 1921; "*Some Wild Oats* Film Owner Gets Himself Arrested," *DMR*, Sep. 21, 1921; "Court Battle on *Wild Oats* Ends," *DMR*, Sep. 23, 1921.
16. Advertisement for *Some Wild Oats*, *DMR*, Sep. 24, 1921.
17. *N.D.D. Inc. v. Faches*, 385 F. Supp. 286 (N.D. Iowa 1974).
18. "Midwest Theaters Ban *Fahrenheit 9/11*," *Chicago Tribune*, July 3, 2004.
19. David Martosko, "Trump Rents Out Movie Theater to Show *13 Hours* Film for Free," *Daily Mail*, Jan. 16, 2016.

Kansas

1. Recent efforts to revive Superman, first as a savior in *Superman Returns* (2006), then as a vigilante in *Man of Steel* (2013) and *Batman v Superman: Dawn of Justice* (2016), stumbled, pleasing neither critics nor audiences.
2. "Near Riot When Film Is Censored," *Dakota County Herald*, Nov. 24, 1911.
3. Ibid.
4. "Film Censors Named," *Concordia Blade-Empire*, Apr. 7, 1915.
5. "Kansas Fight Film," *Fort Scott Tribune*, Apr. 15, 1915.
6. "Won't Show Willard Films," *Coffeyville Daily Journal*, May 3, 1915.
7. "*Sin* Barred from Kansas by State Movie Censors," *Abilene Daily Reflector*, Oct. 16, 1915.
8. "Festus Foster Kissed 13 Girls in One Evening," *Wichita Beacon*, Oct. 23, 1916.

9. James Bone, *The Curse of Beauty: The Scandalous and Tragic Life of Audrey Munson, America's First Supermodel* (New York: Regan Arts, 2016).

10. "Festus Kissed 13 Girls in One Evening," *Chanute Daily Tribune*, Oct. 24, 1916.

11. "Kansas Bars Drink Movies," *St. Louis Post-Dispatch*, Apr. 13, 1915.

12. "Even Movies Must Be Absolutely Dry," *Fort Wayne Sentinel*, Apr. 17, 1915.

13. "Miss Carrie Simpson, Film Censor, Outlines Her Ideal Photo Drama," *Topeka Daily Capital*, Aug. 7, 1915.

14. *Ibid.*

15. *Mutual Film Corp. of Missouri v. Hodges*, 236 U.S. 248, 251 (1915).

16. "*Birth of a Nation* Rejected by State," *Topeka Daily Capital*, Jan. 25, 1916.

17. *Mid-West Photo-Play Corp v. Miller*, 169 P. 1154, 1156 (Kan. 1918).

18. "Censor Board Protects the Morals of Kansas," *Topeka Daily Capital*, Oct. 23, 1921.

19. See entries for "The Pilgrim," "Flesh and the Devil," and "All Quiet on the Western Front," Kansas Board of Review Movie Index, Kansas Historical Society, www.kshs.org/p/board-of-review-movie-index/13820.

20. "Shaky Decision," *Hutchinson News*, Aug. 19, 1942.

21. *Mutual Film Corp. v. Ohio*, 236 U.S. 230, 244 (1915).

22. *Holmby Productions v. Vaughn*, 177 Kan. 728, 729 (Kan. 1955).

23. *Kansas v. Columbia Pictures Corp.*, 197 Kan. 448, 455 (Kan. 1966).

24. *Maguin v. Miller*, 433 F. Supp. 223, 230 (D. Kan. 1977).

Kentucky

1. Sources differ with regard to Griffith's birthplace, attributing the location to either La Grange or Crestwood. See Henry Stephen Gordon, "David Wark Griffith: His Early Years; His Struggles; His Ambitions and Their Achievement," *Photoplay*, June 1916; and Schickel, *D.W. Griffith* (New York: Limelight, 1996), 16.

2. Gordon, "David Wark Griffith," *Photoplay*, June 1916.

3. "Gala Opening for *Birth of a Nation*," *Brooklyn Daily Eagle*, July 3, 1915; "*Birth of a Nation* Stirred Large Audience to Enthusiasm," *Houston Post*, Oct. 19, 1915.

4. "Strand Manager After Original Screen Fans," *Courier-Journal*, Mar. 14, 1920.

5. Gordon, "David Wark Griffith," *Photoplay*, June 1916.

6. "Louisville, Kentucky, History Covers but Ten Years," *MPW*, July 15, 1916, 396.

7. "Louisville," *MPW*, Nov. 8, 1913, 632.

8. "To Censor Pictures," *Courier-Journal*, Oct. 2, 1909.

9. See "Censor for Films," *Hopkinsville Kentuckian*, Sep. 16, 1915; "Owensboro to Censor Films," *Courier-Journal*, Mar. 9, 1921.

10. "Film Censor Bill to Get Senate Hearing Today," *Courier-Journal*, Feb. 9, 1922.

11. "3 Would Censor Films in State," *Courier-Journal*, Feb. 23, 1922.

12. Richard R. Lingeman, "The Ordeal of Fatty Arbuckle," *NYT*, Aug. 27, 1976.

13. "Arbuckle Film Withdrawn Here," *Courier Journal*, Sep. 13, 1921.

14. "The History of the Louisville Division of Police, City of Louisville Police Department, n.d., https://
louisvilleky.gov/government/police/history-louisville-division-police; "Varied Answers Are Given to Question of Fairs Interest," *Courier-Journal*, Sep. 10, 1921.

15. "Policewomen Are Censors for City," *Courier-Journal*, Dec. 5, 1922.

16. "Federation of Women's Clubs," *Courier-Journal*, Sep. 28, 1934.

17. "Film Series and Movie Listings," *NYT*, Aug. 5, 2010.

18. *Cambist Films Inc. v. Tribell*, 293 F. Supp. 407 (E.D. Ky. 1968).

19. *Cain v. Commonwealth of Kentucky*, 437 S.W.2d 769 (Ky. Ct. App. 1969); *Cain v. Kentucky*, 397 U.S. 319 (1970).

20. "*How to Succeed with Sex* Arrives," *NYT*, Apr. 11, 1970.

21. *Johnson v. Commonwealth*, 475 S.W.2d 893 (Ky. Ct. 1971).

22. *Roaden v. Kentucky*, 413 U.S. 496 (1973); *Harry Roaden v. Commonwealth of Kentucky*, 473 S.W.2d 814 (Ky. Ct. App. 1971).

23. "*Disco Dolls in Hot Skin* Out of Prosecutors' Reach," *Bowling Green Daily News*, Nov. 24, 1999.

Louisiana

1. "Death of William T. Rock," *MPW*, Aug. 12, 1916, 1078.

2. "Thomas Armat, 81, A Pioneer in Films," *NYT*, Oct. 1, 1948.

3. "Amusements," *New Orleans Times-Democrat* (hereafter cited as *NOTD*), July 3, 1896; "Vitascope Hall," *NOTD*, Aug. 2, 1896; "Vitascope Hall," *NOTD*, Aug. 9, 1896; "Amusements," *NOTD*, July 18, 1897.

4. Kevin Brownlow, *Behind the Mask of Innocence* (New York; Knopf Doubleday, 2013), 80.

5. Mike Scott, "The Legend of *Tarzan* in Louisiana," *Times-Picayune*, July 6, 2016.

6. *Ibid.*

7. "To Censor the Movies," *Shreveport Times*, Sep. 18, 1912.

8. "Censoring of Pictures," *NOTD*, Sep. 21, 1912.

9. "Censors Stop Picture," *Alexandria Town Talk*, Sep. 1, 1913.

10. "Fifty Baton Rouge Women," *Alexandria Town Talk*, Jan. 27, 1917.

11. "Marguerite Clark, Ex-Actress, Dies," *NYT*, Sep. 26, 1940.

12. "Long Appoints Censors," *NYT*, July 16, 1935.

13. Leonard Shannon, "*Walk* in New Orleans," *NYT*, May 7, 1961.

14. "Film Premiere Shifted," *NYT*, Feb. 20, 1962; "Showing of Film in N.O. Is Cancelled," *Lake Charles American-Press*, Feb. 20, 1962.

15. *United States v. One Carton Positive Motion Picture Film Entitled Technique of Physical Love*, 314 F. Supp. 1334 (E.D. La. 1970).

16. *State of Louisiana v. Gulf State Theatres of Louisiana*, 287 So.2d 496 (La. 1973); *State of Louisiana v. Gulf State Theatres of Louisiana*, 270 So.2d 547 (La. 1972).

17. *Gulf State Theatres of Louisiana v. Richardson*, 287 So.2d 480 (La. 1973).

18. *Byers v. Edmondson*, 826 So.2d 551, 553n2 (1st Cir. 2002).

19. *Byers v. Edmondson*, 712 So.2d 681, 683 (1st Cir. 1998).

20. *Byers*, 712 So.2d at 684.

21. *Schenck v. United States*, 249 U.S. 47, 52 (1919).

22. *Byers v. Edmondson*, 826 So.2d 551, 556 (1st Cir. 2002).

Maine

1. "Anti-Kinetoscope Bill Passes," *Bismarck Tribune*, Mar. 27, 1897; "Old Statute Protects Maine Against Syndicate Invasion," *Los Angeles Herald*, July 7, 1910; also see Barak Y. Orbach, "Prizefighting and the Birth of Movie Censorship," *Yale Journal of Law and the Humanities* 21, no. 2 (May 8, 2013).

2. "Amusements," *Bangor Daily Whig and Courier*, Sep. 1, 1897.

3. "Plays and Players," *Bangor Daily Whig and Courier*, Dec. 1, 1899.

4. *Ibid.*

5. See *A Bill to Amend and Consolidate the Acts Respecting Copyright*, S. 6330, H.R. 19853, 59th Cong. (1906).

6. *Edison v. Lubin*, 122 F. 240 (3d Cir. 1903).

7. Benjamin W. Rudd, "Notable Dates in American Copyright 1783–1969," *Quarterly Journal of the Library of Congress* (1971), 138, http://copyright.gov/history/dates.pdf.

8. "Early Motion Pictures Free of Copyright Restrictions in the Library of Congress," Library of Congress Moving Image Research Center, n.d., http://www.loc.gov/rr/mopic/earlymps.html.

9. Library of Congress, *Report of the Librarian of Congress and Report of the Superintendent of the Library Building and Grounds for the Fiscal Year Ending June 30, 1912* (Washington: Government Printing Office, 1912), 173.

10. Wendi A. Maloney, "Centennial of Cinema under Copyright Law," *Library of Congress Magazine* (Sep.–Oct. 2012).

11. See "Edison General File Series: 1919: (E-19-50) Motion Pictures," in the Thomas A. Edison Papers at Rutgers University, http://edison.rutgers.edu/NamesSearch/glocpage.php3?gloc=E1950&.

12. The business of distributing motion pictures with lapsed copyright protection had been on the sidelines of the mainstream market since at least the 1950s, when Blackhawk Films began exploiting PD or orphaned prints of silent films. In 1955 the initial copyright term for the first talkies registered in 1927 came due. Those films not renewed provided a treasure trove of content for niche distributors. Thunderbird Films and Reel Images sold Super 8 and 16 mm prints to a third-tier market of colleges, libraries, and private collectors. See David Pierce, "Forgotten Faces: Why Some of Our Cinema Heritage Is Part of the Public Domain," *Film History*, Apr. 1, 2007.

13. "Hughes Film Trial Is to Continue," *Lewiston Evening Journal*, July 13, 1976.

14. Dale McGarrigle, "Collector of Vintage Films Converts Hobby into Blockbuster Business," *Bangor Daily News*, Feb. 8, 1991.

15. *Classic Film Museum Inc. v. Warner Bros.*, 597 F.2d 13, 15 (1st Cir. 1979).

Maryland

1. "More Appointments Made," *Frederick News*, May 30, 1916; *United Artists v. Board of Censors*, 210 Md. 586, 588 (Md. Ct. Spec. App. 1956).

2. "Maryland Censors Upheld," *Motography*, June 8, 1918, 1114.

3. "Annual Report: Maryland State Board of Motion Picture Censors, 1920–1921," 6–7, http://msa.maryland.gov/megafile/msa/speccol/sc5300/sc5339/000113/020000/020896/unrestricted/20150277e.pdf.

4. *Ibid.*

5. Stanley Frank, "Headaches of a Movie Censor," *Saturday Evening Post*, Sep. 27, 1947.

6. *United Artists v. Maryland Board of Censors*, 210 Md. 586, 594–595 (Md. Ct. Spec. App. 1956).

7. Jacques Kelly and Frederick N. Rasmussen, "Film Censor Mary Avara, 90, Dies," *Baltimore Sun*, Aug. 10, 2000.

8. "X-Rated Grandma Sees All Films," *Free Lance-Star*, July 26, 1979.

9. *Board of Censors v. Times Film*, 212 Md. 454, 465 (Md. Ct. Spec. App. 1957).

10. *Fanfare Films v. Motion Picture Censor Board of State of Maryland*, 234 Md. 10, 12 (Md. Ct. Spec. App. 1964).

11. Adam Bernstein, "Mary Avara, Staunch Md. Film Censor, Dies," *Washington Post*, Aug. 11, 2000.

12. *Dunn v. Maryland Board of Censors*, 240 Md. 249 (Md. Ct. Spec. App. 1965).

13. *Hewitt v. Maryland State Board of Censors*, 241 Md. 283 (Md. Ct. Spec. App. 1969); *Hewitt v. Maryland State Board of Censors*, 243 Md. 574 (Md. Ct. Spec. App. 1966).

14. *Trans-Lux Distributing Co. v. Maryland State Board of Censors*, 240 Md. 98 (Md. Ct. Spec. App. 1965).

15. *Leighton v. Maryland State Board of Censors*, 242 Md. 705 (Md. Ct. Spec. App. 1966).

16. *Wagonheim v. Maryland State Board of Censors*, 255 Md. 297 (Md. Ct. Spec. App. 1969).

17. *Hewitt v. Maryland State Board of Censors*, 255 Md. 528, 529 (Md. Ct. Spec. App. 1969).

18. *Hewitt v. Maryland State Board of Censors*, 254 Md. 179 (Md. Ct. Spec. App. 1969).

19. *Hewitt v. Maryland State Board of Censors*, 256 Md. 358 (Md. Ct. Spec. App. 1970).

20. *Sanza v. Maryland State Board of Censors*, 245 Md. 319 (Md. Ct. Spec. App. 1967); *John Ebert v. Maryland State Board of Censors*, 19 Md. App. 300 (Md. Ct. Spec. App. 1973); *Star v. Preller*, 375 F. Supp. 1093 (D. Md. 1974); *Mangum v. Maryland State Board of Censors*, 273 Md. 176 (Md. Ct. Spec. App. 1974).

21. "Bill Would Ban 'Snuff' Movies," *Hagerstown Daily Mail*, Jan. 31, 1976.

22. *Freedman v. Maryland*, 380 U.S. 51 (1965).

23. Jacques Kelly and Frederick N. Rasmussen, "Film Censor Mary Avara, 90, Dies," *Baltimore Sun*, Aug. 10, 2000.

24. "The Grandmother Who Fought Porn," *underbelly* blog, Apr. 24, 2014, http://www.mdhs.org/underbelly/2014/04/24/the-grandmother-who-fought-porn-mary-avara/.

25. Ben A. Franklin, "Last State Board of Censors Fades Away after 65 Years," *NYT*, June 29, 1981; Gilbert Sandler, "When Censors Edited Reel Life," *Baltimore Sun*, Apr. 27, 1993.

Massachusetts

1. *Commonwealth v. Wiseman*, 356 Mass. 251, 253 (Mass. 1969).

2. Richard Schickel, "The Frightful Follies of Bedlam," *Life*, Dec. 1, 1967.

3. *Commonwealth v. Wiseman*, 356 Mass. 251, 255 (Mass. 1969).

4. Richard Schickel, "The Frightful Follies of Bedlam," *Life*, Dec. 1, 1967.

5. Vincent Canby, "*Titicut Follies* Observes Life in a Modern Bedlam," *NYT*, Oct. 4, 1967.

6. Roger Ebert, "*Titicut Follies*," *Chicago Sun-Times*, Oct. 8, 1968.

7. John H. Fenton, "Film Stirs Furor in Massachusetts," *NYT*, Oct. 18, 1967.

8. "*Titicut* Film Barred by Massachusetts after Month's Trial," *NYT*, Jan. 5, 1968.

9. "*Titicut* Is Barred to Bay State Public," *NYT*, June 25, 1969; *Commonwealth v. Wiseman*, 356 Mass. 251, 263 (Mass. 1969).

10. Francis Hopkins, "Ban Lifted on Movie After 24 Years," *Pittsburgh Post-Gazette*, Aug. 3, 1991.

11. "Crowd at Hearing on Bill to Censor Movies," *Boston Daily Globe* (hereafter cited as *BDG*), Feb. 11, 1915.

12. "Colored People to Storm State House," *BDG*, Apr. 19, 1915.

13. "Court Hearing on Film Today," *BDG*, Apr. 20, 1915; "Starts Hearing Without Delay," *BDG*, Apr. 21, 1915.

14. "Thinks It Hurtful Play," *BDG*, Apr. 25, 1915.

15. "Kill the Sullivan Bill," *BDG*, Apr. 27, 1915.

16. "Judge Dowd's Order Obeyed," *BDG*, Apr. 23, 1915.

17. Neal Gabler, *An Empire of Their Own* (New York: Anchor Books, 1989), 90–91.

18. "Senate Fights over Bill," *BDG*, May 18, 1915.

19. "Use Mayor to Promote Film Show," *Boston Post*, Sep. 19, 1916; "*Is Any Girl Safe?* Closed by Censors," *Boston Post*, Oct. 4, 1916.

20. "Boston Bars Famous Film," *Boston Post*, May 17, 1921.

21. Joseph J. Huthmacher, *Massachusetts People and Politics* (Boston: Harvard University Press, 1959), 295.

22. "*Blockade* Film Banned," *Fitchburg Sentinel*, July 29, 1938.

23. "Hollywood Boasted Too Soon," *Decatur Daily Review*, Apr. 4, 1940.

24. "Garbo Banned," *Fitchburg Sentinel*, Nov. 28, 1941.

25. "Police Coil *Rope*," *Berkshire Eagle*, Oct. 1, 1948.

26. Bruce Weber, "Anita Bjork, Once 'the New Garbo,' Dies at 89," *NYT*, Oct. 25, 2012.

27. *Brattle Films v. Commissioner of Public Safety*, 333 Mass. 58, 61 (Mass. 1955).

28. *Commonwealth v. Moniz*, 338 Mass. 443, 445–446 (Mass. 1959).

29. Douglas Martin, "Edward de Grazia, Lawyer Who Fought Censorship of Books, Is Dead at 86," *NYT*, Apr. 23, 2013.

30. Justice William O. Douglas recused himself because an excerpt from one of his books had appeared in the *Evergreen Review* published by Grove, which also distributed the picture. As a result the Court was deadlocked at 4–4. See *Karalexis v. Byrne*, 306 F. Supp. 1363 (D. Mass. 1969).

31. David J. Fox, "*Henry & June* Ban Called an Isolated Situation," *Los Angeles Times*, Oct. 6, 1990.

32. Josh Chetwynd, "Banned in Boston," *USA Today*, Mar. 5, 2001.

Michigan

1. "The Film Cycle," *NYT*, July 23, 1891.

2. Waldo Walker, "All Industry Honors Nine of Its Pioneers," *NYT*, Oct. 21, 1928.

3. "Barney Oldfield, Ex-Racer, Is Dead," *NYT*, Oct. 5, 1946.

4. "Sidewalks of New York Put in Film," *NYT*, June 5, 1927; "Projection Jottings," *NYT*, Oct. 2, 1927.

5. Winston Burdett, "The Screen," *Brooklyn Daily Eagle*, Jan. 18, 1937.

6. Gene Blottner, *Columbia Noir: A Complete Filmography 1940–1962* (Jefferson, NC: McFarland, 2015), 109.

7. "Amusements," *Detroit Free Press*, Dec. 15, 1895.

8. "Fall Opening This Entire Week," *Detroit Free Press*, Sep. 25, 1898.

9. The film was most likely *The Passion Play of Oberammergau* (1898); see "Passion Play Pictures," *Detroit Free Press*, Feb. 17, 1901.

10. "Film Men Ask Congress' Help," *Detroit Free Press*, Mar. 20, 1909.

11. *Journal of the Senate of the State of Michigan*, vol. 1 (Lansing, MI: Wynkoop Hallenbeck Crawford Co. State Printers, 1913), 200.

12. "Would Censor Movies," *News Palladium*, Mar. 15, 1915; "Create a Board of Movie Censors in Short Council Meet," *News Palladium*, Mar. 21, 1916.

13. "Potter Talks on Censorship," *Detroit Free Press*, Feb. 4, 1914; "Detroit to Have Police Censorship Again," *Michigan Film Review*, Apr. 2, 1918.

14. "Bullets Check Suspect's Sprint," *Detroit Free Press*, June 28, 1909; "Sprinting Cop Makes Arrest," *Detroit Free Press*, Aug. 25, 1909.

15. "At the Orpheum," *News-Palladium*, Apr. 8, 1915.

16. "Detroit Censor Says 'No,'" *Oregon Daily Journal*, Sep. 12, 1921; "Detroit Bans Normand Films," *Manitowoc Herald-Times*, Jan. 10, 1924.

17. "Detroit Film Inspector Quits After 15 Years," *Winona Republican-Herald*, May 4, 1948.

18. "Rogers-Crawford-Gable Films Banned in Detroit," *News-Palladium*, Mar. 28, 1940.

19. Kristen Pullen, *Like a Natural Woman: Spectacular Female Performance in Classical Hollywood* (New Brunswick: Rutgers University Press, 2014), 40.

20. *Bloss v. Paris Township*, 380 Mich. 466, 470 (Mich. 1968).

21. *American Mini Theatres, Inc. v. Gribbs*, 518 F.2d 1014 (Mich. Ct. App. 1975).

22. *Young v. American Mini Theatres*, 427 U.S. 50, 72–73 (1976).

23. Vincent Canby, "Film View," *NYT*, Mar. 7, 1976.

24. *Swope v. Lubbers*, 560 F. Supp. 1328, 1335 (W.D. Mich. 1983).

Minnesota

1. "Burton Holmes, Lecturer, 88, Dies," *NYT*, July 23, 1958.

2. "Holmes on the Orient," *Saint Paul Globe*, Mar. 1, 1896.

3. "Dramatic," *Saint Paul Globe*, Mar. 27, 1898.

4. "Burton Holmes' Lectures," *Minneapolis Journal*, Jan. 1, 1901; "Burton Holmes' Lecture," *Minneapolis Journal*, Apr. 19, 1902; "Y.M.C.A. Strengthens Entertainment Course," *Saint Paul Globe*, Jan. 18, 1903.

5. Dave Kenney, *Twin Cities Picture Show: A Century of Moviegoing* (Minneapolis: Minnesota Historical Society, 2007), 18.

6. "Regulating the Movies," *Pioneer*, Mar. 1, 1913.

7. *Bainbridge v. City of Minnesota*, 131 Minn. 195, 196 (Minn. 1915).

8. "*The Birth of a Nation*," *Appeal*, Oct. 23, 1915.

9. "*Birth of a Nation* Back to Twin Cities," *Bismarck Tribune*, Dec. 14, 1915.

10. Iris Nathanson, "Remembering the Shubert's Buzz Bainbridge," *Minneapolis Post*, Nov. 19, 2009.

11. "Doctors and Mayor to Censor Moving Picture at Grand," *Pioneer*, June 22, 1916.

12. "Beauty Unadorned Adorned Enough Says Mayor Nye," *Bismarck Tribune*, July 16, 1916.

13. F.A. Wilson, "*Is Any Girl Safe?*," *Pioneer*, Dec. 2, 1916; "Worthwhile if It Saves One Girl," *Brainerd Daily Dispatch*, Dec. 7, 1916; "Vice Film Endorsed by Censors," *New Ulm Review*, Jan. 24, 1917.

14. "Bans: *The Evil Thereof*," *MPW*, July 8, 1916, 283.

15. "Legion of Decency Condemns Movie," *NYT*, Aug. 14, 1947.

16. Kenney, *Twin Cities Picture Show* (Minneapolis: Minnesota Historical Society, 2007).

17. "Ted Mann, 84, Who Owned Theater Where the Stars Preserve Their Prints," *NYT*, Jan. 22, 2001; also see Kenney, *Twin Cities Picture Show* (Minneapolis: Minnesota Historical Society, 2007).

18. "Banned in Winona: The Frozen River Film Festival's Fracking Fiasco," *Star Tribune*, Jan. 24, 2014.

Mississippi

1. Joel Rose, "Robert Johnson at 100, Still Dispelling Myths," National Public Radio, May 6, 2011, www.npr.org/2011/05/07/136063911/robert-johnson-at-100-still-dispelling-myths.

2. Judy Klemesrud, "They Wait Hours—To be Shocked," *NYT*, Jan. 27, 1974.

3. Foster Hirsch, "What the Devil Happened to *The Exorcist*'s Oscar," *NYT*, May 5, 1974.

4. *ABC Interstate Theatres v. Mississippi*, 325 So.2d 123, 124 (Miss. 1976).

5. "Archie L. Shepard's High-Class Moving Pictures," *Vicksburg Evening Post*, Nov. 23, 1904.

6. "Archie L. Shepard's High Class Moving Pictures," *Vicksburg Herald*, Feb. 12, 1905.

7. Robert Grau, *The Theater of Science* (New York: Broadway Publishing Co., 1914), xi.

8. Anne Morey, "Early Film Exhibition in Wilmington, North Carolina," in *Hollywood in the Neighborhood: Historical Case Studies of Local Moviegoing*, ed. Kathryn Fuller-Seeley (Berkeley: University of California Press, 2008), 57.

9. "Give Us Decent Pictures," *Jackson Daily News*, June 12, 1911.

10. "Don't Repeat It," *Jackson Daily News*, June 22, 1911.

11. "Money to Censor Films Needed," *St. Louis Post-Dispatch*, Mar. 13, 1914.

12. "To Censor Movie Love," *Daily Arkansas Gazette*, Mar. 19, 1914.

13. "Mississippi Movie Censors," *Delta Democrat-Times*, Apr. 18, 1940.

14. Milton Esterow, "*Baby Doll* in Dixie and Flatbush," *NYT*, Feb. 26, 1956.

15. "*Baby Doll* Hit by Censors in Only a Few Southern Theaters," *Delta Democrat-Times*, Jan. 20, 1957.

16. "Charge Jackson Censors Movies," *Delta Democrat-Times*, Mar. 9, 1959.

Missouri

1. "Some Remarkable Facts About the St. Louis World's Fair," *Palestine Daily Herald*, July 30, 1904.

2. Mark Hudson, "Eadweard Muybridge," *Telegraph*, Sep. 6, 2010.

3. "President Shot at Buffalo Fair," *NYT*, Sep. 7, 1901.

4. Martha R. Clevenger, "Through the Eyes of a Fairgoer: The 1904 World's Fair Memoir of Edward V.P. Schneiderhahn," *Gateway Magazine, Missouri Historical Society*, 1992.

5. Walter Barlow Stevens, "Edward Vincent Paul Schneiderhahn," *St. Louis, the Fourth City, 1764–1909*, Vol. 2 (St. Louis, MO: S.J. Park, 1909), 717–718.

6. "Film Censor Bill Passes," *St. Louis Star*, Mar. 5, 1910; "House Joyfully Kills Bills of Three Councilmen," *St. Louis Post-Dispatch*, Mar. 30, 1910.

7. "Schneiderhahn Says Art Covers a Lot of Sins," *St. Louis Post-Dispatch*, Dec. 18, 1910.

8. "Wants Blewett as Chairman of Picture Censors," *St. Louis Post-Dispatch*, Oct. 30, 1912.

9. "Women to Censor Theaters of City for Coming Month," *Springfield Missouri Republican*, Feb. 20, 1913.

10. "Bald Knobbers in Jam," *NYT*, Mar. 21, 1887.

11. Rusty D. Aton, *Baseball in Springfield* (Charleston, SC: Arcadia, 2005), 19.

12. "Bald Knob Show Manager Pinched," *Springfield Missouri Republican*, July 6, 1913.

13. "Outlaw Films Banned," *St. Louis Post-Dispatch*, June 22, 1913.

14. "Bennert Defies Powers," *Springfield Missouri Republican*, June 28, 1913.

15. *Ibid.*

16. "Bald Knobber Film Hold Up May Get Into Court," *Springfield Missouri Republican*, June 27, 1913.

17. "Land Given 'Wife'," *Springfield Missouri Republican*, Jan. 28, 1914.

18. "Kansas City Censor Personally Endorses Lying Lips," *Neosho Daily News*, Apr. 25, 1921.

19. Dan Care, "Around Town," *Kansas City Kansan*, Mar. 13, 1921.

20. *State ex rel. Goldman v. Kansas City*, 319 Mo. 1078 (Mo. 1938).

21. *Hallmark Prod. v. Mosley*, 190 F.2d 904, 906 (8th Cir. 1951).

22. See *Hartstein v. Missouri*, 404 U.S. 988 (1971); *State v. Harstein*, 469 S.W.2d 329 (Mo. 1971).

23. *Kansas City v. O'Connor*, 510 S.W.2d 689 (Mo. 1974).

Montana

1. "Man Jailed after Threatening to Shoot Boy over *Star Wars* Spoiler," CBS News, Dec. 22, 2015, http://www.cbsnews.com/news/man-jailed-after-threatening-to-shoot-boy-over-star-wars-spoiler/.

2. Angela Brandt, "Shooting Threat over *Star Wars* Spoilers Leads to School Lockdown," *Helena Independent Record*, Dec. 21, 2015.

3. "Local Motion Pictures to Be Taken This Week," *Anaconda Standard*, Apr. 4, 1911.

4. "Motion Picture Man Takes Many Views of Butte Life," *Anaconda Standard*, May 7, 1911.

5. See Karen C. Lund, "American Indians in Silent Film," Library of Congress Moving Image Research Center, n.d., http://www.loc.gov/rr/mopic/findaid/indian1.html; also see "K.E.S.E. Program for Fall," *Motography*, Sep. 1, 1917, 464.

6. "Builder and Photographer Are Eulogized," *Helena Independent Record*, Feb. 14, 1960; also see Lund, "American Indians in Silent Film."

7. Ellen Baumler, *Montana Moments: History on the Go* (Helena: Montana Historical Society, 2010),172.

8. "Sob Sister Takes Shot at Politician," *Tonopah Daily Bonanza*, Sep. 30, 1916.

9. "Donlan Bill Forbids Moving Pictures That Depict Crime," *Helena Independent Record*, Jan. 11, 1921.

10. "Montana House Kills Bill to Censor Movies," *Courier-Journal*, Feb. 25, 1921.

11. "At the Theaters," *Daily Courier*, June 21, 1927

12. "Red Skies of Montana," *Denton Record-Chronicle*, Apr. 27, 1952; "Only Survivor of Big Mann Gulch Fire Succumbs in Missoula," *Helena Independent Record*, Jan. 14, 1955.

13. "Hedda Hopper's Hollywood," *Tucson Daily Citizen*, Mar. 20, 1954.

14. Brian D'Ambrosio, "Actor Jeff Bridges Talks Montana," *Montana Standard*, Mar. 20, 2016; Rick Newby, ed., *The Rocky Mountain Region* (Westport, CT: Greenwood Press, 2004), 177; "20 Years After the Film *A River Runs Through It*, a River of Tourism Runs Through Montana," *Oregonian*, Aug. 18, 2012; Todd McCarthy, *Howard Hawks: The Grey Fox of Hollywood* (New York: Grove Press, 1997), 683.

15. Manohla Dargis, "The Second Coming of Heaven's Gate," *NYT*, Mar. 15, 2013.

16. Eric Clements, "Screening of Comedic Muslim Film Protested in Missoula," KTVQ.com, Apr. 28, 2016, http://www.ktvq.com/story/31839542/screening-of-comedic-muslim-film-protested-in-missoula.

Nebraska

1. "The State at St. Louis Fair," *Norfolk Weekly News*, Nov. 27, 1903.

2. "Nebraskans at St. Louis," *Omaha Daily Bee*, Nov. 21, 1904.

3. "In Deadwood," *Deadwood Pioneer*, Aug. 15, 1956; see also Richard W. Etulain, *The Life and Legends of Calamity Jane* (Norman: University of Oklahoma Press, 2014), 219; "Nebraska's First Motion Picture," Nebraska State Historical Society, last modified Sep. 14, 2005, www.nebraskahistory.org/publish/publicat/timeline/first_motion_picture.htm.

4. Angela Aleiss, "Who Was the Real James Young Deer?" *Bright Lights Film Journal*, May 2013, www.aisc.ucla.edu/news/files/Young%20Deer%20BL%20Article.pdf.

5. "First All Negro Film Has Been Completed," *Oregon Daily Journal*, Aug. 6, 1916.

6. "Omaha Picture Shows to Be Close Censored," *Lincoln Daily News*, June 12, 1912.

7. "Recreation Places Need Supervising," *Lincoln Star*, Nov. 2, 1913.

8. "Exchanges May Move from Omaha," *MPW*, Mar. 8, 1919.

9. "Nebraska Censorship Bill Defeated," *MPW*, Apr. 5, 1919.

10. "Wolz Would Censor Films," *Omaha Daily Bee*, Feb. 3, 1913; "Nebraska to Have Movie Censorship," *Des Moines Register*, Apr. 28, 1921; "Gov. M'Kelvie Vetoes Movie Censorship Bill," *Alliance Herald*, Apr. 29, 1921.

11. "Governor as a Movie Censor," *Lincoln Star*, Jan. 19, 1929; "Censorship Proposed for Moving Pictures," *Lincoln Evening Journal*, Jan. 27, 1931; "Movie Censorship Has Big Following," *Lincoln Evening Journal*, Apr. 1, 1931.

12. "Can This Be Omaha?," *Lincoln Evening Journal*, May 15, 1937.

13. "Mayor's Board Puts O.K. on *Lady of Burlesque*," *Lincoln Evening Journal*, May 21, 1943.

14. "Doctors Present *Birth of a Baby* in Welfare Movie," *Life*, Apr. 11, 1938, 32–36.

15. "Bans Baby Picture," *Nebraska State Journal*, June 23, 1938; "Butler Is Overruled," *Nebraska State Journal*, June 25, 1938.

16. *State of Nebraska v. American Theater Corp.*, 230 N.W.2d 209, 213 (Neb. 1975).

Nevada

1. Prizefighting prohibitions swept through state legislatures, including New Jersey (1847); New York (1865); Pennsylvania (1867); Florida (1868); Kentucky (1869); California and Rhode Island (1872); Nevada (1877); Massachusetts (1883); Maine and Ohio (1884); Idaho and South Dakota (1887); Connecticut (1888); Missouri (1889); Louisiana (1890); Arkansas, Tennessee, and Texas (1891); Oregon, including the Alaska Territory (1892); Delaware and Illinois (1893); Indiana, Iowa, Minnesota, Vermont, and Virginia (1894); and Nebraska (1895). See Barak Y. Orbach, "Prizefighting and the Birth of Movie Censorship," *Yale Journal of Law and the Humanities* 21, no. 2 (May 8, 2013): n30, n206.

2. See Dan Streible, *Fight Pictures: A History of Boxing and Early Cinema* (Berkeley: University of California Press, 2008), 35–36.

3. "Con Riordan's Last Bout," *NYT*, Nov. 18, 1894; "Fitzsimmons, Pugilist, Acquitted," *NYT*, July 4, 1895; *People v. Fitzsimmons*, 34 N.Y.S. 1102 (1895).

4. Colleen Aycock and Mark Scott, *Tex Rickard: Boxing's Greatest Promoter* (Jefferson, NC: McFarland, 2012), 8.

5. "Corbett and 'Fitz' Matched," *NYT*, Oct. 12, 1894; "No Boxing at Chicago," *NYT*, Dec.17, 1894; "Florida as the Resort of Pugilists," *NYT*, Apr. 14, 1895; "Corbett-Fitzsimmons Fight," *NYT*, Sep. 28, 1895; "May Be Had in Mexico," *Boston Post*, Oct. 4, 1895; "Prizefighters Not Wanted," *Boston Post*, Oct. 8, 1895; "Will Not Have the Fight," *Boston Post*, Oct. 16, 1895; "Pugilistic Fizzle Ended," *Boston Post*, Nov. 3, 1895.

6. "Fitz Wants Some Dough," *Salt Lake City Tribune*, Feb. 11, 1896.

7. Russell R. Elliott, *History of Nevada* (Lincoln: University of Nebraska Press, 1987), 406.

8. "Will Fight in Nevada," *Leavenworth Times*, Jan. 13, 1897.

9. "Fitzsimmons Put Out by Johnson," *NYT*, July 18, 1907.

10. Cecilia Rasmussen, "Boxing Venue Had Heavyweight in Its Corner," *Los Angeles Times*, Feb. 10, 2008.

11. "Crowd Gathers at Arena," *NYT*, July 5, 1910.

12. "Sad Crowd at Ringside," *NYT*, July 5, 1910.

13. "Eight Killed in Fight Riots," *NYT*, July 5, 1910.

14. Act to Prohibit the Importation and the Interstate Transportation of Films or Other Pictorial Representations of Prize Fights, 37 Stat. L. 240 (1912).

15. *Weber v. Freed*, 239 U.S. 325 (1915).

New Hampshire

1. William Dieterle, dir., *The Devil and Daniel Webster* (RKO Radio Pictures, 1941).

2. "Moving Pictures," *Portsmouth Herald*, Apr. 19, 1899.

3. "Gustave Frohman, Stage Veteran, Dies," *NYT*, Aug. 17, 1930.

4. "Daniel Frohman Gets Big Stars to Act for 'Movies,'" *NYT*, Dec. 22, 1912.

5. *Ibid.*

6. "Urges Censorship of Moving Pictures," *Portsmouth Herald*, Apr. 2, 1915.

7. "Cinema: Ramparts in Pennsylvania," *Time*, Oct. 21, 1940.

8. "Court to Hear Plea for Film," *Wilkes-Barre Record*, Sep. 24, 1940; see also *In re Ramparts We Watch*, 39 D. & C. 437 (Pa. 1940).

9. Wolfgang Saxon, "Louis de Rochemont, 79, Is Dead," *NYT*, Dec. 25, 1978.

10. Margaret Lillard, "Landmark '49 Film About Family Passing for White Recalled," *Los Angeles Times*, July 25, 1989.

11. Robert McG. Thomas Jr., "Thyra Johnson, 91, Symbol of Racial Distinctions, Dies," *NYT*, Nov. 29, 1995.

12. Lillard, "Landmark '49 Film," *Los Angeles Times*, July 25, 1989.

13. Thomas M. Pryor, "Hoeing His Own Row," *NYT*, June 26, 1949.

14. "Barred in Memphis," *NYT*, Aug. 21, 1949.

15. *RD-DR Corp. v. Smith*, 183 F.2d 562, 562 (5th Cir. 1950).

16. *Mutual Film Corp. v. Ohio*, 236 U.S. 230, 244 (1915).

17. *RD-DR Corp. v. Smith*, 183 F.2d 562, 565 (5th Cir. 1950).

18. *RD-DR Corp. v. Smith*, 89 F. Supp. 596, 597 (N.D. Ga. 1950).

New Jersey

1. Harold G. Bowen, "Thomas Alva Edison's Early Motion-Picture Experiments," in *A Technological History of Motion Pictures and Television*, ed. Raymond Fielding (Berkeley: University of California Press, 1967), 92.

2. *Ibid.*, 93.

3. *Ibid.*, 91.

4. "Kinetographing a Fight," *Times-Picayune*, June 20, 1894.

5. "Barred by Bradley," *New York Evening World*, July 17 1894.

6. Terry Ramsaye, *A Million and One Nights* (Abingdon, UK: Frank Cass, 2006), 256.

7. "The History of Movies in NJ," Official Website for the State of New Jersey, n.d., http://www.state.nj.us/nj/about/arts/movies.html.

8. "Studios and Films," Fort Lee Film Commission, n.d., http://www.fortleefilm.org/studios.html.

9. Kathleen M. Middleton, *Bayonne* (Charleston, SC: Arcadia, 2003), 94.

10. Tammy La Gorce, "Not Hollywood, But Once Famous for Movies," *NYT*, Sep. 14, 2012.

11. Helene Stapinski, "For Ft. Lee, Film Moments of 100 Years," *NYT*, May 8, 2009.

12. "Montclair to Censor Films," *Trenton Evening Times*, Aug. 6, 1909.

13. "Ban on Motion Picture," *Bridgewater Courier-News*, Aug. 13, 1918.

14. *Public Welfare Pictures Corp. v. Brennan*, 100 N.J. Eq. 132 (Ch. 1926); *Hygienic Productions v. Keenan*, 1

N.J. Super. 461 (Ch. Div. 1948); *American Museum of Natural History v. Keenan*, 20 N.J. Super. 111 (Ch. Div. 1952); "Documentary Film Barred in Newark," *NYT*, May 10, 1952; "Confiscated Film Cleared in Jersey," *NYT*, May 20, 1952.

15. "Jersey Judge Sees *The Moon Is Blue*," *NYT*, Oct. 16, 1953.

New Mexico

1. "War Scenes," *Albuquerque Citizen*, May 31, 1898.; *Albuquerque Citizen*, May 25, 1898; *Albuquerque Citizen*, June 13, 1898.

2. "Cineograph Performance," *Albuquerque Citizen*, May 1, 1900; "The Carnival Will Be in Full Blast Tomorrow," *Albuquerque Journal*, Nov. 20, 1904; "The Britt-Nelson Prize Fight Pictures," *Albuquerque Citizen*, Nov. 2, 1905.

3. "Board of Censors to View *Birth of a Nation* in Interest of Colored Folks," *Santa Fe New Mexican*, Mar. 25, 1916; "*Birth of a Nation* Is Tremendous Spectacle," *Santa Fe New Mexican*, Mar. 27, 1916.

4. "State May Have a Movie Censor," *Albuquerque Journal*, Feb. 16, 1921.

5. "Forget It," *Santa Fe New Mexican*, Feb. 16, 1921.

6. "Herbert Biberman Dead at 71," *NYT*, July 1, 1971.

7. "Actress in Film Under Fire Is Seized as Illegal Alien," *NYT*, Feb. 27, 1953.

8. "Street Fight Halts New Mexico Filming," *NYT*, Mar. 4, 1953.

9. *IPC Distributors v. Chicago Moving Pictures Machine Operators Union*, 132 F. Supp. 294 (N.D. Ill. 1955).

10. "Complete National Film Registry Listing," Library of Congress, n.d., http://www.loc.gov/programs/national-film-preservation-board/film-registry/complete-national-film-registry-listing/.

11. See Albuquerque NM Rev. Ordinances, Ch. 14, Art. XVI, § 14–16–1–5(B), 2009, amended 2011.

12. *City of Albuquerque v. Pangaea Cinema*, No. 33, 693, ¶27 (N.M. 2013); *City of Albuquerque v. Pangaea Cinema LLC dba Guild Cinema*, 284 P.3d 1090, 1101 (N.M. Ct. App. 2012).

13. Michael Williams, "Pornotopia Festival Zoning Difficulties Good for Families," *Albuquerque Examiner*, Oct. 25, 2010.

14. Dan McKay, "NM Supreme Court Reverses Pornotopia Conviction," *Albuquerque Journal*, Sep. 12, 2013; Moriah Carty, "Film Festival Heats Up Albuquerque," DailyLobo.com, Nov. 17, 2014, www.dailylobo.com:8080/article/2014/11/11–18-pornotopia.

15. *Monica Pompeo v. Board of Regents of the University of New Mexico*, Civ. No. 13-0833 MCA/CG, ¶9 (D.N.M. 2015).

16. *Monica Pompeo*, Civ. No. 13-0833 MCA/CG at ¶10.

17. *Monica Pompeo v. Board of Regents of the University of New Mexico*, 58 F. Supp. 3d 1187, 1190 (D.N.M. 2014).

18. *Monica Pompeo*, 58 F. Supp. 3d at 1189–1190.

19. Maggie Shepard, "Free Speech Lawsuit Against UNM Tossed," *Albuquerque Journal*, Dec. 26, 2015.

New York

1. "Mr. Edison's Latest," *Middletown Times-Press*, Mar. 10, 1894.

2. "Edison's Vitascope Cheered," *NYT*, Apr. 24, 1896.

3. See "Machines," *Who's Who of Victorian Cinema*, n.d., http://www.victorian-cinema.net/machines.

4. "No Moving Picture Monopoly," *New York Sun*, Mar. 13, 1902.

5. Christopher Gray, "A Family's Legacy, Burnished Anew," *NYT*, Apr. 13, 2008; Christopher Gray, "So You Think the Empire State Is a Tall Building?," *NYT*, Aug. 20, 2006; *White v. Walters* testimony, in *New York Supreme Court Appellate Division—First Department*, vol. 2308, June 1, 1911; Alan Crosland, "How Edison's 'Black Maria' Grew," *Motography*, Apr. 22, 1916; Rowley Amato, "Midwood's Historic Vitagraph Studios Gets Wrecking Ball," *Curbed New York*, Apr. 18, 2015.

6. Advertisement, *MPW*, May 6, 1916; "The Early Years (1909–1911)," Thanhouser Company Film Preservation Inc., n.d., http://www.thanhouser.org/1909.htm; Robert Levis, "Hooray for Hollywood?" *Newsday*, May 4, 2011. A decade later, in 1920, Paramount opened a facility in Astoria, Queens (see http://www.kaufmanastoria.com/about-us/).

7. Theodore A. Bingham, "Foreign Criminals in New York," *North American Review*, Sep. 1908, 383.

8. "Bingham to Close Sunday Theaters," *NYT*, Dec. 5, 1907; "Picture Shows to Test Blue Law," *NYT*, Dec. 7, 1907; "Picture Shows Fight to Open on Sundays," *NYT*, Jan. 1, 1908.

9. Picture Shows All Put Out of Business," *NYT*, Dec. 25, 1908; "Picture-Show Men Organize to Fight," *NYT*, Dec. 26, 1908; "Court to Pass on Theatre Licenses," *NYT*, Dec. 30, 1908; "Moving Pictures Win," *NYT*, Jan. 7, 1909.

10. "Motion Picture Law May Pass To-Day," *NYT*, May 14, 1912; "Pass Film Bill with Censorship Clause," *NYT*, Dec. 18, 1912; "Folks Bill Vetoed By Mayor," *NYT*, Jan. 1, 1913.

11. "Mrs. Belmont to Testify," *New York Sun*, Mar. 5, 1914.

12. "Sex-Mad?," *New York Evening World*, Mar. 7, 1914.

13. "Movie Censor Bill Signed by Miller," *NYT*, May 15, 1921.

14. "Wingate Is Named State Film Censor," *NYT*, Dec. 10, 1926.

15. "Why Movie Was Stopped," *NYT*, July 3, 1928; "Censors Ban Film on Russian Revolt," *NYT*, May 26, 1928; "Orders Darrow Film Cut," *NYT*, Oct. 31, 1931.

16. "Movie Censorship Nets State Million," *NYT*, Dec. 17, 1931; "Scan 1,651 Miles of Film," *NYT*, Nov. 20, 1932.

17. "State Film Director Joins Staff of Hays," *San Bernadino County Sun*, Sep. 16, 1932. Joseph I. Breen replaced Wingate in 1934.

18. "Irwin Esmond Dies," *NYT*, Aug. 8, 1956; "Regents Ban Film on Narcotics," *NYT*, June 26, 1938; "Polygamy Film Banned," *NYT*, June 17, 1939; "Film Called Dangerous," *NYT*, Feb. 15, 1939; "Censor Ban Lifted from Warner Film," *NYT*, Feb. 25, 1939; "Maternity Film Revised," *NYT*, Mar. 5, 1942; "*The Outlaw* Ban Holds," *NYT*, May 16, 1942.

19. Thomas M. Pryor, "Film Censorship Policy Defined," *NYT*, Feb. 10, 1946.

20. *Ibid.*

21. "Albany Police Ban *Bitter Rice*," *Oneonta Star*, Feb. 8, 1951; "New York Censors Lift Ban on Disney's *Vanishing Prairie*," *Long Beach Independent*, Aug. 13, 1954.

22. *Joseph Burstyn v. Wilson*, 343 U.S. 495, 509 (1952).

23. "Spellman Urges *Miracle* Boycott," *NYT*, Jan. 8, 1951.

24. *Joseph Burstyn, Inc. v. Wilson*, 303 N.Y. 242 (N.Y. 1951).

25. *Matter of Joseph Burstyn, Inc. v. Wilson*, 303 N.Y. 242 (N.Y. App. Div. 1951).

26. "*The Miracle* Happens," *NYT*, June 1, 1952.

27. *Burstyn v. Wilson*, 343 U.S. 495, 506 (1952).

28. "The Law of New York of 1921," in *The Morals of the Movie* by Ellis Paxson Oberholtzer (Philadelphia, PA: Penn Publishing, 1922), 221.

29. *Matter of Commercial Pictures Corp. v. Board of Regents*, 305 N.Y. 336 (N.Y. App. Div. 1953).

30. "Court Sees Banned Film," *NYT*, Jan. 6, 1954; *Superior Films, Inc. v. Department of Ed. of Ohio*, 346 U.S. 587 (1954).

31. *Matter of Excelsior Picture Corp. v. Regents*, 2 N.Y.2d 237 (N.Y. App. Div. 1957).

32. Richard Andress, "Film Censorship in New York State," New York State Archives, n.d., http://www.archives.nysed.gov/research/res_topics_film_censor.

North Carolina

1. Walter S. Hayward, "Harvest of the Storm Gods," *NYT*, June 22, 1952.

2. "Robert Mitchum, 79, Dies," *NYT*, July 2, 1997; Bill Davidson, "The Many Moods of Robert Mitchum," *Saturday Evening Post*, Sep. 1, 1962.

3. Interview with J. Lee Thompson, in *The Making of Cape Fear* (Universal Home Video, 2001).

4. *Ibid.*

5. John Lyden, ed., *The Routledge Companion to Religion and Film* (London: Routledge, 2009), 421.

6. Jacob Crawford Clapp, ed., *Historic Sketch of the Reformed Church in North Carolina* (Philadelphia: Publication Board of the Reformed Church in the United States, 1908), 308.

7. "*The Passion Play*," *Lexington Dispatch*, May 22, 1901; "The World-Renowned *Passion Play*," *Charlotte Observer*, June 6, 1901.

8. Allison Graham and Sharon Monteith, eds., *The New Encyclopedia of Southern Culture* (Chapel Hill: University of North Carolina Press, 2011), 106; "Bible Show and Moving Pictures," *Albemarle Enterprise*, Apr. 27, 1905.

9. "Coming," *Randolph Bulletin*, May 27, 1909.

10. "To Censor Movie Shows in Charlotte," *Charlotte News*, Apr. 6, 1914.

11. "Asheville Film Censor to Have Full Power," *Charlotte Observer*, Jan. 17, 1917.

12. "The Motion Picture Censorship Bill Is Given Favorable Report," *Greensboro Daily News*, Feb. 24, 1921.

13. "Movie Censorship Bill Up to House," *Fayetteville Observer*, Mar. 2, 1921; "Two Bills Killed," *Salisbury Evening Post*, Mar. 8, 1921.

14. *Journal and Proceedings of the North Carolina State Bar* (Raleigh: North Carolina State Bar, 1938), 32.

15. Larry Richards, *African American Films through 1959* (Jefferson, NC: McFarland, 1998), 252.

16. *Drive In Theatres v. Huskey*, 435 F.2d 228 (4th Cir. 1970).

17. David K. Frasier, *Russ Meyer—The Life and Films* (Jefferson, NC: McFarland, 1990), 160.

18. Sara Bonisteel, "*Hounddog* Opponents Crying Foul over Dakota Fanning Rape Scene," Fox News, Mar. 19, 2007, www.foxnews.com/story/2007/03/19/hounddog-opponents-crying-foul-over-dakota-fanning-rape-scene.html.

North Dakota

1. "N.D. Chautauqua," *Bismarck Tribune*, June 8, 1899.
2. "The City," *Bismarck Tribune*, Sep. 26, 1899.
3. "The Exhibit," *Jamestown Weekly Alert*, Mar. 14, 1901.
4. "Additional Local," *Red Lodge Picket*, Nov. 23, 1900.
5. "Moving Pictures," *Bismarck Tribune*, Feb. 17, 1902.
6. "Famous Moving Picture Show," *Bismarck Tribune*, June 2, 1903.
7. *Ibid.*
8. "Better All the Time," *Bismarck Tribune*, Dec. 27, 1907.
9. "*Mutt and Jeff* Will Appear at the Bijou," *Bismarck Tribune*, Mar. 25, 1912; "New Municipal Auditorium Opens Monday with Musical Masterpiece," *Bismarck Tribune*, Jan. 7, 1914; "Mary Pickford to Appear in Big Screen Feature at Auditorium Two Days," *Bismarck Tribune*, June 26, 1917.
10. "No Picture Censor," *Weekly Times-Record*, Feb. 18, 1915.
11. "Western," *Taliban Valley News*, Mar. 4, 1921; "Senate Wants Federal Insp. Of Movie Films," *Bismarck Tribune*, Mar. 1, 1921.
12. "Brief State News," *Ward County Independent*, May 22, 1919.
13. See *United States v. E.C. Knight Co.*, 156 U.S. 1 (1895); *Northern Securities Co. v. United States*, 193 U.S. 197 (1904); *Swift & Co. v. United States*, 196 U.S. 375 (1905); *United States v. American Tobacco Co.*, 221 U.S. 106 (1911); *Standard Oil v. United States*, 221 U.S. 1 (1911).
14. "Acts to Dissolve Big Lasky Concern as Movie Trust," *New York World*, Sep. 1, 1921.
15. "Film Trust Hearing Will Begin Today," *NYT*, Apr. 23, 1923.
16. "Says Film Trust Bars Independents," *NYT*, Apr. 24, 1923.
17. "Movie Owner Says He Was Frozen Out," *NYT*, May 11, 1923.
18. "Famous Players Guilty of Film Trust Conspiracy," *NYT*, July 10, 1927.
19. *United States v. Paramount Famous-Lasky Corp.*, 34 F.2d 984, 989 (S.D.N.Y. 1929); note that a similar verdict was reached against *First National Pictures* in *United States v. First National Pictures*, 34 F.2d 815 (S.D.N.Y. 1929).
20. *Federal Trade Commission v. Paramount Famous-Lasky Corp.*, 57 F.2d 152, 159 (2d Cir. 1932).
21. *Paramount Pictures v. Langer*, 23 F. Supp. 890, 902–903 (D.N.D. 1938).
22. *United States v. Paramount Pictures*, 334 U.S. 131 (1948).

Ohio

1. "The Kinetoscope," *Evening Review*, May 7, 1895.
2. Advertisement, *Evening Review*, Dec. 28, 1897.
3. "Wants to Censor Moving Pictures," *Marion Daily Mirror*, Feb. 10, 1910.
4. "Cleveland Now Has Movie Censorship," *Sandusky Register*, Dec. 12, 1912.
5. "Moving Picture Censor," *Cincinnati Enquirer*, Jan. 8, 1913.
6. "Cox Gets Busy," *Cincinnati Enquirer*, Apr. 16, 1913.
7. "All Movies Censored in This State Now," *Lima News*, Nov. 5, 1913.
8. "Moving Picture Censors," *Cincinnati Enquirer*,
Sep. 4, 1913; "Woman Lands State Plum," *Cincinnati Enquirer*, Aug. 20, 1913.
9. "Censors Will Use Chapel," *Cincinnati Enquirer*, Aug. 27, 1913.
10. "Good-Bye Wild West 'Movies,'" *Lima News*, Sep. 3, 1913; "Censoring Pictures," *Wilmington Ohio Journal-Republican*, Oct. 15, 1913.
11. "New Law Becomes Effective in Ohio," *Town Talk*, Nov. 4, 1913.
12. "Quits Censor Board," *Cincinnati Enquirer*, Dec. 21, 1913. Maddox was replaced by W.R. Wilson in July 1914; see "New Movie Censor," *Democratic Banner*, July 17, 1914.
13. "Censors Must Cut Out Dollar Meals," *Salem News*, May 15, 1914.
14. "It's Mrs. Maude Murray Miller," *Piqua Daily Call*, Dec. 1914.
15. "Vestal Cuts Loose," *Cincinnati Enquirer*, Mar. 10, 1915; "Film Censor Quits Job," *Chronicle Telegram*, Mar. 15, 1915.
16. *Motography*, Jan. 10, 1914, 14.
17. "Those Picture Censors," *New Philadelphia Daily Times*, July 25, 1914.
18. "Again Ban Picture," *East Liverpool Evening Review*, Jan. 6, 1916; "Censors Reject *Birth of a Nation*," *New Philadelphia Daily Times*, Mar. 6, 1925.
19. "Farrar's *Carmen* Is Shown in Cleveland," *Marion Star*, Oct. 15, 1915.
20. *Mutual v. Ohio*, 236 U.S. 230, 244 (1915).
21. "Ohio Censors Reject Films of Title Bout," *Detroit Free Press*, July 7, 1919.
22. "Will Not Pass Ohio Board of Censors," *Marion Star*, Mar. 26, 1921.
23. Advertisement, *Detroit Free Press*, Feb. 10, 1918; "Eastland Films Given Approval by Ohio Censors," *Lima News*, July 28, 1915; "Snappy Comment," *East Liverpool Evening Review*, Nov. 23, 1923.
24. Bruce Catton, "A Pen Fire and a Movie," *New Philadelphia Daily Times*, Sep. 26, 1930; "*Baby Face* Film Banned in Ohio," *Massillon Ohio Evening Independent*, July 25, 1933.
25. "*Outlaw* to be Cut," *Circleville Herald*, June 18, 1946.
26. "State May Ban Bergman Movie," *Dover Daily Reporter*, Feb. 7, 1950.
27. *Superior Films v. Dept. of Education*, 159 Ohio St. 315, 328 (Ohio 1953).
28. *Superior Films v. Dept. of Education*, 346 U.S. 587, 588 (1954).
29. *RKO v. Dept. of Education*, 162 Ohio St. 263 (Ohio 1954).
30. "Censors Remove Ban on 5 Movies," *Delphos Daily Herald*, Mar. 13, 1954.
31. "She Sees 'Em Free," *Ohio St. U. Monthly*, Oct. 1922, 16; "Ohio Film Censors Seek Better Law," *East Liverpool Evening Review*, Dec. 4, 1954.
32. *Jacobellis v. Ohio*, 378 U.S. 184, 197 (1964).
33. *United Artists Corp. v. Gladwell*, 373 F. Supp. 247, 249 (N.D. Ohio 1974).

Oklahoma

1. Kent Demaret, "You Got Trouble in Elmore City," *People*, May 19, 1980.
2. *Ibid.*
3. Rod Lott, "*Footloose*," *Oklahoma Gazette*, Oct. 14, 2011.

4. Kent Demaret, "You Got Trouble in Elmore City," *People*, May 19, 1980.

5. "Texas State Fair Car," *Daily Ardmoreite*, Sep. 15, 1901.

6. Advertisement, *Morning Tulsa Daily World*, Aug. 28, 1910; Advertisement, *Morning Tulsa Daily World*, Sep. 16, 1910; "Live News from Everywhere," *Ada Evening News*, Sep. 13, 1910; "Jeffries-Johnson Fight Pictures Tabooed," *Muscogee Times-Democrat*, July 16, 1910.

7. "Mayor Will Appoint Board of Censors," *Tulsa Star*, Jan. 17, 1914; "Would Censor Crime Movies," *Oklahoma City Times*, Feb. 2, 1915.

8. "Police as Censors," *Muscogee Times-Democrat*, May 27, 1915.

9. "Oklahoma City Makes Mayor Censor," *MPW*, Jan. 8, 1916, 280.

10. Stephanie Shafer, "Hamon, Jacob Louis," *The Encyclopedia of Oklahoma History and Culture*, n.d., www.okhistory.org/publications/enc/entry.php?entry=HA058.

11. "Clara Hamon Freed by Murder Jury," *NYT*, Mar. 18, 1921.

12. "By Special Ordinance Ardmore Puts Ban on Immoral, Criminal and Indecent Moving Pictures," *Daily Ardmoreite*, Apr. 3, 1921.

13. "Crime Pictures Barred in State," *Morning Tulsa Daily World*, Apr. 29, 1921. Al Jennings capitalized on his notoriety by playing a bandit in more than twenty motion pictures 1914–1920; Emmett Dalton played himself as well as his two brothers who had been killed in the Coffeeville, KS, shoot-out in *Beyond the Law* (1918); Henry Starr appeared in one film, *A Debtor to the Law* (1919), and Hamon in one film, *Fate* (1921).

14. "ACLU Remembers Michael Camfield," ACLU of Oklahoma, Oct. 11, 2011, http://acluok.org/2011/11/aclu-remembers-michael-camfield/.

15. Greg Sandoval, "Video Outlets Reverse Ban on *The Tin Drum*," *Los Angeles Times*, July 10, 1997.

16. *Video Software Dealers v. Oklahoma City*, 6 F. Supp. 2d 1292, 1296 (W.D. Okla. 1997).

Oregon

1. See Greg Long, *The Making of Bigfoot: The Inside Story* (Amherst, NY: Prometheus Books, 2004).

2. Leah Sottile, "The Man Who Created Bigfoot," *Outside*, July 5, 2016, http://www.outsideonline.com/2095096/man-who-created-bigfoot.

3. "Did This Dog Find Bigfoot?," *Daily Mail*, Aug. 17, 2016.

4. Larry Langman, *A Guide to Silent Westerns* (Westport, CT: Greenwood Press, 1992), 505.

5. "Censors Organize," *St. Johns Review*, Jan. 8, 1915.

6. "Portland Has Paid Movie Censor," *Oregon Daily Journal*, Mar. 7, 1915; "Mrs. Newill Is Chairman," *Oregon Daily Journal*, Mar. 24, 1915.

7. "May Censor Movies," *Roseburg Review*, Mar. 23, 1915.

8. "Bandit Chief's Dead Recalls Robbing of California Trains," *Pittsburgh Press*, Feb. 23, 1917.

9. "Censors Ban Film of Outlawry," *Seattle Star*, Feb. 17, 1915.

10. "Censor of Pictures is 'Inconsistent' Say the Film Men," *Oregon Daily Journal*, Aug. 1, 1915.

11. "Movie Censor Board Now Attempt to Censor News Films," *Oregon Daily Journal*, Sep. 28, 1916.

12. "Police Stop Show," *Oregon Daily Journal*, Dec. 10, 1915.

13. "*A Fool There Was* Is Censored by the Local Censor Board," *Roseburg Review*, May 10, 1915.

14. "Film Censors Bar *Kreutzer Sonata*," *Oregon Daily Journal*, Mar. 8, 1915; "Manager Clashes with Censor Board over *Serpent* Film," *Oregon Daily Journal*, Jan. 23, 1916.

15. "Pola Negri Barred from Screen in Portland," *Albany Evening Herald*, Nov. 26, 1924.

16. "French Film Banned by Portland Censor," *Herald and News*, Mar. 24, 1950.

17. "Censor Condemned Film Though She Did Not Recall Subject," *Oregon Daily Journal*, July 27, 1916.

18. "Censors Vote to Ban *Fools First*," *Oregon Daily Journal*, June 7, 1922.

19. "Arrested over Censored Film," *Klamath News*, Jan. 28, 1928.

20. "Portland Censors Crack Down on Theater Owner," *Corvallis Gazette-Times*, July 25, 1940.

21. "Showing of First Nazi Film Banned," *Greensburg Daily News*, Jan. 20, 1934; "Protest Nazi Film," *Oregon Statesman*, Feb. 1, 1934.

22. "Portland's Censor Fight Continues," *Herald and News*, June 3, 1950; "Court Overrules Movies' Censor," *Oregon Statesman*, June 8, 1950.

23. *City of Portland v. Welch*, 229 Or. 308, 310 (Or. 1961).

24. "Portland Film Censor Law Declared Illegal," *Oregon Statesman*, Dec. 21, 1961.

25. "Censored Film Draws Full House," *News-Review*, Apr. 14, 1960.

26. *In the Matter of the Seizure of the Films Love Robots and Little Girls v. Juba*, 460 P.2d 850 (Or. 1969).

27. *State v. Graf*, 501 P.2d 345, 347 (Or. Ct. App. 1972).

28. *State of Oregon v. Henry*, 732 P.2d 9, 18 (Or. 1987).

29. Wallace Turner, "Oregon Court Broadens Free Speech Rights" *NYT*, Apr. 15, 1987.

Pennsylvania

1. M. J. McCosker, "Philadelphia and the Genesis of the Motion Picture," *Pennsylvania Magazine of History and Biography* 65, no. 4 (October 1941): 405.

2. Ibid., 404.

3. "Corbett and Knock-Outs," *Philadelphia Times*, Mar. 28, 1897; "500 Realistic Pictures at Maysville Park Pavilion," *Mt. Carmel Daily News*, Aug. 20, 1898.

4. "The Court Record," *Washington D.C. Evening Star*, Nov. 7, 1904.

5. Steve Siegel, "Before Hollywood, There Was Betzwood," *Morning Call*, May 11, 2012.

6. Lauren Ball, "The World's First Nickelodeon," *Post-Gazette*, July 28, 2016.

7. Scott Tady Calkins, "Warner Bros. First Theater to Reopen in New Castle," *Ellwood City Ledger*, Apr. 4, 2013.

8. "State Inspection of Picture Films," *York Daily*, Apr. 12, 1911.

9. "Full Crew Bill Becomes a Law," *Altoona Tribune*, June 20, 1911.

10. "Increased Pay for Election Officers," *Daily Notes*, Apr. 28, 1911.

11. "State Censors of Movies Named," *Gettysburg Times*, Jan. 21, 1914.

12. "Censorship of Films 'Curse of Ages' Say Owners of Movies," *Harrisburg Daily Independent*, Jan. 26, 1914; "Censors to Rob Movies of All Their Thrills," *Delaware County Daily Times*, Jan. 27, 1914.

13. "Censor Board for Movies Completes Code of Rules," *Harrisburg Daily Independent*, Apr. 27, 1914.

14. "Yard of Kiss Is Enough," *Gettysburg Times*, Aug. 3, 1914.

15. "Fight against Film Censors," *Valley Independent*, Mar. 29, 1915.

16. "The Drug Terror," *Morning Herald*, June 25, 1914; "Defies Board of Censors," *Harrisburg Daily Independent*, Aug. 18, 1914.

17. "*Birth of Nation* Riot in Philadelphia Is Quelled," *Chicago Daily Tribune*, Sep. 21, 1915.

18. "Theater Manager Will Defy Mayor," *Pittsburgh Daily Post*, Aug. 26, 1915.

19. *Buffalo Branch, Mutual Film Corp. v. Breitinger*, 250 Pa. 225 (Pa. 1915).

20. "Sweeping Cuts Are Made in New Films by Censors," *Pittsburgh Post-Gazette*, Dec. 3, 1916.

21. "No 'Yeggs' in Movies," *Fulton County News*, Dec. 7, 1916.

22. "Movie Censors Are Particular About What You May See," *Daily Courier*, Apr. 19, 1916.

23. "Seven Films Condemned by Board of Censors," *Pittsburgh Post-Gazette*, Apr. 15, 1917.

24. "Bill Hart Scenes in Wilmington Movies Left to Imagination," *New Castle News*, May 12, 1919.

25. *In re Franklin Film Mfg. Corp.*, 253 Pa. 422 (Pa. 1916).

26. "Banned Film Owners Take Plea to Court," *Evening Public Ledger*, July 15, 1919; "Money Refunded on Tickets," *Pittsburgh Press*, July 18, 1919.

27. "Move to Oust Film Censor," *Harrisburg Daily Independent*, Mar. 19, 1915; "Oberholtzer Named Chief Movie Censor," *Pittsburgh Post-Gazette*, Oct. 20, 1920.

28. Ellis Paxson Oberholtzer, *The Morals of the Movies* (Philadelphia, PA: Penn Publishing, 1922), 172.

29. "C. Chaplin a Fool, Says Oberholtzer," *Evening Public Ledger*, Jan. 17, 1917; "No Booze in the Movie Films," *Indiana Gazette*, Nov. 8, 1923; "Some States Have Prohibited Film of Flaming Youth," *New Castle Herald*, Feb. 23, 1924.

30. "Director of State Movie Board Censors Cut from Payroll," *Pittsburgh Press*, June 24, 1921.

31. "Film Board Bans *Spanish Earth*," *Wilkes-Barre Times Leader*, Sep. 18, 1937.

32. "Police Guard Film Censor after Attack," *Altoona Tribune*, May 24, 1938; "Film Censor Prefers Threats to Bodyguard," *Altoona Tribune*, May 26, 1928.

33. "Judges Expected to Uphold Film Censors," *Mount Carmel Item*, Sep. 27, 1940.

34. "Narcotics Raid Traps Screen Star, Actress," *Albany Democrat-Herald*, Sep. 1, 1948.

35. *Hallmark Prod. v. Carroll*, 384 Pa. 348, 373 (Pa. 1956).

36. *Commonwealth v. Blumenstein*, 396 Pa. 417, 423 (Pa. 1959).

37. *Kingsley International Pictures v. Blanc*, 396 Pa. 448, 472 (Pa. 1959).

38. *William Goldman Theatres v. Dana*, 405 Pa. 83, 104 (Pa. 1961).

39. "Musmanno Backs Film Censor Bill," *Evening Sun*, Sep. 8, 1965.

40. *Duggan v. Guild Theatre*, 436 Pa. 191 (Pa. 1969).

41. "New *Black Fury* Ban," *NYT*, Apr. 6, 1935.

Rhode Island

1. "Lubin's Pictures of the Navy," *Motography*, Jan. 2, 1915, 25;

2. Jeffrey Vance, *Douglas Fairbanks* (Berkeley: University of California Press, 2008), 37.

3. "The History of Film in Rhode Island," Rhode Island International Film Festival, n.d., http://www.film-festival.org/FilmHistory.php; "Rhode Island in the Limelight: Film," n.d., http://www.quahog.org/factsfolklore/index.php?id=18.

4. Richard Curland, "Historically Speaking: Silent Movies Were Filmed in Voluntown," *Norwitch Bulletin*, June 16, 2013.

5. "Joseph Byron Totten," *MPW*, Nov. 6, 1915.

6. "At the Empress," *Des Moines Register*, Apr. 28, 1917; "Gipsy O'Brien, State Favorite, Enters Film," *Seattle Star*, Sep. 13, 1919; "Drops Questionable Play," *NYT*, Jan. 5, 1927.

7. Ashleigh Bennett and Kristie Martin, *Rhode Island Beer: Ocean State History on Tap* (Charleston, SC: Arcadia, 2015), 31.

8. "New Production Company," *MPW*, Sep. 4, 1915; "Hornblower & Weeks Enlarge Offices," *Brooklyn Daily Eagle*, July 8, 1929.

9. "New Production Company," *MPW*, Sep. 4, 1915; "AFI Catalog of Feature Films," n.d., http://www.afi.com/members/catalog/AbbrView.aspx?s=1&Movie=16419; "Graphics Collections," Rhode Island Historical Society, n.d., http://www.rihs.org/library/graphics-collections/.

10. "New Production Company," *MPW*, Sep. 4, 1915.

11. "Writing the Movies," *NYT*, Aug. 3, 1913.

12. Adam Tawfik, "The Elusive Eastern Film Corporation of Providence, Rhode Island," honors thesis, Rhode Island College, 2013, digitalcommons.ric.edu/cgi/viewcontent.cgi?article=1077&context=honors_projects; Maria Fosheim Lund, "Beta Breuil," *Women Film Pioneers Project*, Sep. 27, 2013, https://wfpp.cdrs.columbia.edu/pioneer/ccp-beta-breuil/.

13. "Movie Promoters in Row," *NYT*, Dec. 9, 1914.

14. See *Dintenfass v. Amber Star Films Corp.*, 99 A. 516 (R.I. 1917). Dintenfass incorporated the Champion Film Co. in 1912 and became an early director at Universal Film Mfg. Co. Pushed out of Universal, Dintenfass teamed with Louis Burstein to buy out the bankrupt assets of Lubin Mfg. Co. in 1917 and created the Vim Comedy Company. See Fort Lee Film Commission, *Fort Lee: Birthplace of the Motion Picture Industry* (Charleston, SC: Arcadia, 2006), 10.

15. Blair Miller, *Almost Hollywood: The Forgotten Story of Jacksonville, Florida* (Lanham, MD: Hamilton Books, 2013), 57.

16. "Rebuild Burned Studio," *Motography*, Sep. 15, 1917.

17. David Cantor, "The Reward of Courage," Medical Movies on the Web, National Institutes of Health (Bethesda: National Library of Medicine, 2013), https://www.nlm.nih.gov/hmd/collections/films/medicalmoviesontheweb/pdf/rewardofcourageessay.pdf.

18. "A Moving Picture Exhibition," *Newport Mercury*, Mar. 28, 1903.

19. "Amusement Censor Dies," *Topeka Daily Capital*, Mar. 5, 1922.

20. *Thayer Amusement Corp. v. Moulton*, 7 A.2d 682 (R.I. 1939).

21. *Kingsley Pictures Corp. v. Regents*, 360 U.S. 684 (1959).

22. *Kingsley International Picture Corp. v. City of Providence RI*, 166 F. Supp. 456, 458 (D.R.I. 1958).

23. *Burstyn v. Wilson*, 343 U.S. 495 (1952).

24. *Kingsley International Picture Corp. v. City of Providence RI*, 166 F. Supp. 456, 461–462 (D. R.I. 1958).

25. *Scuncio v. Columbus Theatre*, 277 A.2d 924, 925 (R.I. 1971).

26. "Theater Operators Refused Hearing by Supreme Court," *Telegraph*, Apr. 6, 1971.

South Carolina

1. Complaint filed in Los Angeles Superior Court; excerpt appears in "Bamboozled By Borat?," *Smoking Gun*, Nov. 13, 2006, http://www.thesmokinggun.com/documents/crime/bamboozled-borat.

2. *Ibid.*

3. Meg Kinnard, "Humiliated Frat Boys Sue *Borat*," *Washington Post*, Nov. 10, 2006.

4. "Borat," gross earnings on Box Office Mojo, http://www.boxofficemojo.com/movies/?page=weekend&id=borat.htm.

5. Meg Kinnard, "Humiliated Frat Boys Sue *Borat*," *Washington Post*, Nov. 10, 2006.

6. Carl DiOrio, "*Borat* Judge: No Suit for You," *Hollywood Reporter*, Dec. 12, 2006. Fox answered the complaint with a special motion under California's Anti-SLAPP (strategic litigation against public participation) statute (Cal. Civ. Proc. Code § 425.16), claiming that Baron Cohen had a First Amendment right to portray unorthodox views toward anti–Semitism, racism and sexism. Anti-SLAPP statutes are intended to counter suits brought to chill the valid exercise free speech.

7. "Entertainments at the Court House," *Greenville News*, Feb. 24, 1901.

8. "At the Theatre," *Greenville News*, Sep. 25, 1904.

9. "Gov. Blease Posing for Motion Pictures," *Greenville News*, July 29, 1914.

10. "'Satanet' Fell from Building at Columbia," *Ashville Gazette-News*, June 18, 1915.

11. "Movies of Camp Moore," *Greenville News*, Aug. 24, 1916.

12. "Motion Pictures Being Made Here," *Greenwood Daily Journal*, Oct. 14, 1916.

13. "Does Not Think Clergy Should Be Followed in Motion Picture Issue," *Greenville News*, Apr. 12, 1916.

14. "Chief Points in Cooper's Message," *Gaffney Ledger*, Jan. 17, 1920.

15. "Movie Censorship Is Opposed," *Greenwood Index-Journal*, Jan. 29, 1921.

16. "Movie Measure Not Practical," *Newberry Weekly Herald*, Feb. 1, 1921.

17. "House Would Censor State's Movie Films," *Gaffney Ledger*, Mar. 19, 1938.

18. Sanjeev Bhaskar, "What Did *Life of Brian* Ever Do for Us?," *Telegraph*, Nov. 29, 2009; "New Lease of *Life for Brian* as Glasgow Ends Film Ban after 29 Years," *Scotsman*, June 20, 2009; "Group in Belmar, N.J., Protest *Life of Brian*," *NYT*, Oct. 4, 1979.

19. Wendell Rawls Jr., "*Life of Brian* Stirs Carolina Controversy," *NYT*, Oct. 24, 1979.

20. *Ibid.*

21. *Ibid.*

22. See *Gawker v. Bollea*, 170 So.3d 125 (D. Fla. 2015).

South Dakota

1. Todd David Epp, "Alfred Hitchcock's 'Expedient Exaggerations' and the Filming of *North by Northwest* at Mount Rushmore," *South Dakota History* 23, no. 3 (Fall 1993): 181–196.

2. *Ibid.*

3. Vincent Canby, "Malick's Impressive *Badlands* Screened at Festival," *NYT*, Oct. 15, 1973; see also Vincent Canby, "*Mean Streets* at Film Festival," *NYT*, Oct. 3, 1973.

4. Henry Louis Gates Jr., ed., *African American Lives* (Oxford: Oxford University Press, 2004), 592.

5. Steve Miller, "West River Story," *Rapid City Journal*, July 26, 2010.

6. Kate Kelly, "New Documentary About Black Filmmaker Oscar Micheaux," *Huffington Post*, Aug. 4, 2014, http://www.huffingtonpost.com/kate-kelly/new-documentary-about-bla_b_5448566.html.

7. "Moving Pictures," *Daily Deadwood Pioneer-Times*, Dec. 24, 1899.

8. *Engineering Record* 53, no. 2 (1906), 52.

9. "Promises to Be Good Show," *Daily Deadwood Pioneer-Times*, Apr. 24, 1909.

10. "Moving Picture Censorship," *Daily Deadwood Pioneer-Times*, Jan. 30, 1921.

11. "Movie Censor Bill Approved in S.D.," *Albuquerque Journal*, Feb. 26, 1921.

12. See the documentary's website, http://www.honordiaries.com/about-the-film/.

13. Jonathan Ellis, "Film Provokes Censorship, Tolerance Debate at USD," *Argus Leader*, Mar. 27, 2015.

14. Raheel Raza, "Our Film About 'Honor Violence' Should Not Be Censored," *Huffington Post*, May 31, 2015, http://www.huffingtonpost.ca/raheel-raza/honor-diaries_b_6968630.html.

15. Rachael Krause, "Despite Some Criticism, USD Conference to Show Controversial Documentary Friday," Apr. 10, 2015, http://www.siouxlandmatters.com/news/local-news/despite-some-criticism-usd-conference-to-show-con.

Tennessee

1. "Censor Blames Devil for Ban on Films," *La Grande Observer*, Jan. 27, 1955.

2. "Memphis Bars Beulah Binford Film Shows," *Tennessean*, Sep. 11, 1911.

3. Mara Bovsun, "No Trail to Be Found," *New York Daily News*, June 27, 2005.

4. "Barred by Philadelphia," *NYT*, Sep. 8, 1911; "Binford Girl on Way Here," *NYT*, Sep. 8, 1911; "Bars Beulah Binford Pictures," *NYT*, Sep. 10, 1911.

5. "Moving Picture Censors Named," *Tennessean*, May 8, 1914.

6. "Picture Barred by Board of Censors," *Tennessean*, July 25, 1916.

7. "Offensive Portions of Picture Cut Out," *Tennessean*, July 26, 1916; "Censors Reject Twilight Sleep," *Tennessean*, Aug. 13, 1916.

8. "Noted Photoplay Passed by Censors," *Tennessean*, July 26, 1916; "Answers Criticism on Censorship," *Tennessean*, Oct. 24, 1916.

9. "Censor, Ill, Gets Private Screening," *Tennessean*, Jan. 9, 1922.

10. "Obituary Hamilton Love," *New York Lumber Trade Journal*, May 15, 1922.

11. "Vivian Tupper Named on Censorship Board," *Tennessean*, May 12, 1922.

12. "Most Notorious Hollywood Censor Dies at Age 89," *Monroe News-Star*, Aug. 27, 1956.

13. "He's Built His Business from a Log Cabin to a Skyscraper," *Manitowoc Herald-Times*, Oct. 29, 1929;

Robert Richards, "Aging Memphis Censor, Who Has Banned Many Movies, Is After Forever Amber," *Lubbock Avalanche-Journal*, Sep. 28, 1947.

14. Michael Finger, "Banned in Memphis," *Memphis Flyer*, May 8, 2008.

15. *Binford v. Carline*, 9 Tenn. App. 364, 369 (Tenn. Ct. App. 1928).

16. *Binford*, 9 Tenn. App. at 378.

17. "Lloyd T. Binford Dies," *Wellsville Daily Reporter*, Aug. 27, 1956.

18. "Tennessee Bans Motion Picture," *Statesville Daily Record*, Aug. 3, 1945.

19. "Memphis Bans *James* Movies," *Kingsport News*, Apr. 17, 1946.

20. "Memphis Will Bar Duel in the Sun," *Anniston Star*, Apr. 22, 1947.

21. "Film *The Outlaw* Ordered Banned by Memphis Censor," *Hope Star*, Feb. 20, 1946.

22. "Memphis Will Bar Duel in the Sun," *Anniston Star*, Apr. 22, 1947.

23. "Memphis Movie Censor Bans Charlie Chaplin Film *Monsieur Verdoux*," *Blytheville Courier News*, June 10, 1947.

24. "Chaplin Banned by Film Censor," *Ogden Standard-Examiner*, Jan. 11, 1951.

25. "No, No Ingrid," *Idaho Falls Post-Register*, Feb. 6, 1950.

26. *Brewster's Millions* was first adapted by Cecil B. DeMille in 1914 and remade in 1921 with Roscoe "Fatty" Arbuckle. In 1926 the title character was changed to a female in *Miss Brewster's Millions* with Bebe Daniels. The scenario was repurposed to inspire British versions in 1935 and 1961 and four Bollywood versions in 1954, 1985, 1988, and 1997. Modern audiences will be most familiar with the Richard Pryor version released by Universal in 1985.

27. "Memphis Bans Movie for Too Much Racial Equality," *York Gazette and Daily*, Apr. 7, 1945.

28. *United Artists v. City of Memphis*, 189 Tenn. 397, 401 (Tenn. 1949).

29. "No Segregation, So Memphis Bans Film," *Bakersfield Californian*, Dec. 3, 1948.

30. Robert C. Ruark, "Binford, Banning Specialist," *Tucson Daily Citizen*, Nov. 16, 1950.

31. "Exits and Entrances," *Oakland Tribune*, Mar. 27, 1946.

32. Billy Rowe, "Hollywood Wonders About Motive Behind Censor's New Action," *Pittsburgh Courier*, Aug. 27, 1949; "Memphis Censors Give Approval to Film," *Camden News*, Sep. 9, 1949.

33. Robert Ruark, "Tar Heel at Large," *Daily Tar Heel*, Nov. 19, 1950.

34. See *RD-DR Corp. v. Smith*, 89, F. Supp. 596 (N.D. Ga. 1950).

35. "News from Towns around the Nation," *Tucson Citizen*, Dec. 19, 1949.

36. "*Lulu Belle* Banned," *Wilkes-Barre Record*, July 1, 1948.

37. "Memphis Censors *David, Bathsheba*," *Albuquerque Journal*, Oct. 7, 1951.

38. "*David and Bathsheba* Censored in Memphis," *Cumberland Sunday Times*, Oct. 7, 1951.

39. "Censor Board Bans Private Showing of Russell Movie," *Kingsport Times*, Feb. 12, 1954; William Crider, "Memphis Films Are Censored," *Kentucky New Era*, Mar. 5, 1954; "Dance Too Sexy," *Tipton Daily Tribune*, Oct. 4, 1954.

40. "Memphis Bans *The Wild One*," *Kingsport News*, Jan. 18, 1954; "Memphis Bans Movie About Delinquency," *Kingsport News*, Mar. 28, 1955; Erskine Johnson, "Johnson in Hollywood," *Gastonia Gazette*, Aug. 4, 1955; "Memphis Bans Film," *Bridgeport Telegram*, Oct. 9, 1955.

41. "Rugged Censor to Quit," *Kansas City Times*, Oct. 27, 1955.

42. "Lloyd Binford Dies," *Wellsville Daily Reporter*, Aug. 27, 1956.

43. "Censors Order Film Be Cut," *Kingsport News*, Sep. 11, 1959; "*Baby Doll* Film Banned," *Corpus Christi Times*, Nov. 16, 1956.

44. "Memphis Censor Bans 'Nudie' Movie," *Kingsport Times*, Nov. 7, 1962.

45. *State v. William Kendall*, Criminal Court Case File 94240 (1964); also see Whitney Strub, "Black and White and Banned All Over: Race, Censorship and Obscenity in Postwar Memphis," *Journal of Social History* (2007), http://www.unm.edu/~unmvclib/handouts/black race.pdf.

46. *Embassy Pictures Corp. v. Hudson*, 242 F. Supp. 975, 978 (W.D. Tenn. 1965).

47. See *New Riviera Arts Theatre v. State of Tennessee*, 412 S.W.2d 890 (Tenn. 1967); *Robert Arthur Mgt Corp. v. State of Tennessee*, 414 S.W.2d 638 (Tenn. 1967); *State v. Marshall*, 859 S.W.2d. 289 (Tenn. 1993).

Texas

1. "Fitzsimmons and Maher Matched," *NYT*, Dec. 6, 1895.

2. David Ansel Weiss, "Boxing Impresario Nonpareil," *True West*, Aug. 1, 2005.

3. "Maher Knocked Out," *Austin Weekly Statesman*, Feb. 27, 1896.

4. "The Kinetoscope Play," *Galveston Daily News*, Feb. 28, 1896.

5. "The Wonderful Magniscope," *Bryan Texas Eagle*, Jan. 28, 1897.

6. "Moving Pictures Shows Should Take Care," *Brownsville Herald*, June 17, 1909.

7. "Moving Picture Show Censor," *Houston Post*, Dec. 27, 1909.

8. Matthew Solomon, *Fantastic Voyages of the Cinematic Imagination: Georges Méliès's Trip to the Moon* (Albany: State University of New York Press, 2011), 2.

9. Richard Abel, *The Ciné Goes to Town: French Cinema 1896–1914* (Berkeley: University of California Press, 1998), 14.

10. "'Canned Drama' by the Wholesale," *Palestine Daily Herald*, Dec. 29, 1910.

11. Raphaël Millet, "Gaston Méliès and His Lost Films of Singapore," Apr. 3, 2016, http://www.nlb.gov.sg/biblioasia/2016/04/03/gaston-melies-and-his-lost-films-of-singapore/.

12. Cynthia Littleton, "Ford Films Found in Kiwi Vault," *Variety*, June 6, 2010; "Film Notes: Billy and His Pal (1911)," n.d., http://www.filmpreservation.org/preserved-films/screening-room/billy-and-his-pal-1911.

13. "Stand by the Censors," *Houston Post*, Aug. 2, 1915; "Censors Visited Picture Shows," *Houston Post*, Apr. 30, 1913.

14. "Motion Picture Manager Was Acquitted by Jury," *Houston Post*, July 30, 1915; "*Birth of a Nation* Stirred Large Audience to Enthusiasm," *Houston Post*, Oct. 19, 1915.

15. "Put Ban on Useful Film," *MPW*, Feb. 19, 1916; "Work of Dallas Censors," *MPW*, May 27, 1916.

16. "Censors Bar Children at O'Neil Play," *Abilene Reporter-News*, Jan. 1, 1933.

17. *Gelling v. State*, 247 S.W.2d 95 (Tex. Crim. App. 1952).

18. *Gelling v. State of Texas*, 343 U.S. 960 (1952).

19. *Janus Films, Inc. v. City of Fort Worth*, 354 S.W.2d 597 (Tex. App. 1962).

20. *Interstate Circuit, Inc. v. City of Dallas*, 390 U.S. 676, 690 (1968).

21. Marc Savlov, "Thirty Years on Location," *Austin Chronicle*, June 15, 2001.

22. "History" and "TFC Timeline," Texas Film Commission, n.d., http://gov.texas.gov/film/about/history.

23. Tex. Admin. Code, §121.4(b), 2010, Tex. Film Comm'n, Ineligible Projects.

24. Mark Meier, "Muzzled!," *Santa Fe Reporter*, Aug. 8, 2010.

25. Allan Turner, "Film on Waco Tragedy Messes with Texas' Image," *Houston Chronicle*, May 30, 2009.

26. *Machete's Chop Shop, Inc. v. Texas Film Commission*, no. 03-14-00098-CV (Tex. App. 2016), http://case law.findlaw.com/tx-court-of-appeals/1724593.html.

27. Charles Ealy, "*Machete Kills* Company Sues Texas Film Commission over Denial of Incentives," *Austin American Statesman*, Mar. 14, 2014.

28. *Ibid.*

29. Eriq Gardner, "*Machete* Producer Claims Anti-Immigration Activists Killed Tax Incentives," *Hollywood Reporter*, July 15, 2013.

30. *Ibid.*

31. *Machete's Chop Shop, Inc. v. Texas Film Commission*, no. 03-14-00098-CV (Tex. App. 2016), http://case law.findlaw.com/tx-court-of-appeals/1724593.html.

32. Greg Groogan, "Legal Expert Calls Suppression of Autism Film by Houston Mayor 'Censorship,'" Apr. 8, 2016, http://www.fox26houston.com/news/119346731-story; Cameron Langford, "Anti-Vaccination Activists Back Rejected Film," Sep. 2, 2016, http://www.court housenews.com/2016/09/02/anti–vaccination-activists-back-rejected-film.htm.

33. "Two Efforts to Regulate Motion Picture Shows Fail," *El Paso Herald*, Apr. 5, 1921.

34. "Want Movie Censor," *Corsicana Daily Sun*, May 27, 1921.

Utah

1. Jacob W. Olmstead, "*A Victim of the Mormons* and *The Danites*: Images and Relics from Early Twentieth-Century Anti-Mormon Silent Films," *Mormon Historical Studies* 5, no. 1 (Spring 2004): 203–221.

2. Richard Alan Nelson, "A History of Latter-Day Saint Screen Portrayals in the Anti-Mormon Film Era, 1905–1936," master's thesis, Brigham Young University, 1975, http://scholarsarchive.byu.edu/cgi/viewcontent.cgi?article=5974&context=etd.

3. Objectionable Film Passes the Censors," *Salt Lake Tribune*, Feb. 25, 1912.

4. Olmstead, "*A Victim of the Mormons*," *Mormon Historical Studies* 5, no. 1 (Spring 2004).

5. "Mormonism in Movies," *Reno-Gazette-Journal*, Nov. 1, 1912; "One Hundred Years of Mormonism," *Ogden Standard*, Feb. 18, 1913.

6. Randy Astle, "Glimpses: Nephi's Colored Plates," Mormon Artists Group, July 2008, http://www.mormon artistsgroup.com/mormon_artists_group/Glimpses_Nephis_Colored_Plates.html.

7. "Wetzel O. Whitaker," BYU College of Fine Arts and Communications wiki, last modified Jan. 30, 2015, http://history.cfac.byu.edu/index.php/Wetzel_O._Whitaker.

8. Randy Astle and Gideon O. Burton, "Mormons and Film," LDS Living, n.d., http://www.ldsliving.com/Mormons-and-Film-100-Years-on-the-Silver-Screen/s/4478.

9. *God's Army* (2000) box office returns, The Numbers, n.d., http://www.the-numbers.com/movie/Gods-Army#tab=summary.

10. *The Other Side of Heaven* (2001) box office returns, The Numbers, n.d., http://www.the-numbers.com/movie/Other-Side-of-Heaven-The#tab=summary.

11. Debbie Hummel, "'Mollywood' Shuffle Ahead," *Los Angeles Daily News*, Oct. 30, 2005.

12. *Deadpool* (2016) box office returns, The Numbers, n.d., http://www.the-numbers.com/movie/Deadpool#tab=summary.

13. Ben Winslow, "Utah Movie Theater's Liquor License Threatened for Showing *Deadpool*," Fox13 Salt Lake City, Apr. 18, 2016, http://fox13now.com/2016/04/18/utah-movie-theaters-liquor-license-threatened-for-showing-deadpool/.

14. Lindsay Whitehurst, "Experts Debate Sex and Alcohol in Utah *Deadpool* Case," *Daily Herald*, Nov. 4, 2016.

15. *Cornflower Entertainment. v. Salt Lake City Corp.*, 485 F. Supp. 777 (D. Utah 1980).

16. "Utah Theater Wins *Deadpool* Case Over Law Banning Booze" in The Associated Press, September 1, 2017.

Vermont

1. "Return of a Native," *NYT*, July 26, 1959.

2. Susan Jo Keller, "Footlights," *NYT*, July 2, 2000.

3. *Ibid.*

4. Frederick James Smith, "Foolish Censors," *Photoplay*, Oct. 1922, 40.

5. "Would Censor Movie Shows," *Bennington Banner*, Jan. 10, 1917.

6. "Morality Laws," *Burlington Free Press*, Jan. 22, 1921.

7. "Censorship Bill Is Introduced," *Caldonian-Record*, Feb, 2, 1921; "Movie Censorship Bill Under Fire," *Burlington Free Press*, Feb. 15, 1921.

8. "Legislature Makes Many Changes in Burlington Charter," *Burlington Free Press*, Apr. 6, 1921.

9. Matt Dunne, "Risky Business," *Independent*, July 1, 2004, http://independent-magazine.org/2004/07/risky-business/.

10. *Ibid.*

Virginia

1. "Books Received," *Houston Post*, Feb. 16, 1913; "Teachers Meet at Buckingham," *Times Dispatch*, Apr. 14, 1913.

2. "Oscar Micheaux," African American Trailblazers in Virginia History, n.d., http://www.lva.virginia.gov/public/trailblazers/2012/?bio=micheaux; also see "Oscar Micheaux 1893–1951 Marker K-90," n.d., http://www.markerhistory.com/oscar-micheaux-1893-1951-marker-k-90/.

3. "Richmonders Appointed to Mount Vernon Board," *Times Dispatch*, Apr. 22, 1922.

4. "State Censors Inspect 150 Miles of Pictures," *Times Dispatch*, Sep. 18, 1922.

5. Charlene Regester, "Black Films, White Censor," in *Movie Censorship and American Culture*, ed. Francis G. Couvares (Amherst: University of Massachusetts Press, 1996), 174.

6. *Ibid.*, 174–175.

7. "An Oscar Micheaux Filmography," in *Oscar Micheaux and His Circle: African-American Filmmaking and Race Cinema of the Silent Era*, ed. Pearl Bowser, Jane Gaines, and Charles Musser (Bloomington: Indiana University Press, 2001), 252.

8. *Ibid.*

9. "Society Woman Admits Colored Blood in Veins," *Daily Free Press*, Nov. 10, 1925.

10. Code of Virginia as Amended to Adjournment of General Assembly 1924, §5099(a)(2), "Preservation of Racial Integrity," http://www.encyclopediavirginia. org/Preservation_of_Racial_Integrity_1924.

11. Melissa Ooten, *Race, Gender, and Film Censorship in Virginia 1922–1965* (Lanham, MD: Lexington Books, 2015), 83.

12. "Chatham Man Successor to Chesterman," *Danville Bee*, Feb. 27, 1931.

13. "100 Pictures a Minute," *Roanoke Times*, Dec. 11, 1897.

14. "The Picture Machine Broken," *Richmond Dispatch*, Apr. 6, 1900.

15. "New Movie Ordinance Creates Censor Board," *Times Dispatch*, May 9, 1916.

16. "Here and There in the Legislature," *Times Dispatch*, Jan. 22, 1918.

17. "Chapter 257, An Act to Regulate Motion Picture Films," *Pollard's Supplement to the Code of Virginia, 1922* (Richmond, VA: Everett Waddey, 1922), 1057.

18. "Richmonders Appointed to Mount Vernon Board," *Times Dispatch*, Apr. 22, 1922.

19. "Mammy's White Folks," *Times Dispatch*, Dec. 4, 1919; "Miss Minerva's Baby," *Times Dispatch*, Sep. 1, 1920.

20. "Movie Censor Board Money Maker for VA," *Danville Bee*, Feb. 2, 1927.

21. "Censors Reject College Movie," *Danville Bee*, July 10, 1931.

22. "Movie on Hitler Barred in Virginia," *Danville Bee*, Nov. 14, 1939.

23. *City of Lynchburg v. Dominion Theaters*, 175 Va. 35 (Va. 1940).

24. "Three Grandmothers on Virginia Motion Picture Censor Board," *Danville Bee*, Aug. 30, 1961.

25. "Considers Movie Obscene," *Kingsport News*, Feb. 29, 1964.

26. "Movie Censorship Law Challenged," *Kingsport News*, May 3, 1963.

27. "VA Censorship Law Invalid," *Cumberland News*, Apr. 21, 1965.

Washington

1. Peter Bunzel, "Outbreak of New Films for Adults Only," *Life*, Feb. 23, 1962, 90.

2. See Western Live Stock and Insurance Association advertisement, *Washington State Journal*, Dec. 11, 1907; "Samuel Glasgow Made New City Commissioner," *Spokane Daily Chronicle*, Dec. 2, 1914; "Courthouse News and County News," *Colville Examiner*, Dec. 19, 1914.

3. "Film Confiscated," *Seattle Star*, July 22, 1916.

4. "Seattle Censors Alive," *MPW*, Feb. 19, 1916, 1171.

5. "Griffith Film in Spokane," *MPW*, Aug. 21, 1913, 1344.

6. "May Bar Films," *Helena Independent Record*, Jan. 13, 1927.

7. "May Name 15 Censors," *Tacoma Times*, Aug. 19, 1916.

8. "*Birth of a Nation* is Filling Tacoma Theater," *Tacoma Times*, Aug. 25, 1916.

9. Will Present *Sapho* with No Fear of Being Arrested," *Tacoma Times*, Nov. 6, 1913; "Censors Demand Apollo Theater Trim Its Film," *Tacoma Times*, Apr. 19, 1916; "Censor Board Bans Picture," *Tacoma Times*, Dec. 6, 1917.

10. "Provide for City Censors," *Tacoma Times*, Jan. 10, 1917.

11. "Three Named as Censors," *Tacoma Times*, Feb. 17, 1917; "Censor Board Ready to Act," *Tacoma Times*, Feb. 23, 1917.

12. "Film Banned," *Daily Chronicle*, Dec. 11, 1946.

13. "Film Censors Ban *Rope* in Seattle," *Eugene Guard*, Oct. 23, 1948.

14. "State Supreme Court Hears Obscenity Case," *Spokane Daily Chronicle*, Oct. 21, 1970.

15. *Rabe v. Washington*, 405 U.S. 313, 316 (1972).

16. *Brockett v. Spokane Arcades*, 472 U.S. 491, 499 (1985).

17. *Renton v. Playtime Theaters*, 475 U.S. 41, 43 (1986).

18. Greg Lukianoff, "Feigning Free Speech on Campus," *NYT*, Oct. 24, 2012.

West Virginia

1. "Enoch Rector, 94, Inventor, Dead," *NYT*, Jan. 27, 1957.

2. Charles Musser, *Before the Nickelodeon* (Berkeley: University of California Press, 1991), 45–46.

3. "Sheriffs at Edison's," *New York Evening World*, Sep. 12, 1894.

4. "Want the Big Fight," *Philadelphia Inquirer*, Oct. 27, 1894.

5. "Personal," *Philadelphia Times*, Aug. 4, 1884.

6. "Lambda Company Chartered," *Richmond Dispatch*, Dec. 29, 1894.

7. Stephen Herbert, "Major Woodville Latham, Grey Latham, and Otway Latham," *Who's Who of Victorian Cinema*, n.d., http://www.victorian-cinema.net/ latham.

8. Panopticon Rivals the Kinetoscope," *NYT*, Apr. 22, 1895.

9. "Griffo Immortalized," *Brooklyn Daily Eagle*, May 5, 1895.

10. "Marvels of the Eidoloscope," *Chicago Inter Ocean*, July 28, 1895.

11. "Photographing a Wink," *Ottawa Daily Republic*, July 11, 1895.

12. "James J. Corbett vs. Bob Fitzsimmons," BoxRec. com, last modified June 4, 2016, http://boxrec.com/media/ index.php/James_J._Corbett_vs._Bob_Fitzsimmons.

13. Tom Gunning, *D.W. Griffith and the Origins of American Narrative Film* (Urbana: University of Illinois Press, 1994), 64.

14. See, e.g., *Edison v. American Mutoscope & Biograph Co.*, 151 Fed. 767 (2d Cir. 1907); *Edison v. American Mutoscope & Biograph Co.*, 144 Fed. 121 (C.C.S.D.N.Y. 1906); *American Mutoscope & Biograph Co. v. Edison Mfg. Co.*, 137 Fed. 262 (C.C.D.N.J. 1905); *Edison v. American*

Mutoscope & Biograph Co., 127 Fed. 361 (C.C.S.D.N.Y. 1904); *Edison v. American Mutoscope & Biograph Co.*, 114 Fed. 926 (2d Cir. 1902).

15. "In the Circle of Society," *Washington Times*, Aug. 18, 1906; "Another Latham Tragedy," *Baltimore Sun*, Mar. 27, 1907.

16. Herbert, "Major Woodville Latham, Grey Latham, and Otway Latham," *Who's Who of Victorian Cinema*.

17. Advertisement, *Wheeling West Virginia Intelligencer*, Dec. 1894.

18. "*Birth of a Nation* Upheld by the Court," *Charleston Daily Mail*, Dec. 18, 1915.

19. "Facts and Comments," *MPW*, Feb. 19, 1916.

20. "*Birth of a Nation*," *Raleigh Herald*, June 27, 1918.

21. *West Virginia Senate Bill No. 259* (Charleston, WV: Tribune Printing Co., 1921), 783.

22. "Some Curious Excisions," *Life*, Feb. 29, 1960, 85; see also Albert W. Harris, "Movie Censorship and the Supreme Court," *California Law Review* 42, no. 1 (March 1954), 125n19.

23. "Controversial Film Censor at Memphis Dies at Age of 89," *Lubbock Evening Journal*, Aug. 27, 1956; Sonny Inbaraj, "*Lolita* Sparks Debate on Censorship," *Inter Press Service*, Mar. 20, 1999; "The Night of the Hunter (1955)," The Swedish Film Database, n.d., http://www.sfi.se/en-gb/Swedish-film-database/Item/?type=MOVIE&itemid=16297.

Wisconsin

1. "Critics Praise *Way of All Flesh* Craterian Thursday," *Medford Mail Tribune*, Jan. 4, 1926.

2. Mordaunt Hall, "The Best Pictures of Past Year," *NYT*, Jan. 1, 1928.

3. "*The Way of All Flesh*," *Variety*, Dec. 31, 1926.

4. Mordaunt Hall, "The Best Pictures of Past Year," *NYT*, Jan. 1, 1928.

5. Paul Harris, "Library of Congress: 75% of Silent Films Lost," *Variety*, Dec. 4, 2013.

6. Anthony Slide, *Nitrate Won't Wait: A History of Film Preservation in the United States* (Jefferson, NC: McFarland, 2000), 13.

7. Phillip W. Stewart, "A Reel Story of World War II," *Prologue* 47, no. 3 (Fall 2015), https://www.archives.gov/publications/prologue/2015/fall/united-newsreels.html.

8. For instance, when a theater in South Dakota advertised a non–MPPC-licensed film of the Wolgast-Nelson boxing bout, General Film Co., the MPPC's distribution arm, notified the theater owner "that if he showed the fight pictures he would not be supplied with films for the regular business of the house. At the mercy of the Trust, the theater owner was forced to call the fight pictures off." See "*Wolgast-Nelson Fight* Is Off," *Deadwood Daily Pioneer-Times*, May 17, 1910.

9. "Harry E. Aitken," Waukesha County Online Genealogy and Family History Library, n.d., http://www.linkstothepast.com/waukesha/aitken.php.

10. "Milwaukee Has Censor Board," *MPW*, Dec. 20, 1913, 1529.

11. "Philipp for Censorship of Movies," *Capital Times*, July 16, 1920.

12. "White Slave Films Will Mean Censors," *Janesville Daily Gazette*, June 7, 1916.

13. "Sponsors of Movie Censor Bill Hopeful," *Eau Claire Leader*, May 6, 1919; "O.K.'s Plan for Local Censor Body," *Capital Times*, May 21, 1930.

14. "Plan New Film Censor Methods in Madison," *Capital Times*, Apr. 24, 1930.

15. Frank Crane, "*What Price Glory*," *Sheboygan Press Telegram*, Nov. 15, 1924; "Plan Changes in Censorship of Films Here," *Capital Times*, Apr. 24, 1930.

16. *Mutual Film Corp. v. Industrial Commission of Ohio*, 23 U.S. 230, 244 (1915).

17. "Scarlet Street Banned," *Waukesha Daily Freeman*, Jan. 12, 1946.

18. Matthew J. Prigge, "James Dean Banned in Milwaukee!," *Shepherd Express*, Jan. 11, 2016.

19. Vincent Canby, "Screen: *Woodstock* Ecstasy Caught on Film," *NYT*, Mar. 27, 1970.

20. *Engdahl v. Kenosha*, 317 F. Supp. 113, 1135–1136 (E.D. Wis. 1970).

21. *Borger v. Bisciglia*, 888 F. Supp. 97, 98 (E.D. Wis. 1995).

22. *Borger v. Bisciglia*, 888 F. Supp. 97, 101 (E.D. Wis. 1995).

Wyoming

1. "Rothacker Film Mfg. Co," *MPW*, Feb. 24, 1917; Edward Weitzel, "*The Hell Cat*," *MPW*, Dec. 7, 1918; "*The Wolf of the Tetons*," *MPW*, May 24, 1919.

2. U.S. Census data at http://factfinder.census.gov.

3. "Sherman and *Birth of a Nation*," *MPW*, Nov. 13, 1915.

4. Jas S. McQuade, "Harry A. Sherman Secures Rights to *The Crisis* for the United States and Canada," *MPW*, Sep. 23, 1916.

5. *Ibid.*

6. Stephen Klein, "Cheyenne City Council's Speech Shenanigans," Wyoming Liberty Group, Jan. 14, 2014, https://wyliberty.org/blog/legal-perspectives/cheyenne-city-councils-speech-shenanigans.

7. Mike Hale, "The Cost of Natural Gas," *NYT*, June 20, 2010.

8. Joanna Zelman, "Josh Fox, *Gasland* Director, Talks of Capitol Hill Arrest," *Huffington Post*, Feb. 4, 2012, www.huffingtonpost.com/2012/02/04/josh-fox-arrest-gasland-republicans_n_1251275.html.

9. Richard A. Oppel Jr., "Taping of Farm Cruelty Is Becoming the Crime," *NYT*, Apr. 6, 2013.

10. Wyo. Stat. §40-27-101 (2015), http://legisweb.state.wy.us/2015/bills/SF0012.pdf; revised in 2016 as Wyo. Stat. §§ 6-3-414 (e)(iv); 40-27-101(h)(iii) (2016), http://legisweb.state.wy.us/2016/Introduced/SF0076.pdf.

11. Trevor Brown, "Wyoming Lawmakers: Bill Isn't an 'Ag-Gag,'" *Wyoming Tribune Eagle*, Mar. 10, 2015.

12. *Western Watersheds Project v. Michaels*, no. 15-CV-00169-SWS, July 6, 2016.

13. "Ag Gag Laws Have No Place Under the First Amendment," *Des Moines Register*, Aug. 16, 2015.

Conclusion

1. See *Monica Pompeo v. Board of Regents of the University of New Mexico*, Civ. No. 13-0833 MCA/CG, ¶9 (D.N.M. 2015); George Leef, "College Officials Tell Students: You May Speak Freely As Long As It's Within Our (Tiny) Speech Zone," *Forbes*, Dec. 15, 2016; Dan Flynn, "Idaho Squares Off with Animal Rights Group before 9th Circuit," *Food Safety News*, Jan. 3, 2017; Corey Hutchins, "Will a South Carolina Political Blogger Go to Jail to Protect His Sources?," *Columbia Journalism Review*, Jan. 6, 2017.

Bibliography

Armatage, Kay. *The Girl from God's Country: Nell Shipman and the Silent Cinema.* Toronto: University of Toronto Press, 2003.

Balio, Tino. *Grand Design: Hollywood as a Modern Business Enterprise, 1930–1939.* Berkeley: University of California Press, 1996.

Barnouw, Erik. *Documentary: A History of the Non-Fiction Film.* Oxford: Oxford University Press, 1993.

Bernstein, Matthew, ed. *Controlling Hollywood: Censorship and Regulation in the Studio Era.* London: The Athlone Press, 2000.

Bowser, Eileen. *The Transformation of Cinema, 1907–1915.* Berkeley: University of California Press, 1994.

Butters, Gerald R., Jr. *Banned in Kansas: Motion Picture Censorship, 1915–1966.* Columbia: University of Missouri, 2007.

Cook, David A. *Lost Illusions: American Cinema in the Shadow of Watergate and Vietnam, 1970–1979.* Berkeley: University of California Press, 2002.

Corcoran, Michael, and Arnie Bernstein. *Hollywood on Lake Michigan: 100+ Years of Chicago and the Movies.* Chicago: Chicago Review Press, 2013.

Couvares, Francis G., ed. *Movie Censorship and American Culture.* Amherst: University of Massachusetts Press, 1996.

Crafton, Donald. *The Talkies: American Cinema's Transition to Sound, 1926–1931.* Berkeley: University of California Press, 1999.

Cripps, Thomas. *Slow Fade to Black: The Negro in American Film 1900–1942.* Oxford: Oxford University Press, 1993.

De Grazia, Edward, and Roger Mewman. *Banned Films: Movies, Censors and the First Amendment.* Bowker, 1982.

Doherty, Thomas. *Hollywood's Censor: Joseph I. Breen and the Production Code Administration.* New York: Columbia University Press, 2009.

Fort Lee Film Commission. *Fort Lee: Birthplace of the Motion Picture Industry.* Mount Pleasant, SC: Arcadia Publishing, 2006.

Geltzer, Jeremy. *Dirty Words & Filthy Pictures: Film and the First Amendment.* Austin: University of Texas Press, 2016.

Goodman, Ezra. *The Fifty-Year Decline and Fall of Hollywood.* New York: Simon & Schuster, 1961.

Grieveson, Lee. *Policing Cinema: Movies and Censorship in Early-Twentieth-Century America.* Berkeley: University of California Press, 2004.

Griffith, D.W. *The Rise and Fall of Free Speech in America.* Los Angeles, 1916.

Jura, Jean-Jacques, and Rodney Norman Bardin II. *Balboa Films: A History and Filmography of the Silent Film Studio.* Jefferson: McFarland Press, 2007.

Koszarski, Richard. *Hollywood On the Hudson: Film and Television in New York from Griffith to Sarnoff.* New Brunswick: Rutgers University Press, 2008.

Koszarski, Richard. *An Evening's Entertainment: The Age of the Silent Feature Picture, 1915–1928.* Berkeley: University of California Press, 1994.

Lev, Peter. *The Fifties: Transforming the Screen, 1950–1959.* Berkeley: University of California Press, 2006.

Lorence, James J. *The Suppression of Salt of the Earth: How Hollywood, Big Labor, and Politicians Blacklisted a Movie in the American Cold War.* Albuquerque: University of New Mexico Press, 1999.

Lupack, Barbara Tepa. *Richard E. Norman and Race Filmmaking.* Bloomington: Indiana University Press, 2013.

McLean, Adrienne L., and David A. Cook, ed. *Headline Hollywood: A Century of Film Scandal.* New Brunswick: Rutgers University Press, 2001.

Monaco, Paul. *The Sixties: 1960–1969*. Berkeley: University of California Press, 2003.

Musser, Charles. *The Emergence of Cinema: The American Screen to 1907*. Berkeley: University of California Press, 1990.

Oberholtzer, Ellis Paxson. *The Morals of the Movies*. Philadelphia: The Penn Publishing Company, 1922.

Ooten, Melissa. *Race, Gender, and Film Censorship in Virginia 1922–1965*. Lanham: Lexington Books, 2014.

Prince, Stephen. *A New Pot of Gold: Hollywood under the Electronic Rainbow, 1980–1989*. Berkeley: University of California Press, 2002.

Randall, Richard S. *Censorship of the Movies: The Social and Political Control of a Mass Medium*. Madison: University of Wisconsin Press, 1968.

Rice, Tom. *White Robes, Silver Screens: Movies and the Making of the Ku Klux Klan*. Bloomington: Indiana University Press, 2016.

Scott, Ellen C. *Cinema Civil Rights: Regulation, Repression, and Race in the Classical Hollywood Era*. New Brunswick: Rutgers University Press, 2015.

Schaefer, Eric. *Bold! Daring! Shocking! True! A History of Exploitation Films, 1919–1959*. Raleigh: Duke University Press, 1999.

Schatz, Thomas. *Boom and Bust: American Cinema in the 1940s*. Berkeley: University of California Press, 1999.

Sklar, Robert. *Movie-Made America: A Cultural History of American Movies*. New York: Vintage, 1994.

Slide, Anthony. *Ravished Armenia and the Story of Aurora Mardiganian*. Jackson: University of Mississippi Press, 2014.

Smith, Sarah. *Children, Cinema and Censorship: From Dracula to Dead End*. London: I.B. Tauris, 2005.

Vizzard, Jack. *See No Evil: Life Inside a Hollywood Censor*. New York: Simon & Schuster, 1970.

Wiseman, Frederick. *Five Films by Frederick Wiseman*. Berkeley: University of California Press, 2006.

Wittern-Keller, Laura. *Freedom of the Screen: Legal Changes to State Film Censorship, 1915–1981*. Lexington: University of Kentucky Press, 2008.

Index